CONFRONTING THE GREEK DICTATORSHIP IN THE UNITED STATES

YEARS OF EXILE: A PERSONAL DIARY (1968–1975)

ORESTIS E. VIDALIS

Confronting the Greek Dictatorship in the U.S.

YEARS OF EXILE:
A PERSONAL DIARY (1968–1975)

PELLA
PELLA PUBLISHING COMPANY, INC.
New York, NY 10018-6401
2009

This book was published for The Center for Byzantine and Modern Greek Studies, Queens College of the City University of New York, which bears full editorial responsibility for its contents.

MODERN GREEK RESEARCH SERIES, XV, DECEMBER 2009

CONFRONTING THE GREEK DICTATORSHIP IN THE UNITED STATES

Years of Exile:

A Personal Diary (1968–1975)

Library of Congress Control Number 2009935298

ISBN 0-918618-93-2

PRINTED IN THE UNITED STATES OF AMERICA
BY
ATHENS PRINTING COMPANY
337 West 36th Street
New York, NY 10018-6401

Dedicated to the Greek officers who chose the path of sacrifice and resistance against the dictatorship

MODERN GREEK RESEARCH SERIES

The purpose of this monograph series is to promote and disseminate scholarly works on the history, institutions, and the culture of the Greek people. It is sponsored and edited by the Center for Byzantine and Modern Greek Studies, Queens College of the City University of New York (formerly jointly with the Greek Seminar of the Center for Mediterranean Studies of the American University). This is the fifteenth publication within the framework of the Modern Greek Research Christos P. Ioannides, Professor of Political Science, Queens College of the City University of New York, Director.

MODERN GREEK RESEARCH SERIES

I. *Essays on the Cyprus Conflict.* Edited by Van Coufoudakis. 1976

II. *Foreign Interference in Greek Politics: An Historical Perspective.* By T.A. Couloumbis, J.A. Petropulos, and H.J. Psomiades. 1976

III. *Greek-American Relations: A Critical Review.* Edited by T.A. Couloumbis and J.O. Iatrides. 1980

IV. *The Greek American Community in Transition.* Edited by H.J. Psomiades and A. Scourby. 1982

V. *Education and Greek Americans: Process and Prospects.* Edited by S.D. Orfanos, H.J. Psomiades, and J. Spiridakis. 1987

VI. *Greece, the New Europe, and the Changing International Order.* Edited by H.J. Psomiades and S. Thomadakis. 1993

VII. *Greece and the New Balkans.* Edited by Van Coufoudakis, Harry J. Psomiades and Andre Gerolymatos. 1999

VIII. *Greek American Families: Traditions and Transformations.* Edited by S.J. Tsemberis, H.J. Psomiades, and A. Karpathakis. 1999

IX. *The Eastern Question: The Last Phase. Second edition.* By Harry J. Psomiades. 2000

X. *Realpolitik in the Eastern Mediterranean.* By Chris P. Ioannides. 2001

XI. *Reading Greek America: Studies in the Experience of Greeks in the United States.* Edited by Spyros D. Orfanos. 2002

XII. *The Voice of the People: Mantinades of Crete.* By Stylianos V. Spiridakis. 2004

XIII. *The Greek Junta Phenomenon: A Professor's Notes.* By Theodore A. Couloumbis. 2004

XIV. *My Detroit: Growing Up Greek and American in Motor City.* By Dan Georgakas. 2006

XV. *Confronting the Greek Dictatorship in the United States: Years of Exile: A Personal Diary (1968–1975).* By Orestis E.Vidalis. 2009

Table of Contents

Preface

"To those who cling to power through corruption and deceit and the silencing of dissent, know that you are on the wrong side of history, but that we will extend a hand if you are willing to unclench your fist" asserted President Obama in his inaugural address on January 20, 2009 recognizing the tension between democratic ideals and the pragmatic challenges of the world arena.[1]

And again, six months later in Cairo, "Obama tries to reshape American goal of global democracy" states the front page of the New York Times and its subtitle fills in "but leaves it unclear how to nudge regimes that don't share vision."[2] This was the Times' take, days after the President's speech in Cairo on June 4, 2009 where he reached out to the Muslim world with unprecedented eloquence, conviction and depth of understanding. While Obama's approach to the Islamic world broke new ground, the balancing act between democratic principles and pragmatic interests had been ongoing since America's rise to the status of superpower in 1945. As Henry Kissinger described it in his *Diplomacy* "no nation has been more pragmatic in the day to day conduct of its diplomacy, or more ideological in the pursuit of its historic moral convictions."[3]

This balancing act between principle and pragmatism fell on its face in the case of Greece in the late 1960s and early 1970s under the stewardship of Dr. Kissinger during the Nixon administration. Modern Greece had close ties with the United States since its struggle for independence from the Ottoman Empire in the 1820s. The Greek struggle was warmly embraced by America's people and leaders who had fought for the same ideals a few decades earlier. Greece and the United States fought on the same side in both World Wars of the 20th century. The relationship between the two countries moved to a new level after the Second World War and the tragic Greek Civil War (1946-49) which followed. Through the Truman Doctrine and the Marshall Plan, America literally altered the course of history for post-war Greece. Finally, the bonds with America have been further strengthened by the

[1]Obama, Barack. President Barack Obama's Inaugural Address. White House, Washington D.C. 21 January 2009.

[2]Baker, Peter. "Obama tries to reshape American goal of Global Democracy." New York Times International Herald Tribune. 10 June 2009.

[3]Kissinger, Henry. *Diplomacy*. New York: Simon & Schuster, 1994.

Greek-American Community which grew and prospered throughout the 20th century while retaining strong emotional and spiritual links to its ancestral homeland.

Despite all these significant ties, modern day Greece has developed a broadly anti-American sentiment, punctuated from time to time by riots and demonstrations. This sentiment continues to mark the course of Greek democracy 35 years after the demise of the 7 year military dictatorship that ruled the country from 1967 to 1974. In survey after survey of public opinion across Europe and the European Union, Greece maintains the lead in terms of distrust and dislike of U.S. government policies and practices.[4]

My father's diary, the book at hand, describes in lucid and revealing detail the policy setting during the years of the Nixon administration. American policies on the question of Greece (1968-74) were based on bureaucratic inertia, expediency and convenience resulting in American support for the despised Greek dictatorship. The myopic stance of the Nixon administration, through errors of commission and omission, ignored continuous warnings and principle-based positions regarding the loss of democracy in Greece. Despite a most significant opposition from Congress and the media, the American administration continued with "business as usual" toward Greece. In short, policy stability, once more, was chosen over democracy by the Executive Branch of government exclusively focused on the strategic objective of containing the Soviet bloc.

Decisions, consequently, followed the "reasoning" of ignoring domestic realities in Greece. Such decisions included the strategically insignificant, but politically laden, option to home port the sixth fleet in Greece, as well as the choice to supply military assistance to the dictators without democratic strings attached. There can be many explanations for this policy toward a small country and ally. The more benign hypothesis can be based on bureaucratic inertia, with some credibility, given the momentous conduct of foreign policy by Nixon and Kissinger simply focusing on higher level challenges and leaving the Greek issues to the various agencies and their intramural turf fights. Simply recall the negotiations to end the Vietnam War, the beginning of the process of détente with Brezhnev, the rapprochement with Anwar Sadat and the Yom Kippur War, the China opening and finally the administration's demise with the Watergate scandal.[5] Less benign hypotheses, which focus on the dominance of the CIA and the military industrial complex laced with imperialistic rhetoric, are more popular with Greek intellectuals.

[4]"Anti-American Sentiment up Sharply in Greece-Survey." Reuters. 16 December 2006. http://www.alertnet.org/thenews/newsdesk/L16822173.htm.

[5]Horne, Alistaire. "Kissinger: 1973, The Crucial Year." *The Economist*. 11-17 July 2009. 77-78.

Regardless of the hypotheses one prefers to adopt, the fact remains that the U.S. government supported the military dictatorship in both symbolic and real terms.

Beyond these hypotheses two instructive stories about the workings of the American political system are documented, in my father's diary. The first story is critical and pessimistic, as it focuses primarily on decisions made by the U.S. executive branch of government. The second story is optimistic, and it demonstrates the openness of the U.S. political system to the participation of persons with a moral purpose, reasoned argument and patient tenacity. People, even with modest means, armed with conviction and intellectual ability, can get a hearing, argue their case, and have an impact on policies over time. This book reflects the struggle of a man who left his country with little more than a suitcase and the ambition to witness the restoration of democracy in his fatherland. Pessimism and optimism intersect in the pages of this diary, as my father in the period of 1968 to 1974 set out to help shift U.S. policies toward opposition to the Greek dictatorship.

The diary begins on October 22, 1968 when my father was informed by the military dictatorship that he would be permitted to exit from Greece. The very next day, my father, my mother and I flew to the United States. We left behind a country that had been ruled by a military dictatorship since April 21, 1967. We boarded the plane with our personal effects and little else. My father, a brigadier general in the Greek Army at the time, had been one of the leaders of a move to dislodge the dictatorship from power. It took place on December 13, 1967. The months which followed were marked by the consequences of this brave but unsuccessful act. Stripped of his rank and held in detention (which was followed by house arrest and by continuous surveillance of our family) he was neutralized politically and rendered inactive.

Determined to act against the dictatorship on his own terms, he brought our family to Toledo, Ohio. To achieve financial autonomy he began a managerial career, at age 51, with Owens Corning Fiberglass Corporation in the totally unfamiliar professional environment of U.S. industry. He was helped in this choice by two key executives of Owens Corning who had known and respected my father from their own military days— the Chief Executive Officer, General L. Norstad (previously supreme allied commander of NATO), and the Vice president of Planning, Colonel (ret.) Jim Webel.

Thus, Orestis Vidalis began to fully engage with his "corporate day job" to provide for our family's sustenance, but at the same time he undertook the audacious task to change American policies towards the military regime in Athens. Needless to say, this left him little time to enjoy his precious family environment.

He pursued his single minded objective using a two pronged strategy: The first part of the strategy was to influence and to shift policy of the United States Government (Nixon/Kissinger administration) away from a convenient and short sighted accommodation of an "anti-communist" military regime. His counsel was that the U.S. should move to principled and vigorous support of democratic values leading to outright pressure to restore democracy in Greece. His conviction was always that a democratically ruled Greece would remain part and parcel of the Western world, given the convergence of values and interests of all concerned. The second part of the strategy was to advocate a credible and legitimate political solution to the Greek predicament that would restore the previous constitutional order without resorting to revolutionary violence, which would have surely created chaos and compounded the grave problems already caused by the junta.

My father meticulously recorded in his diary each day his discussions, his reflections and his key correspondence with officials at the State Department and the Pentagon, the U.S. Congress, the editorial offices of major newspaper and media and with the hesitant leaders of Greek American opinion. In parallel, he proceeded with a ceaseless, mostly clandestine, communication with activists inside Greece, both from the world of politics and the armed forces, as well as a very wide network of Greek activists outside Greece, which included exiled politicians and statesmen, intellectuals and business people — all united in their desire to hasten the end of the dictatorship but with vast differences among them as to the methods and strategies of restoring democracy.

For my mother and me, my father's struggle became our family's only project and a near obsession—as we supported him throughout the junta years in preparation of draft letters and speeches, research, filing and logistic support which he generously recognized at every turn. However, it was his intellect which always managed to envision the long term effects of various policies and his wisdom in synthesizing workable policy options in the real world.

It was his persuasiveness and intellectual honesty that earned him the ear of many congressmen (such as Senators Scoop Jackson, Claiborne Pell, J. W. Fullbright, Paul Sarbanes, representatives, Don Edwards, Ben Rosenthal, John Brademas, Don Fraser) as well as the editors of the New York Times, the Christian Science Monitor and Newsweek as well as the BBC in Europe. In wave after wave of visits to Washington D.C. and New York, my father triggered discussions that resulted in Congressional hearings and letter writing campaigns. His moderate style, his ability to listen patiently to all viewpoints yet argue with understated tenacity, and iron discipline, also earned him the respect and the ear of key actors in the executive branch as well, such as Undersecretary of State for Political Affairs, Dr. Joseph Sisco, and Vernon Walters, Deputy Director of the CIA.

My father was a gifted writer and public speaker, yet he chose the rigor of the diary and the discipline of the daily recording of events because he was mindful of the future student of history who would want to have as close a reflection of the events and the subtleties of the actions that unfolded. As a student and admirer of the classical Greeks, my father was aware of Thucydides method which was described in the "Peloponnesian War" in the chapter the "History of Early Times." "The absence of romance in my history will, I fear, detract somewhat from its interest: but if it be judged useful by those inquirers who desire an exact knowledge of the past . . . then I shall be content."[6]

My father was content with the full publication of his diary and archival material presented to the Greek reading public in 1997, thirty years following the colonels' coup. The two volume book received wide recognition in Greece and was awarded a prize by the Academy of Letters and Sciences which my father had the good fortune to receive in person.

He felt, subsequently, that there was an important story to be told by his book for students of international politics and the U.S. Government and he very much wished to have an abridged version with less emphasis on the Greek political detail and stripped of most of the personal and family elements, focusing mainly on his interaction with those that influenced and debated American policy and impacted on official decision making. He did not live to complete this task. It was to be accomplished in phases: The first phase, with the generous financial support of S & B Industrial Minerals and the Kyriacopoulos family entailed the meaningful abridging and translation of the Greek text carried out by the Hellenic Foundation for European and Foreign Policy (ELIAMEP) team under the supervision of professor Theodore Couloumbis, to whom our family is grateful for his friendship and diligence. The second phase, from which this new book has emerged was carried out by our family and has been a collaborative effort with the Center for Byzantine and Modern Greek Studies, Queens College,CUNY. This phase has come to its completion under the watchful care of professor Christos Ioannides. Both these scholars, along with (translators, editors and staff) have helped us capture and convey my father's profound love for democracy, and for this we are deeply grateful.

My father's struggle for the restoration of democracy in Greece was not born of discipline and duty alone. He was deeply offended that a consolidating democracy in Greece was suspended by some of his fellow officers who had hijacked the democratic institutions to which he had dedicated his

[6]Thucydides. *The Peloponnesian War*. Trans. Finley, John. New York: Random House, 1951.

professional life. He was and remained to his last day deeply passionate about democracy. He believed to his inner core that what the ancient Athenians first conceived and practiced is humanity's best hope. Democracy, after all, remains the only form of government that nurtures individual freedom and dignity.

Jean Pierre Vernant, in his "Les origins de la Pensee Grecque," wrote about the ancient Greek democratic city. He identified the causal link from philosophical debate displacing myth and immersing human thought to rigorous and rational argument, measurement and accountability. This led to pure political practices that were separate from religion, with their own vocabulary, principles and premises. The democratic thought paradigm had characterized a civilization which, as long as it survived, viewed public life as the apogee of human activity.[7] For the Hellenes, citizens of the democratic polis were deemed useless unless they actively participated in public affairs. Wisdom and reflection is the right and privilege of a free people. From democracy flow the norms, rights and obligations of a harmonious and self-sustaining polity.

Beyond the ancient Greek city state, the issue of meaningful participation in the democratic processes of large, impersonal and bureaucratized contemporary societies is a central challenge of our times. We hope that my father's story will encourage people to get involved in the affairs of the "polis," pursue their individual and group causes and, regardless of outcomes, contribute through their participation to humanity's collective progress.

Efthymios O. Vidalis
Athens, Summer of 2009

[7]Vernant, Jean-Pierre. *La Pensée Grecque*. Trans. Kakosaiou-Nikolouli, Eleni. Athens: Kardamitsa, 1992.

Introduction

The work, which this essay serves as a prologue, consists essentially of two parts. The major part is a journal or diary covering a period beginning October 23, 1968 and ending August 23, 1974. The only somewhat smaller part consists of a collection of documents (memoranda, correspondence, articles, etc.), almost all originating in the same period and each cross-referenced in the journal in its chronologically appropriate place. Together, the two parts open onto a broad landscape, the foreground rich in intimate and vivid detail. As its title correctly indicates, the work is about the author's years of expatriation, corresponding roughly to the seven-year period of military dictatorship in Greece (1967–1974) and focusing on the collective struggle waged against it from abroad as well as from within Greece.

Orestis Vidalis, by education, vocation, and professional self-identification a military man who rose in the officer corps to the rank of lieutenant-general, had thirty years of army service behind him and was serving in northern Greece as Chief-of-Staff of the Third Army Corps when, in December 1967, King Constantine II unsuccessfully attempted to stage a countercoup against the dictatorship imposed on Greece by army colonels in a *coup d'etat* on April 21 that same year. General Vidalis was sympathetic with the objective of the countercoup and informed about it, though on short notice. He was one of the key leading participants. As a result of its failure, he was placed under detention. Hence his decision to take the route of expatriation, but only as a temporary condition until democracy was restored in Greece and as the best base from which to do battle with the dictatorship.

Here then was a military man taking on a political project. He deeply believed, as he continues to do, that the military should strictly confine itself to military affairs and refrain from any involvement in the political arena, particularly intervention through resort to force. In his introduction he is careful to point out that, but for two exceptions originating in the execution of military duties and eventuating in apolitical personal friendships, he had no contact whatever with political figures before the dictatorship. One reason for opposing the dictatorship was the fact that it constituted, in extreme form no less, armed intervention in politics and was predicated on the questionable proposition that political problems can successfully be resolved through military means. But doing battle with the dictatorship involved his own breach of the boundary between the military and political arenas, his own involvement in politics.

In engaging himself politically, however, he was no longer in active service as a military officer. Moreover, though his expatriation entailed fighting the dictatorship through political means and constituted a political mission in terms of its weaponry, it was, in his eyes, a national project in terms of the larger goals to which it was dedicated and he was, as a private citizen, assuming the most solemn obligations—and costs—of citizenship and patriotism.

Why, if his project was resistance to the dictatorship, did he choose to participate from outside rather than inside Greece? His answer is that it gave him the freedom and opportunity to do things that he could no longer do in Greece. Only one of a growing body of expatriates, he chose as his base of operations the United States, rather than other parts of Europe or Canada, and it took him almost a year to make the necessary arrangements for leaving Greece and getting there.

Why the United States? Ultimately, perhaps, because the United States played a hegemonic role in Greece since the enunciation of the Truman Doctrine in 1947 and its decisive contribution to the victory of the pro-Western side in the Greek civil war that ended in 1949. U.S. policy, therefore, was one of the major factors that could contribute to or work against the viability and survival of the dictatorship. General Vidalis, in turn, was well placed to lobby for a change in U.S. policy, in part through friends and acquaintances within the Greek-American community, in part through prominent American military officials whom he had come to know through professional interaction within the NATO alliance. He was a man who, because he had performed career duties and pursued advanced studies in Washington, could operate effectively in the United States. The fit between an important national field of activity and a man conversant with it became financially and politically feasible when General Vidalis was offered a managerial position by Owens Corning Fiberglas, an American company that was the largest of its kind in the world. This appointment to the company's headquarters in Toledo, Ohio he owed to two of his former and most distinguished American assocciates in the military, both now retired and working for the company: as its Chairman General Lauris Norstad, former Commander of NATO in Europe, and as a recent addition to the company Colonel James Webel, who had served in Greece from 1960–1964 as a NATO liaison officer. Such a position was a *sine qua non* for the entire project because it provided the financial wherewithal to support a family of three (the author, his wife, and thirteen-year old son) and to cover travel, lobbying, and other expenses entailed by his project. In addition to ensuring the author's control over his project through financial autonomy, it also helped him, perhaps decisively, obtain the dictatorship's reluctant but eventual permission to leave Greece.

Expatriation, undertaken as a citizen's voluntary and temporary rallying to the aid of a violated and imperilled nation in crisis, was not only a self-initiated project. It was self-assigned and self-designed as well. There is no suggestion that General Vidalis was designated or even urged by anyone to take on his mission. There is no reason to think anyone designed the project for him or that it was the product of any systematic collaboration in advance of its implementation. Indeed, his was one of many projects independently springing up in various and sundry places. He, like others, had no choice but to define his own project and eventually to fit it into the assemblage of individual projects that emerged. Given the element of surprise in the military coup of April 1967, there was no already established infrastructure of resistance into which he and others could fit themselves and, particularly after the failed countercoup in December, those parts of any official or unofficial infrastructure that could be pressed into the service of resistance were either suppressed, dismantled, or crippled by the dictatorship. He was obviously free to follow his own judgment and feel his way as he took on new employment and explored his new environment. Much in the project as it took shape was *ad hoc* but much in its nature, strategy, and approach eloquently bespoke the man, his deepest values, his political orientation, and his world-view.

This was and is a man whose political orientation is defined by a series of core commitments: to democracy as the best form of government in the instrumental as well as the moral sense; to individual freedom and individual's defense of that freedom as the most solemn obligation of citizenship; to the exclusion of the military from politics and its subordination to civilian rule; and to the national interest as the interest is defined and served by the people alone rather than by or with foreigners, who can only be trusted to serve their own national interest as they define it. Though he embraced and embraces these commitments as ends in themselves, he also argues for them in pragmatic terms as well. He argues that democracy is the most effective path to national development, individual freedom the most effective way of inculcating the duties of citizenship, and a military divorced from politics the best guarantee of the unity, discipline, and professionalism that national security requires of the armed forces. Letting the foreigner define national interest is to forfeit a nation's control over its own destiny. This political credo he identified with the United States as its best, but arguing for those principles on grounds of utility, realism, and *realpolitik* was most probably designed to persuade (and embarrass or discredit) Americans who allowed national security in some narrow sense to override such principies or Greeks who may have given up on democracy in its quest for unity and the resolution of vital issues, and bought into the idea that order and progress depend on authoritarian methods and the use of force to compensate for the weakness of persuasion and voluntary compliance.

The general design of his project may appropriately be characterized as restorationist, hence as conservative, realistic, and minimalist. First and foremost, it was prompted by the wish to maximize the chances and speed the success of reversing the April coup and toppling the dictatorship, lest with the passage of too much time the regime might entrench itself and create new facts that would broaden rather than narrow the power gap between itself and the resistance. Second, it was prompted by the desire to achieve the restoration of democracy at the lowest possible cost in time, money, existing infrastructure, manpower, and blood, therefore essentially ruling out the armed resistance or guerrilla warfare then characteristic of third-world decolonization movements. These objectives meant defining the project in terms of what was considered the most easily achievable because it was the most modest goal: that of restoring the *status quo ante*, when its institutions and instrumentalities were still intact or amenable to restoration, rather than having to rebuild from scratch after the democratic landscape had been decimated, or aspiring to radical, systemic, revolutionary change that was intended to improve dramatically on the past but was in fact unpredictable in its ultimate results. The latter goal, because identified with leftism, might possibly constitute a source of bitter controversy, even civil war within the opposition to dictatorship.

The general strategy of his project has several identifying components. Resistance would be waged largely on the political and diplomatic fronts rather than as armed struggle. It would be as open and inclusive as possible, encompassing as broad a spectrum of the public as possible and confining junta collaborators to as small and ultimately isolated a minority as possible. This openess meant, at the political level, a coalition of right, center, and left parties, ordinarily ideological and political rivals but drawn together now by the common ban against their existence. It would also have embraced the King and ex-Premier Constantine Karamanlis, now both in exile, as rallying points of popular support because both, either singly or together, were symbols of legitimacy and continuity, the best guarantee for an orderly and stable transition back to normality, and, most likely, the only kind of leadership the United States would be willing to accept as an alternative to the colonels. Though neither the King nor Karamanlis were willing to make any formal or explicit commitment to it, this resistance strategy was at the time known as the Karamanlis solution. It meant in effect to keep the issue of monarchy or the nature of a restored democracy from becoming divisive constitutional issues or to settle for the announced minimum goal of restoring representative government and political freedom as the lowest common denominator of consensus within such a broad-based resistance coalition. The final and most fundamental component of this resistance strategy was its aim of winning over the military, domestically, and the United States, internationally to have these two props of the junta withdraw their support from it.

A feature of this strategy—reinstitution of the palace and the political right, for however limited a time, to a position of hegemony in this broad-based alliance—was its weakness as well as its strength. It threatened to wipe out the gains in democratization that took place under the Center Union Party of ex-Premier George Papandreou in the first half of the 1960's in other words, to restore democracy in its formal but restricted form of the 1950's under Karamanlis rather than in its mid-60s form during the heyday of Center Union rule. It therefore made a single, unified resistance movement impossible.

Running parallel to and in competition with the resistance movement built upon the Karamanlis solution, the movement that constituted a major pole of resistance and in which this project eventually became a component part, another major pole of resistance developed. Led by Andreas Papandreou and capturing a broad segment of the center-left political spectrum, PAK (the Pan-Hellenic Liberation Movement) adopted many of the trappings of third-world, anti-imperialist movements in the heyday of their success and ideologically identified its national struggle with the larger global struggle of non-Soviet socialisms against the rising neo-imperialism of the United States, as well as the declining classical imperialisms of Western European states. According to PAK, Greece was the victim of U.S. neo-imperialism, whose main indigenous props in Greece were the dictatorship and the defense establishment on which it was based. Resistance to dictatorship, therefore, had to mean resistance against its chief props; the Greek military, on the one hand, and the United States, on the other. This strategy, from the point of view of the Karamanlis solution, lacked realism. Its success was highly problematic owing to the unequal power balance and success, if it were to come, could only materialize after a struggle to dismantle the first as a whole and expel the U.S. from its hegemonic position in Greece.

What then were some of the component goals that were defined and pursued as part of the resistance project based on the Karamanlis solution? They were formulated with special reference to U.S. officialdom and general American public in order to effect a change in U.S. policy. They are covered by General Vidalis in the following characterization of the one objective of his "temporary voluntary exile": "to contribute, as much as possible, to the creation of conditions that would allow our repatriation to a Greece relieved of dictatorship and with the Greeks free."

The most obvious and least difficult task was at the level of propaganda or, more accurately, of counter-propaganda: exposing myths circulated by the dictatorship and, whether persuading others or not, at least not leaving unchallenged the status assigned them as facts. To the myth that the junta had intervened to avert a communist threat and to the myth that the junta had acted to replace a hopelessly flawed democracy and would eventually restore freedom without prejudice to order and national security, he asserted that the coup had its origins within a fanatical segment of the military at least ten years before it took place, during a constructive period of democratic life when there were no longer any signs of a communist danger on the horizon. He also asserted, with a variety of arguments, that the junta had no intention of restoring genuine democracy or giving up power, whose seizure they pretended to be only temporary. To the colonels' arguments that they enjoyed popular support or, at the very least, acquiescence, he argued that, under the repressive conditions of dictatorship, the people were not free to express their genuine sentiments and that, given the virtually universal assumption that the U.S. stood behind the dictatorship, the people regarded anything but acquiescence either futile or suicidal. The most important of these myths was that the defense establishment, especially the army, given this fact and its loyalty to NATO, constituted the best guarantee of the security needs of Greece, the U.S. and the Western alliance. To this he argued, ceaselessly and increasingly, that the best way to ensure the security of Greece and its value to the Western alliance was a strong domestic front and high public morale, neither of which was possible without freedom and democracy.

A broader task was not merely challenging junta myths verbally but also exposing and remolding reality in such a way as to expose myths through empirical evidence. This entailed encouraging elements in Greece to take whatever action that would and could demonstrate hostility to the junta and disaffection with the U.S. and NATO for collaborating with the junta and tolerating dictatorship within a Western alliance whose ostensible purpose was the defense of freedom, certainly in its member-states if not globally. Another component of this task was, in addition to exposing defections from the pro-junta military, encouraging them so that the dictatorship could only rely on a segment of the army for support and so as to be able to identify the dictatorship with only a segment of the defense establishment. Such defections had two advantages for the resistance. One, the most immediately important, was to persuade the U.S. that the dictatorship was, rather than the surest guarantee of U.S. strategic needs, the greatest threat to them because its involvement in politics had fractionalized and factionalized the ranks of the officer corps and had led to the retirement, dismissal, or resignation of the best educated, most professional, and most authentically pro-Western officers in the Greek army. The other was to ensure that, once the junta fell, the army as an institution would not be totally discredited in the eyes of the Greek public, that the threat of backlash be directed against small segments of the military rather than against the military as a whole.

The third and more complicated task was a lobbying campaign for a change in U.S. policy toward Greece. This entailed lobbying high U.S. government officials: on the one hand, the executive branch of the Government, particularly the State Department and the Pentagon; on the other hand, the legislative branch of the Government, consisting of the two houses of Congress. It also entailed working with the American news media and American academic circles. In addition, it attempted to lobby through the Greek-American community, not only those individuals within it who were part of U.S. officialdom (senators and congressmen, etc.) but also the Greek-language press in the United States as well as its two major nationwide institutions: the largest fraternal organization called AHEPA (American-Hellenic Educational and Progressive Association) and the Greek Orthodox Archdiocese of North and South America, led by Archbishop Iakovos and with its headquarters in New York City. In the normal course of recording General Vidalis' indefatigable lobbying efforts, his journal leaves the reader in absolutely no doubt that his contacts were legion, that he succeeded in finding his way into high places, and that he earned himself a reputation for dependability, moderation, prudence, and knowledgeability.

Among the lobbying objectives pursued, two were especially prominent and elusive. One was that, as a way of restoring democracy in Greece, Washington should adopt a policy of coercion based on threats and fiat and abandon the alternative of relying on suasion with the dictatorship through a policy of maintaining outwardly correct relations while quietly granting positive incentives. To Washington's argument that such a policy would constitute impermissible intervention in the domestic affairs of a sovereign state, General Vidalis argued that the problem of dictatorship was misformulated by Washington and that it had a duty to the NATO alliance, as did all member states in the common interest of the alliance, to intervene to remove the evil that alliance was set up to defend against. The other objective was to persuade Washington to make some public gesture of cordiality toward King Constantine and Constantine Karamanlis, two of the best-known opponents of the regime and the two hitherto most notable for their pro-Western orientation. Its justification was that such a gesture would constitute a tacit designation of one or both as an alternative to the junta, at least an alternative to oversee a transition back to democracy.

The final objective was to thwart, however quietly and non-confrontationally, any U.S. efforts to arrange for some accommodation between dictatorship and democracy, junta and palace or the political world. The possible return of the King to a Greece in which the junta remained in power was opposed on the grounds that his presence would only serve to discredit him and legitimize the dictatorship. Implementation of the authoritarian constitution of 1968 or any other constitution formulated by the junta, rather than one hammered out by a representative, democratically elected, constituent assembly, was opposed because it constituted a way of putting a pseudo-democratic facade on a dictatorship.

Suffice it to say, therefore, that the journal and the documentary section of this work are a mine of fascinating, detailed, and significant information about the junta period, its dictatorship and its resistance. It is particularly illuminating on the subjects of U.S. policy toward the dictatorship, the divisions within the U.S. Government and American society regarding the relations between Greece and the United States, and the nature of the Greek-American community's response to dictatorship in Greece and U.S. responsibility for it. It is inclusive of much else as well, shedding light on changes and divisions within the dictatorship itself and on resistance activities in Europe that converged with that of General Vidalis. It is, finally and most obviously, most informative regarding General Vidalis himself, who reveals himself casually, hence convincingly, because we see him as actor as well as recorder. To be sure, we see the landscape that he records through the prism of his personal experience as it is still fresh, but this champion of freedom, through the record form that he uses and through the way he records, allows us a freedom as spectators of the landscape to see it with our own eyes, mind, and spirit as well as his.

* * *

Thus far we have been writing about this volume as journal and documents, journal of and documents from the period of military dictatorship, journal and documents about resistance as the self-initiated and self-designed project of a self-designated activist answering the call of patriotic duty. We have examined the nature of the project and the record of its unfolding. But, in putting into print this hitherto private corpus of writings approximately twenty-five years after they were completed, in sharing them a generation later with the public at large, General Vidalis is engaged in a distinct though related project and presenting himself in a recognizably similar but not absolutely identical form. His work is enriched and enriching because it adds new dimensions to his project of 1967–1974; the hindsight of a quarter-century on the part of a man who is not just that much older but now engaged in a second project.

A journal or diary, kept concurrently with the activities and processes it records, opens a window to a past experienced as present. Its entries are written *in medias res*, when the future is unknowable and much in the present is still unknown. Everyone, protagonists and antagonists, groping in the dark regarding the future, lives in uncertainty about the effectiveness of what they are doing. That is what gives journals an immediacy, an authenticity, an excitement that is dispelled when hindsight and reflection on the past intervene. Hindsight, however, has a different set of rewards, it allows us to assess the significance of a period and evaluate its projects in terms of their verifiable consequences. What were the longer-term consequences of dictatorship, of resistance, of the dialectic between the two? With access to what once was the impenetrable future, the journal-keeper is better able to engage in self-assessment. By placing one's motivations and actions during that period in a larger diachronic context of unfolding processes, by rethinking the sufficiencies and deficiencies of one's earlier project, one can perhaps confront the opaqueness of one's current future with greater confidence or greater humility. One may be in a better position to decide whether to act or not to act in the present and, whichever the choice, what way to be active and what way to remain inactive.

Though General Vidalis' publication confines itself almost exclusively to his personal journal and related documents from the same period, he does, fortunately, encase them in a slim envelope of introduction and conclusion written some twenty-five years later. Unlike the diary itself, this envelope is not a dialogue with oneself, a personal record of the nightmare that was dictatorship in Greece, or a mix of expressed frustration and euphoria while ceaselessly doing battle for Greece in the United States. It is the late-1990s monologue of a still hardy but older warrior, coming out of retirement a quarter-century later, to do battle once more, but this time a different kind of battle. As in the late sixties and early seventies, he is again a self-designated warrior with a self-designed and self-initiated project.

The weaponry of this project is largely literary rather than political or diplomatic, as it was then. His intended audience is largely Greeks, Greeks of all hues: all citizens of mainland Greece (Helladic Greeks living within the boundaries of the Greek republic) and all those worldwide who identify themselves as ethnically Greek and with Hellenism globally. But this public monologue is particularly addressed to that segment of its Greek audience who are young, who were born after the period to which it relates or born too late to remember it. It is offered—devoutly, one might add—as a contribution to the collective memory, the on-going collective memory of living Greeks regarding their forefathers and foremothers, particularly in moments of extreme crisis. His project, this time, is not directed against a military dictatorship, which is, blessedly, thing of the past. It is directed against the possibility that a dictatorship might repeat itself if it is forgotten or if it is neglected as a legacy of an on-going present. The significance of his project might be described in the slightly paraphrased words of a character in Milan Kundera's *The Book of Laughter and Forgetting*: "the struggle of memory against forgetting is the struggle of human beings against power." As a contribution to the collective memory, this project falls into a long-established and cumulatively lofty tradition of memorialists extending. back to the rise of the modern Greek state, the tradition that received lasting grandeur from another military man who, like the author of *Years of Exile*, also had a natural entrepreneurial or managerial talent to go with his military skills, General Yannis Makriyannis. The writings of that General were memoirs, however, recall of events after the considerable passage of time, rather than a journal, the recording of events as they were taking place. It is the envelope in General Vidalis' work that parallels the memoirs of Makriyannis. Without the envelope he is merely giving the reader access to his private records. With it he is, beyond sharing the value of hindsight with the reader, also helping the reader work through the journal or reflect back on it.

Why has he undertaken this project? The most basic objective is academic and informational: to shed light on the first project. He asserts at the beginning of the final chapter ("Conclusions"): "The history of the activities in the United States for the restoration of democracy in Greece is unknown in its concrete details." Unknown in the United States as well as in Greece or not known well enough, one might add, lest one think his assertion is applicable only to Greece. Unknown in any comprehensive or systematic way, one might elaborate, lest it appear he means only "unknown with any degree of specificity." This project, then, is meant to provide a mass of information that can "contribute to the historical investigation of a critical period in the life of the nation." Reduced to its bare minimum, it makes available raw data for an eventual historical synthesis.

A second objective is to provide, in contrast to the journal format and in only the sketchiest way, an alternative format that he had considered for his subject and subsequently discarded: an analytical and topical account, which would sacrifice detail, complexity, and the rich texture of daily experience, for the sake of summary and necessarily more abstract analysis and assessment. General Vidalis' final chapter is a brief but illuminating attempt to utilize that format when it becomes, in his judgment, an appropriate adjunct to the format of his original choice. Taking three communities in succession—Greeks, Greek-Americans, and Americans—he analyzes the role of constituent groups within each community in supporting or opposing the dictatorship, in contributing to or abstaining from collective resistance.

There is no need to paraphrase the General's analysis, which is notable for its clarity, brevity, and balanced assessment of each community as a whole. Suffice it to observe that many of his judgments, more deeply delineated than in the journal, are unfavorable. But when they are, they are restrained, free of mean-spiritedness, self-righteous moralizing, or personal attack, and accompanied by the acknowledgement of extenuating circumstances. Negative judgments are counterbalanced by laudatory ones, but again with restraint and concern for accuracy. For instance, positive acknowledgements are emphatically and persuasively extended to two figures whose contribution to the resistance has gone unrecognized or, in the judgment of General Vidalis, received insufficient recognition: ex-King Constantine and Archbishop Iakovos of North and South America. Though these or other judgments may be disputed, what seems indisputable is that they are made with the most meticulous concern for equity and accuracy and that, though stated with conviction, they are presented without dogmatism or insistence.

A third objective of General Vidalis' current project is to assess, in long-range historical terms, the damage done by the dictatorship to Greece. There is no need to enumerate the summary list that he compiles after writing, with the help of hindsight, that the dictators "not only did not solve any of the political, social, economic, or national problems that troubled the country, but were the reason for the negative developments that took on the magnitude of national disasters." Suffice it to say that what is most impressive in his analysis is that he goes beyond the obvious types of damage, such as the catastrophe of the Turkish invasion of Cyprus in 1974 and the de facto partition of the island that has continued since then, to say nothing of the poisoned relations between Greece and Turkey as a legacy of that event and the dictatorship's contribution to it. He is deeply sensitive to the less tangible but real and lasting damage of the seven-year dictatorship, damage in the form of lost opportunities or loss of time and human labor which might otherwise have been used to take them. Among the things he finds most deplorable is the necessity, prompted by dictatorial rule, of redirecting Greek energies from the path of single-mindedly promoting Greek development in general to that of getting Greece back on the constitutional path.

Fourth and fifth objectives stem from his attempt to assess the performance of the resistance as a whole, parallel to the third objective of assessing the impact of dictatorial rule and in contradistinction to the second, which is confined to an analysis of the alignment of forces in the clash between dictatorship and resistance. If the junta was so damaging in its impact and if it was able to last so long, what is one then to conclude about the value or effectiveness of the resistance? The General reminds us that the dictatorship was not toppled by collective resistance or by the United States. The former was not able to, the latter never tried. He admits that, in spite of his lobbying efforts and those of others in the United States, the resistance, albeit more effective with Congress, never succeeded in getting either the Johnson or Nixon administrations to withdraw the support that the dictatorship needed to stay alive. Rather, it self-destructed after gross adventurism on its part. In retrospect, which is to say in the "envelope" of introduction and conclusions, his assessment of resistance is mixed: on the one hand, balanced, realistic, and nuanced; on the other, complicated and ambivalent.

His introduction acknowledges and summarizes important resistance initiatives over time and contributions to resistance by individuals and groups, especially in the political world, the armed forces and ultimately the student population of Greece and in the world of academia, news media, and Houses of Congress in the United States. His emphasis is on the positive, according all these efforts a cumulative contribution to the weakening and deterioration of the dictatorship, and a fourth objective appears in the form of acknowledging those who fought the good fight, including himself. In this introduction he writes of himself:

> "The nature and extent of a Greek military officer's activities must be made known, the difficulties he encountered, the help he gave others, the assistance given him by others, and the reactions of the dictatorship, which culminated soon enough (August 1970) with the 'withdrawal' of his citizenship."

In the next paragraph he goes on:

> "That narrative also constitutes an obligation I bear to all those who helped in all possible ways in the attempt to restore political normality, prompted by their belief that democracy ought to return as soon as possible to Greece, the land that gave birth to it."

In his conclusions the author takes up the matter in a more striking way, though in this case regarding citizens of the country that generously hosted him even as its government was propping up the regime he was so ardently fighting:

> "The writer absolutely believes that the time has come, after roughly three decades, for the Greek state to search out the eponymous American citizens who took a basically activist position against the Greek dictatorship, to reward them ethically and to honor them for their unselfish contribution to the restoration of political freedom in Greece. This book can serve as the basis for searching out such eponymous figures."

But, concurrently, General Vidalis shifts to a markedly negative focus in posing a very important historiographical question that adds depth and significance to his first objective of calling attention to the necessity of source materials for an eventual historical synthesis of the period of dictatorship. Why, he trenchantly asks, did all these efforts fail to liquidate the dictatorhip? The question is made more difficult and the charge of failure made more agonizing by having already acknowledged the magnitude of the human efforts and sacrifices that went into the resistance. He answers in a characteristically responsible and self-critical way: in so many words, because we did not do enough or do what we did effectively enough. A fifth objective is to engage, quietly but unmistakably, in an act of confession and expiation.

He starts with himself. He blames himself for two failures: not anticipating the coup of April 21 and hence being taken by surprise, not playing a sufficient role in the countercoup of December 13 and hence having to choose expatriation if he wanted to actively resist. Then, of course, the moral imperative of later promethian efforts to undo what might with greater vigilance have been avoided. On behalf of his generation he confesses to the youth of Greece that it has failed them by not avoiding conditions that made military intervention possible, by not organizing a resistance that was effective enough to nip the dictatorship in the bud, and not passing on to the next generation conditions making their burden easier but, instead, adding problems that need never have existed. We find him, then, engaged in a project of deeper moral purpose, a mission, raising the question of accountability for deficiencies and failures in the land and the question of how Greeks can use the imposition of dictatorship and the deficiencies of resistance as a mirror capable of reflecting back to them the flaws in themselves that need to be overcome. Realizing that casting blame on others is a more frequent human response than self-criticism, especially in times of crisis, and realizing that the assignment of blame is likely to be divisive rather than constructive, he is careful to caution that, though the dictators and those who supported them in one way or another bear a heavy responsibility for the seven-year dictatorship and the national crisis it precipitated, they are not the only ones. By deeds of omission if not of commission, he asserts, all are somehow complicit and hence accountable as well. All need to avoid accusing others as a way of exonerating themselves and to be self-critical so that all, feeling themselves accountable, will engage in a collective and concerted effort to purge the land of its deficiencies.

A final objective is formulated as a hope:

> "It would be a blessing for us to be taught something from that national vicissitude of ours and for us to create the conditions that would allow us to anticipate the future with optimism."

What conditions would these be? His entire work is an attempt to answer that question and, in the larger sense, show how one might use the lessons of the past in order to shape the future. General Vidalis is engaged in exercising and encouraging others to exercise the citizenry's right—and duty—of self-determination, but doing so through memory and the guidance than can come from memory's recall. He is explicit about his belief that the personal experience he acquired in carrying out his earlier project permits, perhaps even obliges, him to try his hand at answering that question. He tries to turn to account the first project by using it to facilitate the second one, this second one, like the first, entailing for him a time of crisis in the history of the nation.

The larger context of the current crisis is the international watershed precipitated by two processes: the dissolution of the Soviet Union and the unification of Europe. Apart from what it entails for the economy and international standing of Greece, the crisis incorporates, in the eyes of the author, a variety of components: among them, the deterioration of mores, mistrust of virtually everything, lack of confidence in political leaders, pessimism about the future, insensitivity to the needs of the weak, nurturing the young in an environment that fails to teach the riches of the national heritage or to inculcate decorum and civility, and, most of all, the frenzied political partisanship that has overtaken and lost sight of the national interest.

> "All these factors", he concludes, "tend to work against all those national virtues that kept us standing in incomparably more difficult periods of wars and national catastrophes."

Not only is he responding to a new and in many ways a greater crisis in this second project, he sees an integral relationship between this crisis and the earlier one, a relationship of cause and effect.

> "Though the result of many causes, a main one (for the current crisis) is a consequence of the interposition of the dictatorship, which, among all its dreadful consequences, stood in the way of modernization and renewal in persons and ideas."

Whether or not one agrees with the content of the author's response—his diagnosis of the current challenges and the best way to deal with them—at the very least one has to accord him admiration for keeping so knowledgeably current with the rapidly changing world in which we live and for dealing as comprehensively as he does with the problems it poses for and the opportunities it offers Greece. Even more, one has to appreciate one of the most impressive features of the work as a whole: that it provides us with material and leaves us the room to draw lessons beyond those that he enumerates; in short, to draw some lessons of our own as we anticipate the future. Allowing us this freedom is perhaps the most profound way in which we might find this valuable and illuminating work by so earnest, generous, and modest a patriot and inspiring paean to freedom.

John Anthony Petropoulos
Department of History
Amherst College

The exiled Brigadier General Orestis Vidalis

ORESTIS E. VIDALIS (1917–2001)

The long career path of Orestis Vidalis has cut through three different sectors; the military, the political and the corporate.

His military career began in 1937 when he was commissioned as a second lieutenant of the artillery and ended on December 13, 1967 when he became chief of staff of Greece's 3rd Army Corps. He participated in combat operations against the German invasion of Greece (1941) and during the Greek Civil War. He studied, and later taught, in major Greek institutions for the training of military officers. He also graduated from the U.S. Artillery School and the Command and General Staff College in the United States. He was the first Greek military officer to serve in the, then, Supreme NATO headquarters, at the Pentagon in Washington D.C.

His political career began in conjunction with his involvement with NATO. He studied political science at Georgetown University from where he received his master's degree in 1957. His opposition to the dictatorship, and his active pursuit of the restoration of democracy in Greece led to the loss of his Greek citizenship in August of 1970. In October of 1988 his book, "The Contemporary Geopolitical Setting and our National Policy" was honored with an award by the Athens Academy of Letters and Sciences. From 1988 until 1993 he served as chairman of the Center of Political Research and Further Education (ΚΠΕΕ) which was the most preeminent think tank in Greece at the time. During these five years, research programs of great national significance were completed.

His corporate career was a result of his exile from Greece to the United States. He started working at Owens Corning Fiberglass in November of 1968, reaching the level of Vice President. In 1976, he returned to Athens where he was assigned to expand the company's activities in the Middle East and Africa. He left the company in December of 1987. In November of 1992, he became Chairman and CEO of «Amfiktyonia 1992 S.A.»

CHAPTER 1

1968

Arrival in the United States

I opted for self-exile very early, while I was still under house arrest after the failed December 13, 1967 attempt. The United States, I felt, would be the best host country for me. It was a difficult and risky undertaking to relocate my family, my wife and my thirteen-year-old son. Being financially self-sufficient was the first requirement; it never crossed my mind that I might operate in the U.S.A. against the regime while being financially supported by others. If this condition were not met, I would remain in Greece.

I must now explain how it became possible for me to leave Greece. I will begin with the former American Ambassador to Greece, the late Henry Labouisse, who was an enthusiastic supporter of my views against the Junta. Labouisse came to Greece especially to discuss my plans with me and to see how he could help. Although I was closely followed by the Military Security Police at that time, one night I managed to escape surveillance and meet Labouisse at my sister's house.

At that time, Labouisse was Head of UNICEF and the discussion revolved around whether or not I would be interested in working at the United Nations. We left the issue open, mainly because we both agreed that it would be impossible to take public action against the dictatorship from within the UN. We agreed to keep in contact.

Following Labouisse, a good friend of ours came to Greece. The late Dr. Petros Koumandouras, a Greek-American scientist, humanitarian, founder and president of MEDICO. We met with him at the Hotel *Kostis* in Kifisia with great precaution, where we were staying in order to have access to a telephone since our own line at home was cut after my release from detention following December 13, 1967. I gave him detailed instructions to meet with Colonel James Webel in the U.S.A. and explained what was happening in our country and to me. As soon as he returned to the States, Koumandouras got in touch with Webel whose first contact with me was by letter on February 18, 1968.

From 1960 to 1964, the now retired American Colonel James Webel was in Greece as NATO's liaison officer with the Greek General Staff. We had worked together closely, when in charge of the office of the late General Frontistis, who at the time was Head of the Joint Chiefs of Staff.

In this capacity—and because of my earlier service with NATO's High

Command with the Standing Group in Washington—I participated in all the meetings between the Head of the Joint Chiefs of Staff and NATO's highest ranking officers. As NATO's liaison officer, Webel also participated in most of these meetings. Webel was an outstanding staff officer: tireless and perceptive. He also was a valuable supporter of Greek views and a model NATO representative to Greece. Our cooperation was extensive and close, particularly over the first study (which I think was also the last) of NATO's military assistance to Greece until the American military assistance was abruptly cut off in 1962. On many occasions we worked late into the night on the study code named *Athena*, which ended up providing Greece with the significant sum of 70 million dollars in assistance from NATO. This collaboration and the considerable esteem we held for each other bound us closely.

At the time the dictatorship took over, Webel had left the army and was employed by Owens-Corning Fiberglas (OCF), the largest firm of its kind in the world. At that time (1968), General Lauris Norstad, formerly NATO Supreme Commander for Europe was chairman of the company. Norstad knew me from meetings with General Frontistis, which I always attended. I discovered later during our long period of working together at the company, General Norstad was a military man who firmly believed that soldiers on active duty should not under any circumstances get involved in politics, much less intervene in the political process using force.

The coincidence of James Webel and General Norstad (both of whom I knew well) working for the same company provided the golden opportunity. As soon as Webel heard about my situation from Dr. Koumandouras, he began working to get me out of the country. Initially, escape by sea was planned. Although considerable effort was put into such a plan, escape by sea was not feasible, so we decided I should leave with a regular passport. Webel arranged for me to be hired by the company. When this was done, the firm sent me an official offer of employment on April 11, 1968. At the same time, they notified the American Ambassador of the offer.

Next, our departure had to be arranged. With support from the Director of Prefectures, Kostas Koukouridis, I met with Pattakos who was Minister of the Interior, and requested that I be issued a passport. Pattakos agreed on condition I sign a brief statement that I would refrain from political activity. Indeed, I did sign such a statement but was nevertheless not allowed to leave. Webel had to come to Greece, on September 1, 1968, to influence events.

On September 30, 1968, after his return to the U.S.A., Webel sent letters to Papadopoulos, Makarezos, and Ambassador Philip Talbot on behalf of the company to get the issue reconsidered. Talbot met with Pattakos on October 4 and received an encouraging response, but was not given a firm date. On October 22, 1968, the Head of the Military Security Police, Brigadier Spyros

Velianitis, a capable officer but an active participant in the regime, surprised me with a phone call that I could leave. Within 24 hours my wife Matina, son Efthimios, and I had left.

Departure from Greece and Initial Contacts

October 23, 1968, Wednesday
New York in ten hours

Nine months of patience and persistence have come to an end and today we are free and flying to the free world. The bitterness of exile is intense but mitigated by the feeling that this adventure is being undertaken to help liberate Greece. The first phase of patience has paid off. The only decisive factors were James Webel and my own withdrawal from center stage in Athens. Papadopoulos had faced the dilemma of either formally revealing his fear (that I might cause the Junta serious difficulties) or risking my freedom and thereby demonstrating his own courage. He chose the second, so today the second phase begins. The purpose of the first phase was for me to leave the country, openly or otherwise. The purpose of the second phase is to return to a free and happy Greece. How this goal is to be achieved, however, remains unknown. Nonetheless, I believe that I should follow certain principles:

a. Avoid making waves, at least for a while;
b. Get in touch with prominent Americans, inform them of the situation, and get them involved;
c. Restore contact with Europe;
d. Maintain secret contacts with Greece;
e. Wait for the results of the American elections before deciding on a specific strategy and tactics;

The Gotham Hotel was our first home in this land. The first people we met in this new and difficult phase gave us, apart from a warm welcome, optimism and joy.

October 24, Thursday
Breakfast meeting with the former U.S. ambassador to Greece, Henry Labouisse

I went to see Henry Labouisse at his office. He greeted me warmly and told me how surprised and pleased he was to see me at the UN. He recalled our last, 'illegal' meeting at my sister's house in Athens. We both spoke constantly about Greece. Actually, I monopolized the conversation at first. I described the situation since he'd left, especially the circumstances of the referendum. He was up to date. He seemed surprised when I said that the next hope to be dashed would be that the regime would restore democracy on its own. I explained to him that these people act on the basis of a deeply held belief that, for Greece, democracy falls between disaster and luxury. None of them believes in the need for proper democracy. This conviction is their foundation and they have no intention of leading the country back to normal conditions. They will try to keep the dictatorship going for as long as possible. They understand only blunt language from genuine free world democracies. Tolerance and appeasement will only keep them in power longer.

Labouisse followed my argument thoughtfully and concluded: "So, restarting aid was another mistake?" I replied "Yes, without a doubt, unless they have ensured that democracy be restored." He asked me to visit him again and to keep him informed and recommended that I meet with Daniel Brewster who was in charge of the Greek desk at the State Department.

October 27, Monday
First visit to the State Department

Meeting at the State Department with Daniel Brewster. Polite and interested, he listened to me carefully. His basic question was: "Do you believe they will want to return to normal conditions?" My reply was explicit: "They have no intention of returning the situation to normal quickly and will do so only under pressure. Any other interpretation is romantic and unrealistic, ignoring the junta's psychology, motivation, and beliefs."

When he asked me how I planned to deal with the issue of Greece, I replied, "I will brief responsible people and do not intend to use Greece's troubles for self-promotion." He told me to feel free to do whatever I wanted and to communicate with him whenever I wished.

October 29, Tuesday

Meeting with an old teacher of mine from Georgetown University: Professor Atkinson, a conservative anticommunist who specialized in Soviet Cold War strategy and tactics. He expressed the opinion that, forced to choose between sliding toward communism and the present situation, the latter was much to be preferred. When I asked if he would agree to this situation being continued for years, he reacted strongly against this prospect, describing such a development as a disaster for both Greece and the West.

Arriving and Settling in Toledo, Ohio— First Acquaintance with the Company

October 31, Thursday
A hesitant Webel

The first day in Toledo ended with many questions, the main one being: "Have I simply changed my place of banishment or will I actually be able to help my country?" The questions are agonizing and it only gets worse as I see Webel hesitant. Patience, however, is imperative for a gradual clarification of the position, with honesty and courage and, if necessary, a change of venue.

November 2, Saturday

House-hunting with the Webels since this morning. Several prospects but no decision. Webel always willing and polite but hesitant whenever I raise the subject of Greece. I proceed slowly and carefully. I don't want to upset the psychological climate through haste. The conversation does, however, give me Webel's impressions of General Norstad's views about Greece:

- He is not favorably disposed to the Junta;
- He thinks the King should under no circumstances return while the Junta is in power

This is the first optimistic indication so far.

November 6, Wednesday
A victorious Nixon

Woke-up at 6:00 AM. Television reports that the situation has changed since midnight, but nothing is definite yet. The contest is still too close to call.

Around 10:00 AM Nixon was declared the winner. Now Norstad is my only hope. Labouisse, Koumandouras and Brademas (a Congressman and friend of the doctor) are all Democrats. I am therefore well placed close to Norstad. On Friday things will become clearer. In the meantime, we are still hesitant to take the decisions that will bind us with Toledo.

November 8, Friday
Cordial meeting with General Norstad

I asked to meet with General Norstad and was told that he would see me that afternoon. That afternoon, around 4:00 PM, we were sitting in Webel's office discussing possibilities for my personal employment when the general arrived, sat on a chair, and began the conversation. We spoke about Greece for a full hour. In what follows, I will attempt to convey the general's thoughts as accurately as possible.

> "Clearly, the situation is a disgrace for Greece. There are repercussions upon all NATO officers and on me, personally. The King reacted properly and I believe that his action, even though it failed, saved the reputation of Greece, the army, and the throne. The King is capable and intelligent. He proved his democratic credentials. The Queen, young and likeable, comes from a family with a democratic tradition and is a marvelous companion for the King. The King must not return under the current regime but when he does return, he will be the only force capable of uniting the Greek people.
>
> "At our most recent meeting two years ago in New York, Karamanlis expressed bitterness at being abandoned by the Americans.
>
> "The men ruling Greece today hate democracy and clearly have a dictatorial mentality. They claim to have saved Greece from communism, but it is still not clear to what extent this is or is not true.
>
> "Kanellopoulos is a wonderful man but not an effective politician.
>
> "Despite these tragic times, Greece will emerge stronger from these tribulations."

At this point, I explained to him that the Colonels had no desire to bring democracy back to Greece. There was a great deal of evidence showing that they had no such intentions. The people, despite what was being said, were turning against the army and the Americans. Sooner or later this would lead to increasing sympathy for the political left.

"That would be a disaster for Greece and for all of us," he replied, "and if the Junta does not realize that extending their rule would be catastrophic, they must be pressured into understanding. The American government cannot do this immediately. But if some responsible people here make the effort, it may be possible to achieve something."

I told the general that I agreed wholeheartedly with his assessment and confessed that the goal of my presence here was precisely that: to inform responsible people so that there might be activity that would bridge the chasm appearing between the two peoples. Taking advantage of this excellent opportunity, I asked Norstad, "Would you like me to write down the events and my impressions?"

"Yes, by all means, please give me your views in writing. I will try to convince Mr. Nixon. Maybe we can achieve something," he replied enthusiastically.

I thanked the general warmly and, not hiding my emotions, gave him to understand that I already had achieved something very important. In this one hour, I experienced the greatest satisfaction I could have expected. Already there might be an opening to the new president, I had acquired a powerful new ally, and I was encouraged that I had chosen the right path. But now I had to write down my thoughts.

Webel followed the discussion silently, nodding his head at the points the general and I raised. He surprised me by intervening decisively at one point to add something very important that I could not say myself. He told the general that shortly after April 21, 1967 I was offered a very high post at the Foreign Ministry, which I declined. The general immediately said to me, "You were wise and cautious. It would be terrible if everyone were involved with the dictatorship." The day ended, with the first substantive success coming on Matina's name day.

November 23, Saturday
Communication with Greece begins

The first letter sent (November 10) by my classmate and very good friend Brigadier Panourghias contained important information about the funeral of George Papandreou and other matters, such as:

a. I never imagined that there would be such a crowd. According to the BBC, it was some 250,000 people.
b. Kanellopoulos was received enthusiastically everywhere all the way to the Cathedral. When his car stopped at one point, people rushed up and kissed his hands.
c. The King was not allowed to send a wreath.
d. All the palace guards are to be transferred because their present commander, a Gendarmerie Lieutenant Colonel, reported that "they do not inspire confidence as they are loyal to the King." (This is the precise wording of his report.)

It is gratifying that my system of communicating with Greece, however rudimentary, is starting to work, even though less than a month has passed.

December 13, Friday
First Anniversary of December 13, 1967

Today is the first anniversary of December 13, 1967. I am thinking of those hours.

The uprising in Kavala on the morning of December 13 proves how much the people supported the King's attempt to take power from the Junta. If the attempt failed, those least responsible for the failure are the people and the King. In the end, the responsibility lies with us all; the people who planned the action and the commanders and staff officers who rushed to carry out the plan but failed to take advantage of the King's initiative. Of course, much of the blame must be borne by many generals and other high-ranking officers who failed to uphold their oaths out of fear and selfishness.

A year ago today we lost a battle but not the war. That is why I am here. By coincidence, today I finished the report for the general and I gave it to Webel in the evening. It is dated December 13, 1968. Webel now seems very willing to help me. He has not yet read the report.

Communications Established with the King and Konstantinos Karamanlis

December 18, Wednesday

That afternoon the flight from New York for Toledo, for the first time, was delayed two hours. I arrived home late, not expecting any surprises, but I certainly found one. Matina told me that the King had telephoned from London. He called twice, asked when I was expected, and requested that I call him back by 11:00 PM his time. I had to call, therefore, between 4:30 and 5:00 in the morning.

December 19, Thursday
First contact with the King

I woke at 4:15. At 4:30 AM precisely I placed the call. When his familiar deep voice came down the line he told me: "Good morning, Brigadier, I am very glad you are there." He asked me for details about my departure and I briefed him about my position with the company. I then told him of General Norstad's position against the Junta. I assured him that Norstad was not only clearly against the junta but positively disposed to help return conditions to normal. The conversation concluded with the idea that I should propose the King be invited to meet with Nixon.

December 20, Friday
My first text on the dictatorship

Webel read the final text and was enthusiastic about the idea of the King being invited. He suggested that the King should be invited to the new president's inauguration. I said that would be ideal, but difficult. He thought a while and asked me what I thought of the idea of the King coming here and decorating General Charles Bonesteel, who led the mission to study aid for

Greece. I told him that if the State Department agreed, I was certain that the King would have no objections.

December 23, Monday
Communication with Greece continues

I received two new reports from Panourgias. The general assessment with which he concluded the December 5 report goes as follows:

> Under pressure from the Americans, Papadopoulos is being forced to negotiate the return of the King and announcing elections. Also to satisfy the Americans, he is discussing the participation of a few politicians in his government. Familiar as we are with his tactics, we strongly doubt his sincerity. Papadopoulos is probably using delaying tactics to strengthen his hold on power. Proof of this is the lack of reaction from the Junta's extremist factions, who are well known to be against the King's return. In the last analysis, Papadopoulos already controls everything and the armed forces through Angelis, remaining the dominant figure in the country. Any return of the King would at first glance seem highly unlikely and would mean his complete submission to the Junta.
>
> The *Daily Express* article and the associated rumors could be serving Papadopoulos's aims to promote his image as a moderate leader both at home and abroad.

December 24, Tuesday

I sent the following letter to Karamanlis:

> *Mr. President,*
>
> *I have been in America for a few weeks now. In April I had decided to try to leave Greece, when I became convinced that I had been neutralized at home and came to believe that I could help put an end to Greece's troubles if I were outside the country.*
>
> *You will be wondering what my capabilities are. Let me explain. From 1950 to 1953 I studied at two American military colleges, one of which was the War College. From 1954 to 1957, I served at the Pentagon as the first Greek staff officer of the Standing Group, NATO's largest Headquarters at the time. At the same time, as a private citizen, I went to Georgetown University and earned an MA in political science.*
>
> *I then served with our own Joint Chiefs of Staff, as director of General Frontistis's Office, where I was directly involved with important NATO matters, including the Athena study, through which, as you may recall, we*

received 70 million dollars over a three year period. As I am sure you realize, this background enabled me to develop personal relations with a large number of American officers, many of whom now occupy critical positions. In particular, I came into contact with General Norstad.

I felt this background had potential but also carried responsibility. The problem was, how would I disengage myself in order to exploit this potential? For eight months the functionaries conferred, then decided to let me go, and then reversed their decision after three days. I would not have been able to leave (with my family so as to avoid pressure later) had General Norstad not intervened. One of his staff and a personal friend of mine, a retired Colonel who had served in Greece from 1960 to 1964, came to Greece in September and presented the Junta with the choice either of admitting that my activities abroad could be a threat to them or of appearing strong. They chose to let me go, not really having an alternative.

So I am now here, free to use my connections and convinced now more than ever that I took the right course. In Greece I believed, and I am even more certain now, that if our troubles are to be ended, the solution can only come from America. There are now two unique opportunities, the new administration and the upcoming review of the NATO treaty.

I have been able to get in touch quietly with many officers, including your old acquaintances, Mr. Labouisse and, of course, General Norstad. Labouisse is an excellent man who sees things correctly, but he is a Democrat and therefore powerless. Norstad, in contrast, is a Republican and has a great deal of influence. He is particularly well disposed, aware of the general terms of the problem, and determined to speak with Nixon. I cannot predict the result because vast powers are besieging the White House. It is already a major step forward that the general, a person of great standing in industrial and economic circles, will become personally involved.

I am obliged to take this opportunity to tell you that in all our discussions the general has spoken of you highly and is a firm believer in you.

That is all from here for now. If you would like, it would not be difficult to keep you regularly informed of progress here. I am in contact with Greece—unknown, of course, to the dictators—and I regularly receive reports on the domestic situation. These reports are not always accurate, but they exist and I think they are improving. These, too, I can forward to you for your personal information.

Long before my sudden departure, I had informed Messers, Kanellopoulos, Papalighouras, Chrysanthopoulos, and Frontistis of my intentions. Since having arrived here, I also informed the King.

Please keep this letter and my intentions secret for now, until General Norstad proceeds, after detailed briefing from the undersigned.

That is all for my first contact with you and your first report.

I am at your service. I believe 1969 must be decisive and that everyone must concentrate their efforts on Nixon. I hope Mrs. Karamanlis and yourself will accept my warmest wishes for a happier 1969. I wholeheartedly wish that in the new year you will be able to help our troubled country decisively return to calm and peace.

Everyone, both here and there, expects very much of you.

Respectfully,

Brigadier Orestis Vidalis

December 25, Wednesday

Christmas Day. We are alone but not lonely. We are so close to Greece, to all of Greece, that we believe we are simultaneously in Athens and Thessalonica, in Veroia and in Kavala. My studies, the cards, and the final letter today to Karamanlis make us live only for Greece. We don't feel exiled at all. It is wonderful to live with a sense of mission properly thought out and—so far—correctly carried out.

While writing the cards I found myself again and again wishing, "that our country be calm and at peace once more."

December 28, Saturday
Regime's intentions clear: Stay in power

Today I received another two reports from Panourghias, but I did not find out if he had received my letters. The final assessment in the December 12, 1968, report is as follows:

1. Notes again the extensive effort to prepare the ground for politicizing the junta and legalizing the dictatorship.
2. Superficially lenient measures will be used to strip the arguments from the regime's opponents both inside Greece and abroad.
3. Papadopoulos is implementing the communist tactic perfectly. He is creating the impression of benevolent expectation. This deceptive tactic has brought significant results in political circles, so that no one believes that the only purpose of Papadopoulos's maneuvers is to perpetuate his power and nothing else.
4. In order to curry favor with the Americans and NATO and Pentagon officers, he is imposing the formal chain of command in the army, easily using Angelis, high ranking officers, and the Colonels. It seems that the lower ranking officers of the mutineers are falling into line and will not be able to react against it, at least in the near term.

The assessment in the December 19, 1968 report:

1. Papadopoulos's intentions are revealed in his speech. No word on elections. Though it would not be difficult for a "National Revolutionary Party" to win more than a hundred seats in parliament, who among them would elect Georgios Papadopoulos their leader? Freedom of the press is not an issue given that the press knows that Papadopoulos or a substitute will run the elections. With part of the old political world participating in the elections, a sham democratic climate is fostered particularly for external consumption. Papadopoulos's main idea seems to be to gain time, for the same purpose as ever: to perpetuate his rule.
2. Greece's reputation has been destroyed.
3. Is it possible that the U.S. is trying to find a compromise solution?
4. It may be possible to penetrate and organize active officers to overthrow the Junta.
5. The general public and the armed forces must be informed. Even officers outside the army are the objects of whisper campaigns and unverified rumors.
6. An attempt must be made, by blackmail if necessary, to unite Greece's political world.

December 31, Tuesday
1968 comes to a close

This morning Webel suggested we both go to the King and Karamanlis to give them information if Nixon changes his position and decides to talk to the King. We should also prepare them, so there may be a comprehensive solution. Webel's suggestion and attitude heartened me and I fully accepted his idea. He said that on a visit to OCF factories in Belgium and Italy we could also travel to Paris and Rome. All of this, however, depends upon Nixon changing his position.

Webel seems increasingly interested.

An unusual amount of activity has taken place in the last two months, capped by the report to Norstad.

Today ends a year full of anxieties and bitterness, but also with some hope.

CHAPTER 2

1969

The New Year Begins—General Norstad Favorably Disposed

JANUARY 7, TUESDAY

Today I received the general's first reaction.

Norstad met with Webel and told him that my report was excellent, contained some fine ideas and that he would see me at the end of the week to discuss it. The general is going to Washington over the weekend to meet with the new Secretary of Defense, who wanted to meet with him.

During the discussion, Webel suggested that one of the first steps might be replacing the Ambassador in Athens. The general agreed and responded that Labouisse would be an appropriate choice. Webel was thrilled with this idea, which the two of us had already discussed, and added: "Sending a new Ambassador and inviting the King to America will change the climate immediately." The general agreed. Webel left him deep in thought.

JANUARY 23, THURSDAY

The next letter to arrive was from Konstantinos Karamanlis:

> Paris, January 18, 1969
>
> *Mr. Vidalis,*
>
> *I am happy to learn that you are close to Mr. Norstad, for whom I feel deep respect and genuine friendship. The general is experienced in European matters and clearly perceives what his countrymen, apparently, do not. This is that day-by-day Greece's problem is also becoming their problem. There are two reasons this is happening. The first is that anti-Americanism is increasing and the second is that, strategically, Greece can become an open wound for America and NATO.*
>
> *I must tell you that, personally, I feel badly when I consider that, after making a mess of things, the Greeks find themselves in the position of calling upon foreign assistance to restore freedom to their homeland.*
>
> *Please convey my regards to the Norstads and to a good friend of mine who lives in Ohio, Mr. Canaday, 500 Security Bldg. Toledo, Ohio.*
>
> *Friendly regards,*
> *Konstantinos Karamanlis*

It is typical of Karamanlis that he does not hide his bitterness that "Greeks turn to America after they have made a mess of things." He is absolutely right. I wrote the same in my report to Norstad.

I also received a long letter from Panourghias.

In this letter, dated January 11, 1969, Panourgias expresses his pleasure that I have made contact with the King and Karamanlis and considers that, for everyone's efforts to bear fruit, the following are needed:

- A radio station or airtime on an existing station to broadcast news of the resistance and instructions to military officers and other leading groups opposed to the regime;
- Establishing a group in Europe to represent all the resistance;
- Direct communications between this group and the resistance inside Greece.
- Financial support for efforts within Greece.

Cooperation with the Resistance Begins

FEBRUARY 4, TUESDAY

Letter to Karamanlis.

Mr. President,

Thank you for your letter; it was a great encouragement. The general was particularly pleased.

I agree fully with your not liking that we have to appeal to foreigners. Unfortunately, at present it a prerequisite for some kind of solution, provided, of course, that we also help ourselves. The situation here, as I am experiencing it, can be summarized as follows:

- *The dictatorship is calmly tolerated, largely because of the stock phrase that Greece was saved from communism;*
- *This calmness is extended by Greek Americans, who return from visits to Greece with reports of apparent calm;*
- *In the United States there is a Committee for Democracy in Greece, whose honorary president is Melina Mercouri. The prominence of leftists as defenders of democracy increases perplexity;*
- *Most of the press is against the Junta but remains silent without stimulation. This already long silence further extends the calm;*
- *The concentration of Greek politicians and leaders within Europe and the constant harping by some that America is solely responsible for what hap-*

pened irritates the Americans, distancing them from our cause. They fear leftist chaos after the Junta.

The general is an exception. He considers the dictatorship a "disgrace" (his term) for Greece, its army, and even for the NATO militaries.

After our first meetings he was determined to speak to Nixon and asked for my personal views and predictions in detail.

I gave him a report, approximately 120 pages, on December 26. On January 10 he told me how impressed he was with its content, which he described as excellent, and said that he would forward it to influential friends of his in Washington. On January 27, when I gave him your greetings, he told me that the new administration is reviewing its policy towards Greece, noted his special ties to Kissinger, and confirmed that he would visit Europe in late spring.

I asked him formally if he agreed that I should let you know and he replied: "Certainly, please write to Mr. Karamanlis that I thank him for his greetings, ask him to accept ours, and that I hope he will receive me in Paris in late spring."

That's all as far as the general is concerned. I will let you know in time exactly when he is expected to travel.

Apart from this I have learned that General Quinn is to be the new Ambassador to Athens, though it is not yet official. From 1953 to 1956 he served with JUSMAG. I am trying to meet him.

I am concerned now with Nixon's forthcoming trip to Europe. On no account must he visit Greece. Instead, he should meet with you and the King. I don't know what can be achieved in this regard.

I have not yet seen your friend, Mr. Canaday. I have spoken with him twice on the telephone. He seemed particularly pleased, expressed his admiration for you, and asked me to convey his warmest regards. I hope to see him this week.

I will send you my report to the general as soon as possible, for your own information.

Mr. President, I am fully aware of the great difficulties, of all kinds, I will encounter. I know how powerful the forces of darkness—which reach all the way to Nixon—still are. And I know how hard it is to convince people who either don't care, or are prejudiced. I cannot predict the results of my efforts. I do not overestimate my capabilities, but I feel obliged to use all the strength I have.

I hope you will permit me to express the opinion that a coordinated and concentrated effort is needed now to shake things up here, improve morale back home, and force the junta to reconsider its position.

I have informed only yourself and the King of my activities. Nobody else knows anything.

To repeat what I have already written to you, I am at your disposal.

Respectfully,

Orestis Vidalis

February 8, Sunday

Dinner at Carl Staelin's, head of the company's legal division. The Canadays, whom Karamanlis recommended to me, were also present. Canaday is a powerful businessman who respects Karamanlis. He believes that the King acted hastily. He wants to help. He is afraid of both communism and the dictatorship. He let it be understood that he considers Andreas Papandreou, not George Papandreou with whom he had spoken and agreed, to be responsible. He wants us to talk, but he also wants the opinion of Tom Pappas. In any case, he was well disposed. He needs to be convinced that the Junta has no intention of leaving on its own accord, and then he might be able to offer something. He is afraid, but I don't know why. He was sent greetings from the King but did not reciprocate. He does not write to Karamanlis. He is thinking of going to Paris and Rome to see them but does not want to write. He is planning to visit Greece in May with others about the American School of Archeology. It seems that he has raised money.

Conclusion: interesting meeting. Fear dominates even those with nothing to fear. Perhaps his reluctance can be explained by concern about possible retaliation against the School of Archeology, with which his group is connected.

February 12, Wednesday
News from Greece

A dispute between Papadopoulos and Talbot appears in Panourghias's latest report.

> 1) Reliable sources close to the situation informed me that the last meeting between Talbot and Papadopoulos was dramatic. The outgoing Ambassador made clear to P. that his government wanted the Junta to leave immediately and that a new civilian government should return the country to democratic rule as soon as possible. P. replied that he was not about to bow to pressure or tolerate intervention in the country's internal affairs.

When the subject of NATO was raised, P. said that Greece would insist that the Alliance be revised and that whoever disagreed—meaning the Scandinavians—could withdraw. T. threatened that his government would denounce the Junta officially. It seemed, for a moment, that matters would take a serious turn for the worse.

P. threatened to announce that Greek-American relations had been damaged.In the end, apparently, tempers were controlled and further developments must await the arrival of the new ambassador. P. then called a meeting of the Council of Ministers Military Group at which Pattakos and Makarezos were in favor of complying with Talbot's demands. P. while the others were unrelenting.

2) The same sources believe that the Americans and others are beginning to see that the Junta will not leave peacefully.

3) For the post-dictatorship period these sources see a broad based, Karamanlis-led government that would hold elections within one year. The parliament would have the power to amend change the constitution. Karamanlis himself would not stand for election. It is also said that Andreas Papandreou agrees with all this, on condition that the parliament would be empowered to draft a new constitution, although this is not necessarily his immoveable position.

February 17, Monday
Nixon not in a hurry

Webel and I spoke about the Greek situation this morning, as we do every Monday. I confessed that I am distressed: I see no momentum. Nixon must meet with the King and Karamanlis soon. Webel acknowledged the delay and expressed his faith in Norstad, but offered to send telegrams to Nixon and Kissinger himself. I dissuaded him. I urged him to see Norstad immediately and learn what he wants to do. I told him that I have decided to send Norstad a second report with all the new information I have. He agreed with both these points and undertook to see Norstad.

Webel spoke with Norstad around midday and dejectedly told me that Norstad has discussed the subject with Kissinger extensively and thinks that it would be a very delicate matter for Nixon to see the King and Karamanlis now. The conclusion is that unless Norstad is operating without telling me what he's doing—and I wouldn't blame him—progress will be very slow. Nixon is in no hurry and obviously wants to explore the consequences of any changes before he acts, if, in the end, he does act.

In any case, I'll write the new report and keep up the pressure on Norstad.

February 27, Thursday

We had dinner at the Canadays, alone. Ward Canaday is primarily interested in the American School of Archeology. He has written to Papadopoulos. He wants to learn clearly and definitively what can be done. He is hesitant when I tell him that prominent people need to speak out. He fears for the school. Clearly, he wants this story to end, but cannot see how. At the end of the discussion he said that Nixon should clearly challenge the junta to set a date for restoring democracy. He was pleased when I told him that I would give him a copy of the report (the second report, given to Norstad on February 21). His case is typical of someone who loves Greece, wants to help, does not know how, and refuses to accept the status quo continuing. We ended the evening agreeing to continue the conversation, saying, "We must do something."

February 28, Friday
Answer to Oliver Marshall

Today, with some delay, I replied to Colonel Marshall, a former U.S. military attaché in Athens, who had written to me on 28 January. The letter described all the activities to date.

March 9, Sunday

I arrived in Washington in the evening. At 7:00, Professor Theodoros Couloumbis picked me up from the hotel with his car. I let him speak first. The Junta is well entrenched. Their people here are watching everyone. Everyone is afraid, no one speaks, no one knows what to do.

Couloumbis continued talking until we reached his home. I showed him my report to Norstad, and it fascinated him. He skimmed through the text, agreeing with everything. I showed him a letter dated January 30, 1969, from army Captain Ch. Rozakis. A new surprise. He agreed completely. The capstone was his question, "What must we do?"

"We need academicians to help, young people who do not yet have senior academic posts," I told him. He began giving names, and we agreed that he would send me a detailed list. He suggested inviting the director of the Voice of America Greek program and someone from the State Department to his house, so tomorrow night at 8:30 PM. I will continue the discussion with both of them, as well as Harilaos Lagoudakis of the State Department and T. Stavridis of the Voice of America.

MARCH 10, MONDAY

I went to Congress. At 2:00 in the afternoon John Brademas and a couple arrived, and we began talking immediately. I had prepared a presentation in order to restrict myself to the basics. He expressed himself freely as being against the Junta. He had met with them and had believed that they would hold elections, but, of course, elections were not held. He had met with Karamanlis, who shared his views.

He agreed with the Karamanlis solution. He told me I should meet all the Greek-American congressmen and described the positions each held. I asked him to send me a list of these congressmen, and he said he would. He will try to have the issue raised again despite there being many other issues of concern. We will meet again.

In the evening, I met with Harilaos Lagoudakis and T. Stavridis at Couloumbis' house. Both of them are solidly against the regime and both believe that the U.S. will not begin to take any steps unless obliged to do so. I asked Stavridis if a speech could be broadcast by the Voice of America. He answered that it will be broadcast if it is entered into the Congressional Record or published by more than two major newspapers.

Contacts Established with the State Department

MARCH 11, TUESDAY
Meeting with Brewster

I called Stavridis and we met at Congressman Nedzi's office, where I was introduced to James Pyrros. At dinner we were joined by Mrs. Luverne Conway. She was passionate about Greece. I explained the situation to them and emphasized that they both need to ensure a great deal is said about Greece over the next two months in Congress and the press. Both of them are liberals and both of them blamed American apathy and conservatism. They are fanatically against the regime and understand that only the Karamanlis solution can work now. They agreed that my presence, especially now with a conservative administration, is extremely useful. They will see that many articles appear in the press. Since I was not in the States when the developments in Greece began, I asked James Pyrros, who lived through the American responses from the beginning, to tell me what had happened.

Immediately after lunch, I went to the State Department, where I was welcomed by Daniel Brewster. This time, given the Talbot disappointment, I took the initiative and said

> "I believe that by now you must be convinced that Papadopoulos has deceived you. I imagine that Mr. Talbot has described the situation fully to you. My information convinces me that the situation is getting worse, that everyone is turning against the Americans, and that this dislike is turning into underground action. If we do not to intervene soon, we will no longer be able to intervene."

He listened to me carefully, agreeing. When I asked, "How is it possible that he has the support of the people and yet still maintains martial law?" Brewster responded, "Would it be useful to lift martial law as a first step?" I replied, "Certainly, but this must happen within the framework of a broader agreement and a general plan of action."

I put the idea of the King coming to the United States to him, and he did not object. Finally, I concluded, "This is a time for review. Current policy has failed. We must see how we can go forward together."

When we met the first time, Brewster had told me that they could do nothing, but he accepted my assessment now, agreeing that they must reconsider their policy and say something, but that it would be better if the Greeks raised the issue first. After the issue was raised, then the State Department could respond. In any case, the new administration has not yet dealt with the Greek issue, nor has it decided on a new ambassador. Other sources confirm this.

MARCH 12, WEDNESDAY
What is the revolution? A conversation.

At 4:00 in the afternoon Princess Irene called, and at 4:30 I arrived at her hotel. I told her my life story. She was attentive and interested. I asked if I could send a man whom I trust completely to the King. She replied, "If you trust him, so will the King, but we should call him in Denmark and ask."

She phoned Denmark right then and there and I spoke with the King. I asked if I could send a completely trustworthy messenger to Rome to brief him. He asked if it was anything urgent and I replied, "No, but I want to bring you up to date."

He agreed and said, "He should ask for Thomas, say that he is coming on your behalf, and I will see him." That evening I saw Petros Koumandouras. I begged him to go brief the King and explained what he was to say.

Afterwards, Koumandouras told me he had just finished reading a book by a political science professor who examined the historical consequences of large-scale global upheavals. The book's message was that since developing countries will go through a revolutionary phase in order to replace the old order with a new one, the U.S. should not obstruct the process by interfering in the internal affairs of such countries. Koumandouras was afraid that, perhaps, the State Department also considers the regime a new development that should not be obstructed.

My response was that social revolutions derive from spiritual and social unease, are positive and progressive, and bring new vision. First, the Greek Junta is not a revolution in this sense because it does not have any new vision, but believes only in the antithesis of democracy. Second, it is not a revolution because neither the people nor the intelligentsia support it, as is shown by martial law still being in effect after two years. Third, it has not replaced the old order because it remains based on the same supports (the army, foreigners) as in the past. New faces do not mean a new order. The fourth and most important point is that the violent overthrow of democracy only will hasten the real revolution which, when and if it comes, will take everything in its path, including Greece and the American position in Greece.

Briefing the King and Karamanlis with Special Messengers

March 13, Thursday

At 12:30 pm I met with Petros Koumandouras. I gave him my letter to the King and its attachments, explained exactly what he is to do, what he is to discuss, and when he is to go. The letter briefed the King about my actions with Norstad and Labouisse and their own positions; my meetings at the State Department and Congress; the negative stance (with a few bright exceptions) of the Greek-Americans; my contacts with Greece and particularly my contact with Karamanlis; "whom everyone here considers the only politician now capable of being useful in the solution."

I asked Petros to discuss only the following:

- Details of how I left Greece and who helped me;
- What I am doing at the company;
- What opportunities and obstacles exist;
- That progress is being made even though I am alone;
- That results can be achieved despite the difficulties;
- That nobody is aware of Koumandouras's mission.

Koumandouras discreetly asked whether the King might be angry with me for the failure of December 13. I explained that this should not be the case and told him that I spoken with the King in Denmark yesterday.

March 17, Monday

A copy of Issue 4 of the mimeographed publication *Eleftheroi Ellines* (Free Greeks) dated February 22, 1969 arrived today. [This was a conservative mimeographed publication, pro-King and anti-Junta, organized by General Sophocles Tzannetis.]

In an article entitled "Ideas and Guns" I read the following:

> On April 18, 1967, Prime Minister Panaghiotis Kanellopoulos, at one of the last cabinet meetings, prophetically said: "In our time there are two kinds of leaders. Those who have ideas and those who have weapons. My friends, ideas are not enough. . . .

Eleftheroi Ellines adds, "None of the attending ministers took his words seriously."

March 18, Tuesday

Meeting with Canaday in the afternoon. He tells me he is to go to Rome and Paris. He is enthusiastic about the text I gave him. He fears that Nixon is swamped. I tell him that intervention must be now because soon it will be too late. He is quite reluctant to take any initiative. I suggest that he investigate the Junta's intentions in Athens. He will learn that they do not intend to back down. When he returns, we'll speak again.

March 21, Friday

Bruce Lansdale arrives. We meet at home in the morning. His general impression:

- Damage to American standing in Greece is irreparable;
- The junta does not intend to leave;
- He cannot see how the matter will end;
- General Eaton of JUSMAG and most Americans stationed in Greece, with the exception of the agricultural attaché, are for the Junta.
- The Junta's standing will suffer if the new ambassador does not arrive quickly.
- A Greek voice must be raised. The King ought to appoint someone prominent to speak for him.

March 24, Monday
Koumandouras meets the King

Koumandouras calls to tell me that he has met with the King. He was well received and they spoke at length. The King asked him if I am optimistic.

Koumandouras replied that, alone and without support, I already had achieved a great deal. With assistance and coordination, therefore, I should be able to achieve much more. The King asked if we had ever discussed December 13 and Koumandouras answered "never." The King was happy with the contact established and asked that we keep it up but he seemed troubled by developments in Greece. Koumandouras asked him if he would come to the U.S. and was told he would do so only if invited by the president. Koumandouras had been doubtful before going, but he returned pleased and convinced that it had been a fruitful meeting.

March 25, Tuesday

Greek Independence Day. I write to John Nicolopoulos.* Among others things I describe my impressions from my contacts so far with influential Americans.

March 26, Wednesday

Webel is assigned to meet with Karamanlis.

Between OCF meetings, I write Karamanlis:

> *Mr. President,*
>
> *Colonel (ret.) Webel will be in Paris from April 7 to April 10. He served in Greece and is a philhellene. I owe my presence here to him, and he is a close associate of General Norstad. I have asked him to bring you the material I have written for Norstad. It is a good opportunity for you to meet and speak with him without reservations and to stress the dangers inherent in continued American inaction.*

After an extensive analysis of the situation, the letter concludes:

> *The moment is critical. If we do not hurry we may lose all hope. Then everyone will be irrevocably compromised with the regime and we will have complete enslavement of Greece to violence, which will slowly but irresistibly worsen. I must add that Canaday's question is echoed in many circles, "Why does Karamanlis stay silent?" No one believes that you are not involved in politics.*
>
> *I believe the time has come for you to lead a crusade of renewal. That we are outside Greece is not a disadvantage, being so increases our freedom of action. It would be good for you to visit the United States either now or, at least, after your meeting with Norstad.*
>
> *I wish I could meet with you. I wish I could circulate copies of various texts, such as the Anastaplo article, in the thousands. I wish I had complete freedom of action. But all this will come when you decide.*

These are my thoughts today. I will continue my efforts even though I am alone, without coordination, without being considered in the thoughts and actions of others.

My conscience is clear because in the King and yourself, the last remaining assets of national importance, I have unreservedly entrusted my actions, fears, hopes, and suggestions. I will continue to keep you informed and await instructions.

Respectfully,

Orestis Vidalis

PS. If you would like to have more copies of the Anastaplo article, please write to me.

I spoke to Webel before I left the office. He is enthusiastic about going to meet with Karamanlis.

Eisenhower's Death and the King's Arrival in the U.S.A.

March 28, Friday

Eisenhower died this afternoon. Everything here is slowly coming to a halt because of sad but expected event. I wonder who will come from the Greek side.

March 31, Monday
The King in America

Princess Irene calls me to tell me that the King wants to speak with me. I tell her that I very much want to see him, wherever and whenever he chooses.

April 1, Tuesday
Congressmen and professors seek an audience with the King

I called Irene in the morning. I told her that in the meantime I have learned from Sismanidis that Pattakos will stay for four weeks.

Petros Koumandouras called me in the afternoon. He met with Brademas today.

Brademas is now considering gathering congressmen and senators to ask Archbishop Iakovos to request a meeting with the King. Koumandouras also said that Sismanidis called to say that the King will meet the vice-president and the Secretary of State but also that Pattakos will see the same people. He fears that they may seek a compromise. I don't think so.

At 11:30 P.M. Princess Irene calls and the King comes to the phone. He seems happy and optimistic. "General, I want to see you. Can you come to New York?"

"Certainly." I explain that Brademas is trying to collect a group of congressmen and senators and Couloumbis is trying to collect a group of professors to meet him. He agrees and tells me that they should call Papagos in the morning. I tell him that Puschinsky has asked to see him, and I explain that he is a supporter of the dictatorship. The King was not aware of this. I stress that he must meet with Puschinsky and the King agrees. The same is true of Kousoulas. He tells me that he'll let me know when he is in New York so that we can meet there.

April 2, Wednesday

After the meeting the professors issued a short statement setting down the main points raised during their audience with the King:

Present: His Excellency, King Constantine; Her Excellency, Princess Irene; the King's Chief of Staff, Leonidas Papagos; Professors Theodore Couloumbis, Artemis Emmanouil, Phillippos Emmanouil, Dimitris Kousoulas, Nikolaos Stavrou.

The positions expressed during this audience were the result of many years of individual and collective research by the five professors. Each of them has published significant papers about modern Greece and all of them have been working together recently on a volume about modern Greek politics.

I call John Brademas, Democratic congressman from Indiana. He is pleased that contact with the King has been reestablished. He explains that even though Congress is on its Easter break he has assembled about ten congressmen to meet with the King. He tells me that my Toledo speech was "excellent" and that he will enter it into the *Congressional Record* and send me a copy. I thanked him warmly for all his support.

April 3, Thursday
Meeting with the King

At 11:30 the King called and I went to the hotel. The King greeted me warmly.

"Who have you seen, your Majesty?"

"The Secretaries of State and Defense and I spoke with Kissinger on the phone."

The Secretary of Defense informed the King that he had informed Pattakos that no decision was taken on aid and that the matter was being reviewed.

Kissinger, with whom there had been a scheduled meeting, called to say he had to go and was sorry they would not be able to meet. Kissinger told him, "Your Majesty, it is not possible now for you to meet with the president. You should come back when you can see him at leisure."

The King replied that if this were to happen, it must be before the summer. Kissinger told him to come back in May. The King remained noncommittal.

The King had an interesting meeting with de Gaulle, who insisted that he should come to Paris.

When the King finished telling me this, he added that his meeting with Vice President Agnew was unexpectedly good. Agnew was very interested. Later on, the King of Belgium told Constantine that Agnew had said to him, "King Constantine speaks clearly and frankly. I really like his position."

"Your Majesty, I have told you that they are reviewing their policy. The May invitation is an excellent opportunity. You must accept it and come fully prepared. Today Norstad told me that they are reconsidering their position, the secretary of defense told Pattakos that they have not decided yet on aid, and they haven't sent an Ambassador. All this is compatible with the May invitation. Your Majesty, in personal terms you must feel bitter that you did not meet with Nixon, but this bitterness should not be any deeper."

"Now, what is going to happen before May? I believe that Karamanlis must come here. I sent him a lot of material through Norstad's assistant. I suggested that he should take the lead and come here. His silence is helping Papadopoulos."

The King said, "I'll call Karamanlis tomorrow afternoon and tell him to come."

He seemed happy because we were getting somewhere. His disappointment was equally justified and unjustified.

We discussed the organization of the resistance in Greece. He will wait to meet with Pipinelis to find out what he meant when he said, "You go, your Majesty, and make all your contacts" after the King had phoned him from Rome to say that he was going to the U.S.A.

He asked me about December 13, and I said, "What do you want with the story, your Majesty? Don't worry about it; despite its failure it was an investment. You should be thinking of the future."

"I agree that it was an investment, if things develop as we want."

I stopped that discussion there and asked if all politicians had gone to see him. He answered, "All, except Papandreou."

The conversation ended around 2:30 in the morning. I bade him goodnight and stressed that everything would be all right.

I returned to my hotel, deep in thought for hours. How much that young man is trying to do, alone, unaided, without affection, misunderstood. And how much did he accomplish, how much responsibility did he shoulder when, young and inexperienced, he was abandoned by politicians, betrayed by soldiers, disappointed by those who stood by him, and now faced with the absence of coordinated activity by those inside and outside Greece.

April 5, Saturday
New meeting with the King

I arrived at the Drake Hotel at 9:30 in the morning. A short while later, the King invited me up as he was calling Karamanlis and telling him his impressions. When Karamanlis asked him if he had seen me, the King responded, "He is here with me. Speak to him," and passed me the receiver.

> K.K.: I received your letter and have met with the Colonel. We stayed together for an hour and discussed matters. I asked him to convey some points to the general.
>
> O.V.: Mr. President, I am repeating to you now verbally that it is an opportunity and a necessity for you to come here.
>
> K.K.: That needs preparation. I will study everything and see.
>
> O.V.: Certainly it needs preparation and we will do it.

Then the King and I were left alone. He told me of the difficulties he had encountered in order to meet with U Thant, the UN General Secretary.

I then began presenting my thoughts about our future efforts. I explained that the whole issue is psychological. All the people he sees, de Gaulle, Wilson, etc., must condemn the regime publicly. Secret diplomatic denunciations are of no use. They give the regime the pleasure of ignoring them. He agreed completely. I proposed that the May visit be very well prepared, with an earlier visit by Karamanlis if possible, on the basis of a detailed, specific program. When he meets with Nixon everything must already have been clarified. He agreed.

He recalled that Pattakos said Papadopoulos wanted to hold municipal elections but that Pattakos and the others did not let him do so on the grounds that such elections would be the first step toward their departure. The King concluded, "I will meet with Karamanlis, we will arrange everything, but I think that you should be present. Can you come to Europe?"

"Your Majesty, I can take leave but there is the matter of cost, because I cannot justify a trip to Europe with the company paying. I am sorry to bring up the issue but it is a factor."

"Why should you be sorry, it can't be ignored. I'll handle it. When we are ready, I'll telephone you to come to Europe."

"Agreed, your Majesty."

"Expect my phone call around the end of April, perhaps earlier." We parted. I do not know how the Greek story will play out but I thank God for giving me the strength to be optimistic and keep up the struggle. I believe the King is making the right moves. Nonetheless, what can he do alone, without a solid political base in these trying days?

I forgot to note the King's answer to my question about Archbishop Iakovos. "The Archbishop is clearly against the Junta. He sent them a letter setting January, 1970 at the latest for a complete return to normal. Pattakos was furious with him."

The King told me to see Clairborne Pell, the Democratic senator from Rhode Island.

Karamanlis—Webel Meeting in Paris

APRIL 7, MONDAY

April 5, 1969
Paris 12:15 PM

Dear Orestis,

I delivered your package to Mr. K yesterday at his apartment. I arranged to see him today again and I met with him one hour in his apartment. He said he had read your report fully, and your letter too. He did most of the talking but I was able to brief him on our feelings and on your special efforts. We will talk at length when I return but I wanted you to have a digest of his views now. The principal views he has are as follows:

1. For the regime to attempt to continue indefinitely will be a disaster for Greece and present a major problem for the United States.

2. He cannot state exactly the time period but he used the time of 3 to 6 months or perhaps a year as being the outside *limits for a safe solution for transfer of power.*

3. He insists it would be naïve for anyone to think the regime could merely call for free elections. There must be a very strong *and* very competent *political leadership and government as a transitional measure. He is prepared to do this and to obtain what he considers a critical reforms for the entire country as a preliminary step for free elections within a one or two year period.*

4. He insists that the U.S. Govt. must see Greece as a problem for them as well as for Greece. If they recognize this he is ready to come to Washington and counsel the president and to take an active part in preparing a detailed plan to transfer power to a government led by himself.

5. Mr. K. believes that only a carefully thought out plan with full U.S. support can succeed.

6. His popularity is still high inside and outside Greece.

7. He believes he is the only "bridge" left for the Junta away from disaster. Everyone else wants to hang them, but he offers a way to safely transfer power. If another six months goes by he may be forced to speak against the regime and this will destroy the bridge *and only a* violent *solution would come afterwards.*

8. He is prepared to come to Washington to advise the president but only if the president and U.S. Govt. feel they have a problem in Greece and ask for his advice.

9. He says the regime is "2nd rate Latin Amerian dictatorship" and this can never succeed in Greece where the people are not like the Latin Americans.

10. If the Junta attempts to retain power there will be a violent reaction in Greece.

11. The Communist block—in the future—could attempt to move into Greece. They want détente now but this picture could change and Greece become another Viet Nam.

12. Politics is a psychological state. You can let one or two trains go by but perhaps by the third train you are lost. He feels the time is now *to have the U.S. decide on a joint solution to the problem.*

13. He is prepared to advise and to lead a new government provided he is given freedom to run a strong government to solve many basic problems as the prelude to return to free elections.

14. He has been to New York 4 times but no one in Washington ever asked for his counsel or advice.

15. He does not force himself on the U.S. Govt. because he does not want them to say—"OK, it's your problem—go ahead and do it"—and then turn away. He feels it is a joint problem and needs a joint solution but wants U.S. support of the plan.

16. He feels that his value of his remaining status as the only "bridge" open to the Junta is a valuable link which he should not destroy by making statements against them when there is still a chance for a satisfactory transition of power from them to him which will save them and the country from an eventual disaster.

17. He suggested Norstad be named by the U.S. Govt to prepare a suitable plan for them. He would be prepared to assist and to lead in its execution. He repeatedly stressed his confidence in and admiration of Norstad.

18. He feels that for his own reasons he must soon bow to tremendous pressures from all over Greece and from other Govts in Europe to speak against the regime. However, he felt if he does this without a definite plan it will only serve to destroy the "bridge" and end the opportunity for a smooth transfer of power. He repeatedly said, "History will soon require me to speak for myself and the good of the country."

19. He feels the regime will probably have to make some type of future commitments on the 2nd anniversary of their Coup.

20. He looks and and feels strong and confident. When I first saw him yesterday after nearly 9 years I thought he had gotten old but today his eyes flashed. He has the steady gaze of confidence. He speaks powerfully and with great confidence. I believe he has the stuff to carry this off. He is a superb politician.

21. He stated he had no desire to return to politics or power but that he saw a great duty to save the country from disaster and he was prepared to return to head a government for that purpose.

22. He will only move in a major way to participate in a return to power if the U.S. sees this as a problem for the U.S. as well as Greece. He says he is the only hope to the Junta members for their personal survival and they need him.

23. He has not *been contacted by the Junta. They had meetings about him prior to the King's coup attempt but after he spoke against them, they have made no attempt to contact him.*

24. One of the reasons he has been quiet against tremendous pressures to speak is to retain the "bridge" which is an out *for the Junta. If the bridge is destroyed that option is finished forever. They need him both for a "solution with dignity" and for their survival.*

25. He is ready—willing and able. He waits for a call from the president for his counsel and advice and to participate in a careful plan. He believes Norstad could play an important role to head the U.S. side.

Orestis—this covers the main points of our conversation. I of course briefed him on what you are doing and the role you have played and on my own impressions of what is happening in Greece. My personal opinion is he would jump at the chance to participate in a plan that had U.S. support. He feels if he speaks on his own it will only "destroy the bridge."

He is personally strong, confident *and* well able *to carry this off. He wants me to report fully to Norstad when I return. He is* ready *and* waiting. *He feels he has more than 70% support in Greece now.*

We . . . will return to Toledo on either Saturday April 12 or Sunday April 13. . . .

I will brief General Norstad fully on this meeting with Mr. K. on April 14. In the meantime, please tell the general I have seen Mr. K. If the general comes to Europe Mr. K. would like very much to see him and talk on this matter. He sends his warm regards and respect. . . .

Faithfully,

Jim

April 14, Monday

Webel saw Norstad for only five minutes. He told him that they must meet at ease for at least half an hour. Norstad told him that he had seen the Secretary of State, who informed him that General Quinn in particular and the idea of any military Ambassador in general had been rejected. They have made another selection, a good one. Norstad insisted that they delay the announcement for as long as possible. He also told Webel that he had spoken with Pipinelis, who repeated that the junta needed to leave as soon as possible. Webel's new meeting with Norstad had not taken place by the end of the day.

April 15, Tuesday
Letter from Webel to General Spivy

Webel wrote a strong letter about Karamanlis to General B.E. Spivy, who is a member of NATO's Military Committee (the alliance's highest level).

Meetings in Washington and Reports to Karamanlis

April 21, Monday
Meeting with the Deputy Secretary of State

I went to the State Department and met with Stuart W. Rockwell, the Deputy Secretary of State, who was polite and willing to talk. I told him, "I have heard about you" and he answered, "Me too." I said that today is April 21st and exactly two years ago my deception began with the first communication I received that night. I also told him of my conversation with Pattakos a few days later when he offered me an important post at the Ministry of Foreign Affairs, which I rejected, stressing that I did not want to leave the army. He asked me about morale in the army. I emphasized that morale had never been worse and explained why it was so low in each branch, in the army, in the navy, and in the air force. I stressed that military discipline was dangerously lax, that effectiveness had been undermined by the removal of able and experienced officers, and that constant surveillance by the Junta's lackeys had bad psychological effects upon officer morale. I pointed out that serving Greek officers who were in the U.S. for training had tried to communicate with me, lamenting the unusual situation in the army and the low morale. Rockwell asked me how Greek politicians in and outside Greece were planning to coordinate their actions to help restore political life in Greece. He also asked me if the regime was in contact with influential people abroad, such as Karamanlis. I said, "I know Karamanlis has been in contact with other politicians abroad and with the King and that he is ready to undertake further responsibilities. "However," I added, "before Karamanlis proceeds with any new steps, he must have assurance from the United States that, if they cannot support his efforts, at least they won't work against him."

Rockwell answered, "It is our long-standing position that it is up to Greek politicians and the Greek people to take the most suitable measures to restore representative government in Greece."

I replied, "This position is a theoretical oversimplification because the problem is psychological. Everyone believes, rightly or wrongly, that the United States supports the regime and politicians, such as Karamanlis, cannot help until the American position changes."

He answered, "Karamanlis is intelligent enough to realize the difficulties involved in interfering in a country's internal affairs." Certainly Rockwell has closed his eyes to the fact that the Americans are prolonging the junta's life.

April 23, Wednesday
Karamanlis informed

Yesterday I returned to Toledo. In the morning Webel explained Norstad's position, which is:

- a His relations with the Administration are such that he cannot raise the issue unless asked.
- b He has already done everything possible and has asked that the appointment of a new Ambassador be delayed for six months.

Webel wrote to Karamanlis.

Clearly, Webel is distressed by Norstad's reservations. He has decided to write to Vice President Agnew, to General Wheeler, and to Kissinger since Norstad will not proceed. He showed me the letters and I agree.

Webel is fired up. He will try to see all of these people when he goes to Washington on May 2.

May 7, Wednesday
Letter to Karamanlis

Webel returned around noon. In Washington he met with Kissinger's aide and with Brewster and his aides.

Kissinger's aide was the more flexible. They talked for an hour and a half. Webel explained the situation and gave him a copy of my summary. Kissinger's aide told him that he sees no prospect for an American initiative but that they would not react against a successful Greek one. There is also no prospect of an invitation to Karamanlis. If he came, they would see him. He promised to relay everything to Kissinger and inform Webel soon of Kissinger's views.

Brewster firmly squashed the idea of a U.S. initiative.

I learned nothing new, just confirmation that if we don't start, nothing will happen.

My disappointment was obvious to Webel. He, too, was deeply saddened. He had expected more. I will write to Karamanlis and to the King.

May 8, Thursday
Letter to Karamanlis

I write the following letter to Karamanlis:

May 8, 1969

Mr. President,

Please accept my best wishes for your name-day.

Since Norstad and Webel have been working on our problem for some time, I now can tell you what I think will happen with your suggestions.

I believe that:

a. *Everyone (the Administration, but much more so Norstad) wants to get rid of the Junta as soon as possible.*
b. *Now they are applying more specific pressure directly upon the regime.*
c. *They will not commit themselves to third parties, such as the King or ourselves.*
d. *They will not invite you to Washington or discuss a joint plan of action.*
e. *They will applaud, silently at first, any positive initiative. They will increase pressure on the Junta and will move more to the fore as the effort appears likely to succeed.*
f. *They are not convinced that your following among the people is so high (70%). The American officers stationed in Athens have disastrous influence.*

Given all this, which I expect Norstad or Webel to confirm in the near future (they have both been in Washington recently), the question arises:

Should the Greek side take the initiative or should we wait for time to wear down the Junta?

I believe that there is no choice, because time will wear all of us down in the eyes of the Greek people and there is no guarantee that it will wear down the Junta.

I insist that now is the time for you to take a decision.

I believe that it would be useful for us to meet.

I also am writing to the King today about this matter.

The prospect is not distressing but neither is it pleasant in terms of your specific position.

Clarification of the situation would be of practical use.

Perhaps this prospect is even preferable since we will remain free of restraints for now and the future.

I am hurrying to put these thoughts down for you today so that no time will be lost. Please consider them as you make your decision. If the situation here changes in the meantime I will be pleased even though I will have acted to no purpose. Unfortunately, I don't expect it.

Please convey my respects to Mrs. Karamanlis.

Respectfully yours,

Orestis Vidalis

I am preparing an essay and other information for Greece. The people in Greece must understand that without activity within Greece nothing can happen.

May 9, Friday
Karamanlis on Webel's letter

I receive a letter from Karamanlis:

Paris 7.5.1969

Dear General,

Although Mr. Webel's letter does not fully convey my intent, it does capture the essence of my evaluation of the Greek situation. In any case, I was impressed by his love and enthusiasm for our country. I received the documents you sent me and congratulate you for the actions you have taken, although, as you know, I believe the restoration of democracy in our homeland to be primarily an obligation of the Greek people. The truth is, unfortu-

nately, as recent events have shown, that this has not yet been understood in Greece.

I must assure you, however, that I am following developments in Greece. I will not shrink from helping, if at some point I judge that my intervention would be substantively useful.

Friendly regards,

Konstantinos Karamanlis

P.S. I hope that Webel's letter has not been shown to others, apart from the general.

May 10, Saturday
News of Andreas Papandreou

Koumandouras called me. Andreas Papandreou made a speech saying that the Junta will be overthrown by the army. The American Administration did not receive him, he met with Senators including Kennedy, and he denounced the CIA again.

May 12, Monday

I telephoned Andreas Papandreou. Washington disappointed him. He was afraid that there will not be a peaceful solution. He spoke in Montreal and stressed the need for action in Greece.

Communication with Andreas Papandreou and His Colleagues

May 14, Wednesday

A new telephone conversation with Andreas Papandreou in the morning. He was disappointed with Washington. He agreed with my view that Greek politicians must unite and he agreed to see Karamanlis. In addition, he agreed not to speak of the army as if it and the Junta were one and the same. He believes that the resistance must get organized. He agreed that he ignored the psychological issue of serving officers who do not support the Junta. He thinks that Kanellopoulos should send a representative to Europe. He tried to persuade me that his relations with Karamanlis are very good and that the King needs to help promote the political issue. He disagreed with the constitutional issue as promoted by the *Greek Report*. He considers the 1968 Constitution a disgrace that must be replaced on the basis of the 1952 Constitution, and I agreed fully. He told me that Pell maintained that the Greek people have accepted the regime and that he had a difficult time persuading him that this was not the case. In any case, this convinced him that the resistance needs to act and he will instigate action in Greece as soon as he gets back to Europe. Andreas Papandreou's assessment that there must be substantive action within Greece is absolutely correct. The main problem is how such an effort can be undertaken without the forces inside and outside Greece opposed to the regime first being unified. [The *Greek Report* was published in London by the prominent *Kathimerini* editor-in-exile, Eleni Vlachou; the editor was Panaghiotis (Takis) Lambrias.]

May 17, Saturday
Meeting with Anastaplo and Deros

Yannis Deros came in the afternoon. A follower of Andreas Papandreou, he told me that Andreas was greeted by a cavalcade of cars and motorcycles and that they raised $14,000 for Andreas's cause.

We went to his office where I was met by a group of Andreas's followers who were clamoring for a common front against the Junta composed of the King, Karamanlis and Papandreou.

"Why does Karamanlis keep silent? Why does the King do nothing?" they pressed.

May 18, Sunday

In the morning I called Deros. I told him the three conclusions from yesterday's meeting.

- You must broaden the party base, because otherwise you will not be able to proceed;
- You must organize the mailing of copies with a catalogue of recipients;
- I will provide you with a copy of my speech of March 25 to broadcast over the radio on the day of the parade.

He agreed with everything but noted that the first would be difficult.

May 21, Wednesday

Bombs have started going off in Athens.

The *Toledo Times* wrote of bombs in Syntagma Square and at the Ministry of Finance.

May 29, Thursday
Article in Look*—Officers exiled*

The May 27th edition of *Look* magazine has a three-page article, "Greece: Government by Torture" subtitled, "The frightening military regime against the people today ruling Greece is responsible for a system of terror whose victims number in the thousands."

Couloumbis called me in the evening to say that someone had heard over the radio that there had been a royalist counter-coup which failed, and that officers have been arrested.

At 9 PM we hear from London that "23 officers have been arrested Wednesday night. Most were retired but some officers were still on active service."

I am deeply concerned for Generals Tzannetis, Vardoulakis, and Panourghias.

May 31, Saturday

That night Couloumbis called saying that a source, which cannot be disclosed, told them that the failed plan was to take Crete and bring in the King and Karamanlis. I told him this could not be believed because of the factional diversity of the group and because I knew the intentions of both Karamanlis and the King (without saying what they were, of course).

June 3, Tuesday
The King will not come to America

In the evening the King called from Switzerland. He is upset with the lack of action. He sent a messenger to Karamanlis saying that he sees no action, nobody in Greece is doing anything. My letter has convinced him that nothing is expected from America either. I answered that I had the same impression. Then he told me that he would not be coming to America because the administration does not feel that the timing is right.

June 5, Thursday
Thoughts on creating an organization

Had lunch with Dr. Koumandouras. We spoke of tomorrow's meeting with the Archbishop. I told him that I'm thinking of moving closer to the center of things, to Washington or New York, and that perhaps some academic post would be more closely associated with Greece. The doctor agreed and said that he would look into it. Then we discussed the possibility of establishing an organization throughout the U.S. He said that this is both necessary and feasible.

First Meeting with Archbishop Iakovos and Meetings in Chicago

June 6, Friday
The archbishop's actions

At 10:30 A.M. I arrived at the Archbishopric and was soon called up to his office. He began, "I received your speech from Mr. Koumandouras, the one that Mr. Brademas entered into the Congressional Record. I found out who you are." He then began explaining what his actions had been:

- He told both Pattakos and Papadopoulos that after two years it was time to give up power, but they would not listen. In fact, Pattakos became furious and said that he would "fix him." He may already have gone to Pythi [Greek village near the Turkish border] to meet with the Patriarch and speak against Iakovos.
- He has written to all the politicians, telling them to "Unite in backing Karamanlis."
- He is trying to see Kissinger to explain that Greece is a volcano ready to erupt unless they intervene.
- He believes Nixon's position is much harder than Johnson's.

He also related some typical incidents:

- The other day he bluntly told a diplomat that he was no diplomat but, instead, a government functionary, and the man replied, "What can I do? It is my duty to support the government; don't forget the majors, they are worse still."
- Nixon told Pattakos, "I have decided not to interfere in the internal affairs of other states, but the Atlantic Alliance is unhappy with the military government. You must soon restore parliamentary rule." Pattakos answered, "Instead, I think the Atlantic Alliance and you need our system." Nixon replied, "Then we have nothing left to discuss," and Pattakos left.
- The other day Skouras told Vovolinis that it is time for democracy to be restored. Although they were in the cathedral, Vovolinis shouted, "Why should we become a democracy, so we can be a mess as you are?"

I told the Archbishop my own position. He listened attentively and told me that he was particularly pleased. At the end, he told me to see him again and escorted me out.

JUNE 12, THURSDAY

I called the State Department and asked to have lunch with Vigderman, the new head of the Greek Desk at the State Department. They called me an hour later to tell me that he would be pleased to accept for Friday, June 27.

JUNE 16, MONDAY

In Chicago in the evening. I had to rent a car since Anastaplo doesn't have one.

After wandering around lost for a while I finally found his house around 9:00 PM. We discussed prospects. I stressed that each of us must do whatever we can without waiting for solutions from others. We discussed what can be done to mobilize the Greek community in Chicago. He had many reservations but proposed that I go see a Greek-American judge who might be able to give me information about whether or not Greek-American sentiment can be changed.

JUNE 17, TUESDAY
Andreas Papandreou declaration

Deros called around 5:00 in the afternoon and proposed that we meet in the evening. At 7:00 PM we met at a hotel near his. I presented my assessment and stressed that one-sided political positions repel, that differing groups should unite behind the single goal of overthrowing the dictatorship. He explained to me that they have worked in a nonpartisan way, that they set up the Committee for Human Rights, and that they plan to start distributing material to change public sentiment. I asked how they intended to accomplish this and offered to see if Anastaplo would help them. He asked me if the King would come to Chicago in August, if invited by the mayor. I said that I didn't know. Finally, we agreed that they would try to organize document distribution with Anastaplo's help and that we would talk again.

JUNE 18, WEDNESDAY

This morning I met with Javis, a rich Greek-American involved in many things. He came to the hotel and we had breakfast together. He said that he does not believe that Greek-American sentiment will change unless there is some kind of government in exile or something similar. I asked, "Who would recognize such a government? I agree that some voice must be raised, but until then, what do we do?" "Whatever we do will not be effective," he replied. I told him that "the problem is psychological and the voices of influential people here would be heard, welcomed, and effective." He understood the value of the idea and claims to know people, such as Rockefeller's brother and others. He agreed to try. I asked to send me the articles he's written and we agreed to stay in touch. I recommended that he read Anastaplo's article.

Had lunch with Anastaplo. He read Papandreou's declaration and agreed with me that it is going in the wrong direction.

I called Deros in the afternoon and explained to him that Papandreou's declaration is a political program for the post-dictatorship period. As such, now it helps the Junta because it does not help set a realistic course of cooperative action for all political figures and parties inside and outside Greece to bring down the dictatorship. I gave him Anastaplo's telephone number and address so they could get in touch directly.

Meetings in Washington

JUNE 26, THURSDAY

At 12:40 P.M. I arrived at Undersecretary of State Harold Saunders's office in the Executive Office Building, an extension of the White House. I outlined the situation and proposed the idea of progressively harsher measures as psychological preparation for a solution. He listened to me, agreed with my assessment, and admitted that given Greece's strategic importance, they are faced with a terrible dilemma. I stressed that they should evaluate the situation on the basis of developments five years from now, not today. At that point neither the Junta nor the people will need them. He was thoughtful, without reaction or arguments and without indicating that he had reached any decision. He thanked me for the visit and requested that I stay in touch.

Petros Koumandouras came by at 2:30 PM and we left to see Senator Pell. He was busy. As soon as he was finished, he came out in person and led us into his office while apologizing. He began by telling us that he had issued a statement on Greece today, trying both to commit the Administration and have a fact-finding team to go to Greece to confirm the *Look* article. He then told us that he is furious with the situation and asked what could be done. I outlined the situation and told him that the Pentagon was digging in its heels and that nothing was happening. He tried to excuse the military, saying that they had their problems, too. I told him that they could begin a series of measures imposing psychological pressure.

- "Such as? Should they tell Truman to speak out against the Junta?"
- "Even that would be something," I answered.
- "I'll write to him tonight and send you a copy, Petros. What else can we do?"

- "We can form a group of select Americans concerned about Greece and mobilize public opinion."
- "I agree and will be the first to join, but I don't have time to organize the group myself. Names such as the general's and yours, Petros, are valuable and I'll join you. They told me to go to the Fraser committee, which has Melina Mercouri, but I won't go because nothing is happening there. I am at your disposal. You are the first responsible Greek, apart from the King, I've met. Good luck. Now, however, you should go see the Secretary of the Senate Foreign Relations Committee. Tell him exactly what you told me and talk it over with him."

He called the Secretary, told him to draft a letter to Truman, and to talk with us. "Let's stay in touch, general. I am at your disposal. If you want to see Undersecretary Joseph Sisco or anything else specific, write to me."

I thanked him and we went to see the secretary. I explained the situation. He agreed and said that the issue is one of access to public opinion. The committee will be good because it will broaden support and maintain it over time. Money will be needed, of course, but it can be raised. Organization and prominent names will be required.

Couloumbis called me later to say that he was with the professor and former Minister Nianias and asked me to come to his house for dinner to meet with Nianias. I arrived at 10:30 PM. Nianias was in the country at the invitation of the State Department. He had passed through London and seen the King, who had given him my telephone number and his greetings to me.

Nianias railed against the Junta, hinted that the bombs had been placed by their organization, said that Markezinis ought to be hanged, that Stefanos Stefanopoulos was working on the ambassadors. He had seen Panaghiotis Kanellopoulos and Panaghis Papalighouras before leaving. Both sent greetings. We talked until midnight.

JUNE 27, FRIDAY
Meeting with State Department's Vigderman

Vigderman, the new head of the Greek Desk at the State Department, arrived at the hotel at 12:30. We sat down to lunch. He was an old acquaintance who had served at the Athens embassy. Our first meeting after so many years was particularly warm. I launched into the story at his request, and he was very interested. I stressed the decade old preparation for the coup. We reached the present. He spoke openly against the junta.

He said, "The new administration is reviewing all international problems and devising new policies. The Greek issue is coming up. Something new will be formulated on this as well. But don't forget that Greece provides us facilities we do not want to lose."

The conversation became interesting, and I told him that they must also consider the Greek people, who will resist. They need to look at the problem in terms of two, three, five years down the line to decide on a series of measures that will allow them to sound out public opinion and progress at the same time. Aid without commitments would be a tragic mistake. They could launch a psychological campaign. They could order their officers visiting and stationed in Athens not to praise the regime. They could advise Greek-Americans to change their position. Finally, they could send a special presidential representative to seek an alternative solution and ascertain the junta's strength. After all, why press for elections in Vietnam and not in Greece? All this is not interference, it is disengagement.

"I agree," he said. "Generally, your views are very close to mine with minor variations. What do you think? Should we send an ambassador or not?"

"Clearly not, until you decide on a new policy. It will be harmful if you send one before the policy review is determined. When you do send an ambassador, he should be a capable career diplomat and not a general or political supporter of Nixon."

"I agree. We find ourselves in a tragic position with Greece. No one wants to be involved. The embassy is furious. Everyone is furious, but everyone avoids the issue."

"Everyone else perhaps, but not you now."

He laughed.

We stayed until 2:45 PM. He told me to come see him when I was in town.

Conclusions: A marked improvement over his predecessor Brewster and confirmation that the pot is boiling. As he said at one point, "Papadopoulos must live now in a constant agony."

In the afternoon I went to see Saville Davis of the *Christian Science Monitor*. He told me that he had seen the King and was very pleased. I asked if he wanted me to provide him with documents to broaden the subject of the exiles into an article. He accepted enthusiastically.

At 5:15 PM I arrived at the hotel where Nianias was waiting for me. We stayed until 7:00. I stressed what the Americans need to understand. The people hate the regime, the army, navy, and air force oppose it, the people fear and dislike Americans. The solution is disengagement, not involvement. Measured steps toward a new policy are needed. A new ambassador should not be posted until policy has crystallized. Aid should not be given, or at least not given without specific conditions. I told him to be careful about the Greek-Americans and not the Americans and to trust Couloumbis and anyone he recommends.

He wanted to discuss December 13, telling me that I did everything I could in Athens. I replied, "We all made mistakes, we all did our duty."

We agreed to stay in touch and exchange views and to meet again before he left.

I believe that later he could be a useful connection.

At Couloumbis' place in the evening. At first, when we were alone, I brought him up to date and asked him to keep trying. Later we were joined by Emmanouil, Kyriazidis, Nicolopoulos and Lagoudakis.

They all agreed when I stressed the need to mobilize the Greek-Americans. The Greek nation extends beyond its borders to here and this is the first time that the Greeks of the U.S. have the opportunity to save Greece. If this happens, the bond will be eternal. If it doesn't, then the bond will be in jeopardy.

Lagoudakis gave me a note that congress had sent 116 letters to the State Department as a result of the *Look* article. Up to the 23rd of June, 103 letters had been sent directly to the White House and 374 to the Secretary of State. Altogether, 593 letters were sent by American taxpayers worried about the situation in Greece.

The breakdown:

May 19	68	to the State Department
May 26	95	to the White House
	71	to the State Department
June 2	8	to the White House
	66	to the State Department
June 9	64	to the State Department
June 16	67	to the State Department
June 23	38	to the State Department
	116	to senators and congressmen

July 5, Saturday

I called Nianias. He seemed pleased with his meetings but vague. When I asked about Kissinger, he told me that they had met and spoken for an hour, that he does not want the meeting to become public knowledge, and that they would continue on Monday. Kissinger was cold and unresponsive, he just sat and listened.

July 9, Wednesday
Sisco's testimony

Yesterday Joseph Sisco testified before the House Committee on Foreign Affairs for the Middle East and South Asia. In his testimony, Sisco also referred to military aid for Greece and Turkey. This part of Sisco's testimony is interesting:

> 28. Turning to military aid, most of the funding for the region will be spent on programs in Greece and Turkey, both NATO members and forward defense countries.
> 29. Important defense interests are tied to our relations with Greece and Turkey. They border on the communist countries of eastern Europe. Their political and military strength is needed for protecting NATO's southeastern flank and, in addition, is useful in providing a measure of stability to the eastern Mediterranean. Increased Soviet naval activity in the Mediterranean is a serious reminder of the need for continuous U.S. presence in the region, the importance of NATO's southern flank, and of our need for friends in the region. Greece and Turkey, therefore, take on added importance, since they border on the Aegean Sea through which Soviet naval units must pass on their way to or from their base in the Black Sea.
> 30. One of the keystones of Turkish foreign policy is NATO membership. This, combined with Turkey's military position, the strength of the country's armed forces, and its close relations with the United States, makes it particularly desirable to provide Turkey with the requested level of military aid.
> 31. Here I must make special mention of the military aid program to Greece, since there has been much discord both here and abroad. When the coup occurred in Greece, in April of 1967, the administration had to decide how to deal with the new situation. Should it support the junta, isolate it, or adopt a position intended to encourage the regime to eventually restore the country to constitutional, representative government?
> 32. In consultation with the legislative branch, the executive branch decided that the third option offered the best prospects for U.S. policy, which had to take into account not just the internal situation in Greece, but also the strategic interests of the United States in the Mediterranean and Greece's position as a NATO member. That is why the government of the United States decided to restrict the basic kinds of military aid to Greece while encouraging—as we continue to do—the regime to move toward a return to a constitutional government. At the same time we have maintained shipments of spare parts so that Greece can continue to fulfil its NATO obligations effectively.
> 33. Political developments have proceeded slowly in Greece. A new constitution was presented, a referendum was held, and some of the most repressive measures have been relaxed. However, social freedoms continue to be repressed, political life has not been restored, and an authoritarian government remains in power.

34. On the other hand, Greece has fulfilled all of the international obligations undertaken by previous governments, especially those which concern the Atlantic Alliance.
35. In the fall of 1968 it became clear that our policy of restricting the distribution of certain basic kinds of military aid to Greece would have to be reconsidered in the framework of international events, including the Soviet invasion of Czechoslovakia. There was no point in encouraging our allies to bolster their defenses for NATO and then deny the opportunity to one of them, to Greece. Thus, following the necessary consultations with the legislative branch, the president on October 18, 1968, approved the delivery of part of the proscribed aid.

First Contact with AHEPA

JULY 13, SUNDAY
Speech to AHEPA

AHEPA dinner meeting. I was impressed by the remarks made by a young woman, president of the Maids of Athens group. With few words, but vigorously, she posed the questions, "What is AHEPA? Why is it ailing?" I was the penultimate speaker. I tried to look at the riveted audience as much as possible.

JULY 15, TUESDAY
Article about exiles

I spoke with Saville Davis of the *Christian Science Monitor*. We agreed that the article should be published after Monday 7/21/69, when the moon landings would be finished and before Nixon's trip. He sent me a copy of the article he wrote based on his trip to Athens and the information I gave him about officers imprisoned and in internal exile.

I wrote to Brademas, who had sent me a letter apologizing for not being able to meet me in Washington. I sent him a copy of my speech to AHEPA.

JULY 17, THURSDAY
Unhappy letter from the archbishop and my reply

I received an unsigned letter from the archbishop, writing clearly about our failure to take action and promoting a Greek initiative. He is right. His letter is below:

July 12, 1969

Dear General,

I read your letter [Vidalis to the archbishop, dated July 1, 1969] with care. I found it pained, a bit more than I had expected. Have you have reached the point where you believe that there is no one left inside the fortress, that it must be taken from the outside? Heaven forbid. All our epics must be inspired by illusion, imagination, and the spirit of Don Quixote.

Where are the politicians and the soldiers? Why must the Greeks abroad—this extension of metropolitan Hellenism—bear the full burden of responsibility or take the full curse of the homeland? To help, yes. They did it in the revolution of '21. They did it in the disaster of '40. They did it again after the wars, both the first and the last one. They will do it again, through church guidance and influence. But, in which direction? In cooperation with whom? To what purpose? And should any action or endeavor fall flat, then what? Then the overseas Greeks, as a symbol of hope or influence, also will be lost. Coordination is needed. Who will draw up the battle plan? Shouting and slogans and abuse never won a battle. The battle must be fought. And it must be fought in both capitals, Washington and Athens. Simultaneously. Fiercely, decisively. The capitals of Italy and France must be aware of it. London and Bonn must be mobilized. That is when the Greeks of America will be needed. I assure you that they will not desert the cause. This time, too, they will be present.

P.S. My signature, which you know by now, does not need to be repeated on such documents.

I replied immediately:

Your Reverence,

The fortress does not need to be "taken from the outside," our efforts are not inspired by Don Quixote. The fortress needs to be freed from the suffocating U.S. embrace. That is realism.

The Greeks abroad do not have to "bear the full burden of responsibility." But at all cost they must avoid "the full curse of the homeland." The Greeks of America must not take any steps or action that would fall flat. God forbid. But is it necessary to have so much flattery (see the statements made by AHEPA's High Commissioner) given to the regime? Is it necessary to hold the 1970 conference in Athens?

"Where are the soldiers?" you ask. In the islands, prisons, and recently, apparently, in graves (Major Kourkafas died or was executed during recent interrogation. When I confirm it, I will inform you.) Others, unaided, pow-

erless, alone, are fighting to take the fortress. They crash against the police state, the lack of coordination and light and against the conviction that the U.S. supports the violence as the only solution (see the Symington letter.) They keep on fighting, even though they are being sacrificed.

The primary need is for a coordinated battle plan.

That is the fortress's problem.

All the fortress needs to feel is that the Greeks in America are aware of the tragedy and, at the very least, remain neutral.

The fortress expected that at least Greek-American "unease" would be felt in Washington. (I am not talking of "fighting spirit.") Now, unfortunately, Washington believes that the Greeks here have welcomed developments.

"Hope and influence" are neither endangered nor lost through all this.

If a battle is to be fought, should not everyone be coordinated? Shouldn't they know that they can count on the Greek-Americans to help fight the battle in Washington "fiercely and decisively?" Do they have any signs of such a prospect?

My letter was not pained, but it might have been bitter. Alone, unaided, I fully share your basic worries and bitterness towards the capitals. I mean to draw strength from being let down or encountering indifference and I am pleased because without "slogans and abuse" the fortress can feel the effect.

I am proud because God gave my humble self the opportunity, fortune, strength, and decisiveness to fight for this cause.

I am happy because I have remained a soldier.

I will continue as long as my strength allows, because I believe that we must safeguard:

1. *The nature of Hellenism.*
2. *The prestige of the Greek Army.*
3. *The nation's unity.*
4. *Relations between Greece and America.*

Before I conclude I must clarify one more point.

We of the fortress are responsible for the tragedy. None of you, outside the fortress, is responsible. We are responsible because, through our actions or lack of action, we allowed the fortress to fall. We are responsible because, apart from everything else, we helped create national division. Because of us the Greeks of America have the problem today.

Up to now they have dealt with it, and there are excuses, in a way the fortress interprets as approval for abolishing institutions and damaging the nation's structure.

The fortress is beginning to react.

(See excerpt of a report to the State Department submitted by a Greek-

American supporter of the coup after a quite recent visit to Athens. I will tell you his name when we meet.[1])

At this point the fortress is wondering if the Greek-Americans will continue to hold the same position in the future.

Your Reverence, I am pleased you have given me the opportunity to express some of my concerns to you. I am even more pleased to ascertain that you are upset and worried by the lack of action. Discussing our disquiet by correspondence is not the ideal method. I would be pleased, when and if you desire it, to visit you. I await your availability.

Respectfully yours,

Orestis Vidalis

P.S. 1) Statements made by the High Commissioner for AHEPA were published in the National Herald (Ethnikos Kyrikas) a few days ago. I am sorry that I do not have a copy available.

2) I enclose:

- *The Symington letter [Senator Stuart Symington, D Missouri]*
- *Excerpt from the report to the State Department.*

3) I am also sending you a copy of my short speech to the AHEPA conference on July 13.

July 20, Sunday

The world held its breath for the moon landings tonight. Men have set foot on the moon. Men from the free world were first. Unbelievable moments. It became a reality only through the coordinated use of individual initiative and freedom.

[1]Professor Kousoulas, who concluded his report with, "The above observations lead me to propose that the continuation of the present non-democratic regime undermines realization of the 'aims of the revolution' (modernization), causes apathy, alienation, and even hostility within society towards the Armed Forces and the United States and, therefore, gains peace and order at the expense of the future."

The Effort to Publish a Periodical and Organize a Cause Committee Begins in New York

July 26, Saturday
Contact with Kostas Karras

Kostas Karras called me in the morning from New York. He told me that they have found a public relations firm for promoting a sound solution and are seeking people to form a committee "For Responsible Government in Greece." He asked to meet me.

I arrived at the estate of Karras's mother, now Mrs. Rolfe. The Rolfes were there, along with Kostas Karras, Hovey of the *New York Times*, and Nianias. Discussion ensued about the committee. They wanted Norstad to be president, and I realized that they wanted me to convince him to accept. I explained the general's attitude, temperament, and preoccupations. I believe Norstad would be willing to help only if he saw the issue as an American problem and our methods as acceptable to the administration. If the subject were raised as a Greek request or effort, he would refuse.

I told them that the thought of such a committee had preoccupied me for a long time. I agreed completely with their effort and recommended that they be particularly careful about people and coordination.

After dinner we discussed possible members for the committee. The criteria: serious individuals and big names. I told them a lot they did not know and they listened with evident surprise.

Fifty Congressmen against the Dictatorship

August 1, Friday
The Congressmen's letter

Zotos of the *National Herald* (*Ethnikos Kyrikas*) phoned me to say that 50 congressmen have sent a letter against the junta to Secretary of State Rogers.

I received a letter from Nicolopoulos, with the congressmen's letter enclosed. Among other things, he wrote, "And something unpleasant: The Pentagon is leaking rumors to Congressman Don Edwards's (D-CA) office that you are lobbying for a compromise solution with the Junta. A certain Manolas, who appears to be working very closely with Tsiliopoulos and Kousoulas, is at the Greek Desk of the Pentagon's International Security Affairs. I think that if you were to meet with Edwards, we could dispel these small-minded maneuvers of the Junta."

I asked that they arrange a meeting with Edwards as soon as possible.

The Congressmen's letter is below:

Congress of the United States
House of Representatives
Washington D.C. 20515

July 30, 1969

The Honorable William P. Rogers
Secretary of State
Department of State
Washington, D.C.

Dear Mr. Secretary:

We are writing to you because of our deep concern over the situation in Greece, the only European nation in the Western Alliance in the post World War II period to fall to a military coup.

Authoritative reports indicate that in junta-led Greece the economy is in decline, fundamental civil liberties are suppressed, and people continue to be arrested and jailed without charge. What's more, anti-Americanism is reportedly on the increase because our long-time friends believe the United States is the principle support of a military dictatorship which has no popular base.

Our policy of occasional, tepid expressions of "hope" that the Junta will return to democracy stands in rather hollow contrast to the repeated instances of high-ranking American military figures being pictured and quoted in the controlled Athens press lavishing generous comments on the junta.

Thus we find ourselves in a situation where at a time of moral and political crisis in Greece, our traditional friends of liberal, centrist, and conservative persuasion believe with bitterness that the United States supports the dictatorship and the dictatorship, on the other hand, boasts about it. In the short term, and in the long term, we are in danger of reaping the whirlwind of anti-Americanism, especially when the junta falls, as it inevitably must.

America's attitude is critical to the survivability of the Junta. The sooner the junta falls, the greater the prospect that a responsible, democratic, western-oriented successor government will emerge to bind the economic and political wounds. The longer the Junta lasts, the grimmer the prospect of political polarization, turmoil, bloodshed, and unpredictable consequences to Greece and our own political, moral, and military interests.

Accordingly, we respectfully urge your consideration of the following action:

1. *Since the post of U.S. Ambassador to Greece, presently vacant, has taken on a growing symbolic and practical value, that it be filled by*

> *an experienced, civilian-oriented diplomat of superior credentials and not be treated as a political reward or routine promotion.*
>
> 2. *That a clear sign of U.S. moral and political disapproval of the dictatorship be given and sustained.*
> 3. *That U.S. military aid to Greece should not be increased, and indeed, should be curtailed.*
>
> *Sincerely,*

August 6, Wednesday
In New York with the Archbishop

Flew into New York. Meeting with Iakovos around noon. He has received my letters. Obviously, he had planned our meeting carefully. He began by describing his meeting with Aslanidis. "He exaggerated and was generally incoherent. But he did say something serious. If elections were held today, we'd get the same result as we would have had in May 1967."

Clearly, Iakovos told Aslanidis that the best thing they could do was remove themselves from power. They were not going to gain anything. When Aslanidis asked him to intercede with the administration, he replied, "It is not the job of the Orthodox Church in America to intervene either for or against the regime."

I asked him if he had seen the Congressmen's letter and told him that I wondered why three Congressmen of Greek descent did not sign it. He answered that they acted correctly, that it does not mean that they are for the Junta, and that perhaps even Brademas should not have signed it. Then I explained that we are past appeasement, the Junta is susceptible only to pressure. It is painful to see many Americans concerned about finding a solution while the Greek-Americans remain indifferent. After this initial discussion he invited me to have lunch with him.

We continued our conversation over the meal. He told me that Rogers had told him that he was following the right policy, that is, not dividing the Church. Then I said, "there is a difference between the Church and the community. Obviously the Church cannot make statements, but the community? Why should AHEPA hold its conference in Athens? Why should its president banter with Vovolinis and Pattakos? Can't they at least remain neutral?" He then told me that he would talk to Tsoumas and others at AHEPA. He was not certain that the conference would be held in Athens. He promised to apply pressure on them.

Then I asked if he could bring me into contact with Skouras. "Certainly, when he gets back from Greece I'll invite you over for lunch and then I'll leave the two of you alone to talk." I thanked him.

Conclusions: He is warm hearted, careful in speech and action, willing to help. He concluded our meeting by saying, "You proceed with your efforts and I will proceed with mine. Let each of us do what he can." I fully understand his position, the difficulties are real and his work is important.

The State Department responded to the congressmen's letter. The text of the reply follows:*

August 5, 1969
Joseph P. Addabbo
House of Representatives
Washington D.C.

Dear Congressman Addabbo:

In the absence of the Secretary I am replying to your letter of July 30, also signed by a number of your colleagues, concerning our policy towards Greece. I am sending a copy of this reply to the other Members who signed the letter.

Your letter points up the dilemma we face in determining our policy toward Greece. On the one hand we see an autocratic government denying basic civil liberties to the citizens of Greece. We think such an internal order does not coincide with the best interests of Greece, whose stability in the long run, we believe, depends upon the free play of democratic forces. We have been pressing this viewpoint upon the Greek Government, and our policy on military assistance has been motivated by our desire to see Greece evolve toward representative government.

On the other hand, Greece is a NATO ally which has scrupulously fulfilled its treaty obligations. It is important to our strategic interests in the Mediterranean area and has extended full cooperation in this field.

This, then, is the dilemma—how to deal with an ally with whose internal order we disagree yet who is a loyal NATO partner working closely with the United States in furtherance of the purposes and obligations of the NATO Treaty.

Our policy toward Greece is now under intensive review. As we consider this difficult problem we will keep the suggestions of yourself and your colleagues very much in mind.

Sincerely yours,

William B. Macomber, Jr.
Assistant Secretary for Congressional Relations

*Appears in Congressional Record, August 12, 1969, pages H7320–H7321.

AUGUST 15, FRIDAY

I received the following letter from Karamanlis:

Dear Mr. Vidalis,

I received the documents you sent me and I thank you for your regular updates, which I would like you to continue.

Yesterday I had a visit from Mr. Nianias who told me his impressions from the discussions he had in the United States. Obviously, the issue concerns them theoretically. They do not want, or do not know how, to approach the situation practically.

Rest assured that I am following developments in Greece with interest.

Friendly regards,

Konstantinos Karamanlis

AUGUST 19, TUESDAY
Rolfe-Norstad meeting

In the evening I called Rolfe. He had met with Norstad, who seemed enthusiastic but also cautious. He had been well received. Norstad had spoken against the Junta and was thinking of going to Greece to speak against the regime, but Rolfe told him that no one would hear what he said there, that he ought to be making statements to the BBC, etc. Norstad asked if Rolfe knew me and whether or not we had met. He praised my work with the company. Norstad also asked if Rolfe knew Karamanlis and received an affirmative reply.

He seemed disposed to respond positively to our proposal. At least he did not say "No." He has to clarify his position both with the company and with the administration. That he did not say "no" is significant. Presumably, he will think about it and discuss it with Webel. Another critical meeting ended as well as could be expected. We will await the results.

AUGUST 27, WEDNESDAY

I set off in the morning and arrived at the Rolfes' in Easthampton six hours later. They were sorry that my wife, Matina, had not come with me.

I explained that we would have to persuade Norstad and proposed that the 28th of October would be a good opportunity to announce the formation of the committee. We wrote a letter to Norstad and then drew up the operational plan should he accept. Karras had written them that the Junta might call snap elections and that they should ask me what would happen then. I had written Rolfe on this subject.

August 29, Friday

Saville Davis had his second article on the exiled officers published today in the *Christian Science Monitor*. Entitled "Blow to NATO. Are the Greek Armed Forces Disintegrating?," the article described the effect that losing some of the best officers to internal exile and discharge has had on the combat readiness of the armed forces. Davis had gathered his information in Greece and from the documents I provided him.

September 18, Thursday
New document to Norstad

I finished the following letter and sent it to Norstad:

September 18, 1969
To: General Lauris Norstad
From: Orestis F. Vidalis

Dear General Norstad:

I am fully aware of your interest in the problem of Greece. It has been some time since we discussed this matter, and I believe I have a duty to bring to your attention some facts and some possible future developments.

In my December 13, 1968, report to you I made the following statements:

- *"The sole objective of the junta was and still is to seize and retain power at all costs."*
- *"The methods in achieving this objective comprise:*
  - *A strategy of deceiving the Hellenic and world opinion by pretending that they are building a new democracy.*
  - *Their tactics aim at complete neutralization of all opposition combined with a major brainwashing of public opinion."*
- *"They believe that* democracy *is for Greece something between a* DISASTER AND A LUXURY."
- *"Present conditions within the Armed Forces and the extremely bad relations with the population is such that the morale, overall fighting efficiency, and total war potential of the nation are seriously impaired."*
- *"Despite all efforts by the regime, its popularity is steadily declining."*
- *"In the final analysis, the people are distressed and confused. If the regime is permanently left to its basic belief (toleration and support by the U.S.), nothing but catastrophe will be the end result of the Greek Drama."*

These were some of my beliefs nine months ago.

Unfortunately, developments confirmed all my predictions. There are two areas, however, where my predictions have proved to be extremely moderate, i.e.:

- *The growth of anti-Americanism, even among the conservative segments of the Greek population.*
- *The decline in popular support for the Junta*

Based on the above, let us review what is now likely to happen in Greece.

A campaign has been placed in effect by the junta, through the Greek press, against the King. The King himself has very recently rejected a proposal by the Junta for him to return to Greece unconditionally, and has laid down three prerequisites for his return:

1. *Free elections under international supervision*
2. *Full restoration of press freedom*
3. *The release of all people arrested by the regime.*

Within the last three weeks, an official spokesman of the Junta accused Mr. Karamanlis of working in close cooperation with the leader of the communist party to overthrow the regime.

After the psychological preparation is complete along the above lines, the Junta will soon stage trials, sentence some recently arrested officers and civilians, and then move to their immediate interim objective for solidifying their police-state, i.e., TO DEPOSE THE KING.

Thus, through no effort of the communists but by actions taken by the junta itself, the half-century-old dream of the communists *might become a reality in Greece.*

In addition, on September 8, 1969, the Junta premier stated:

> *Economic developments in Greece cannot be materialized under parliamentary government . . . . Priority should be given to economic development and the maturity of the Greek people under the guidance and influence of the state.*

This is a very clear redefinition of the dictatorship by the dictator himself.

In light of past experience and these likely future developments, we should again pose the question of what the official United States attitude should be.

The latest expression of the position of the present United States administration is, "We face a dilemma." [See August 6 entry on pp. 69–70 above for State Department dated August 5 in reply to letter from 50 congressmen.] This really means, "We do not want the dictatorship, but the free world is unable to outsmart *the dictators," and I can't really believe this is true.*

Two main approaches are taken in this country in connection with Greece. Some people are primarily interested in maintaining Greece under non-com-

munist control at any price, *and others are concerned that the price for this non-communist control is* too high. *The first group is satisfied with the present; the second is worried about the future.*

We have reached a very critical point indeed in terms of preparing for likely future events.

Even at this point, there is no question of the United States imposing solutions upon the internal problems of Greece. The requirement continues to be the disengagement *of the United States from supporting a government that has done nothing but establish a* police-state *in Greece. It has violated all concepts of democracy and free society advocated by the United States in opposition to communism and dictatorship in any form.*

The requirement continues to be the creation by the United States of a new psychological climate, within which developments planned by the Junta can be stopped, enabling new initiatives reestablishing freedom and rational behavior to materialize.

It is time that the belief held by Greece and the entire world in the leadership and ideals of the United States be reconfirmed by words and action.

In my December 13, 1968, report which I updated on February 21, 1969, I submitted to you certain proposals, which I believe are even more valid now than they were before. I would like to suggest that you reconsider these proposals now, with a view to positive action before any assistance from this country becomes either impossible *or* useless.

Above all, I urge you to take any possible action to support the KING and his three conditions for re-establishing rational life in Greece. By assisting the KING in his stand against the dictatorship, one supports Greece, its people, its democratic institutions, the ideals of our world, thereby strengthening NATO and the defense of the United States and the Free World. There is still time to avoid another Vietnam in Greece—but that time is running out.

Orestis E. Vidalis

Setbacks Concerning the Committee

SEPTEMBER 19, FRIDAY
Norstad declines

The Rolfes telephoned late at night. First, Maria said, "We don't have good news." Sydney Rolfe then told me that Norstad called and apologetically told him that his advisers "don't recommend such a role because at the appropriate time [Norstad] will be called upon to mediate. He is the only person suitable for such an assignment who knows the situation." Norstad went on to add that, "this decision is a victory of cold logic over my emotional impulse." The general found the memo I had sent him "excellent" and recommended Milton Eisenhower or Dean Acheson to head the committee instead. A clearly distressed Sydney Rolfe asked for my opinion. I answered that we must persevere and not lose heart. He must find prominent individuals for journalists to interview. We must create a fuss in the press and examine the prospect of publishing a periodical. Maria Rolfe agreed with me. I said, "I believe that we have important work ahead of us and we can succeed. I started this alone and accomplished what I have. Together and with money we can do much more." They agreed with me. I tried to boost their morale. We agreed to think things over and discuss the matter in detail on Sunday, October 15.

September 20, Saturday

Anastaplo came by train from Chicago around midday, on his way to Rome, Greece, Paris, and London. We stayed together for six hours, during which I explained my position in full and how things might develop. I gave him a letter for the King and coded messages for Nianias and Papalighouras. He was worried that he might not be allowed into Greece.

September 21, Sunday
Briefing Karamanlis

I wrote to Karamanlis:

Mr. President,

In a previous letter I raised the idea of a non-governmental effort. On August 19 General Norstad was asked to lead it. He did not reject the proposal. During the discussion he expressed the thought that he might "go to Greece and speak out publicly against the Junta." At that time he declined to give a final answer so that he might discuss it with the Owens Corning board of directors, of which he is the chairman.

Since then he has received my written memo and I sent him the attached document on September 18. I had not directly raised the matter because it was judged that it should remain a clearly American initiative.

On Friday, September 19, he gave his final answer, "My advisers don't recommend such a role because there is the prospect that I will be required to mediate at the appropriate time. I am, it is thought, the only one conversant with the situation and the only suitable person for such an assignment." He apologized for this position, which he described as "a victory of cold logic over my emotional impulse." He did not explain who his "advisers" are. Presumably, the government intervened.

This decision, which at first sight looks bad, may hide developments I do not yet know.

Of course, I am not discouraged. Now it seems that there may be some funds available. I will continue my work, with some help this time. The target audiences are again, congress, the press, the Greek-American community, and, certainly, the goal is for there to be repercussions in Greece.

The greatest possible pressure must be brought to bear. It improves morale back home and is, unfortunately, the only way to influence the American system. The reality of pressure unfortunately trumps the idealism of principle. The Christian Science Monitor article (August 29) was sent to Generals Wheeler and Goodpaster via General Spivy. Wheeler distributed it to all handlers of the Greek issue at the Pentagon. In Greece the article was described as "stunning." The next important article will be published in the October 7 issue of Look. I will send it to you as soon as it comes out.

And now I feel obliged to raise the issue of the King, on a completely confidential basis. If my information is correct, and I think it is, the dictators are thinking of going to extremes. They calculate that by deposing the King they will please the anti-royalists and thereby reverse the sentiment rapidly rising against them.

If the initiative is left to the regime, I fear that we will be left reacting to a fait accompli. The reaction will impress no one. It will be without effect. So I pose the question to you, "Shouldn't we all, and especially you, try to persuade the King to clearly state his position concerning the dictatorship, before the regime makes its move?"

In his isolation he needs your counsel. I make the suggestion because I believe that the time is critical. No longer are we all distracted by the sins of the past, and we are obliged to avert further disaster. Right now the King needs support and advice of a higher caliber than he has yet received. The country and the King have suffered enough from irresponsible advisers and their counsel. You know this better than anyone.

I may be in Europe in November. Will it be possible to see you then?

Mr. Anastopoulos visited me yesterday. We talked at length about the situation here, except for Norstad's refusal and, naturally, my thoughts about the King. He is a valuable asset.

I enclose the document I sent to General Norstad on September 18. I am also sending you some articles from the American press.

Yours,

Orestis Vidalis

September 29, Monday

Today I received the *Congressional Record* for September 18. Pell proposed blocking new credits to Greece until democracy is restored.

Karamanlis Speaks Out Against the Junta—Efforts to Spread His Message

September 30, Tuesday
Meeting with Rolfe

I arrived in New York. Karamanlis has made a statement.

I met the Rolfes at 3:00 in the afternoon. Kostas Karras had called from London and will call again. Mike Moynihan also came. He had no idea about the problem. We explained what we wanted and he kept notes. He undertook two things: First, to print a letter with the main articles against the Junta from the most important newspapers (*New York Times*, etc.) along with Karamanlis's statement and mail it all over America. He also undertook to study the usefulness and cost of a monthly publication. Karras called and said that they would take out a page in the London *Sunday Times* to print Karamanlis's statement. He asked if we should do the same here. I told him that we should wait to see how the press reacts first. We told him we were thinking about a periodical. He was afraid that it would be a big problem. We say otherwise and he agrees that we should do it.

Moynihan left to work on the immediate task. He and Rolfe asked me what we should write in the letter. I remembered that Karamanlis had told Khrushchev, "You can destroy the Acropolis but you cannot destroy the spirit that built the Acropolis." They agreed.

The *New York Times* published a report from London and a fine editorial, but they did not have the full text of Karamanlis's statement, and it was not on the front page. The editorial, however, made up for it.

October 1, Wednesday

Today The *New York Times* published an editorial entitled, "Caramanlis Fights The Junta." Among other points, the editorial noted, "Caramanlis's statement presents the Nixon administration with the moment of truth for Greece. The State Department is obliged to face up to the fact that their policy in Greece is bankrupt. The influence of the United States at this critical juncture could be decisive."

October 3, Friday

Delighted with Karamanlis's statement, Webel wrote strong letters and forwarded the text to General Earle Wheeler, Chairman of the Joint Chiefs of Staff; General B. E. Spivy, U.S. representative to NATO's Military Committee; Harold Saunders of the White House Office for International Security Affairs; Colonel Alexander M. Haig, White House military aide; and Senator Howard H. Baker, Jr. He also wrote to Karamanlis to say how everyone was pleased with the statement.

October 6, Monday

Meeting with Nicolopoulos. Vournas, a long-time follower of Papandreou, called Couloumbis from Washington to say that he agrees with the Karamanlis solution. They have started setting up a new organization and have already paid dues.

The *Christian Science Monitor* today published a main article beginning, "The dramatic appeal by former Prime Minister Constantine Karamanlis for national unity against the current dictatorship in Greece presents the best opportunity for restoring democracy that has appeared since the military coup two and a half years ago."

The *New York Times* also published a new editorial, which concludes, "Mr. Caramanlis is an extremely cautious man, as witness his long silence while other Greek democrats were making precisely these points. The Nixon Administration cannot ignore his warning that entrenchment of the Colonels will, in the end, not protect but rather jeopardize strategic American interests in the Mediterranean, in addition to crushing the hopes of the Greek people for freedom, decency, and peace."

October 7, Tuesday

Meeting with Mike Moynihan around noon. He showed me the draft plan for the first announcement. It includes three elements: an announcement by his office, a statement from Rolfe, and the Karamanlis statement. I modified two of them slightly. Apart from that, it was very careful work. He told me that he had been in contact with Wilson, the personal aide to Secretary of State, Rogers. They discussed the entire matter and agreed that a committee is the only way results can be achieved. It seems that he also communicated with his brother, who is Undersecretary of Housing. He now appears eager to take on full responsibility for the public relations of the effort we are planning with Rolfe and Karras. At our first meeting he was noncommittal, but now he believes that this way we can achieve substantial mobilization.

October 8, Wednesday
Eisenhower[2] approached

We met at the Rolfes' at noon. Mike Moynihan brought the draft plan. Sydney Rolfe agreed with it, with minor modifications.

We discussed the committee. We decided to approach Eisenhower. We discussed the periodical. I insisted that the periodical must be completely different from the *Greek Report.* It was noted that there is very little time. The meeting broke up with the decision to send the first text; to approach Eisenhower with the prospect of setting up the committee by October 28, if possible; and to announce the formation of the committee with a full page ad in the *New York Times* and other newspapers.

October 14, Tuesday

I received the following letter from Karamanlis:

> *Dear Mr. Vidalis,*
>
> *I received your telegram and I thank you for it as well as for your regular reports.*
>
> *As you know, the results my statement will have depend upon how all those who can influence developments in Greece react and, in the final analysis, how the Greek people react.*
>
> *I enclose two copies in case the entire text has not been published in the American press, though I am afraid that the English translation is incomplete.*
>
> *Friendly regards,*
>
> *Konstantinos Karamanlis*

October 15, Wednesday

I arranged meetings for Anastaplo, who just returned from Greece, with General McChristian at the Pentagon and Richardson at the State Department. He is to see Couloumbis and meet with reporters. His news was as expected, except for the effect of Karamanlis's statements. Everyone, from the right all to way to the extreme left, has sided with Karamanlis. I asked him to write a memorandum for Agnew, Nixon, Kissinger, Rogers, Laird, and everyone else he will meet.

[2]Milton Eisenhower, President Dwight David Eisenhower's brother.

October 30, Tuesday
More committee discussions

At noon I left for New York. Moynihan stressed the need for the committee. I agreed completely. Sydney Rolfe joined us. We discussed the committee's charter. That is, that it should call for free elections, curtailing aid until democracy is restored and resuming aid immediately afterwards, having U.S. government representatives stop praising the Junta, informing Congress and public opinion. Moynihan said he would draft a text and send it to us for final approval.

We also discussed alternates for chairmen of the committee if Eisenhower were to decline.

Sydney told us that Norstad called, wanting to speak with him, but did not find him. He'll return the call in the morning.

Then Rolfe brought up the periodical. Though he has agreed to finance it he is concerned that it be of high quality. Moynihan agreed that the periodical should be published even without the committee having yet been formed. The first issue should circulate before December 13, 1969.

We reached three basic decisions tonight: to intensify our efforts to form the committee, to not be dependent only upon Eisenhower, and to prepare for the periodical, which will become the committee's vehicle.

October 31, Friday

At Labouisse's at 11:30 AM. He told me that he had seen Rogers and told him his impressions. He thinks that Rogers is not well informed though, of course, he does not know what Rogers will do. He then described his meeting with Markezinis, who considers the Junta an unavoidable fact. If he became Prime Minister with broad backing for a while, then he would call for elections within 45 days. He maintained that the lower ranking officers don't want to be involved in politics and that a solution will be easy. He wants American support in the form of instructions to the Junta.

November 4, Tuesday
First contact with Tasca, the new ambassador to Athens

11:00 AM at the State Department. Spoke with Vigderman first. His statements were cold though he was warm to me. "What kind of people are these?" he asked me. "One step forward, two steps back. Some in the Pentagon are complaining that we are not helping them decisively."

Then Tasca came in. I explained my position to them. Tasca did not say much, but he was attentive and willing to hear me out. He asked about Karamanlis, the King, and the army. he found my answers unconventional and I emphasized that "pressure" is the only policy that can work. All other strategies are a waste of time. We agreed to meet again before he leaves for Athens.

NOVEMBER 9, SUNDAY
My second speech to AHEPA

I was invited to be the main speaker at AHEPA's dinner meeting. My speech was applauded, and I was well received.

Straight away I met with AHEPA's chairman, Manesiotis, who told me my speech had so impressed him that he had changed the text of his prepared speech after hearing mine. He said Agnew had changed. Manesiotis and Fatseas had visited him a month ago to invite him to the Athens Conference. Agnew refused, saying that the situation is critical and that they should press for elections. We agreed to meet the next day.

Meeting with Konstantinos Mitsotakis

NOVEMBER 14, FRIDAY
Meeting in New York

Trip to New York. I called Mike Moynihan to arrange a meeting in the early afternoon.

He told me again that he had found an editor for the journal. He had met with Wilson, personal aide to Rogers, who repeated the need for pressure. He discovered that an acquaintance of his is an aide to Eisenhower and suggested that we approach this man. Moynihan stressed that Sydney Rolfe must be pressured because, though very intelligent, he needs to be pushed. When we complete matters, the editor will have to come to Toledo to be briefed. I gave him the minutes of the senate, the British *Intelligence Report*, Senator Pell's amendments, and my speech to AHEPA. I also told him about Manesiotis. I recommended that he should see Mitsotakis and he agreed.

In the afternoon I met with Mitsotakis myself. Granitsas and Nicolopoulos were also present. I told them about my meetings with Tasca and Manesiotis, and about prospects for the journal and the committee. I spoke about obtaining permission to republish sections of the *Greek Report* and Mitsotakis said that he is one of its founding members, so permission can be taken for granted.

After the others left, Mitsotakis told me about the situation in Europe. His main points were:

- Karamanlis sent his statement to the King 24 hours before he published it. The King thanked him and asked what he recommended. Karamanlis replied, "Do what you think best." In other words, since his advice to date had been for the King to remain silent, now the King was to understand that he should speak out. The King did not and, according to Karamanlis, this was probably for the best since the junta would have declared him deposed.
- The Council of Europe will expel Greece, and NATO will follow suit (I have my doubts.)
- Karamanlis is not happy with Greece. He expected a more vigorous reaction from the press and a reaction from the Chiefs of Staff, which had been agreed, but they did not react.
- Guerrilla warfare is possible in Crete.
- The King maintains good relations with the Turks and, perhaps, some day, if Makarios reaches a settlement with the Turks he could receive the King there.

We agreed to stay in touch, and that night we had dinner together.

NOVEMBER 17, MONDAY
Letter from Karamanlis

Today I received the following letter from Karamanlis:

Dear General,

I sincerely appreciate your efforts to make the most of my statement.

As you know, I wanted to use the statement to dispel the dangerous confusion surrounding the issue of Greece. I tried to present an accurate picture of the situation in Greece and propose practical solutions.

This intervention of mine has created a new climate. The practical results, however, will depend on this climate being appropriately used by people, both Greeks and foreigners, who can affect developments in Greece.

Unfortunately, I cannot say that I am pleased with the reaction in Greece.

Please convey my greetings and thanks to our mutual friend, Mr. Webel, and to Mr. Sydney Rolfe.

I am truly sorry that the general did not wish to make use of the opportunity offered him by the Greek issue.

Friendly regards,

Konstantinos Karamanlis

Couloumbis called to say that he had phoned Markezinis and told him, "Be aware that any cooperation with the Junta will taint you and should not happen without the consent of the political world." Markezinis replied that he would restore democracy, elections would be held, but that the "army must have a say." When Couloumbis countered: "What do you mean, the army? What will happen with the purged officers?" Markezinis replied, "Now you are confusing things, Mr. Couloumbis," and hung up.

November 24, Monday

Meeting with Senator Saxbe in the morning. He greeted me with the, as he described it, good news that we are moving toward elections. The *New York Times* reported it today. I let him see my surprise. In the unlikely event that pressure leads the junta to call elections, they must be free, the army must withdraw, and a transitional government must be formed. He told me that he will enter these thoughts on the record and asked me to put them in writing. I thanked him and left.

November 25, Tuesday
The journal and the committee

Nine in the morning at the Rolfes'. Moynihan and Williams, the proposed editor for the journal, were there also. We provided Williams with instructions. He will prepare a general plan that he will mail to Sydney Rolfe, Paris, and myself.

At some point Maria told me of the financial difficulties and that we must use American money. That is why Karras and Kulukundis agreed that the funds would be channeled through the latter, who is an American citizen.

I had lunch with Moynihan and told him about my meeting with Saxbe. He insisted that we meet with Eisenhower before December 9, when I have to be back in New York. According to Moynihan, the journal could be ready within three weeks.

I arrived back in Toledo in the evening. I called Mitsotakis from the airport. He said that he had seen Iakovos and that their meeting was "completely positive" and that I should continue cooperating with the Archbishop.

November 26, Wednesday

I wrote to Saxbe to thank him for "helping return rational behavior, freedom, and responsibility to the people of Greece." I also sent him the thoughts I had expressed during our meeting of Monday, November 24. I pointed out the following:

- Karamanlis's statement provides a good opportunity for new American initiatives.
- Pipinelis's recent statements about restoring democracy are worthless because they do not provide a timetable.
- If the Junta really wanted to move toward democracy, it would:
  - Set a date for elections
  - Define the conditions under which elections would be held
  - Guarantee that the army would take no part
  - Accept a transitional government under a credible leader such as Karamanlis.

November 29, Saturday

The *New York Times* had news of the Human Rights Committee report on Greece, which is categorical. The position of the junta and its supporters is difficult.

The Committee Again—The Approach to Professor Eisenhower

December 9, Tuesday

I left for New York in the early afternoon. Mike Moynihan and his wife came, and we talked about the journal and the committee. Moynihan had prepared articles of incorporation, upon which we agreed with some observations. We decided to publish an issue summarizing the situation, to be followed by six-page bulletins every fortnight. I insisted upon an American look, with Greek support.

For the umpteenth time, we agreed that Sydney Rolfe should call Eisenhower to set up a meeting for us to see the professor, while also looking into other candidates. In any case, it seems the periodical will start, even in this form.

December 12, Friday
The junta quits the Council of Europe

Bruce Lansdale called me in the evening. He was very pleased with the European stance.

The Junta walked out of the Council of Europe [to avoid a vote of censure and suspension] and ordered the country to be drenched in flags and military music for three days. Unfortunately, at this time of maximum isolation, the only country standing with the regime is the United States. Immediately after the walk-out/suspension, ten congressmen led by Don Edwards tabled a question in the House of Representatives.

DECEMBER 13, SATURDAY
Questions about December 13, 1967

Two years ago today we tried to stop Greece's descent into shame. We did not succeed. The unchanging question asked by the layman in Greece remains alive in my mind, "Why did you fail?" No one asked us, "Why did you do it?"

DECEMBER 14, SUNDAY
Dispelling the myth of unanimous Republican support for the Junta

On Friday the Senate debated the aid package to Greece. Senator Pell fought well. Senator Dodd, also a Democrat, irritated the administration by arguing against the aid. Senator Fulbright submitted a letter from 37 former congressmen of Greek descent and Pipinelis's disgraceful speech in Switzerland. In the end, Pell's amendment to end military aid was rejected by a vote of 45 to 38. The vote demolished the myth that Republican support for the junta is unanimous. Of the 45 votes against the amendment—and, therefore, against Greece—23 were Republican and 22 Democratic, while 25 Democrats and 13 Republicans voted for us.

DECEMBER 15, MONDAY

I wrote to Pell congratulating him for the amendment he tried to pass blocking military aid to Greece.

DECEMBER 16, TUESDAY

Papadopoulos showed his true colors today. He declared that elections would not be held. The Junta's fear of elections stands revealed.

DECEMBER 17, WEDNESDAY

The periodical's editorial team has been working in New York since Monday. An irritated Bruce Lansdale called to say that Walter Silva told him that the Senate will confirm Tasca's appointment as ambassador tomorrow. He asked me if it could be delayed, even for 24 hours, to show some sign of displeasure with Papadopoulos's declaration. I told him that I would look into it.

December 18, Thursday
Friendly disagreement with Tasca

I called Pell at 9:00 in the morning. I explained the problem to him and he will act. He asked if I am to see Tasca, and I replied that I am waiting for notification. Later, Silva called to say that Tasca, at Pell's request, would like to see me.

In the afternoon, I met Mike Moynihan and together we went to see Dean Wilcoat, of the Johns Hopkins School of Advanced International Studies (SAIS). We discussed Eisenhower. I explained that it would be an important experiment to have a group of prominent people attempt to modify a foreign policy position that the Administration itself cannot or will not modify on its own. Wilcoat was polite but cold. I do not expect him to do much.

At seven in the evening, I met Tasca at the Metropolitan Club. We spoke about the situation for two and half hours. He is not prepared to accept prevarication by the dictatorship. I stressed the need the to curtail the practice of American officers praising the regime. He told me he would impose silence because no one knows what instructions the president (whom he would see tomorrow) would give him.

I also stressed that the Junta has no intention of holding elections and explained the situation within the three branches of the armed forces. In the end, as he was escorting me to the door, he said: "I am not in need of a job. I will not consider my mission successful if the regime is still in power when I leave Greece in a couple of years. I will do everything in my power to restore democracy." I answered: "Your statement pleases me a great deal but I am afraid that if you continue the policy of friendly persuasion instead of determined pressure, you will fail." I asked if he would see the King when he went to Rome. "There are many reasons for me to see him. I have to request this and I will." He praised Senator Pell, and he said that he would tell me what he thinks when he returns in three months.

I believe that his meeting with me, our discussion, and his knowing that Pell and I will be following his actions, will prove useful.

December 19, Friday

Brief visit to the State Department to see Silva. He expressed faith in Tasca, saying that he will not be doing Papadopoulos any favors. I concurred and said how satisfied I was with our meeting, while noting again that the friendly persuasion policy will not bring results.

December 21, Sunday
Mitsotakis article

Webel told me he had just seen Mitsotakis's article in the December 19 issue of the *Wall Street Journal* and that he had sent it with a covering letter to General Wheeler, Chairman of the Joint Chiefs of Staff. The article is particularly important because it reveals the dismal economic developments of the first two years of the dictatorship.

December 24, Wednesday
Intense disappointment in Greece

Today I received Panourgias's report of December 16, 1969 detailing:

- Junta policy against the Council of Europe
- The importance for Europe of the decision to suspend Greece
- The importance for Greece of the decision
- U.S. government policy
- The provision of heavy weaponry
- Russian policy
- Greek reaction against the junta

The report ended with an epilogue that vibrantly expressed Greek disappointment with the American position:

> After extended analysis my proposals are: It is fundamentally necessary to fully inform President Nixon and the American administration of the consequences of their policy and the dangers that are appearing. Essentially, two points need to be stressed: First, the junta, which is using methods no different from those of Hitler and Mussolini, will never leave power of their own accord. Second, apart from the moral responsibility of the U.S. government, the longer this regime remains in power, the greater the danger of the complete and permanent loss of Greece as a factor for stability in the eastern Mediterranean. American policy ought to be determined clearly, honestly, and publicly, on these points. If the United States decides continue support, at least they should declare it openly and say for how long so the Greek people and the resistance can consider the consequences of their actions. If, however, the United States decides, as it should, that the Junta must go, that it is a disgrace, a shame and a blot on Greece, civilization, and the United States that supports it, then the Junta must go immediately. There are innumerable ways this can happen. I still maintain that the best solution is Karamanlis because he will be able to restrain the extremists among his followers from persecutions and reprisals.

> Epilogue
>
> I think I've wasted enough ink. I am completely disappointed by U.S. government policy, particularly its hypocritical, indecisive, opportunistic, and self-contradictory stance. My friendships with Americans, my life in the U.S.A., has affected me deeply. They think that the U.S. truly represents the spirit of freedom. Already, I am disgusted.
>
> Please, if you think this text expresses any substantive arguments, distribute it wherever you can. I do not think, however, that regular channels will be of any use. Only if another direction is followed can it possibly have any value. It is the cry of despair from a tormented former officer, a friend and admirer of the United States who for six months was subjected to the psychological torture of isolation, a method Hitler used extensively to wear down his opponents. I will not annoy any more Americans nor will I even appeal to my friends, because I fear that my bitterness and disappointment would make me use harsh language. I would like to keep my old impressions of good friendship, affection, and genuine collaboration. Strong words confirming the disappointment of a Greek who was always at the forefront of his nation's battles, a military officer who knows America and the Americans well and had believed in their principles.

Unfortunately, today he has reached the perfectly understandable point of giving up on any further effort to help change American behavior.

This is tragic confirmation of the consequences of the insistence, mainly by the Pentagon, upon continuing to appease and support the dictatorship.

DECEMBER 28, SUNDAY

I received a letter from Pell. He sent me the *Congressional Record* of the December 19 Senate debate for which I had asked. The Senate discussion was extremely interesting and Pell ended up with support from 37 senators.

CHAPTER 3

1970

1970 Begins with Attempt to Form a Committee of Prominent Citizens

JANUARY 12, MONDAY
A visit to Professor Eisenhower

At the Rolfe household. Discussion about tomorrow's visit to Eisenhower. An exchange of thoughts about the visit. I stress that decentralization is counterproductive for us. Sydney Rolfe agrees and believes that a central coordinator is needed. He asks if I accept, and I say no; this cannot be my role. This role must be filled by an American professor or lawyer who can appear in public and coordinate the committee's actions. The two of us must remain behind-the-scene supporters of the project. Certainly, I must come to New York or Washington. Sydney Rolfe agrees and asks me if Owens Corning has offices here that could justify my transfer. I tell him no. Then we must look somewhere else, perhaps a university.

JANUARY 13, TUESDAY
Meeting with Professor Eisenhower in Baltimore

We board the train for Baltimore at 7:30 in the morning—Sydney Rolfe, Moynihan, and myself. On the train we discuss strategy for the meeting. Moynihan has prepared a letter/invitation to the members of the committee, a list of the members, and the committee's statutes. Everything is in order.

We arrived in Baltimore with a half-hour delay. Eisenhower's office was on the second floor of an old mansion. We were taken directly to his office as soon as we arrive.

He receives us very politely. He asks Moynihan what his relationship is to Secretary Moynihan. He becomes more trusting when he learns that they are brothers. Sydney Rolfe introduces our subject. Moynihan hands him the relevant documents. He asks for time to read them; and he reads carefully. He discusses the list of names of potential committee members. He is enthusiastic about the list, and says, "It is an excellent choice of level headed, middle of the road public personalities. I know most of them."

I interject and point out the basic points. I mention the King and Karamanlis. Upon hearing the King being mentioned, he asked, "Would the King agree to come?" "Of course, if he is invited by the president," I replied. Last time when he was here for your brother's funeral, the King was obviously saddened by your government's behavior."

After listening to us very carefully, he said, "It is a shame that the cradle of democracy is under a dictatorship. I am excited by your thinking. But, in addition to the committee, the administration must do something as well. Then we will have immediate results. In the past I have avoided getting involved with so-called pressure groups because of my ties with five consecutive presidents. This is different, however, and it is possible that the government will want the committee to exist in order to apply to Greece through it."

He asks Moynihan: "Did you talk this over with your brother? What does he say?" Moynihan replies "Of course, and he thinks this is the correct approach. And I must tell you, in confidence, that the assistant to Secretary of State William P. Rogers, with whom I have discussed this, warmly supports this solution as the only realistic one."

"In that case" says Eisenhower, "I will see Rogers and handle the matter so it appears as help for the Administration. You must understand I cannot appear all of a sudden without warning; that I cannot do. Tomorrow I leave for California, and I will try to see Rogers on the 21st of the month. We will talk afterwards." He asked for our addresses and phone numbers.

If this materializes, it will be a major boost in morale for the people, the political leadership, and the King. "An invitation to the King will be a decisive step," he says. We thanked him warmly and left.

We were quite pleased. He did not reject the idea, he liked our thoughts and preparatory work, and he understood that this was a serious effort.

Sydney Rolfe and I returned to New York by train. Moynihan left for Washington.

An hour after arriving in New York, I met Oliver Marshall, who had served as the U.S. Military Attaché in Athens. His morale was pretty low—he had seen Labouisse that morning looking for a job. I explained my strategy. He read the paperwork on the committee and the magazine. He was pleased. I asked if he could write. He said that a year had to pass from the day he retired from the military. I asked if he would be willing to become the committee's coordinator, with a salary, if such a position were created. He thanked me for the thought and said it would be very pleasant work and he would consider it when there are positive developments.

We talked about the past for a while. I asked if, in fact, the CIA had any involvement with April 21, and he replied, "It is my personal understanding that the local CIA people knew absolutely nothing and were taken by surprise. There is no chance that anybody was sent from Washington. Talbot asked me the same question, and I gave him the same answer. When I came back to Washington, I briefed the Pentagon, as is always done. I told them that this was not a coup, it was a mutiny, but they wouldn't listen. I also told them that the administration must always repeat in every statement it makes that it does not approve of the regime. Vigderman agreed, but the others didn't." Vigderman used to tell him that General Hightower would be better than Eaton, who had taken a clear position in favor of the junta. He showed me the copy of *Newsweek* with the infuriating picture of Papadopoulos on the cover.

The First Light of Hope. Norstad to the King. Interesting Document from the Archbishop.

JANUARY 26, MONDAY
First notice of a meeting between Norstad and the King

Alexandros Lykourezos arrives at the airport at 10:45 in the morning. Matina meets him. We stay together until 6:00 in the evening. He is positive, realistic, and with obvious political ambitions. He has connections with the King and correctly advises him not to return and not to compromise. He believes that the King's work must be promoted.

He knows people and things. In Karamanlis, whom he believes to be an excellent politician, he sees hesitation.

I brief him on the Greek-American situation, as well as Iakovos and Vigderman, and we discuss his program in detail.

We will meet again. He wants to talk about after the Junta. About the prospects for political development and responsibility in Greece.

Webel and Chicles arrived just after Lykourezos left.

Webel told me that during a discussion with the general in Briley's office (the company's legal counsel) that afternoon, the general received a telephone call. It was from the Undersecretary of State, who asked him if he would agree to meet the King in Rome within the next 60 days. He agreed and told Webel and Briley that he will give this meeting wide publicity.

The matter is still secret and requires careful handling.

I immediately write to the King. Throughout the night, I was thinking about what this means and what triggered it. Webel suggested that this may be the result of pressure from the magazine or Eisenhower's intervention.

January 30, Friday
Eisenhower does not accept

Moynihan tells me that Eisenhower does not accept. I ask him if Eisenhower's meeting with Rogers had anything to do with this decision. He replied that Eisenhower said that he had decided before the visit. "Of course, what else would he say?" In view of Norstad's initiative, which was still not known, I am not upset. They don't want Eisenhower in the forefront as well. But, Eisenhower's denial now, coming after Norstad's denial on September 19, suggests to me that Nixon, Rogers, or Kissinger insist on a policy of dealing with the Junta gently.

January 31, Saturday

I communicate with Lykourezos. I tell him about Eisenhower. He wants to get in touch with Harold Saunders, Undersecretary of State. He already has communicated with Anastaplo.

February 3, Tuesday
Secret document by the archbishop

Detroit in the afternoon—to welcome Princess Irene. Iakovos, Bishop of Detroit, is at the airport. He has been notified by the Archbishop. Irene and myself are left alone. I brief her on Archbishop Iakovos, the Norstad mission, and the possibilities in the U.S.A. She shows to me the report of a discussion between Archbishop Iakovos and Nixon given to her by the Archbishop. It is a very interesting document, secret at the time. I get a copy, which follows:

> I saw the president last Thursday, January 22, 1970 at 3:30 PM. His main international political advisor, Dr. Henry Kissinger, was also present. The meeting lasted 35 minutes and the discussion was for the most part about the political problem in Greece. The president told me: "Between the two solutions of completely isolating today's government as the Council of Europe is planning to do, and having politically normal conditions return to the country through action taken within Greece, we chose the second. We believe that persuasion and logic can achieve more than isolation. What is your opinion?"
>
> I answered that I am not a political person and, therefore, have no political opinion. "I am of Greek origin," I said, "and my interest and concern derive from the stressful conditions under which the Greek people are living, both here and in Greece. This is because we know something the Colonels, apparently, are ignoring. That there is such a thing as a disciplined democracy, as was the case under Mr. Karamanlis. Such a disci-

plined democracy could come after the present situation instead of the bloodshed awaiting Greece if the present dictatorship is removed by force. Violence will come," I added. "Since the famous Metaxas dictatorship (famous because of 'Ochi' on October 28) was followed by the incredible, unbelievable barbarity of 1944, why should we believe that today's dictatorship will have the good fortune to lead the country to democracy, taking into consideration the daily arrests, expulsions from the military, trials, and convictions?"

To this question he replied, "So, what is your opinion?" I said that I did not have an opinion, but a wish, if he would like to hear it. He said that he would very much like to hear my wish. "Some time ago, in Greece, I heard that the Americans are responsible for the whole situation. Some accuse us," I continued, "of organizing the revolution itself through the CIA, and others accuse us of supporting the revolution in the beginning either by our indifference or because the revolutionaries threaten to leave NATO." At this point he interrupted me. "And what do King Constantine and the successful former prime minister, Mr. Karamanlis, think? I am interested in their opinion because I respect them both. Furthermore, I have great affection for the Greek people. Because of this affection I, personally, chose Mr. Tasca, a very able diplomat and gave him clear instructions. I expect him here in a few weeks to brief me on the subject. One of my instructions is to convince them to broaden the government's political base and to gradually implement the constitution, leading the country to elections." To this I observed, "They will not broaden their political base because no politician will come. They will not lead the country to elections because they are afraid. Even though they say they have the Greek people on their side, the people (except for a few individual cases) stubbornly deny it." The president interrupted me again. "Since the old politicians refuse to help the government, why doesn't the government look to other Greek citizens? Isn't it true that every Greek is a politician?" I laughed with him at this point and said, "It is precisely because every Greek is a politician that the people refuse to support a government they did not vote for, did not ask to take power, and do not want on their backs."

At this point, the president returned to the question neither he nor I had answered. "What is the opinion of the King and Mr. Karamanlis?" I said, "I believe the King has informed you through the vice-president, whom he saw during his brief stay when he came on his own accord, out of respect, for the funeral of your great predecessor, President Eisenhower. I saw his Majesty," I added, "briefly in New York when he was on his way back to Rome. I know the King will not return unless the revolutionaries announce a specific time for elections. As for Mr. Karamanlis's opinion, for a long time now he has believed that a transitional government, backed by the army and including one, two, or even three ministers from the army, must be formed. This government will rule for at least one year, revise the constitution, and proceed to free, open, and fair elections. I also know that at one time he was willing (I don't know if he still is) to head such a government, to guarantee the military's smooth (without revenge) return to their barracks, take the country to elections, and retire from political life, believing this the ultimate political service to his country." Here, the president asked, "Would he really do that?" "As far as I know, he would," I answered. Then he added, "I was under the impression that he is a remarkable Greek politician. I am glad that I am not proven wrong."

As the discussion was coming to an end, he said, "You must see Mr. Tasca when he comes. I feel somewhat relieved after our discussion. I would like to have the chance to meet with you again in the future. You can tell his Majesty that I have good memories of his father and great respect for himself since I met with him some time ago in London, even if it was unofficially. I always remember the pleasure of meeting Mr. Karamanlis, whom I also met in New York in 1961, and whose service to the country has been truly beneficial." I answered, "I will be glad to do so at the first opportunity, Mr. President, and I am at your disposal for any service I can provide as an American citizen."

January 27, 1970

February 7, Saturday

At my house I find the following letter from Mitsotakis:

January 29, 1970

Dear General,

I am late in replying to your letter of the 26th of last month.

We went through a period of political calm and I was waiting for new developments. I do not yet have anything certain from Greece about Tasca's activities there. All information is that the Junta is not considering any withdrawal.

Information about Makarios "intervening" with the King is not true. Makarios has made no suggestions and does not think the junta has in any way changed its position towards the King. It still does not want him to return under any circumstances.

Lambrias has sent the material he was asked to get for the magazine. He is ready to cooperate in any way.

I am glad you are going ahead with the magazine. I firmly believe that a one-hour radio program (Greek-English) also would be very useful for Greeks abroad.

In London, from which I returned yesterday, I had a conversation with Makis [Arnaoutis] about the usefulness of the Greek-American community in the States, especially the Cretan supporters of the former member of parliament G. Voloudakis, who left together with Nikitas Venizelos. I imagine he will write to you.

Here, we are again turning our focus towards Europe. The Advisory Committee of the Council of Europe is meeting today in Strasbourg. There will be an introduction by Van Der Stoel and a discussion will follow. Also in Strasbourg, the European Parliament (of the EEC) is convening on Monday, February 2 and will discuss Greece. I will also be there. We are focussing all our efforts on the EEC and I am hopeful of some success. We will do the same with NATO. Nevertheless, it is our impression here that the center of gravity has moved to Washington and, mainly, to the interior of Greece. On this last subject we must soon talk in person.

Many warm regards from my wife,

Yours truly,

K. Mitsotakis

Difficulties with the Magazine as Well

February 10, Tuesday
Written confirmation of Eisenhower's refusal

I get in touch with Moynihan. I suggest we move ahead with the magazine, leaving the committee for the second phase. He will discuss this with Sydney Rolfe.

I receive a copy of a letter from Eisenhower to Moynihan confirming that the government discouraged him from proceeding with any action and advising us to meet with Vigderman.

February 16, Monday

In the afternoon at Moynihan's office. He is late. I read what has been prepared, and I am not enthusiastic. It is not enough, and all of it is well known. Moynihan arrives. I discuss my basic disagreement about the NATO article. He agrees with my objections; apparently he is having trouble influencing the writer.

February 17, Tuesday
The magazine

At the Rolfe's before the reception. Sydney Rolfe talks about a change in strategy, he wants to meet with congressmen. I refuse. My position is, "forget about the committee and move ahead with the magazine." "Legally, there must be a publisher," says Sydney Rolfe. "You be the publisher," I tell him. Finally, he is convinced. Moynihan brings a page to the reception announcing the magazine. Most, including myself, like it, but I suggest emphasizing 1970.

February 18, Wednesday

Morning. Sydney Rolfe quarrels for the first time with Mike Moynihan because Williams left, because nothing has happened, and because he is afraid nothing will happen. He suggests we take the *Greek Report* and publish it with slight alterations. I disagreed completely.

Rolfe is upset and blames Moynihan. If the magazine is not up to the standards we want, he will be obliged not to publish it, in spite of the money already spent.

The subject of the committee is discussed. Mike Moynihan is convinced that it is pointless to keep trying.

In the evening, I call General Vander Heide, who agrees to having his answers to my questions being published.

February 20, Friday
Proposals to Lykourezos

Lunch with Lykourezos. In summary, I suggest:

a. This team (those now fighting against the dictatorship) must not become involved in the political contest immediately after the country is freed from this unusual situation;
b. Old, worn-out politicians must not be supported;
c. Theotokis, Mylonas, Venizelos, and Lykourezos seem to be a good choice as a first team;
d. He will write to me as soon as possible about his meetings in Europe.

In Toledo at night.

FEBRUARY 27, SATURDAY
Spyros Theotokis's impressions

Theotokis telephones me from Switzerland. He met with the King. According to Theotokis the King appears optimistic because:

a. Many ambassadors, such as from France and Germany, are meeting with him;
b. A special envoy from Nixon came to meet with him;
c. In Greece they have clearly understood what the King's intervention means; When the King's name is mentioned in the cities, it is warmly received;
d. Tasca seems to have difficulties bridging the gap between the old politicians and the junta. He will visit the King either before or after his return to the U.S.

MARCH 5, THURSDAY

After the failure to form a committee headed by Milton Eisenhower and in view of the natural reservations of the Rolfe family, I feel I must clarify my personal position with Sydney Rolfe. I will try to replace reservations and pessimism with a new emphasis on the need for aggressive action. I wrote to Sydney Rolfe today.

Meetings in Chicago, New York, and Washington

MARCH 18, WEDNESDAY
From Chicago to New York—The magazine is progressing

Direct trip to New York. Meeting with Elias Kulukundis and Sydney Rolfe. Rolfe understood that the magazine is good. Much of the text was edited in London by Lambrias, Lykourezos, and others and was greatly improved. I saw the introduction, and it is better. At my insistence, we agreed on the following:

a. To publish the magazine and have it in circulation before April 21;
b. For Nicholas Gage to undertake the publishing from now on, if he agrees to do so on a volunteer basis;
c. To hire a permanent secretary who will coordinate activities;
d. To continue cooperation with Moynihan;
e. As soon as the magazine is in circulation, to send letters to all the people we are going to invite to serve on the committee. Rolfe did not hide

> the fact that they are beginning to get tired in London. I told both him and Kulukundis that, since now there is a slump, what is needed is an attack. Later we met with Nicholas Gage. He is young, positive, informed, capable and a realist. He accepts to be in charge of the monthly publication of the magazine. He accepts to cooperate with Moynihan and supervise the secretary. Gage is a gifted journalist and writer. It is a blessing that he accepted.

MARCH 20, FRIDAY

John Williams sent me General H. J. Vander Heide's (former head of JUSMAG in Greece) answers to the questions I had sent him. These answers are particularly important because they reflect the opinion of the responsible American general for the condition of the Greek armed forces during 1959—61. The questions and answers will be published in our magazine, *Common Heritage.*

MARCH 26, THURSDAY
Letter from Saxbe of Ohio

Letter from Senator Saxbe of Ohio, with 50 copies of a long text in the *Congressional Record.* The text of his statement before the Senate is calm but draws the correct conclusions and poses some questions to the "Athens government."

APRIL 3, FRIDAY

Bruce Lansdale telephones in the evening. At the Greek embassy, he tells us, they believe that "The Junta sees you as their number one enemy."

I get in touch with Marketos. He is enthusiastic about the article [written by Vidalis for April 21]. We agreed to publish it instead of the main editorial on April 21.

Three Publications Are Associated with Our Activities: *Ethnikos Kyrix* (*National Herald*), *The Christian Science Monitor*, *Common Heritage*

APRIL 21, TUESDAY

Three years of irresponsibility and humiliation for Greece and the Greek people. Today, April 21, the *National Herald* must have published my article, "The restoration of Greek responsibility." I do not know what the *New York Times* and other newspapers did.

The day has gone by and no one has called me, indicating that the American newspapers did not print it. I hope it is broadcast on European radio stations.

April 29, Wednesday
Superstitions that divide

California Senator Nicholas Petris calls me. He is very happy with his European trip, especially with his meeting with the King. I told him the general work plan and he agreed, adding, "It is time for the politicians to stop hiding behind the throne." Petris told me they are going ahead with a national assembly. I stressed that they should include all democratic political viewpoints. He answered that the extreme conservatives will not change their minds; they don't wish to get involved. He will try to see Christopher again after he receives my article. I advised him to be careful.

May 6, Wednesday
An article in the Christian Science Monitor *mentions my position.*

The *Christian Science Monitor* for the first time mentions my name in a very well-written article. This article, dated May 6, 1970, is titled, "Nixon-Congress collision" and has a subtitle, "Back-door U.S. arms aid to Greece strikes Congress sparks."

The following is mentioned in the article:

> For three years—since the military Junta took over control in Greece—the United States has restricted the flow of "heavy" weapons to this NATO ally. This was done to express displeasure with the military regime's removal of democratic freedoms. Now, however, while the junta is celebrating the third anniversary of taking power, here (Washington) it has become known that the value of military aid sent to Greece this year will be almost twice as large as what Congress has approved.

The article explains that this was done by using "surplus" material, which does not require Congressional approval:

> In mid-April, Sen. Stephen M. Young (D) of Ohio registered strong congressional opposition to continued U.S. support of the Greek Government. He introduced legislation which would require "officials of the Pentagon to make complete and prior disclosure of all proposed disposals of surplus weapons.
>
> He believes that in the long run, U.S. support of that government will go against America's best interests. He says that, "in the end these dictators will be ousted.

> "Then," he adds, "the people will remember whose guns and tanks were used to help oppress them."

The article continues:

> Greek expatriates have joined to condemn the regime . . . . mostly in Europe—Paris and London. But the U.S. Senate has been the center for such efforts as well—like the time Melina Mercouri, the Greek film star, spoke to the press from Senate leadership offices.
>
> But one group that until now has been silent is the former military men.
>
> But now, even that silence is breaking.
>
> In a statement made to this paper, former Brig. Gen. and chief of staff Orestis Vidalis declares that the current regime has launched a "nationally disastrous experiment."
>
> " The present regime is a failure," he says. "Old problems remain frozen, while new and complicated difficulties are resulting from the decomposition of institutions, the persecution of enlightened Greeks, the neutralization of able and principled men. . . ."
>
> He says he believes that the present government in Greece is hypocritical because it pledges a return to new democracy some day, while at the same time scorning democracy. "The regime," says General Vidalis, "rewards opportunism, aimlessness, flattery, servility, and betrayal."
>
> He says Army involvement in government has been particularly dangerous. The entanglement of the armed forces in "political responsibilities and activities," he says, has done "incalculable damage to the nation."
>
> The U.S. Congress is taking note of the rising din of dissent around the world, coming from the King's exile in Italy, to the Common Market centers, from NATO powers, to men like General Vidalis.

The article concludes by urging the U.S. government to apply pressure "by withholding even some of the 'surplus' arms material," especially if "the U.S. Congress moves as it has been to restore its vital constitutional role in foreign-policy decision-making."

May 10, Sunday
Common Heritage *becomes reality*

Sydney Rolfe sent out a press release today announcing the circulation of the magazine *Common Heritage*. The press release mentions that, "the purpose of the magazine is to help change the American position from support of the Junta to support Greece's return to democracy."

The title *Common Heritage* was borrowed from the NATO introduction.

"The members of this alliance are determined to safeguard the freedom, common heritage, and civilization of the people who support the principles of democracy, individual freedom, and the rule of law."

Common Heritage is a reality. Thank God.

May 15, Friday

Telegram from Lykourezos. From London they are asking me to make sure that the visit by the American Undersecretary of the Air Force to Greece is cancelled. I call Pell. "I am disappointed, but not surprised," he tells me. "They are getting ready to renew military aid. The Pentagon is determinedly on their side. In any case, the State Department is not interested. The only choice we have is to continue our efforts." I ask him to make a statement in the Senate, and he will.

June 4, Thursday

By extraordinary chance, I come across the *Congressional Record* for May 28, containing the statement by Congressman Sikes, which concludes, "to perform the mission we—and NATO—have assigned to them."

I am furious. I write a letter to the Ambassador, which, in the end, I do not send. I decide to write a long letter to Sikes. I call Vlachou, we will meet at the reception. From Deros I get the answer he received from Andreas Papandreou to his letter dated May 8 about meeting in order to coordinate resistance. Andreas Papandreou's letter is below:

PAN HELLENIC FREEDOM MOVEMENT—PAK
Andreas G. Papandreou
President

May 18, 1970

Dear John,

Thank you for your letter dated May 8. Your suggestion that there be a meeting of different individuals is, unfortunately, in disagreement with my position which, as you know, only recognizes political parties and resistance organizations.

I am always ready to meet with leaders or representatives of political parties and resistance organizations. Cooperation outside this framework tends to destroy the characteristic structure of the struggle.

Regards,

Andreas G. Papandreou

Congress Debates Aid
My Strong Letter to Congressman Robert Sikes

I write the letter to Congressman Robert L. F. Sikes and send copies of it to 65 congressmen and senators. It was a good letter, strongly worded and soundly supported.

June 10, Wednesday
Meeting with Pell, Sisco, Theotokis, and Vidalis

Senator Pell had arranged, after meeting with Senator Fulbright, Theotokis, and myself, for a breakfast meeting at the Senate for himself; Undersecretary of State Joseph Sisco, responsible for Eastern Europe and the Middle East (i.e., Head of the Greek desk), and the two of us. Immediately after the introductory niceties, Sisco wanted to speak, and said the following:

> I mainly want to make clear so there is no misunderstanding but also in order to stress that United States policy:
> a. Insists on Greece returning to normal parliamentary life;
> b. Is obliged to take into consideration specific defense interests in the area;
> c. In any case, is completely opposed to Greece returning to the situation before April 21, 1967.

I interjected with the observation:

> I am particularly pleased with the statement regarding the wish of the United States for Greece to return to normal parliamentary life, but I have observed that the position of the United States on this point is not clear. This is the first time I have heard such a definitively clear statement from an official source.

When Sisco answered that Secretary of State Rogers had repeatedly stated this position, both Theotokis and I pointed out that it is precisely these statements that appear unclear when seen in conjunction with other issues, and that it would be good to publicly clarify these statements. Senator Pell intervened, agreeing that the government's statements often can be interpreted in opposing ways or contradicted by developments.

Sisco agreed that it is possible that the spirit of Rogers's statements may be misinterpreted, but, nevertheless, the official line is to restore normal parliamentary life in Greece, and added, "I would like to learn how you think this can be achieved." Theotokis stressed that the King, as a permanent constitutional element, can play a decisive role toward this end.

Sisco: I agree completely.

Theotokis-Vidalis: While the King is being ignored, generals, Admirals and other officials exchange pleasantries with the dictatorial regime. . . . Recently, the Undersecretary of the Air Force visited Athens, and the government took political advantage of this. Even when the King came here for Eisenhower's funeral, he was shunted aside.

Sisco: Since we are maintaining relations with the Athens government, we are obliged to follow certain rules of protocol.

Vidalis: Yes, but, as it happened, the meeting between the King and Kissinger (President Nixon's foreign policy advisor) that had been arranged for that time was cancelled by the U.S. The King, understandably, was offended by this.

Pell: Do you think the Colonels will give up power because the King wants them to? Perhaps the dictatorship will shift towards the East?

Theotokis: The Athens regime is facing many problems and many difficulties.

Sisco: It is true, the Junta has many problems and many worries.

Vidalis: It happens that I hear from many young officers who, because they cannot see what else can be done, are obliged to keep silent and bear it.

Pell: How can the United States act in such a situation?

Vidalis: First of all, by creating a new impression that the United States does not wish the dictatorship in Greece to continue.

Sisco: Yes. There is no question that any developments in Greece require the active support of the United States.

Vidalis: That is a basic requirement for any progress.

Sisco: Obviously, elections must be out of the question for some time because they would be quite dangerous.

Theotokis: I agree, because elections can be valid only if they are genuine, not held under martial law. Elections held by the dictatorship would generate many problems. In any case, cleaning up the extensive damage left by the dictatorship will require a substantial transition period for dealing with issues of highest priority. By these I mean constitutional, political, economic, and other problems.

Sisco: The truth is that Greek history over the last 20 years is full of transitions from democracy to dictatorship and vice versa.

Vidalis: It is precisely for this reason that we must return to a situation in which the people are responsible for their fate and not have their fate dictated to them by others.

Theotokis: Obviously, Mr. Sisco, your opinion refers to earlier periods, because since the end of WWII, we have had stable parliamentary rule in Greece.

Sisco: You are right; my reference was to earlier periods. You are right.

Vidalis: I understand your interest in this area. You have your strategic interests, but I don't believe that they are protected by the dictatorship in Greece. On the contrary, by prolonging this situation your interests are harmed because the people believe that you support the dictatorship in Greece. This makes the people bitter, convinced that the dictatorship continues because of you.

Pell: Really, what are these extra military supplies needed for so much that the Pentagon has to ship them to Greece in secret?

Sisco: The issue is not important because, in any case, civil war in Greece today is out of the question. I accept that the junta took political advantage of this fact, as is natural. Any government would have done the same.

That was the end of the discussion. Sisco left. Senator Pell kept us a while longer and asked us to convey his admiration and respect to the King for his stance.

June 22, Monday

I received the following letter from Konstantinos Mitsotakis:

Paris, June 12, 1970

Dear General,

I have been late in answering your letter of May 17 because I was waiting to receive a copy of Common Heritage, which, the end, I never received, obviously because of the trouble here with the post office strike. Fortunately, Lambrias is sending me a copy, so I will see it.

There is very little news here. Our friends in Europe are numb and the shadow of the crisis in the Middle East is heavy upon us. We are trying to motivate them as much as possible. The political committee of the NATO (parliamentary) assembly that will convene at the beginning of next month under the Presidency of Javits will, I hope, carry out the plan it is discussing to invite former members of the Greek Parliament who were part of the Greek parliamentary team to NATO in 1962 to appear before the assembly. We probably will not have any developments in the EEC before September, but the chances of blocking the agreement for Greece to join the EEC are favorable.

I hear that recently, with Mrs. Vlachou and Mr. Theotokis there, you are having some interesting conversations, and now Tasca is going there as well. I would be grateful if you would write me of any news.

With my wishes for your name day, I warmly thank you. Warm greetings from my wife.

Yours truly,

Konstantinos Mitsotakis

July 17, Friday
Meeting with Norstad

Meeting with Norstad in the morning, which lasts 45 minutes. He is trying to explain American policy. It probably is an apology. These are the basic points:

- The American government is worried and is seriously looking into the problem
- The colonels will not give up power on their own accord
- The King must not believe that he is forgotten. Proof of this is that the State Department asked him to visit the King a few months ago.
- Military aid is not necessary. What is necessary is keeping Greece in the alliance.
- The situation in the Middle East is highly critical, and no one is thinking of starting anything in Greece.
- The King's silence is correct.
- Karamanlis's statement was premature. Karamanlis is the only successor.
- Rolfe is an excellent young economist. He did not agree to participate in overt anti-junta propaganda because doing so would make him unable to make any other positive contribution.
- He agreed that the Russians are in the Mediterranean to stay and, therefore, the issue of Greece must be solved with long-term criteria.
- He agreed that I should see Kissinger after I return from Europe and asked me to remind him.

- He stressed that the climate against military dictatorships is growing within the U. S. and the moment of absolute condemnation is coming.
- He asked me to convey his greetings to the King and Karamanlis.

My overall impression is that he feels guilty for not pushing the issue and because his attempt was unsuccessful.

Meetings in Washington and the Trip to London

JULY 21, TUESDAY
Meeting with General McChristian

In Washington I met with General McChristian (son-in-law of General Van Fleet), who told me that my report (first document to Norstad, dated 12/13/68,) is excellent. It is now being read by people in the higher levels—he did not tell me who.

He makes it clear that the goal of American policy is to have democracy reinstated; "the question you pose in the report does not apply." I tell him that aid must be used as a political weapon since that is the purpose. He indicates, silently, that he agrees.

JULY 25, SATURDAY
Meeting with Opropoulos

I get a visit from Voloudakis, former member of parliament with ERE. He talks about unifying resistance groups. He dreams about action in Crete and naively asks me if the Americans would oppose its being taken back again by the Junta, to whjch I reply, "of course not."

At noon, Lykourezos and I visit Dimitris Opropoulos. He is in a miserable condition, sitting in a chair with his legs paralyzed. [The result of an accident.]. He feels better when he is involved in discussions about resistance and politics. I brief him on the American side and he briefs me about what is going on. He feels that politicians and members of the resistance must come together to get rid of the Junta. Especially on the subject of the left, he thinks it is a good opportunity to draw them closer to us, now that they have cut ties with Moscow. He believes that everybody agrees. It was funny at one point when, convinced of this development, he asks, "And you, Orestis, are you going to take part in the national assembly or are you going to continue working behind the scenes in the States?" "Of course," I answered, joking. "Have you moved so far along, without telling me anything, that you are now passing ministerial positions around? My dear Mimi, you are overoptimistic.

I hope your visions become reality. I think the indigenous left is an excellent development, and I will support it as much as I can." I left happy because I saw him looking better, in a good mood and ready to do something, even if it was from bed.

July 26, Sunday
Meeting with Sorokos

At noon with Sorokos. He tried to start talking about the past, and I stopped him, stressing that nobody has anything to gain from the past and it would be better for us to talk about the future. The main points of my position were:

- The present regime must be convinced that its mission is over and its national duty is to help the nation return to normal life;
- Everybody's patience, including that of the U. S., has run out
- All the requirements needed for the country to return to normal life exist because there are indestructible forces to that purpose;
- Of course, the present regime enjoys the taste of power and will want to stay on, but, in that case, instead of a renaissance, the nation would be led to slaughter.

He listened attentively and asked if I think that elections will be held, to which I answered, "not if things go well."

He disagreed, saying, "Elections will be held within 1971."

"Do you know this or are you making a conjecture?" I asked.

"I am making a conjecture," he replied.

"Then what kind of elections are they going to be? Like the referendum with the army breathing down the Greek people's necks," I retorted.

"No, Orestis, but have there ever been elections without force and fraudulent counts? We must go through first, second, and more elections in order to recover."

"In that case, the regime is continued in power by wearing a mask and the problem is not solved. Bloodshed will not be avoided."

"Why aren't the politicians working together, Orestis?"

"You must be kidding," I tell him. "This is not realistic. The Greeks will solve the problem when they are free, now or when the first people's revolution takes place."

He does not insist and changes the subject. "Should the King have attempted the December 13 coup?" he asks.

"Of course, for the simple reason that sooner or later this regime will fall, but the nation must go on, and the King, trapped and betrayed, at least will be a reserve that can be used. For the first time in history, the King and the people, the two constant factors, are united in their opposition to the people being deprived of responsibility by force."

He agrees without saying so and tries to maintain that many people in Athens, including Papadopoulos, want the situation to return to normal.

"Perhaps, at first, he wanted to become a Nasser, then maybe a parliamentary Prime Minister, but now he sees that not even this can be done. He cannot do what he may want, other than continue the dictatorship."

He then spoke against Karamanlis because he left, against Frontistis because he accepted Papadopoulos's committees, against Angelis, Patilis, and the politicians who did not react in time.

"We must all put pressure on them Orestis, you, too, even if you do not have the power right now. Why don't you submit a memorandum to Papadopulos explaining the dangers as you see them?"

"You are joking," I said. "You pass it on to him."

In conclusion, I tell him, "Greece's problem is not economic, nor is it Cyprus. It is nothing other than restoring and caring for the people's responsibility. If the present regime has any patriotic feelings, it must take heroic decisions and let the nation move on. The regime is entirely responsible for what happens next. When this drama comes to an end, history will judge all of us, Yannis, according to our stance and the steps we play in returning the situation to normal. You, too, can play a role."

"I play that role, as much as I can," he said.

We said goodbye after he asked if he could write to me, and I answered, "Of course."

Meeting with Mylonas, Theotokis, the King, and Karamanlis

JULY 29, WEDNESDAY
with Mylonas

I leave for Geneva. Theotokis meets me at the airport. I tell him I must see Mylonas. We go to Mylonas's neighborhood. Theotokis sits in a café, and I visit Mylonas in his apartment.

He receives me with great pleasure and politeness and we talk in a very civilized manner. I tell him about the situation in the United States because he does not know the details. He tells me about developments within the left. He was elected president of Democratic Defense. They refused to work together with Andreas Papandreou. They are seeking to unify the resistance groups because they see that political unification is impossible. He asked if I wanted his representative in the States to get in touch with me and I said, "Of course, I would be particularly pleased." We discussed the issue of the King, whom he said he wished would move to the fore. "Without a reason he can't offer anything," I replied, and he agreed.

At 11:30 PM the King called and said that Karamanlis would expect me Friday or Saturday.

August 3, Monday
To the King

The King's aide is trying to find a seat for me for the trip to Spain. At 1:30 PM the King's car picked me up and took me to Porto Ercole, where they live.

The King is happy to see me. I have prepared the briefing. He listens with great attention. He cuts in and tells me following:

- Angelis came to visit, asking him to denounce the resistance groups, but he refused;
- Pipinelis is putting pressure on him to return, and the King keeps repeating the same conditions;
- Two months ago the "uncompromising ones" asked for Papadopoulos to resign and Angelis to take over. Papadopoulos refused, wanting things to remain unchanged because the revolution would be blown to bits;
- Hill, the American Ambassador to Spain, probably will replace Richardson at the State Department. This will be excellent if it happens because they have met and spoken at length in Spain. Hill, in spite of his extreme conservatism, supports normal conditions and the King.
- Tsoumbas came to visit and said that if his proposals concerning promotions and postings are not accepted, he will resign. But he stays on. Angelis asked the King's opinion about making Zagorianakos head of the army. The King did not agree.
- The Shah of Iran, whom he met in secret, told him he raised the subject of Greece with Nixon. Nixon told the shah that, as soon as the Middle East issue is resolved, and he predicted positive results within two months, the Americans would proceed with positive solutions for Greece.

August 4, Tuesday
To Spain with Karamanlis

It is a strange coincidence to be travelling on August 4 [reference to August 4, 1936 when General Metaxas imposed a quasi-fascist dictatorship] to Marbella, Spain, in order to meet with Karamanlis and talk against the current version of August 4 in our country.

The beginning was somewhat reserved. "I don't want politics, general. It is only historical need and everybody's pressure that force me to break my silence." Slowly, as my briefing went on, he got more and more involved.

In general, he was impressed with:

a. Norstad's visit to the King
b. The crisis that will follow if the junta holds elections.

He is not afraid that the elections will stabilize the dictatorship, but he is afraid of the chaos until a new revolution or street unrest takes place as soon as any dialogue begins. This thought alarmed him, and for that reason he will put pressure on Greece as soon as he gets back to Paris.

He had many complaints about the politicians inside Greece and the effort politicians waste. "There are five of us abroad, and we do not want to see each other." The main issue is the change in his position about the transitional government, of which he does not want to be a part so he may run in the first elections, for whether or not reform comes, will depend upon these elections.

August 5, Wednesday

Meeting with Karamanlis in the morning. He has written down the points he wants to discuss.

- How does the King feel? I said, "Alone, worried, but courageous."
- Elections held by the junta must be avoided. Speed up Norstad's visit and apply pressure upon NATO;
- A powerful transitional government, without him, consisting of prominent politicians and generals—he, too, will make suggestions. He agrees that the members of the transitional government must not stand in the elections, something that I, also, have stressed to everybody with whom I have spoken;
- Efforts to organize those who are in Greece. He will try again, as soon as he returns to Paris.

He asked me to tell this only to the King. We spent two hours together. I left for Rome.

August 6, Thursday
New meeting with the King

Meeting with the King in Rome. I gave him a detailed briefing.

He thinks Karamanlis's change of position about the transitional government is constructive. I add that will make all our jobs easier. He asks if I think

Makarios is a suitable mediator. I say, "Of course, but mediation will have to be after Papadopoulos has been weakened so we are talking from a position of strength." He told me that they had taken Papapostolou and someone else out of Cyprus, and this can be used positively.

He asked me if Karamanlis had clarified whom he had in mind for members of the transitional government. I answered, "No, he avoided the subject and I did not insist." I explained how I now see our activities in the U.S., beginning with my meeting with Kissinger.

The main points of this meeting will be:

a. Avoid talking about the past;
b. Discuss two solutions: Elections by the junta and elections by the transitional government;
c. The disadvantages of the first and the advantages of the second;
d. The central idea is to make the two constant factors of Greek life, the people and the King, responsible;
e. Having the King be the transitional link will enable responsibility to be returned to the Greeks progressively.

He fully agreed with the central idea. I then told him about the schedule in the U.S., with the Senate, the press, etc. "But funding is needed," I said. "My resources have been exhausted."

"I fully agree," he said. "I will look into it personally and believe I will find a solution. I must tell you that Hartke's statement about discontinuing military aid shook them. They even reached the point of Pipinelis calling Papagos and telling him that Tasca insists the King must announce that the aid is necessary. Papagos replied, 'The King has made no announcements for months now, how can he make such a declaration now? I will tell him this if I find him.' He did not find me; I was in Denmark. Pipinelis called Papagos for a second time and repeated the point. He found me that time, and I replied, 'If the Americans want such a statement, they can tell me themselves; let Tasca come here.' They didn't come back on the subject. I assume this was a trick on Pipinelis's part to persuade me to take actions favorable to the junta in the hope that he would succeed in having me return."

He told me about the situation in the navy. Soulis was ready to abduct Zoitakis, Papadopoulos, and Tasca at one point when he once had them all on board ship. He did not do it.

"But, your Majesty, you must now appoint a general, in the style of *Mission Impossible*, who could organize pressure within the army for a transitional government. If General Dimopoulos tells you he will do it, he will. Arbouzis does not seem interested. It would be better if this person were on active duty."

"Before I do this, I need to find the funds for this as well."

"Of course. Do you want me to convey your greetings to Archbishop Iakovos and ask him to apply pressure for a transitional government?"

"Of course. Let's keep in touch."

I left at 4:15 in the afternoon.

Trip to London, where I met with Lykourezos, Lambrias, and Arnaoutis. I told them about my trip in very general terms. They told me:

- Sorokos is in a difficult position because it was he who sent Sir Hugh Greene to Greece.
- Davies's statements about the Junta have been cold.
- Davies invited Kanellopoulos, Mavros, Averof, Markezinis, and Stefanopoulos. Kanellopoulos did not accept. [Rodger Davies was Deputy Assistant Secretary of State for Near Eastern and South Asian Affairs.]

Mavros told him that we have reached a dead-end; the economy is not doing well.

Markezinis, talking too much, said that he is willing to cooperate with the regime, that the economy is fine, but that he has not recognized the Constitution of 1968. Because he was going on, the others interrupted him and this created an episode.

Averof said he accepts cooperation. Greece's position on the international level is worse than he had ever seen.

Stefanopoulos made no commitment and added that the economy is sick.

Arnaoutis confirmed the information about Papadopoulos's being asked to resign and Angelis refusing to replace him.

Lambrias said the British embassy in Athens agrees with the position of Sir Hugh Greene in believing that Henry Tasca is a failure.

AUGUST 18, TUESDAY
Meeting with Norstad

I saw Norstad in the afternoon. I explained that we have entered a critical period and that the danger now is elections staged by the Junta. I explained the consequences. I stressed that the solution is a transitional government, not political in nature, and then elections. He asked if there had been such a government in the past, and I reminded him of General Dovas. "Certainly, in that case we have a precedent." I told him the King was particularly pleased with the news about his visit and believes it to be important. I added, "If this visit were to materialize, it would be an important first step."

He then asked me to draft a brief note for him to use as a base for writing Martin J. Hillenbrand, Assistant Secretary of State for European Affairs, so I can meet with him. I asked him about Kissinger and he said that his role would not be decisive if the State Department did not agree. "Let's start with the State Department and then the White House," he said. He praised the royal family. I then told him that I have never been to the Palace. I had never appeared in front of the King before the dictatorship. The regime brought us together, especially the King's attempt to restore democracy and normal conditions to the country on December 13, 1967. He thought that was strange. He then asked me about possible members of the transitional government. I told him this is not difficult. Judges, Professors, generals. He asked me about Margaritis and Koniotakis, believing that Koniotakis was going to be freed. I told him that only communists are set free. He was surprised. We ended with his saying that he would try to see the King and Karamanlis. He wanted the draft by Friday, so he could write Hillenbrand.

AUGUST 20, THURSDAY

I receive a very warm letter from Senator Edmund S. Muskie:

> UNITED STATES SENATE
> COMMITTEE ON BANKING AND CURRENCY
> WASHINGTON D.C. 20510
> Aug. 17, 1970
>
> General Orestis Vidalis
> 2204 Innisbrook Road
> Toledo, Ohio 43606
>
> *Dear General Vidalis:*
>
> *Thank you for your note of June 22 and the attached copy of your very thoughtful letter to Congressman Sikes. I appreciate your taking the time to bring your views to my attention.*
>
> *In your letter to Congressman Sikes, you have presented a strong argument for a proposal such as that offered by Senator Hartke recently and which was, unfortunately, defeated in the Senate.*
>
> *I agree with your final statement in the letter to Congressman Sikes to the effect that respect for democracy cannot be bought. Unfortunately, this seems to be a lesson which is difficult for all Americans to learn.*
>
> *I am grateful for this opportunity to hear from you. I hope that you will feel free to write to me again in the future on matters which are of concern to you.*
>
> *With all best wishes, I am*
>
> *Sincerely,*
>
> *Edmund S. Muskie*
> *United States Senator*

August 22, Saturday

Nicolopoulos and Couloumbis call me from Pyrros's office about Senator Cranston's text on Agnew's position. It is in the *Congressional Record* for August 18 (page S 13607) and says, "I know that he had acted quietly and with great dignity to bring the moral weight of his office to bear against the military junta in Greece."

Monday, August 24
Norstad's letter to the new Assistant Secretary of State for European Affairs, Martin J. Hillenbrand

In the afternoon I receive a copy of Norstad's letter to Hillenbrand. It is the first time I learn about any action he has taken. It is a good sign. I will wait. The letter follows:

August 21, 1970

Mr. Martin J. Hillenbrand
Assistant Secretary for European Affairs
Department of State
2201 C Street
Washington, DC 20520

Dear Marty,

The enclosed memorandum, "The Greek Situation—The Most Critical Phase in Sight—Action Steps [see appendix]," has been given me by a former Greek Army general who, before the present regime, was a leading force in the Greek General Staff. He is General Orestis Vidalis who has been in Toledo for about two years but during this period he has maintained contact with the King and with Mr. Caramanlis, both of whom he has just seen in Rome and Paris respectively. He is intelligent, well educated in both Greece and the United States, politically knowledgeable, and therefore more restrained in word and action than other exiles from his country.

I think it would be useful for you or some other influential State official to talk to General Vidalis while his discussions with King Constantine and Mr. Caramanlis are still very fresh in his mind. He can come to Washington for that purpose at any time convenient for you and I can assure you that the subject will be treated with discretion and restraint. He is an exceptionally fine man and I strongly recommend that you see him.

Warm regards.

Sincerely,
Lauris Norstad

I write Saville Davis of the *Christian Science Monitor* and send him information about Greek officers and citizens held in jail and in internal exile.

September 4, Friday

I received a letter from Kennedy. It was late, but at least he did answer:

Edward M. Kennedy,
Massachusetts

Senate
United States of America
Washington D.C.

Brigadier Orestis Vidalis
2204 Innisbrook Rd.
Toledo, Ohio 43606

September 2, 1970

Dear General Vidalis,

Thank you very much for sending me a copy of your June 8 letter to Congressman Sikes referring to the role Greece plays in NATO.

I share the concerns you expressed in your letter that continued support of the Greek dictatorship by the United States government, based entirely on the need for Greece to continue to carry out is NATO mission effectively, further distances the Greek people from the principles the country had adopted for many generations.

It is unfortunate that the senate's attempt to cut off military aid to the Greek government on July 29 was unsuccessful by a vote of 50 to 42.

In any case, I assure you that I will continue my efforts for the government to use its power and influence to free Greece.

Thank you again for your letter and your thoughts.

Sincerely yours,

Edward M. Kennedy

September 12, Saturday
Meeting with the Archbishop

Meeting in Chicago with Iakovos in the morning. He is convinced that the regime is in disarray, divided, and will establish a time frame for elections.

I stress the danger of elections held by the Junta and tell him he must intervene for a way out.

"Norstad," he says "is very capable. You try and I will as well." In the afternoon, I rewrite the letter to the King, describing my meeting with Iakovos in detail.

SEPTEMBER 15, TUESDAY
New York

Meeting with the Rolfes in the evening. With morale low, the newsletter still being written, we speak about encouragement. They assure me it will go to press on Monday. I tell them this situation cannot continue; they must hire someone. They agree but do not know whom. Complete disappointment.

Military Aid to the Regime Is Resumed

SEPTEMBER 22, TUESDAY

The renewal of aid is announced. We do not have the full text. The *New York Times* editorial is harsh. This brings to an end an important phase, at first glance one that the junta seems to have won. I imagine the distress in Greece and the further fall in public morale. Under different circumstances one would think that, after this, it is all over. On the contrary, those who stick to their principles must increase their efforts—efforts of all kinds.

SEPTEMBER 24, THURSDAY
Meetings with Vigderman, Silva, McChristian, and, most importantly, with Assistant Secretary of State Hillenbrand

Today's editorial in the *Washington Post* blasts the decision to renew military aid. Some of the main points are:

> The game is over: fullscale shipment of arms to Greece is to be resumed. For three-plus years, since the Colonels deposed an elected government in 1967, the United States had maintained a "selective embargo" on arms to its NATO ally. . . . Ostensibly, its purpose was to pressure the colonels back towards representative government.
>
> And the United States is back in the unbecoming position of rendering its full sanction, with no semblance of official reluctance, to a regime which looks like it is enduring . . . .
>
> A case can be made that the United States had exhausted whatever leverage its "selective embargo" had given it, and that nothing further was to be gained by holding out. If that was so, however, then a new case can now be advanced: the Nixon administration has, by increasing its involvement, increased its leverage too. One way to put the new involvement to some good purpose is to press harder for return to democratic rule.

Meeting at 11:00 in the morning at the State Department with Vigderman in the presence of Silva.

O.V.: Up to now I have been doing most of the talking. Today, probably, I should listen to you.

M.V. Of course. Do you have the formal text of the announcement?

O.V.: No.

M.V.: You should get it, it is interesting. Nothing has changed, and we want to help restore democracy. This decision has been postponed for months. Your colleagues in the Pentagon were pressing, the Middle East situation gave them more arguments, and the decision was taken. In any case they would get it anyway, and they would get it from a third party. What matters is that our policy is confirmed and we will continue with greater ease to work towards that end.

O.V.: What is done cannot be undone. The future will show the importance of this decision. If this decision was taken within a framework of genuine willingness to restore democracy and if tangible, visible, and fundamental action is taken towards that end, then this decision may prove to be a positive step. If, on the other hand, nothing follows and everything is left up to the good will of the junta, then the decision will prove to be full, unconditional surrender to the Junta's blackmail. Time will tell if you have helped Greece return to normal conditions or have led it to utter conflict and disorder.

M.V. The economy is healthy, they released prisoners and passports, *Macedonia* is publishing bitter comments against the Junta, the people do not react, and the armed forces are calm. All this and the situation in the Middle East contributed to this decision being taken.

O.V.: The problem is not how the situation appears on the surface, but what forces are developing beneath the surface. You may be underestimating the patience of many people and you may be overestimating what the junta can do. In any case, now that you have officially undertaken part of the responsibility, you also have a responsibility to the Senate and public opinion for restoring democracy quickly. Establishing a policy without a schedule for action will lead nowhere. You have many capabilities, which you are afraid to use. Do you remember what I told you during our first meeting? "If you really do not want the dictatorship but cannot help remove it, then you are showing that you cannot outsmart the dictator." Learn what is deep within the Greek soul and you may become wiser then.

M.V. We recognize that there is a great deal we must do, but we move more slowly than you want. Patience is needed. Of course we agree that there must be—and there is—a program.

O.V. If the junta holds elections, what will you do? Are you going to let them go ahead with elections? You must realize that would be a great tragedy.

M.V. I do not think they have decided to hold elections, but I agree that the problem will not be solved if they do so.

Silva intervened, saying that they will begin to fall apart as soon as they decide to hold elections. I told them that Sorokos had told me in London that elections were going to be held and on no account should they ignore that possibility in their evaluations.

I left convinced that the decision to restore military aid was imposed by the Pentagon, that the White House took advantage of Middle East problems to push the decision through, and that from now on the State Department would play the major role.

At 2:30 in the afternoon I met with Assistant Secretary Hillenbrand at the State Department. He was polite and honest with me and gave the following explanation for renewing the aid.

M.H. The Middle East crisis affected the decision in two ways. First, it made improving our position in Greece more urgent and, second, it made announcing the decision, which, of course, is not popular, easier to do. We expected a stronger reaction from the press and Congress, but the Middle East situation somewhat overshadowed the decision. The conservative leaders who were asked agreed that the aid is separate from political issues and expressed no objections to the aid.

The Junta was negotiating military supplies from the French and was near agreement. Later, they might have purchased weapons from Germany, I don't know. In any case, discussions with France were in the final stage. general, you must make a distinction between the two issues.

O.V. Mr. Assistant Secretary, of course I make the distinction. I am certain, however, that the Greek people do not. The aid means the Junta dominates psychologically because it confirms that the U.S. supports the Junta. What is important is what will follow. If the aid is a means of implementing the policy you say you have and as stated in the announcement, and if measures are taken to confirm this policy, then the decision to renew aid will be a positive step. If, on the other hand, nothing happens, then the conviction will be strengthened that you are not interested in a return to normal conditions but only are looking after your own interests.

Other measures you can take lead to the King. And since, by making this decision, you now are free from the annoyance, why not go ahead with General Norstad's visit to the King, as you had told him?

M.H. This is possible, of course. We are looking into it. It will be decided mainly by Sisco, and I will talk with him soon. I will telephone the general tomorrow—he brought up the subject again. He will be in the area in October and needs to know if he will visit the King. I suspect it is only a matter of timing, if, that is, it is a good idea for General Norstad to visit Italy right after the president's visit. We will decide soon.

O.V. Mr. Assistant Secretary, since President Nixon will be in Rome, why doesn't he meet with the King?

M.H. I don't know, it is a thought, but his schedule is so full and in any case a direct meeting of the two sides without preliminary work is not a good idea.

General, I wanted to ask you if the Junta hard-liners do, in fact, have the power to oust Papadopoulos, or are they being used for intimidation?

O.V. They are used for intimidation, Mr. Assistant Secretary. They know that the minute the first public crack within the junta appears everything is in jeopardy for them. Papadopoulos always played this game, with both external political forces and the hard-liners. To the external political forces he said, "Watch out for the hard-liners," and to the hard-liners he said, "Be careful, because we will fall apart."

M.H. You know, general, we are exceedingly irritated by the noise NATO member states such as Denmark and Norway make. Every time there is a NATO meeting we must make great efforts not to have a flare-up. It is always the Greek problem. This is not an alliance.

O.V. Mr. Assistant Secretary, the only way to restore order is for the situation to stop worsening. Instead of letting the Danes take the lead, you should take the initiative first and then the other member states will accept you as a factor for peace and progress within the alliance, and Greek morale will be raised. Mr. Assistant Secretary, your initiative is needed. Start with the King and go on from there as I explained in my brief note. Perhaps, now that you have given in to everything, you can start making requests. Send General Norstad to the King first and then go ahead with a specific plan implementing your policy.

M.H. What is your opinion about the steps taken toward liberalization?

O.V. They are of no importance internally and of great importance externally. They give an impression of change to the outside world without changing anything inside the country. Proof of this is the discussion about a 50 member legislative committee.

M.H. You are right. A copy of the Spanish prototype.

O.V. I will tell General Norstad about our discussion. Thank you.

M.H. I thank you, general, and please come see me whenever you are in Washington. I probably will call the general tomorrow.

• September 22, 1970, announcement of resumption of full military aid:

United States policy towards Greece has been under review by the administration for the last 18 months. During this time the United States continued to exclude major weapon systems from the program of military aid to Greece, a policy established by the previous administration after the April 1967 coup in Greece.

The administration now has decided to resume the regular supply of military equipment to Greece. The resumption of making these weapon systems available will improve the capability of the Greek armed forces to carry out their responsibilities for defending NATO territory and will be a major assistance in uniting and strengthening NATO's southern flank. Greece provides military advantages to the Atlantic Alliance that are of great importance to the security of the West. In recent months this importance has become particularly significant because of developments in the eastern Mediterranean. The decision to again provide military equipment that had not been available until now is a direct result of these developments.

Although the United States had hoped for a quick return to representative government in Greece, movement toward constitutional rule is being re-established. Large segments of the constitution have been put into effect and partial restoration of human rights has been scheduled. The Greek government has declared that it intends to adopt a parliamentary democracy.

The United States shares the concerns of its NATO partners about speedy progress in restoring political rule in Greece. This is the policy we have steadily maintained.

Friday, September 25
Meetings at the Pentagon

At the Pentagon at 9:00 in the morning, meeting with Vice-Admiral John Weinel (Director J-5 Plans and Policy Director, Joint Chiefs of Staff). He is new in this very important position. I explained my view. "Since your policy is for democracy to be restored, there must be a program. Your plan of persuasion failed. A realistic plan based on pressure is needed, the only language they understand. Otherwise, your long-term interests are at stake."

"How much time do we have, general?"

"1971 is the crucial year. The situation must be resolved during this period and it must be resolved in a way that is beneficial to the Greeks, " I answered.

"Let's stay in touch, general."

Afterwards I saw Major General Stewart (air force) of the DIA (Defense Intelligence Agency). I explained to him my position and he offered that I notify him the next time so that he could assemble various responsible parties from the Petagon and the State Department to hear me out. I told him to focus the effort on the Pentagon which has the responsibility for the military assistance.

The Norstad-King Meeting is Set

SEPTEMBER 30, WEDNESDAY

Meeting with General Norstad in the afternoon. He asks me how the meeting went. I told him that Hillenbrand explained the reasons behind the aid decision to me. The main reason was an impending purchase of weapons from France.

Norstad was annoyed, and told me that some time ago he had spoken with the people responsible for this and told them they "should not tolerate blackmail because the Junta needs the U. S. and NATO more than NATO needs Greece. Heaven help us if we give in to blackmail."

He then said, "I had called them and told them to make sure there is communication between Nixon and the King. They didn't think it was possible. In the afternoon of Friday, September 25, Hillenbrand telephoned and said, "After a meeting between Sisco and Rogers, we ask you please to go ahead and meet with the King."

"I told them," said Norstad, "since the president did not see him, how will I go? They insisted that the meeting must take place."

I then told Norstad that I also had talked with Hillenbrand about the Nixon visit, but he said it had not been prepared for.

He asked for my opinion. I said that the meeting must be held as soon as possible. The people will be encouraged and the junta will realize that the beginning of the end is coming. Then he looked at his calendar and said, "I will go during the first week of November. I will notify Vigderman to alert the embassy, so the King will be officially asked to meet with me. I will go only for this reason, because my Middle East trip was cancelled. I may go through Brussels. We will talk before I leave."

"General, may I inform the King?"

"Of course. Even if he has only half an hour available it will be enough."

"It is not enough, you must stay a while."

He asks, "What is Karamanlis's relationship with the King now? Does the Queen Mother have difficult relations with Karamanlis?"

"The relationship between the King and Karamanlis is very good. The King already is very experienced and tried," I told him.

"I understand."

Immediately after the meeting, I wrote to the King and sent the letter by registered mail. Today's meeting was important because Norstad probably had decided to postpone the trip for much later.

OCTOBER 2, FRIDAY

A long letter from A. Lykourezos.

September 25, 1970

Dear Orestis,

I am writing to you with some delay because our return from Paris was delayed.

1. *The Makarios-King meeting. Makarios told the King that the Cypriot situation is at a dead-end because the Turks are inflexible. He cannot see a solution for the moment. As for the conspiracy against him, he knows now—he has proof—that it was organized by Greek officers. He does not know if Papadopoulos was aware of it personally or if it was initiated and directed by the government. There was no discussion about the King's return.*
2. *Meeting with Karamanlis: Takis [Lambrias] and I had a long and warm discussion with Karamanlis. Conclusion: He believes that a single coordinating organization must be established, but he does not want to undertake any initiative. He probably will not bend on this point. He is bitter about how his initiatives have been received up to now. He is determined to maintain his silence until there is an organized entity ready to take specific political steps. He repeatedly stressed that he is willing to contribute his authority on condition that the necessary conditions have been established within a serious movement able to mobilize the anti-junta forces within Greece and abroad. He stressed his fears about the possibility of elections, that the political world with its characteristic inertia will find itself completely unprepared, unable to face such a move by the junta. He is saddened and angered by the essential absence of the political world and is afraid that the junta will be able to move ahead with its plans without opposition, tricking everybody and having the blessing and help of the Americans. In any case, he is willing to be in touch with us.*

3. *As you probably have been informed, there is a serious crisis within the Junta. The hard-liners pressured Papadopoulos to abandon the idea of lifting martial law by threatening to move against him. Papadopoulos then made his "resignation" maneuver, which created a serious situation until about September 20, 1970. The hard-liners turned to Angelis and asked him to become prime minister. Angelis refused. It seems that they then turned to another general, whose name is not known, but he, too, refused. At the same time, Pattakos stood by Papadopoulos, who, in turn, began the counter-attack. Petanis and Konstantopoulos were transferred. (Kitsos, who publicly swears on Papadopoulos's name, was put in Konstantopoulos's place.) The recent episode with Aslanides seems to have widened the rift between Papadopoulos and the hardliners. Apparently Roufoghalis did some research and discovered some financial scandals involving Makarezos and Aslanides, which he passed on to several officers. After this, Papadopoulos assigned chartered accountants to look into the management of the General Secretary of Athletics. Aslanides got very angry and turned in his resignation, saying that such an audit would be justified only if it were undertaken for all services. Papadopoulos kept the resignation and tried to calm him down. After this, Aslanides wrote a harshly critical article against Papadopoulos and asked Vradini to publish it. Apparently, Athanasiades was not eager to publish it and, with the help of Makarezos intervening, the matter was dropped. The following day, Yeorghalas called Aslanides to his office. Not only did Aslanides refuse to go, he replied, "I will meet with Yeorghalas only in my office during the hours the office is open to the public." Yeorghalas did go to Aslanides's office and asked, on behalf of the prime minister, to be informed about how the Alkimoi Project [the junta youth project] was progressing. Aslanides answered, in front of other people, "Tell your prime minister that I will not report anything to an arch-communist and an enemy of the country," and threw him out of the office. The prognosis is that, with the help of Angelis, Pattakos, and the Americans, Papadopoulos will survive the crisis and establish full control.*
4. *Markezinis and Averof, without the political leaders knowing, are negotiating with Pattakos about standing as candidates in the elections. If elections are proclaimed, apparently Pattakos will head the "Revolutionary" party and Papadopoulos will be made prime minister. Pattakos assures Markezinis and Averof that, in accordance with the election law they are preparing, the second party will receive 30% to 40% of the seats in parliament. Markezinis and Averof say that the number of seats must be according to the percentage of votes. Pattakos will not commit to this!*

5. *Allamanis and G. Rallis recently arrived here and in Paris. Rallis is going to meet with Karamanlis in the next few days, and he intends to pressure him to take action. They are both worried because they have not yet succeeded in organizing and coordinating political struggle within Greece. They say that there is no space.*
6. *Opropoulos's effort has not progressed, and I do not think it will.*

• *The renewal of aid and the Laird visit announced are very distressing events. Karamanlis is very unhappy, believing them to be particularly discouraging developments at this time, strengthening Papadopoulos, especially within the army.*
• *After our meeting with Karamanlis, we are reviewing and reconsidering the issue of a single organization. When we reach conclusions we will write to you.*
• *As far as the newsletter [Common Heritage] is concerned, now is not the time for any articles on "statutory" and "electoral" laws to be written. No "statutory laws" exist, only "drafts of statutory laws." It would be ridiculous for someone to write something now only to have it contradicted by the final form these drafts will take, since they are still being worked on in many ways. Also, how can anyone write responsibly about elections when there is no electoral law yet and the "statutory laws" concerning parties are not in their final form? In any case, Takis and I will look into this and send you whatever material we can.*

With our affection,

Alexandros Lykourezos

[Footnote: Colonel Dimitrios Opropoulos, after a serious accident while in internal exile, was confined to a wheelchair. The Junta allowed him to seek medical care in England. During his stay in London he worked tirelessly to coordinate anti-junta officers, serving and retired, with a representative group of Greek political exiles functioning in Europe, including King Constantine, Helen Vlachos, Panayotis Lambrias, Marion Saraphis, and others.]

October 6, Tuesday

I spoke with Anastaplo today. He had a two-hour meeting with Pattakos. Pattakos had the *Congressional Record* in front of him and was shouting at him angrily, "What business is it of yours to get involved in our internal affairs?" Anastaplo wrote a letter to the *Chicago Tribune* about this meeting. I asked him to send me a copy. He is downhearted.

OCTOBER 8, THURSDAY
I write Hillenbrand

I finally write the following letter to Hillenbrand:

Mr. Martin J. Hillenbrand
Assistant Secretary for European Affairs
Department of State
2001 C Street
Washington, D.C. 20520

Dear Mr. Secretary,

I wish to express my most sincere thanks for your kindness and for the opportunity to exchange some views with you on the problem of Greece.

I do not underestimate the complexity of the situation, and I do not feel that hasty actions will assist Greece or NATO.

May I suggest, however, that almost four years after the coup, initiatives in the direction of implementation of your announced policy are in order now.

I was happy on my return to Toledo to learn that a first step [Norstad meeting with the King] will be shortly taken.

If such initiatives and other concrete actions are taken in the near future, we will find ourselves at the beginning of a peaceful development of a new situation leading to responsible parliamentary democracy in Greece and smooth relations in NATO.

Lack of concrete actions by the United States on the other hand will further reinforce the position of the Junta. Further inaction will destroy the potential leverage you may have gained by resuming military assistance in the environment of the crisis in Jordan. Even now many Greeks despair at the publicity given to the visit by Secretary Laird and the Chairman of the JCS. They ask "Is this the end?" "Has the United States really given in to the Junta?"

The people of Greece and the NATO countries should be encouraged to interpret the decision of resuming military assistance as a calculated step of decisive importance toward your stated objective and not as a decision you HAD to make.

This country's "firm commitment toward restoring the country to political government", presumably a return to democratic processes in Greece, requires a specific program of action be developed and implemented. Important leaders of Greece and Greek public opinion, at the highest levels, stand ready to support the United States in any such program. The people of Greece and of the other NATO nations will then credit this country with its rightful leadership role in resolving this very embarrassing internal NATO family problem.

In this reasoning, I wish to add the thought that although patience is necessary, time is not unlimited. Initiatives, other than the Junta's own schedule of events, are required before it is too late (i.e., before they drive the situation towards their own type of elections or before violence replaces rational opposition to the regime).

It is in this spirit that I provided the brief outline on the Greek situation prior to my visit with you. I consider the thoughts contained in that outline even more valid and with proper planning and active programs, perhaps even more practical today despite the United States' resumption of military assistance.

Please accept my sincere appreciation for the opportunity to meet and discuss this problem with you. I am ready to meet with you again at your convenience if I can be of further assistance.

Sincerely yours,

Orestis Vidalis

OCTOBER 10, SATURDAY
Letter from Saxbe of Ohio

Letters from Kennedy and Saxbe. In his letter Senator Saxbe mentions, among other things, the following [Translated back into English from the Greek translation.]

> Some people maintain that we must support the Greek government for military reasons. Greece now has at its disposal enough weapons for defense against foreign enemies, in addition to the nuclear shield provided by the United States. It is true that Greece is of military importance to the southeastern flank of NATO. If, however, we destroy the form of civilization within the country, that NATO is supposed to protect, then the defense of the geographical area becomes meaningless.

NOVEMBER 5, THURSDAY
Details about Norstad's visit to the King

"General," I asked him, "would you object if the meeting were publicized? Would you mind being photographed together with the King and have that picture distributed to the press?"

"I am going to see the King in order to achieve something substantial. That is what the State Department also wants. It depends completely upon the King. If he wishes publicity, let him decide on how much. I will even go ahead and make a statement to the press if the King wishes so. I have no objections to doing this, as long as I know it in advance and speak with the State Department. For me, for us, the purpose is to help the King. I will go to the State Department before I leave and talk with Rogers and Hillebrand. The way the matter was handled by Secretary Laird and the Head of the Joint Chiefs of Staff was pointless and damaging. I only hope they achieved something positive in providing aid. I will learn about all this and tell the King. This meeting is very useful because I will bring the King's point of view back to them."

He continues speaking because I am only listening. "The idea that the junta would turn towards Russia is ridiculous. Therefore, they should not have been blackmailed. Either their evaluations were wrong or they received something positive about which we do not know. That is why this trip is important. And let's not forget that the State Department asked me to do it, as a result of your visit to Hillenbrand. I know they feel bad knowing that the King believes he has been ignored, and he is the only responsible factor."

November 7, Saturday

I wrote to the King. The main points are below.

- The Nixon administration wants the meeting to be held and is working to achieve it.
- The general is a warm supporter of the King's position; he detests dictatorships with an ideological fanaticism. If he is convinced that he can play a decisive role, he will do so effectively.
- Since the Junta will learn of this visit, I suggested that at least one picture of the meeting be made public, even if it is under the pretext of a friendly visit by the former Commander in Chief of European Forces to the King.
- The patience of the Greek people has been exhausted and such publicity will boost their morale.

November 25, Wednesday

I completed the report on the formation of American policy, based on the opinions of responsible people from the administration and the Senate. I forwarded it to the King along with a letter, the last before Norstad's visit, with my suggestions about the main points that should be addressed at the meeting.

November 25, 1970

Your Majesty,

Enclosed please find my briefing to the general, today. I assumed that he has been completely briefed on the administration's position, so I thought it best to inform him mainly about opposing opinions in Congress before he visits you. I hope this synopsis will be helpful to you as well in the forthcoming discussion.

The main point is that the positions held by Nixon and his advisors can be interpreted in three ways:

a. *They want the dictatorship to remain in power and are only pretending to apply pressure for rule to be returned to you and the people.*
b. *They do not want the dictatorship but believe they can do no more than what they are doing.*
c. *They do not want the dictatorship, recognize that they are in a position to influence the situation decisively, but believe that the time has not yet come for decisive measures.*

I suggest that these three interpretations be presented to your visitor. To you, at least, they are obliged to answer clearly and directly as to which of them is correct.

This is the least they can do for you and the visit suggests that they are willing to help you.

The next step, of course, would be for them to take specific steps, such as:

a. *Appoint General Norstad as the president's envoy to speed the return to normal conditions.*
b. *Have General Goodpaster and other Allied commanders make specific recommendations.*
c. *Stop economic support from private funds.*
d. *Support change by increasing criticism in Congress, etc.*

Your Majesty, you know that the general has supported my work in many ways. I would like to encourage you to tell him that you are grateful for his help. This would reinforce his interest and, in the future, help me in getting in touch with the administration and the Republican leadership in Congress directly.

I will try to come to Europe after the general returns. It would be useful to tell you about the initial results of the visit and receive your instructions for further action.

Respectfully,

Orestis Vidalis

November 28, Saturday
My citizenship is revoked.

Two registered letters arrived this morning for Nikos Antoniou. [Nikos Antoniou is General and Mrs. Vidalis's nephew, who was staying with the Vidalis family while teaching at the University of Toledo and studying for his Ph.D. The papers were forwarded to him by his parents for General Vidalis.]

"It must be his papers," I remarked to Matina.

I was upstairs with Efthymios when Nikos came down to read his mail. When I came back down, I asked, "Was it your papers?" Matina, with tears in her eyes said, "No, it wasn't his papers, but don't be upset." "Of course I will not be upset," I said, and read the two sheets of paper announcing, "revocation of citizenship" and "pension cancellation." "We are proud," Matina said. "Revocation of citizenship is a badge of honor for a free Greek."

This is formal recognition of the effectiveness of my actions against the Junta.

The revocation of my citizenship was made known to me officially in a document from the Pensions Office in the Ministry of Finance dated September 7, 1970 because they did not have the courage to inform me directly. The document is below.

> "Ministry of Finance
> State General Accounting Office
> Pensions Office
>
> September 7, 1970
>
> Subject: Information included
>
> We are informing you that, in accordance with the decision taken by the Minister of the Interior on August 25, 1970 revoking your citizenship, the necessary documentation has been presented to Computer Services to implement the provisions of Chapter B, Paragraph I of Article 63 of Law $18^{54}/1951$ to remove your name from the registry of retired officers and stop paying your pension.
>
> For this reason we are asking you to return your checks for the December 1970 pension payment and 1970 Christmas Present, un-cashed, in order to avoid the legal consequences."

I must think of how to best use the junta's most recent stupidity to help our efforts.

December 1, Tuesday
Nixon administration message to the King

Norstad called me for a meeting. Briley, the company's legal advisor, was present. Norstad said that Rogers gave him a message from the government to the King, which says, roughly, the following:

- Greetings from the American government.
- Assurance assurance that the government is working toward the return of democracy in Greece.
- The government trusts the King and believes that any solution should have the King at the center.
- Best wishes

He then said that it would not be wise to make a statement opposing the dictatorship now, in view of the regime's pledge to take steps toward democracy within the current year.

I said, "General, I advised the King to make your visit public with a photograph. The Junta will know about your visit and, therefore, the rest of the world and the Greeks should know as well."

"That is an excellent idea and I agree."

Today the State Department informed Tasca about Norstad's visit to the King. In contrast with the American ambassador in Rome, Tasca knew nothing about the visit.

Then we discussed the general's response in case he is questioned by journalists. He will say that he has known the royal family for many years and it was his duty to visit the King. That he has informed the State Department, as he does whenever he meets prominent people. That he wishes, as do the American people, the Greek people, and the current regime, for democracy to return to Greece,

He then said, "I expect to find the King worried and bitter, which is understandable. But, if the subject arises, I will tell him that he must overlook the details and be patient."

How the discussion will go will be up to the King.

At the end I said, "General, General Goodpaster can exert the greatest amount of influence."

"I agree completely and will see him on Friday. I will mainly discuss the issue of military aid with him."

December 3, Thursday
Norstad visits the King today

After two years of such bitterness, such disappointment, and such hesitation, General Norstad is visiting the King today.

I do not overestimate the importance of the visit, but I do believe that much can come from it. If Norstad sees that the King is informed, realistic, a determined representative of the will of the nation in restoring responsibility to the Greek people at all costs, he will convey a message of action and initiative. If, on the other hand, he sees the King as cautious, hesitant, influenced by the Junta's terror, then nothing will be gained from this visit.

December 4, Friday
The King's first impressions

The King telephoned me from Rome at 4:00 in the afternoon. He was obviously pleased. He was completely satisfied by the visit. He thanked Norstad for all he had done, they made a thorough analysis, and Norstad will intervene to achieve a meeting between the King and Rogers. They discussed the issue of the King's representatives, and the King told him, "They should deal only with me." The King would like General Norstad to keep in touch on very important and urgent matters, so they will be able to have frequent communication.

December 8, Tuesday
Norstad's first impressions

I met with Norstad in the afternoon. He gave me thorough description of his meeting with the King. He gave him Roger's message, and the King thanked him. Then the King asked him what the American government was thinking. He insisted on this point and brought it up again later.

"I told him," said the general, "that the government is expecting positive measures to be announced by the end of the year. Whether or not they will be announced will be determined soon. Then, the American administration will have to decide what to do.

> We then discussed the issue of his return. He set three clear conditions: free elections, free press, the release of prisoners.
>
> We discussed the priority of these conditions and also his meeting with Secretary Rogers. I will see Rogers on Thursday and will brief him about the visit.
>
> It is very important that I saw a mature leader ready to undertake serious responsibility. He was a completely different man, and I was impressed by how changed, realistic, and informed he is now.

> From the house, I spoke on the telephone with Mountbatten, who tried to organize a meeting between the King and Rogers in Belgium, at the Belgian King's palace. Unfortunately, Rogers left and the meeting could not take place. But I will begin providing Rogers with fresh information.
>
> I told the King that I have learned from many sources that the members of the junta are quarreling among themselves. The Onassis issue, corruption, debauchery, extremism, etc. could blow them apart. For this reason preparations must be made for the situation that will follow after the junta leaves. I agreed that the King must not return unless his terms are met.
>
> I was surprised that many people with whom I spoke told me that most people accept this situation. Only thinking people oppose it because they are not free.

I interrupted him then, and said, "General, how can people still believe in this theory when they know that the junta does not dare go to elections because it will lose?"

He thought, and said,

> Of course, but there is also the possibility that they do not want a parliamentary system. But what ever they do under pressure, if they choose elections it will be the end. I will see Rogers on Thursday and will let you know.
>
> In any case, the King talked enthusiastically about you and trusts your opinions and suggestions. He asked me to convey his greetings to you.
>
> He complained because he has had no contact with Americans. Even at receptions the American Ambassadors obviously avoid him, whereas all Ambassadors of the free world have visited him in Rome. He asked me to keep in touch with him. I told him that would be an honor, but normal communication with the U.S. must be restored.

The University of Thessaloniki, Greek Journalists, and Mitsotakis's Valuable Briefing

DECEMBER 10, THURSDAY
Letter from Greek Journalists—Letter from Kostas Mitsotakis

Today I received the text of the letter Greek journalists living abroad sent to Rodger Davies, Deputy Assistant Secretary of State, contradicting the State Department's claim that "the shift towards constitutional order has begun in Greece."

I received the following letter from Mitsotakis, dated November 27.

Paris, November 27, 1970

Dear General,

I want to say again how much I was pleased with the chance to meet you and personally discover the quietly positive work you do. It was a pleasant surprise for me to discover that such a serious effort is under way. I also want to thank you for the friendly help you so willingly provided during my trip there.

I saw Karamanlis last night for some time. I told him about the situation there and what you had asked me to tell him. He was particularly pleased with the magazine and the committee. I will go to Rome within the next few days, but I do not yet know exactly when, as I have many trips to take right now in different directions. Lambrias came from London today and I briefed him on matters that concern him. He is ready and willing to cooperate closely. He said that he never received your letter of last spring. He will write to you to that effect himself.

Here, attempts are under way to influence European governments for a ministerial conference. There are unexpected difficulties, but the general impression is encouraging. The impression here is that the American government is working behind the scenes to prevent the junta from being overthrown. Do you have any reliable information about this?

I thought that now the office will be organized, Granitsas could send a news bulletin with American news concerning Greece to Greek radio stations whenever needed. I already have discussed this and they will broadcast material if they receive it. Particularly the press, Congress, anti-junta activities by different organizations, and anything else. What do you think of this idea?

We haven't talked about it yet, and I forgot to ask you about a radio hour. What do you think? The news bulletin, of course, if decided, will complement, not substitute, for sending the material we talked about by mail.

Unfortunately, there is no news from home. Dead silence and lower morale. A considerable contribution to this is the news the junta made known and the New York Times printed about renewing military aid. As far as I know, for the time being at least, the information is not accurate. Is there a way to lighten this impression? Please consider this. Perhaps the letter from Edwards and other senators could serve that purpose. If this is done, give it as much publicity as you can and let us know.

I will be away for several days on short, 1-2 day trips. I will, therefore, be close to Paris.

Greetings from my wife.

Friendly regards,

Yours,

Kon. Mitsotakis

PS. This Intelligence Digest *that justifiably annoyed you is published by some stupid half fascist. It is a private publication without any importance.*

December 23, Wednesday
Norstad writes Secretary of State Rogers

Norstad asked to meet me in the afternoon. He showed me the report he sent Rogers about his visit with the King. He could not give me a copy but asked me to keep notes.

December 24, Thursday

I wrote the following letter to the King after meeting with the general yesterday:

December 24, 1970

Your Majesty,

Yesterday afternoon I met with the general.

He asked me to read his report to Rogers. He explained he could not give me a copy.

It was a three-page report. He described your meeting and concluded that the report confirms the Norstad-Rogers meeting on December 11. During that meeting he gave an oral report of his meeting with you.

In the text he describes what you know. He describes your conditions, stresses your determination, your realistic approach, and insists on the need to restore regular, official communication between you and the American government.

In the report he repeats the proposal he made to the Secretary of State about the person who will be the official liaison with you. He suggested, and Rogers agreed, that Cabot Lodge play this role. After I read the report, he told me about his meeting with Rogers, who told him the following:

a. The Nixon administration wants and will work to achieve direct communication with you.

b. The Nixon administration believes that tough young officers want the dictatorship to continue, while Papadopoulos wants constitutional order to return. That Papadopoulos is not taking steps to implement a constitution shows the power of these officers.

c. They do not know how they can find a realistic way out.

d. Rogers does not have positive and specific ideas about what should be done, although no one wants the dictatorship to continue in power. All the information from Athens is that the "regime is strong" and that "the people are not prepared for dramatic moves."

From the Norstad-Rogers meeting it is obvious that they do not want the dictatorship to continue in power, are concerned that the current regime may be overthrown by sudden moves, and honestly want to learn whether or not you can actively participate in developments.

The general told me to report the above to you, and he will write to you immediately after the decision is taken about Cabot Lodge. He plans to return to Rome and introduce you to Lodge. He added that Lodge is powerful, known to him personally, and a man of action.

He believes he will meet with Rogers again towards the middle of January. He asked me to convey his best wishes.

When I come to Europe towards the end of January I may have the decision about Lodge.

Respectfully,

Orestis Vidalis

December 28, Monday

Today I received a very interesting letter dated December 21, 1970, from Professor Daniel P. Tompkins of the Department of Classical Studies at Wesleyan University in Connecticut.

In this letter he sends the results of a study made on the positions taken by members of Congress on the Greek issue during the years 1967 to 1970. Professor Tompkins and a Wesleyan University working group on Greek policy issues worked on this study.

The study was based on the *Congressional Record* and articles written or statements made by members of the House and Senate. The report contains the results of the study from April 25, 1967 to November 17, 1970. The report clearly presents Congress's interest in the Greek issue and the positions for and against the regime. The report leads to the conclusion that the people supporting the regime and its arguments are far behind those opposing the regime. Those who are for the regime base their arguments on official information coming from the regime, while those who are against the regime express original thoughts and positions in defense of the principles of political freedom and democracy.

CHAPTER 4

1971

New Year
Citizenship Revoked
Trip to Europe

MONDAY, JANUARY 11

In the evening, I telephone the journalist Saville Davis of the *Christian Science Monitor* and tell him that my citizenship has been revoked. He is surprised. I tell him I will send him the announcement. He will talk to the *Washington Post*, the *New York Times*, and, of course, the *Christian Science Monitor.*

JANUARY 14, THURSDAY

My statement about my citizenship being revoked

It is my duty to inform the Greek people and the friends of Greece that the dictatorship has revoked my citizenship. I learned of this action indirectly from the Ministry of Finance, which informed me that my military pension is being cancelled in accordance with the Ministry of the Interior's decision to revoke my Greek citizenship.

The only comment I will allow myself to make at this point is that my relationship with the Greek nation has been determined by only one factor; an entire life dedicated to the nation, unconditionally devoted to the ideals the Greek nation represents.

No arbitrary decision taken in secret by self-proclaimed despots can alter this relationship. Their action confirms my belief that the nation is in extreme danger and only utmost determination and a spirit of sacrifice on the part of us Greeks will enable the nation to survive the current, unprecedented crisis.

This crisis can be dealt with only if the wisdom and genuine patriotism of all are placed at the service of the highest national interest, which requires that the sovereign rights of the Greek people be restored without any further delay.

Orestis Vidalis

January 18, Monday

Jim Pyrros called in the evening and said he had read about my citizenship being revoked in the *Christian Science Monitor.*

January 20, Wednesday

The *National Herald* (*Ethnikos Kyrix*) printed the news about my citizenship.

January 22, Friday
Discussion with Norstad. The administration is irritated by Papadopoulos's statements

In the afternoon, I met with General Norstad from 3:00 to 4:00 o'clock. In the beginning he showed me a letter from Lord Mountbatten dated January 1, 1970. The letter said that he was waiting for an answer about Secretary William P. Rogers's response to his suggestions.

Then he showed me a letter dated January 16, 1970 he received from Rogers. The letter thanks Norstad for the report on his meeting with the King and adds that the framework for restoring better communication with the King is being examined.

Then he told me,

> I started writing a letter to the King and tore it up three times. It is not wise to put everything on paper, and a formal letter would be improper. That is why I am asking you, please, to personally tell the King about my report to Rogers, which you can read again if you would like; Roger's letter; the letter that Cabot Lodge sent me; and the letter I sent him. Also, please tell the King that if Lodge is given this mission it would be the perfect solution because he is a personal friend of mine and has political support no one can ignore. I saw him in Rome after my meeting with the King and discussed the subject with him. He would like to be actively involved. If, again, they do not make up their minds, I will force the issue. How? I will ask the King to invite me for lunch in Rome and also will ask if I may bring my friend Cabot Lodge along with me. After this unofficial meeting, Lodge can continue with him. But, I think they will make a decision. You must also tell the King that the administration is annoyed by Papadopoulos's statements of December 19,* but they believe that a sudden reaction would not be productive. They already have noticed the rise in public opinion against the dictatorship in Greece, which is very disturbing to the regime.

*In these statements, Papadopoulos said, "There will be no be constitutional changes during 1971. Only I, as authorized by the people, will decide when the time is right for the safe return to parliamentary life, in accordance with the constitution."

And he added,

> I do not think the King should be more disappointed today than he was during our meeting. The December statements, regardless of the reasons for which they were made, raised many questions.
>
> Please convey to the King my request to either bring you into contact with Lord Mountbatten or, if he prefers, for himself to respond to Mountbatten that the State Department is investigating the possibility of establishing a permanent, official, but unorthodox liaison with the King. Perhaps, in his letter to Rogers, Mountbatten can mention that he was informed by the general that this is under consideration.

He wrote a telegram to Mountbatten saying, "My associate from Toledo will meet with your friend next week. He is bringing an answer to your letter of January 15. You can communicate through your friend. Regards."

Finally, he said, "The King must know that I have not stopped and will not stop keeping him informed. Please convey my respects." He then said that he would meet with the State Department during the first week of February.

I interrupted him only twice during our meeting. The first time was when he said that patience is needed. I said, "After four years of patience they have strengthened their positions and will become even more implacable towards the King, NATO, and the U.S."

"They understand this at the State Department," he replied, "but they don't think they should have reacted immediately." He added, "The government machinery in our country is very conservative and slow moving. It is extremely difficult to collect all those of high ranking officials to discuss one extraordinary and pressing subject."

I then said," General, have you talked with Henry Kissinger? I think it is difficult for things to progress without him."

"I have not seen Kissinger because I am talking with Secretary Rogers now and it would not be helpful to interject Kissinger into this. The Middle East area, of which Greece is a part, is Rogers's responsibility. If I happen to meet Kissinger, then I will tell him. But I do not think I should involve him right now."

January 23, Saturday

Yesterday's discussion with General Norstad confirms that a very great deal of patience is needed, for the Junta is helped by basic factors, such as the apparent apathy of the Greek people, international events that draw the world's attention, and the slow movement of the American government.

Activity within Greece has to be developed in such a way as to spur developments. At the same time, activities here must be intensified as fast as possible.

January 28, Thursday
In London

Lunch with Eleni Vlachou. We discuss the idea of forming a national association. She is going to publish a book with speeches by those who have spoken against the Junta.

January 29, Friday
Visit Opropoulos

I arrived late for my meeting with the King. I told him of Norstad's points. He listened and then, at one point, interrupted and told me how he had happened to meet U.S. Secretary of Defense Laird in Rome, while Nixon was visiting Italy.

They happened to be staying in the same hotel and Laird asked to see him. When they met, Laird asked if he knew that he was going to Athens and that they were going to provide the aid. The King replied that he knew. Laird then asked him what he thought about the aid decision. The King said that if military aid were a step toward guaranteeing the return of parliamentary life in Greece, then it was a very good move. If, however, it was given without that stipulation, then it was very bad. The King then asked if they had any guarantees before going ahead with the aid and Laird answered, "Of course we do."

The King then told me that Tasca was concerned about Papadopoulos's speech on December 19 and met with Pattakos to express his dissatisfaction. Pattakos replied, "If you don't like it, then go find another job." At the same time, Sisco called Ambassador Vitsaxis to the State Department, raised the issue with him, and requested clarification within three days. Vitsaxis sent a coded message describing his meeting with Sisco to Papadopoulos, with a copy to the Ministry of Foreign Affairs. Later, Papadopoulos met with Tasca. Another point is that Tasca told Christopher G. Janus from Chicago to tell the King to get in touch with the Junta and return without conditions. The King was angered and told Janus, "If this gentleman wishes to give me such advice, he should come see me in person."

We stopped for dinner and continued in the evening.

We agreed on what I should tell Norstad when I return:

- Expressions of gratitude
- The King is pleased with Norstad's proposal concerning Cabot Lodge.

- When this happens, there should be a plan of action.
- Request that Norstad be present at the first meeting between the King and Cabot Lodge
- What is happening concerning General Goodpaster's visit to the King?

The discussion then turned to how the Navy must be encouraged so it can be used if the need arises.

Return to U.S.A.—Information about the Situation in Greece (Navy, Moose-Lowenstein* Report)

JANUARY 30, SATURDAY
In New York

I met with Richard Moose of the Fulbright Committee in New York. We discussed the overall situation. He kept notes on my opinions and insisted on the need to separate the issue of aid from political disapproval of the junta. It was a long and interesting discussion. We agreed to meet again after he returns from Greece.

FEBRUARY 4, THURSDAY
Long talk with Norstad

I saw Norstad in the afternoon. I conveyed the King's greetings and gratitude. I told him that the King is awaiting information concerning the Cabot Lodge appointment and would like Norstad be present at the first meeting. The general replied: "Of course, that is how it will be done." He knows that Rogers does not object and that Lodge wants it. In addition to the meeting with Lodge, if the King and Queen would like, he would be glad to visit them in Rome in the meantime.

I answered, "The King would like this and would meet with you with great pleasure as often as you can."

"Another matter the King has in mind," I said, "is that when Lodge is appointed, there must be a detailed plan of action, so there will be progress."

"That is exactly what is going to happen with Lodge, who can talk with the president from a position of political power, and then any plan can be discussed," he said.

Then I raised the subject of publicity. "Because the issue is psychological, the meeting must be made public at some point."

*Richard Moose and James Lowenstein are senior staff members of the Senate Foreign Relations Committee, chaired by Senator J. William Fulbright (D Arkansas).

"I would be happy even now to ask Sulzberger of the *New York Times* to publish something about the last visit."

"I don't think this would be of particular help now," I replied, "but the issue must be faced in the future."

"It is easy, providing the King wishes," responded Norstad.

He then said that the opposition is raising the subject, probably because of Greek urging. "I do not think the subject should be raised because of urging from the Greek side unless someone is asked, in which case he will give his opinion. Making this a political issue would only make it more difficult. We should not forget that the solution will come from Nixon."

I said, "Perhaps this would facilitate the pressure that the Nixon administration wants applied indirectly."

"Perhaps," he said, "because they are annoyed."

I then asked if there is any chance that the King will meet with General Goodpaster. "I discussed this with the general and we agreed that the meeting is premature. But I could arrange for them to meet in Rome at a reception I could organize."

I replied that I did not think this would serve the purpose of changing the psychological climate.

February 10, Wednesday

I called Christopher Janus, who told me about his meeting with Tasca and then later with the King. I asked him to describe these meetings for me in writing. I stressed the need to form a small group of selected Greek-Americans. He asked to meet me and also to meet Graham Hovey of the *New York Times*.

In the afternoon, General Norstad's secretary asked me to read the general's letter to Rogers before she mailed it. The letter, dated February 10, reads, "A Greek colleague in this company returned with renewed optimism after meeting with King Constantine recently. It is thought that this approach can lead to restoring parliamentary rule. I suggest that the steps needed for appointing an experienced, capable, and influential official representative of the American government to the King be expedited. The choice of Cabot Lodge seems excellent."

February 27, Saturday

I drove to Cleveland and sat in on the end of the Archbishop's conference, sitting with him at the table. After dinner, the two of us stayed behind. I told him the latest news, the need to rekindle our efforts because if another year or two go by they will have solidified their position and be able to reconsider their stance toward the United States, NATO, and the Archbishop.

He seemed to agree. Finally, I asked him to help me, behind the scenes, to motivate prominent Greek-Americans to voice their disapproval. He said he would go to Washington to meet with Greek-American senators such as John Brademas and others. He will ask them to make announcements on March 25. He also will see Cabot Lodge in Boston.

March 1, Monday
Information about navy officers.

I received a registered letter from Pierros Panaghiotareas with the names of navy officers with a mark by each name showing their position *vis a vis* the junta. The list has 5 rear admirals, 8 commodores, 32 active duty captains, 65 active duty commanders, and 30 technical support officers characterized as anti-junta. According to Panaghiotareas, more officers among the lower ranks are against the Junta, and more fanatically so.

March 4, Thursday

I telephone the Archbishop. He had met with John Brademas and others. They will make a statement on March 25. He provided them with the necessary material. He saw Senator Charles Percy of Illinois, who was in full agreement and most willing to help. The two senators said today that the United States must exert the greatest possible political pressure in order for Greece to return to parliamentary rule.

I received a letter from Christopher G. Janus, dated February 21, in response to our February 10 telephone conversation. In his letter he writes:

> *What these unscrupulous dictators have done to you only proves once again their ruthlessness and stupidity.*
>
> *Regarding the confirmation of my conversation with Ambassador Tasca in Athens last October, here, based on my notes, is the way the conversation went: I called on Ambassador Tasca to confirm a rumor that Papadopoulos had resigned. Tasca started the conversation by saying that he was the son of an Italian immigrant and he therefore knew how to deal with Mediterranean peoples. He said, "I don't tell Greek rulers what to do, I ask for their help and that's what I did with Papadopoulos when he resigned. I told him of the Russian threat in the Middle East and that we had enough problems, and that I wished he would help me by staying on. After more than an hour's conversation, Papadopoulos agreed to withdraw his resignation."*
>
> *Then Ambassador Tasca asked me if I would do him a personal favor when I returned to the States through Rome. He asked me to give the following message to King Constantine: "Please tell the King that Papadopoulos is his best*

friend. Also tell him—but not in these words—that he should act like a King and speak out in behalf of Papadopoulos."

I passed this message on to King Constantine and his reply was, "Please tell the American Ambassador to Greece that he is the only Ambassador at NATO who had not had the guts to call on me.

Sincerely,

Christopher G. Janus

March 5, Friday
Moose-Lowenstein Report

I called Moose in the afternoon. He was pleased because the response to the report was positive. The goal now is for the committee to make an official investigation. Today's articles in the *Washington Post* and the *New York Times* on the Moose-Lowenstein report are very good. He is sending me three or four copies of the report. The report is very good and quite harsh about the failure of American policy.

March 9, Tuesday
Letter from the Secretary of State

Norstad's secretary telephoned me to say that Rogers had sent him a letter dated March 2, in which he, "thanks him for his letter of February 10 and that they are working on the appointment of an official permanent liaison to the King." I thanked her.

March 16, Tuesday

I went to the *New York Times*. Other than Graham Hovey, I met the editor-in-chief and another member of the editorial staff. I explained my position to them. I stressed that the conservative world also is against the Junta and insisted that they stress this point. I told them about March 25 and my speech. Hovey was interested in the speech, saying that an article could be made out of it. He kept a copy.

In discussing what should be done now, I proposed they should begin suggesting that Tasca should be recalled because he failed, and they agreed. I stayed with them until 2:30 in the afternoon. We agreed to stay in touch. Hovey asked me to keep him informed about any important issues.

March 25, Thursday
Meeting with Sir Hugh Greene and Senator Pell

At 10:00 in the morning I meet with Sir Hugh Greene. He conveyed the King's greetings. I explained my position. He told me about the effort to form a European—Atlantic committee for Greece. We discussed the need—and I insisted upon this point—for the committee to have a multiparty line. I told him about my meeting with Professor Eisenhower. I suggested they look for a conservative to head the committee. If they cannot find one, they should turn to Averell Harriman. He gave me the text of the statement that is scheduled to be released in May. He asked for my address and gave me his.

In the afternoon, I met Senator Pell. I told him about our being optimistic that something will come out of the Nixon administration's disappointment. Now that the Junta is tired, we should increase our efforts. This is a contest of exhaustion. He who wins is he who tires last. I told him that the King always thinks of him with affection because he has been one of our first and main supporters. He asked what he, himself, could do.

"Motivate the new senators, those who have never spoken out, to make brief, regular statements."

March 31, Wednesday
Letters to Norstad and the King

I write Norstad about the latest developments:

> Dear General Norstad,
>
> I think it is appropriate to brief you on some developments of the last 10 days:
>
> a. President Nixon addressed a message to King Constantine on the occasion of the 150th anniversary of Greek independence. In this message the president makes reference to the "spirit of classical Greece."
> b. King Constantine replied to this message by thanking the president and stating that "The people of Greece will extremely appreciate the participation of the American people in this celebration of the struggle for freedom, a struggle inspired by the democratic spirit of classical Greece.
> c. Both messages have been published by the press in Greece and the Greek-American press in this country. The impact on the morale of the people is already more than what one could have expected.
> d. Mr. Panayotis Kanellopoulos issued a joint declaration with Mr. Mavros—a leading member of the Center Union—supporting

democracy. Mr. Kanellopoulos stated: "The declaration shows that the two big parties are united and ready to assume responsibility. It is important for the people in Greece and for the policymakers in Washington who have said until now that there is no alternative to the present regime."

e. Former Greek Premier Stephanopoulos issued a statement on his own behalf calling on Greeks to rally behind King Constantine. He has refrained all these four years from making any statement against the regime. He was a member of the Papandreou party.
f. One hundred and thirty-three prominent, largely non-political Greeks, including two highly respected Lt. Generals, signed a proclamation in Athens similar to a manifesto supporting democracy.
g. During the military parade on March 25*th* in Athens, Papadopoulos was mysteriously absent. He still is not appearing publicly.
h. General Angelis, who is, as you know, visiting this country as a guest of General Westmoreland, cancelled his appearance at a reception in his honor in the Greek Consulate in New York, at the last moment, for security reasons.
   At a reception yesterday for General Angelis at Fort Meyer Officers' Mess, four out of the five Greek-American Congressman declined the invitation of the host, the Greek Military attaché.
i. I was invited by a large Greek-American community (800 families) in Canton, Ohio, to be their main speaker on Sunday, March 28*th*, when they celebrated the 150*th* anniversary of Greek independence. I accepted the invitation. My address, which I delivered in English, was enthusiastically received by an audience of at least 400. A copy of my address is attached. The address was published by one of the Greek American dailies, in Greek, in its entirety.

Orestis Vidalis

Fifteen minutes later, he asked to see me. We talked for about 45 minutes.

I immediately wrote a report of this meeting for the King. The letter to the King, dated March 31, 1971 is below:

> The most important development since my last letter, of course, is Nixon's message to your Majesty.
>
> In a long discussion with the general today, I learned the following:

a. He thinks the message is extremely important, even more so than the Cabot Lodge proposal. They are waiting and will study the ramifications of the exchange of messages very carefully.
b. They have not yet decided about Lodge.

c. The general is planning to visit you again toward the end of May. This is a first sign, not yet to be considered, of a request for an audience. As soon as his schedule is set and after he meets with Rogers he will inform me so I will be able to report to your Majesty. Please inform me of your schedule toward the end of March so I will be in a position to talk with the general. It would be good if I were to know if your Majesty will be in Rome and will be willing to meet the general. Of course, in case of anything urgent I will request your Majesty's instructions by telephone.
d. He is planning to visit Lord Mountbatten.
e. Without explanation, for the first time he told me, "I am beginning to see developments during this year."

After discussing his possible trip, he told me about a meeting he had with Ambassador Stathatos in New York. Mrs. Norstad knows the couple and Stathatos asked to meet with the general.

They did meet and Stathatos tried in a very diplomatic way to clarify the general's attitude.

The general's positions as described to Stathatos are the following:

a. The American people are not in favour of the regime.
b. The regime has lasted much longer than necessary and has not kept its promises.
c. The fate of dictatorships is well known. They are detested by the people, they are structures long out-of-date, and if the military does not give up power in time, chaos ensues.
d. The King is not only needed in Greece as a guarantor of stability, he is today a tried and experienced leader. Of course, the King must return when there is a specific schedule for return to parliamentary rule.
e. I have paid my respects to the King and discovered a leader fully prepared to undertake the responsibilities of the nation's leader.
f. If the regime recognizes the King's importance, then a peaceful transfer of power is possible.
g. I concluded, "Military rule has been prolonged too long."

In Washington I met with Sir Hugh Greene, who is truly remarkable, and Senator Pell.

The statements made by Kanellopoulos-Mavros and Stefanopoulos, as well as the proclamation of the 133, General Pavlos Dimopoulos among them, have had an effect.

Angelis is, literally, surrounded by guards. Their fear that something might happen to him has gone beyond reason.

On Sunday I spoke at the services of a large Greek-American community in Canton, Ohio. I enclose the text of my speech in English. I did not know anybody, but accepted the invitation. The result was acclaim from an audience that is considered largely pro-junta.

The *National Herald* (*Ethnikos Kyrix*) of New York printed my speech in Greek and, I am told, will comment on my position.

Your Majesty,

Slowly but surely we are making progress. The regime is in miserable condition. I am expecting a report on this matter and will forward it to your Majesty immediately. I will try to come to Europe after the general's visit.

We Move Ahead with Planning Action by the Navy

April 2, Friday
Information about naval officers

I receive a letter dated March 26, 1971 from Pierros Panaghiotareas, asking for instructions. Panaghiotareas forwards information he has from Commander N. Pappas, who is studying at the NATO Defense College together with the fanatic pro-junta Lt. Colonel Papapostolou. Because both of them are in the same school, Pappas was able to gather information about divisions within the Junta.

a. There is a group of hard-liners (to put it mildly), now numbering about 80 and consisting of captains, majors, and lieutenant colonels. Their leader is Makarezos; number two is Stamatelopoulos. They seek to advance the revolution's goals by changing the prime minister, who is accused of letting corruption and nepotism reach extreme levels. They consider him a traitor and hate him. They would have Makarezos become Prime Minister, and his first step would be to hold a referendum on democracy. The second most hated man for this group is the King. Members of the group are said to consider both of them [Papadopoulos and the King] "dead." It is made clear that if the King comes back during the Papadopoulos/Angelis coalition, and if any one of this hard-line group is still free, he is to kill them. They can be compared only to fanatical ELAS members. It is horrible to listen to them.
b. Anti-American sentiment is growing constantly. The greater the divisions within the Junta, the greater the fear of bloodshed, and hatred against Americans increases because they do nothing whatsoever to

solve the Greek problem. The measures the Americans have taken up to now are hypothetical, and in fact ridiculous.

c. The final struggle between the contesting groups for dominance will come any day.
d. In the meantime, our supporters are increasing but, unfortunately, there is a leadership problem. The higher ranks are not helping as much as needed.
e. After July we could take 6-7 destroyers and leave. But then what? Who of the higher-ranking officers will survive? How can his Majesty help us? They tell me I should try to meet with his Majesty on my return trip. The people are expecting us to do something—they are worried. If quarrels inside the Junta become obvious, it would be an opportunity for action.

In the afternoon, I talk with Saville Davis of the *Christian Science Monitor*, who reads his article to me. I make some suggestions; he accepts them, and the article is set for Monday.

April 10, Saturday
Another meeting with Panaghiotareas

I met with Pierros Panaghiotareas, in the afternoon for two hours, who told me in person what he had written me. He asked my opinion about what can happen with the navy. I told him to continue with the planning carefully and secretly—no use of the King's name. Only when everything is ready should there me any meetings with the appropriate people in Europe. Let's refer to the organization as "Omega." He asked me to draw up instructions, and I promised I would do so. Since nothing can happen before the annual transfers and promotions are announced and we know who will be commanding what ships, he will keep me informed. He will wait for my instructions.

April 12, Monday

I write the text Pierros Panaghiotareas and I discussed. I make it in the form of a contract between the Royal Navy and the people of Greece. When Matina reads it, she does not find it enthusiastic enough. I change it and set it aside so it will mature more in my mind. By chance, I ask if the *Congressional Record* has arrived. I discover that my speech in Canton was included in the April 7 issue, with a brief, complimentary introduction by Senator Bow, whom I have not met.

April 22, Thursday
The contract

I got in touch with Hovey of the *New York Times.* He will write an editorial that will refer to my speech.

I sent my thoughts and instructions and the draft of a "Royal Navy National Contract" to Pierros Panaghiotareas.

Omega 21/4/71

Thoughts—Instructions

The worries the Royal Navy has are the worries all Greeks have. But the Royal Navy worries can be transformed into historic acts.

Clearly, the time has come.

Discussions and worries must be replaced by realistic action.

Four years of humiliation are more than enough.

A draft of a Royal Navy National Contract with the people of Greece has been prepared.

The contract describes the struggle and its purpose. It is a summon for national salvation.

Its acceptance by R.N. officers will show their courage, readiness for self-sacrifice, and mature judgment in performing their national duty.

Converting the contract into reality will guarantee the R.N. the first place in the effort to free the country from the suffocating embrace of violence and the dictators' foreign supporters.

The contract does not explain how this goal will be reached.

Basic steps could be:

- Immediately establishing a leadership nucleus for the Ramrod organization consisting of R.N. officers on active duty.
- Begin initiations into Ramrod based on the triad system. Initiate only those who are 100% loyal.
- No leaking of information about Ramrod to outsiders. Ramrod members take formal oath.
- Attempt to complete Ramrod as soon as possible.
- Members of the nucleus group meet with Alexander (O. Vidalis).
- Study the possibilities of expanding Ramrod in the following order:
    - R.N. officers not on active duty
    - The Royal Air Force by establishing the Ikaros organization.
    - The Royal Army by establishing the Philippos organization.
- Study how the nucleus can act and discussions with Alexander.
- From the first Ramrod meeting, study measures for immediate action

in case the junta is pressured by outside factors into actions such as staging fake elections.

- No member of Ramrod, Ikaros, or Philippos will seek any benefits or position after the goal is achieved.
- The first steps require utmost care. Communication while Ramrod is being established must be undertaken extremely carefully.
- From now on, not a minute must be lost. Time is valuable.

If the R.N. acts now, success is certain.

For four years the Hellenes have patiently suffered their martyrdom. Their support will be tremendous.

Everybody is waiting for the resurrection. No one doubts that the resurrection is coming.

But none of them know the source of the resurrection's inspiration and courage.

You, the young officers of the R.N., are called upon to bring to the Greek people, even to your army colleagues held in bondage, the ultimate joy of freedom and resurrection in a new Greece.

ROYAL NAVY NATIONAL CONTRACT.

For four years the R.N., robbed of its character and humiliated as have been all the people of Greece, has been watching the modern tragedy of Greece in great distress.

The R.N., fully conscious of its great historic responsibility, believes that it no longer has the national right to passively observe the tragic dead-end our country has reached and has decided to take decisive steps to return our beloved country to Greek ideals and destiny.

The R.N., faithful guardian of Greek heritage,

BELIEVES

- That Greece and Greek culture can be understood only as a denial of violence and an expression of responsible freedom.
- The purpose of the armed forces is to serve the nation and, therefore, the people, protecting the territorial and spiritual heritage of our fathers.

The R.N. is now convinced that further rule through violence will devastate the country, because:

- It renders the historical bearers of responsibility, who are only the people of Greece and his Majesty, the King, useless.
- It divides and degrades the armed forces, robbing them of their tradition, altruistic nature, and unity of purpose.

- It generates feelings of hatred within the Greek people towards the glorious uniform of an officer.
- It creates a dangerous mistrust of national values in the souls of young people.
- It mortgages the country's economic well-being under onerous terms for future generations.
- It proclaims national independence but is supported by outside forces, all the while knowing that the people will never serve any interests other than those of the nation.

In view of this immediate danger, the R.N. CALLS UPON the armed forces and the people of Greece to a national alert to save the country.

The specific purpose of this historical R. N. call is to "restore political responsibility to the Greek people."

This will be achieved when his Majesty, the King assumes responsibility and a government of national salvation is formed.

The mission of the government of national salvation is to prepare for and hold free elections within a specific time period, no longer than twelve months. None of the members of the government of national salvation will stand in the elections.

The R.N., in its efforts to achieve this supreme goal, PROMISES the Greek people that it will use all its forces, that it is ready for any sacrifice, and that no member within its ranks participating in this initiative will seek any form of benefit or political power.

If it is true that the Greek people are in no hurry to respond to dangers not immediately obvious, it is also true that when they judge that the moment for action has arrived, they give everything for their country in an admirable way.

THE MOMENT IS HERE.
THE R.N.'s BRAVERY AND VIRTUE ARE SPEARHEADING OUR NATIONAL SALVATION.
THE MATURE AND VIRTUOUS GREEK PEOPLE TOGETHER WITH THE TWO OTHER PATRIOTIC BRANCHES OF THE ARMED FORCES ENDORSE
THIS HISTORIC NATIONAL CONTRACT
LONG LIVE THE NATION

Briefing Politicians in Greece Kanellopoulos—Mavros

April 23, Friday

I received a letter from Congressman John Brademas with the *Congressional Record*, in which he has finally taken off the gloves. Many other congressmen made serious statements along with him. All five of the Greek-American congressmen made a joint statement. All this is good.

May 2, Sunday
Letter to Kanellopoulos and Mavros

In the morning, I meet with Peter Agris, owner of the *Hellenic Chronicle*. I explain my position, give him the recent *Congressional Record*, and insist that the "moment has come" for all to wonder "until when?"

His reaction seems quite positive. He tells me it is the only position he understands as "positive and realistic." He wants me to return to Boston.

This is followed by a discussion with General Frontistis. At one point, he tells me that, in Greece, two people have increased prestige, "Kanellopoulos, and yourself. Everybody has talked to me about you and everybody has insisted that we meet."

Before leaving, I gave him the following letter for Kanellopoulos:

April 17, 1971

Mr. President,

Tomorrow is Easter.

Please accept our warmest wishes to you and Mrs. Kanellopoulou. May this four-year ordeal of the Greek people, which coincides with your ordeal, end with the resurrection of a completely new Greece.

I follow your national patience and perseverance with emotion. Your example is an inspiration. Your stance is admirable.

The recent successful unity is an investment of the utmost importance; it may be a sign of further developments. At this time I feel it is my duty to contribute to your national effort with all my strength. At the same time I feel I also would very much like to have your full and continuous support.

I begin with my evaluation of the current American position.

This, of course, is a first step. I assume that a safe system for regularly exchanging information can be established. I am writing also to Mr. Mavros in the same frame of mind. The common course with the Center Union makes my work here much easier. It will be even easier if the unity achieved proves, in practice, to have significant results domestically.

At this point, the American position towards the Greek problem consists of both positive and negative factors.

The positive factors are:

a. *Nixon's policy is irrevocably focussed on the restoration of constitutional order (while studiously avoiding any reference to the type of constitutional order).*
b. *The administration is in a weak position in regards to both the Senate and public opinion. It cannot retract its policy because doing so will bring accusations that its "friendly persuasion" tactic has failed and it has been deceived by the regime.*
c. *The administration is particularly sensitive to European pressure, especially within the NATO framework.*
d. *The junta's inability to lift martial law and move towards elections have convinced the administration that the Greek people oppose the regime and, therefore, long-term American interests are at risk.*
e. *The Democratic party leadership and most Democratic politicians clearly support us.*
f. *Except for the Greek-American press, the American press as a whole is a valuable ally.*
g. *The average American loathes the dictatorship in Greece.*
h. *The continuation of the dictatorship strengthens our support while undermining the regime's support.*

The negative factors are:

a. *The Nixon administration believes that Papadopoulos is in a strong position.*
b. *They believe that the entire armed forces support the regime.*
c. *They believe that the Greek people, suffering from a crisis of trust against everybody, have no taste for open confrontation.*
d. *They recognize that proponents of pragmatic compromise in order to reach the goal are becoming more numerous, in addition to Averof and Markezinis.*
e. *They believe that the economic situation does not create immediate problems for the regime*
f. *They consider that the police state is powerful and ubiquitous, so that, for the time being, any opposition would be crushed at birth.*

The above assessment of positive and negative factors demonstrates that most of our weak points are within the country.

In spite of its weaknesses, the Nixon administration must produce some dramatic result by the spring of 1972, when the election campaign begins.

I believe that pressure will continue to increase during this period. Already, during the first quarter of 1971, the effects of this pressure were publicly revealed first by Sisco, then by Rogers, and, finally, by Nixon with his message to the King.

Together, these facts show that some developments may arise that I believe can be extremely dangerous.

The danger lies in the possibility that outside pressure will push the Junta to stage elections, without, largely because of the psychological climate imposed by the regime, the free forces being able to make adequate preparations.

I cannot rule out this possibility, which the American side would present as the best possible under current domestic conditions. Such a development would be touted as a success for Nixon's policy and would temporarily neutralize our supporters, at least until the 1972 elections.

Obviously, such a possibility must be averted. Every effort here will be expended to that end. Domestically, however, the country must actively be prepared to deal with this possibility if it cannot be averted.

It would be naïve of me to suggest what steps should be taken inside the country to deal with this possibility.

I considered it my duty to clearly present the problem to you and add just a few thoughts that would help our work here if they could be implemented:

- a. *Concentrating all strength around the new unity of purpose. Public announcement, if possible, of the united stand. New names in addition to the ones already known would add considerable weight.*
- b. *Galvanizing the armed forces, universities, and other centers of national concern.*
- c. *Liberating ourselves from the delusion that the problem can be solved only by foreigners.*
- d. *Determining a clear and simple national/political goal for ERE-EK cooperation. [ERE—National Radical union (Karamanlis, Kanellopoulos). EK—Center Union (Mavros)]*
- e. *Expressing trust in the King from as many concerned national sources as possible.*

Mr. President,

I ask you to please look into the possibility of sending an authorized representative of the Union so we can discuss this phase in detail.

I believe we are reaching a very delicate phase of our national adventure. We must productively coordinate activities and agreed objectives.

The time has come to pass the baton to the interior of the country for the race's final lap.

Abroad, we will continue working hard under unfavorable conditions, but the times require the interior of the country to take action, in spite of the difficulties. New exiles and new violence by the regime will lead both it and its supporters to a dead-end. I await your news.

Please convey my respects to Mrs. Kanellopoulou.

Sincerely yours,

Orestis Vidalis

PS. Please inform Mr. Mavros of my assessment.

I gave the following letter for Mr. G. Mavros to General Frontistis:

April 17, 1971

Mr. Minister,

The achievement of a common path for the two great bearers of national responsibility is an investment of great importance, a milestone.

The union achieved makes our work here much easier and it will become even more so if developments show that the union has serious consequences inside the country.

A gathering of all forces around the union, public expression of approval, and especially new names in addition to those already known, would make the union an undeniable reality.

Please accept my sincere congratulations for your contribution to this. I wish you full success in achieving your goals.

I have written to President Kanellopoulos in the same spirit. I also included my respects to you, which I asked him to convey.

At present it is my duty to help your national effort with all my strength.

Sincerely yours,

Orestis Vidalis

May 20, Thursday

Meeting with Norstad. I relay General Frontistis's greetings and stress his impressions that the Junta is divided, that public hatred of the U.S.A. is growing, and that the King is the center of any solution even if the young accuse him of doing nothing.

He tells me about the administration's dissatisfaction with Maurice Stans,* that he has had no news from Cabot Lodge, and that he is thinking of visiting the King in early July. He asked how the King could gain most publicity. I replied, "There should be press coverage when you go there and he should be invited by the president to visit the U.S." He asked for us to meet again next week to talk about promoting the King.

May 25, Tuesday
Initiation of selected naval officers

I received a letter from Pierros Panaghiotareas with the names of those who accept the contract, i.e., Commander Sekeris (Kiel), Commander Pappas (Rome), Commander Papadongonas (Athens), and the diplomat Sekeris (NATO/Brussels). Panaghiotareas writes that they will meet in Germany to arrange details.

Washington Dilemmas and Hesitation

June 14, Monday
Silva briefs me after his return from Greece

Lunch with Walter Silva. His recent visit to Greece made him even more uneasy about the future. In Thessaloniki he asked to see Zagorianakos and Gandonas. The first said he would see him for five minutes, the second not at all. He stayed with Zagorianakos for over an hour. Silva told him:

> It is time to move towards implementing the constitution—NATO cannot take it any more. Europe is upset, pressure from Congress is unearable, the press is taking aim at the government, and this cannot be tolerated anymore. Within Greece, the army is in a terrible state, officers do not follow orders. Special forces are rising up against the regime and eight officers are arrested and imprisoned. Young people in universities say that Greek society is rotten and that the regime is just an example of this decay—they will overturn everything.

Zagorianakos listened to the monologue and admitted for the first time—Silva had met with him in the past—that the military plays a political role. Objecting, he said, "Why don't you leave us alone to take care of our own back yard?"

*The Secretary of Commerce, Maurice Stans, visited Greece on April 23. In an article published Sunday, April 25, the *New York Times* wrote that Stans "surpassed the American Ambassador Henry Tasca in unnecessary praise of the Greek regime, especially during the week it was celebrating the fourth anniversary of its removal of constitutional government in Greece."

Silva replied, "Since we all belong to this club, in accordance with its statutes we have the right to demand proper conduct from members. And how could the United States not be interested when every gun and every shell in the armed forces, which have taken on a political role, are American?"

Zagorianakos concluded, "Although I don't agree with all the points, there are some points that do need attention."

In the evening, although he had not originally accepted an invitation to a party held in his honor, Silva went after all and stayed a long time.

At the same time, Gandonas notified him that his schedule had changed and he could see him. According to Silva, he said the same thing to Gandonas in even stronger terms, to which Gandonas responded, "Why don't you push for developments? I am just a public servant and do not influence the policy set by the prime minister." Silva replied, "I know you are a member of the revolutionary group and, therefore, you have an opinion."

In Athens, Silva saw two new members of the Center Union. He had the feeling that even the more peaceful ones already are talking about a violent overthrow. The military does not obey; they do not follow orders for transfer. Angelis and Zagorianakos see the dead-end, that it is not easy for officers to return to their barracks. Angelis and Papadopoulos disagree on who should be Chief of the Army. Papadopoulos insists on Zagorianakos. Angelis insists on Broumas so a lot of officers would not have to retire all at once. [The tradition in the Greek armed forces is that when a relatively junior general is promoted to chief of the army, all his seniors are retired automatically.] The decision was postponed. The politicians believe that the King is a vital factor because developments can take place through him. Tasca is exerting pressure only on Papadopoulos. Silva explained the need for developments to Ambassador Lagakos, using the same language he used with Zagorianakos and Gandonas.

When Lagakos told him he had never heard this American point of view before, Silva asked, "Since you are responsible for the American desk in the Ministry of Foreign Affairs, aren't you present at the meetings between Tasca and Palamas?"

"Of course," he said, "but I have never heard such vehemence before."

Tasca did not let Silva see political leaders such as Kanellopoulos. He only let him see the younger ones.

Silva returned deeply concerned. During our discussion, I asked him what happened with the Cabot Lodge issue, and he told me that the White House disagreed with assigning Cabot Lodge for this task. He then told me that the King must do something, however difficult, to dispel the worry officers have (a worry the junta cultivates) that when the King returns, "heads will roll." "Also," he said, "and this, too, is difficult, for the same reason the King must declare that he will not recall back to active service those officers who now are outside the service. The basic idea is for the King to cultivate a deeper level of communication with serving officers." He went on, "This can be achieved by a carefully written article describing his well-known point of view vis-à-vis the political problem while also dispelling the strong concerns officers have that keep them immobile and under Papadopoulos's power."

At this point I said, "Nobody can speak for the King, but if I were asked my opinion I simply would say that a strong King can decide even to ask forgiveness, while a weak King, no matter what he does, will appear to be begging. Therefore, strengthening the King's position comes before any other consideration. Tasca is the only ambassador who has not gone to Rome. General Goodpaster could invite the King to NATO exercises. President Nixon could invite the King to Washington. And definitely, after Nixon's message to the King on March 25, Stans's improper visit and statements should have been avoided."

Silva listened attentively. He said, "You are absolutely right, we must take the first step," and then he revealed two things. First, that the visit of a secretary (he did not tell me who) to Greece in the end of June was cancelled and, second, that Tasca's visit to the King is in the works. Secretary Rogers, who has decided to order Tasca to go to Rome officially, handled the issue. As soon as the State Department receives the White House's decision on this matter, it will officially notify the Greek Ministry of Foreign Affairs about the decision. At this point, Silva expressed some doubts about Tasca's willingness; Tasca, apparently, believes that the King should denounce the acts of violence against American installations. I told him that Tasca seems to be in the clouds since he ignores the fact that the King has not made any statements at all for approximately two years.

I told him that Tasca's visit to Rome would be a clear declaration of U.S. policy, but it is not enough.

"What else can we do without making the Pentagon an enemy?" he asked. "Many things. First, VIP visits from the U.S. and NATO must stop." He said nothing. "Second, the administration should use the Senate as an ally and not an opponent. It should encourage voting for a resolution condemning the junta and warning that unless democracy is restored within a certain time period, the military aid policy will be reviewed."

He thought a little and, as if he had discovered America, said, "That is powerful and effective. I will get in touch with the Senate to prepare it and will make sure it is approved so there will be no opposition from the State Department. I have reported all this to Sisco. Please don't tell him of our discussion. Sisco is worried and much looking forward to meeting with you. His role in the Middle East gives him a special place in the White House, so whatever he starts will bring results."

Before we parted I told him that the general line should be:

- Declaration of policy;
- Implementing this policy steadily, without hesitation;
- Strengthening the King's position;
- Getting free from the fear that the Junta will turn to the East.

Pierros Panaghiotareas came by the house in the evening. He believes that the R.N. promotions help the Omega effort.

June 15, Tuesday
Meeting with Sisco

In the morning I went to the office of Senator Saxbe (Ohio). His trip from Athens had been delayed, so he was not there. I saw two of his assistants. Michael H. Gertner is his assistant on foreign policy issues. He will help promote the resolution, which will have a good chance of receiving the majority of votes. He asked me to send him a draft with arguments.

11:30 AM at the State Department. I saw George T. Churchill, the new director of the Greek section. I told him some general information about my life. We did not get to the basic subject because we were waiting for Sisco.

At 12:00 noon we went to the office of Joseph J. Sisco, Undersecretary of Near East Affairs. R. Davies greeted me first and then Sisco came into the reception room to greet me and lead me to his office.

Also present were Rodger P. Davies, Deputy Assistant Secretary, Near East Affairs, and George T. Churchill, Country Director for Greece, Near East Affairs. Churchill kept notes.

I began by thanking Sisco for accepting my request for a meeting. He said, "We delayed this meeting general, we should have done it sooner. In any case, I am glad to see you."

Then came the following discussion:

O.V. I had to see you now because all of us, except for one, are at a dead-end. I will explain. The regime is not moving ahead because it is afraid of the Greek people and of itself. The Greeks are not moving ahead because they are afraid of the regime, believing that it is supported by you. And you do not move ahead because you are afraid that the regime may turn to the East. The only one not facing a dead-end is the Soviet Union. It is the first time in our history that the Soviet Union is able to exercise such influence without using communism. The Soviet Union maintains excellent relations with the regime because doing so helps the regime blackmail you and, therefore, prolong its life. This prolongation angers the Greek people. This anger will benefit the Soviet Union because the leftist movement will be strengthened as it was after the Metaxas dictatorship. Furthermore, the Soviet Union is rejoicing because the issue of the King is in limbo and surely you are aware that ending parliamentary monarchy in Greece was the dream of communism.

J.S. General, how do you see the King's position today? What are they thinking in Greece about the King?

O.V. That is a very serious issue. The regime is in conflict with the King because it would like the King to surrender to their anachronistic state. Many blame the King for his silence, for not constantly attacking the regime. Most people, those who think more responsibly, believe that any solution able to guarantee peaceful transfer from today's mayhem to reason must pass through the King. If the King decisively contributes to restoring normal conditions, then everybody will wish him long life and will appreciate the importance of his decision to stand against the regime. As protector of the sovereign rights of the Greek people, the King will be considered the savior of modern Greece.

J. S. Yes, I understand. The King and the people, a beautiful and stable combination. Right, general. How do the young people feel?

O.V. The same as young people in the rest of the world, with the added disappointment that they live without freedom. Their opposition to the present regime is absolutely justified. If we do not pay attention to the young, soon we will have a tragic surprise.

J. S. General, my daughter is opposed to me because I am the establishment, even though no one has taken away her freedom. I understand what would happen if she were in the position of Greek youth—it is truly tragic. The situation in Greece is completely different from that of the United States. In Greece there is a regime that does not follow democratic procedures. Therefore, the typical revolt of the youth there is intensified by the existence of an oppressive government, giving young people the feeling that there cannot be any change without violence.

We then discussed Papadopoulos's position and the effects of the pressure he is under, mainly from abroad.

O.V. Papadopoulos has created the situation. Everyone in the regime believes in the "value of the dictatorship." Whatever pressure is applied to Papadopoulos is not transferred to his associates. Whatever private conversations Ambassador Tasca has with Papadopoulos are not passed on.

J. S. I told Papadopoulos that we want him to move towards parliamentary government. The regime has not moved as fast as we had hoped or as fast as we were led to believe. The United States is not happy. We will continue our two-front policy, meeting our NATO obligations and encouraging the regime to move in the correct direction. General, the Greeks remain passive and blame us for creating this situation in Greece. What is your opinion?

O.V. We Greeks, alone are responsible for creating this situation, even if there were—I do not know—foreign collaborators in the coup. Although we are responsible creating this situation, we are not responsible for prolonging it and we definitely will not be responsible for its aftermath if our voice is not heard. Since you, for strategic reasons, work closely with the regime, you also have become responsible for its prolongation, which has robbed the Greeks of their responsibility. As for the "passiveness" you mentioned, what is perceived as passiveness is the people realizing that they cannot do anything without help. The aftermath to this drama is of enormous importance. The future of Greece and the future of its relations with the western world will depend upon what form this aftermath takes.

J. S. I agree general, but, as you know, our policy is the return of democracy while keeping a strong Greece within the alliance. From our schools we know that Greece is synonymous with for democracy. We have a longstanding sentimental tie with Greece; we are "in love" with Greece. For these reasons we are applying considerable pressure but things do not move. We express our disappointment, but what can we do? Truly, we face a dilemma.

O.V. Please let me interrupt you to discuss the points you raised. Your policy is known, you have repeated it, but you have not taken steps to implement it. This is the first serious point. implementing your policy makes the dictators insolent and the people your enemy, not in their feelings but, in essence, because the question, "Whether the U.S. cannot or does not wish to implement its own policy, the result is the same: Dead end." gets rooted in the Greek soul. Slowly but surely your prestige and the trust the Greeks have in your great country is being shaken to the core. Excuse me for using the language I know, but I assume you will respect it.

J.S. General, I am very pleased and ask you please to continue in this language, from which I expect only substantial results.

O.V. The second point is that you are applying pressure. Yes, you are, but, as I already have told you, you are applying pressure only to Papadopoulos, ignoring the fact that the regime is a group, led, of course, by

Papadopoulos. For this reason the others have not understood what is going on, they are not responsible. You have not even checked how much they can stand and you start from the assumption—without even applying any pressure—that they will turn to the East if pressured.

J. S. I agree, general, it is a group leadership, but how can we make our pressure known to all of them?

O.V. During the next presidential press conference, have a question and the president's answer prepared. If the president says that NATO has done its duty towards Greece and is strengthening the country's defenses but the current government is not moving fast enough towards restoring the conditions embodied in NATO's ideals and goals, then all supporters and opponents of the regime will understand the message. The pressure will be word-wide. At this point Sisco turned to Churchill and said, "Write this down," which Churchill already had done.

J. S. General, you talked about implementing our policy. What do you mean? Cutting off military aid? If not that, what else?

O. V. A general plan you could follow is this:

a. The president makes a public statement about the return to democratic procedures and keeps repeating it.
b. VIP visits to Greece should stop.
c. Strengthen the King's position.
d. Send a special presidential envoy to stress, candidly, the U.S. position to Papadopoulos.

Mr. Secretary, at the point where we are now you must start with simple things and go on gradually to the more complicated. First, distance yourselves from the regime. There is no reason for government officials to visit Greece. Both Junta supporters and the Greek people at large consider visits such as those made by Stans and Packard political actions that demonstrate the weakness of the U.S. government.

J.S. The Stans visit was a bad accident. Packard did not speak, but I agree they strengthen the government's position, general.

O.V. Second, you should put together a long-term program for specific steps with continuity and follow-up. Do something each month in support of your policy.

Third, strengthen the King's position, i.e.:

• Support General Norstad's actions

- Have Mr. Tasca go to Rome, officially and publicly.
- Have General Goodpaster invite the King to NATO exercises.
- Finally, President Nixon should invite the King to Washington for talks.

> If the above steps, combined with instructions to all Americans stationed in Greece about fully implementing the spirit of your policy are carried out systematically, there will be a chain reaction. Given the present dead-end for everyone, what you call "your dilemma," only well planned steps taken by you will move things along.
>
> J.S. General, I fully understand what you mean, you are a realist. We will consider all this. Please, let's meet again soon if that is convenient.
>
> O.V. I am available for discussion or clarification any time of the day or night.
>
> J.S. General, time clearly is working on the side of those who realistically strive for the return of democracy to Greece.
>
> O.V. I suppose Mr. Secretary, you mean time is working in favor of Greece, because people are just volunteers called into action for this purpose. If you help, as I believe you will, time is working in favor of maintaining excellent long-term relations between the "lovers."
>
> J.S. I must go to Greece. If, indeed, I do go, there will be results.

The meeting lasted for one hour and five minutes.

On our way to his office, Churchill said, "It was an excellent meeting. Mr. Sisco showed great understanding of your positions. I believe the visit will bring results. He is working on Greece now, he is worried, and your visit will help him."

"Let's not be in a hurry, Mr. Churchill, and let's hope you will proceed with one verb, to 'implement' your policy."

Senator Pell insisted on speaking with me on the telephone, he had telephoned from Rhode Island to have his secretary make sure we talk. I called him at his house from the airport. I told him I saw Sisco. He, too, believes they are worried. He is preparing a draft amendment, not interrupting aid, but he has not yet decided on the wording. Toward the end of June or beginning of July, he will go to Rome and he asked me if I could arrange a meeting with the King. I told him I would be glad to let the King know of his wish.

June 16, Wednesday

Meeting with Hovey of the N*ew York Times* in the morning. I explained to him the need for more frequent articles now to help the administration focus on the political problem, stressing the need to implement its policy. He said he would intensify his effort.

June 24, Thursday
Letter to Sisco and letter from Couloumbis

Joseph J. Sisco
Undersecretary
Department of State
2201 "C" Street, NW
Washington, D.C. 20520

Dear Mr. Undersecretary,

I want to express my sincere thanks to you for our recent meeting.

I am well aware how valuable and tightly scheduled your time is and how difficult your position must be when you constantly hear the same arguments.

I hope I have helped in making the meeting useful for you and perhaps more productive towards our common goal.

Of course, I am concerned for many reasons. First, I am concerned whenever I consider the fact that "nothing is permanent except change." It is the change that concerns me. It is the future reality I wish to see develop in a way and in a direction that will serve the long-term interests of both Greece and the West. I believe this is the greatest challenge for all parties concerned.

According to its stated policy, the United States has undertaken the obligation and developed a determining influence in shaping this future situation. I believe that wisdom and realism, together with this country's decisiveness, will help in facing this great challenge.

For me, our meeting was encouraging, and I thank you again.

Sincerely yours,

Orestis Vidalis

I received the following letter from Couloumbis:

June 21, 1971

My Dear General,

I was very glad to see you last week when you honored us with your presence in my home Saturday evening.

I am writing this brief letter mainly to convey some of my impressions from my last meeting with Walter Silva. In general, I was pleased because he returned from his recent trip to Greece with clear impressions that are similar to your assessment of the situation.

I had lunch with Silva the day after your meeting with Joseph Sisco. Naturally, I asked him about the effect of your meeting and their impressions.

He told me approximately the following:

1. *You made an extremely good, positive impression on Mr. Sisco, who liked you as a person and would like to continue the productive communication with you.*
2. *Compared with how others have presented themselves, yours was a serious, useful, and welcome visit.*
3. *He believes that the administration's pressure on the junta will increase considerably and that actions such as public meetings with King Constantine will follow.*
4. *He feels that his influence on Sisco is increasing. For example, Sisco told him that Vidalis's opinions strengthen Silva's suggestions, and more in this vein. My general conclusion is that your meeting with Sisco is of great importance and is based on mutual feelings of respect and good sense. For this reason your meetings with him, at all costs, must continue frequently on a serious and responsible basis.*

Warm regards,

Theodore Couloumbis

PS. Greetings from the family

July 7, Wednesday
Tasca to the King

A letter from Arnaoutis informs me that on July 2, 1971, the Americans asked for an audience with the King. He says the meeting will take place within one week. They ask me not to report this to anyone.

July 10, Saturday

Colonel Oliver Marshall will appear before the House. The House Foreign Affairs Committee invited him. He told me he will keep me informed about the discussions with the committee and will call me again for a long talk.

July 12, Monday

Letter from Arnaoutis. Tasca went to Rome. A milestone and a step forward.

The Senate and House Examine the Law on Aid

July 13, Tuesday
Oliver Marshall's testimony

One hundred and thirty-three prominent, largely nonpolitical Greeks, including two highly respected Lt. Generals. John Nicolopoulos describes the committee's session yesterday as triumphant. The atmosphere was definitely against the junta. Oliver Marshall, with whom I spoke, was only relatively pleased because he did not have the chance to say much since they had him speak together with the Pentagon representative, who was seen to be completely unacceptable.

Wednesday, July 14

I receive an unsigned letter from General Frontistis, as we had agreed. He says that Kanellopoulos totally agrees with my positions (*see* p. 149 above) and will be in touch with me.

July 15, Thursday
Lunch with Senator Pell

Lunch with Senator Pell at the Senate. He hands me a statement he had made. He is afraid of his Greek-American voters, who think Greece is just fine under the regime. He will propose a resolution and will send it to me. He will make a statement in favor of Tasca's visit to the King. He asked me to give him two proposals for the King's role. He will visit him during the summer if he goes to Europe.

I saw Pierros Panaghiotareas in the afternoon.

I asked him:

a. For the people in Europe to come into contact with me;
b. Toward the end of August, have somebody from Athens come here and brief me on progress, if possible;
c. I gave him Hǫgg's address to send me mail from Greece;
d. I gave him two copies of the correspondence code I improvised and showed him how to use it.

Reception at Sismanides's in the evening. The atmosphere is pleasantly charged because of the unexpected vote by the Senate Foreign Relations Committee, which was 17 in favor and 12 against cutting off aid to Greece. The State Department they said they have "less room for negotiation."

July 16, Friday
In Boston

Meeting with Elias Dimitrakopoulos. Euphoria, because of the vote. He blames Margaret Papandreou for raising the issue of the King and Greene for speaking of the King having a diminished role in the future. I leave for Boston. Meet with Karayannis and Agris and we talk until 1:30 AM. Agris is impressed by the latest developments. In spite of their pro-junta attitude they agree that the situation must end. Agris believes there will be developments and I tell him, "Only if there is pressure."

July 17, Saturday

Dinner with Silva and Couloumbis in Washington. In our discussion, we agree that the main goal for the Americans is for Papadopoulos to hold elections. The other interesting points were:

a. Angelis was pressured while he was here by the Undersecretary of Defense on the issue of elections. For a month, relations between Papadopoulos and Angelis were strained because Angelis insisted on elections.
b. Averof met Papadopoulos and told him to set the election date any time. That, Papadopoulos said, he could not do because the country would become paralyzed. Averof then told him to send confidential letters to the NATO countries announcing the date so the statement would bind him. He is still waiting for an answer.
c. That the Senate committee's decision will be undermined on legal grounds and Papadopoulos will be the winner.
d. That Tasca will meet with Karamanlis before he comes to the States.
e. Since nothing better can be done, pressure for elections by the regime would be the best development.
f. Pressure will continue whenever possible. Silva told us he prepared an announcement in case journalists ask what the State Department's opinion is on the Senate resolution. This announcement includes facts that will appear for the first time.

July 18, Sunday
The administration is unhappy and tries to overturn the resolution

Defense Secretary Laird pressured the committee's president for a re-vote to be taken on the resolution. The president was cautious. Laird asked that he, himself, and Secretary Rogers testify instead of Undersecretaries Sisco, Nutter, and Hillenbrand. They are very annoyed and are trying to overturn the resolution.

I notified Senator Hartke to add the following to the resolution he is preparing: "Military aid will be automatically restored to the levels proposed by the administration immediately after free parliamentary rule is restored in Greece." I stressed to him that the text he had prepared would create problems in the future for us because it downplays the need for aid.

I later called the journalist from the *Christian Science Monitor* to ask the State Department tomorrow, "What is the State Department's position on the decision taken by the Senate committee?"

July 19, Monday
Editorial mentioning Marshall

The lead editorial in the *New York Times* on July 19, 1971 is mainly based on Colonel Oliver Marshall's testimony. Part of the editorial is below.

> Action to halt aid to Greece resulted directly from testimony last week before a Foreign Affairs subcommittee headed by Representative Benjamin Rosenthal of Queens. Here some members learned, evidently for the first time, that the 1967 coup had not been an action of military leaders to head off Communism, as so frequently represented, but "an open mutiny within the armed forces and a rebellion by those mutineers against their King and the constitutional Government of Greece."
>
> The man who said this was Col. Oliver Marshall, now retired, American Defense and Army attaché in Athens, 1963-67. He sees "the greatest danger to future Greek—American and Greek—NATO relationships" in the widely-held belief that "the United States supported this military mutiny and continues to do so." In other words, by sustaining the junta this country will jeopardize its own and NATO's security rather than protect it.
>
> Colonel Marshall advocated an all-out effort to convince Greeks that the United States does not back the Junta and to persuade the Junta to keep its promise to restore democratic government. Contradicting the State-Pentagon line, he said this effort should take priority over "our immediate military needs on Greek soil."

I called Marshall and thanked him. He said he is at my disposal.

Walter Silva said something very important the other evening. He said that the Cyprus problem is at a particularly critical stage right now. The Turks are ready and determined to settle the issue. The Turkish Joint Chiefs of Staff is estimating possible losses during a landing and the numbers of Turkish-Cypriots who might be killed if there were a landing. They are waiting for the outcome of the Palamas-Erim meeting before they take final decisions.

July 20, Tuesday

The lead editorial in the *Washington* Post is about the committee's vote freezing aid to Greece and Pakistan.

July 22, Thursday

John Nicolopoulos discussed the two questions I posed with Silva. Mainly, what do they think would the reaction be to the Tasca-King meeting. "Clearly discomfiting the junta. Clearly a good effect on the people. New steps are being prepared. Panic among the extremists. Then, kowtowing and expressions of faith in the "administration." The Pentagon will fight. Kissinger must be approached."

July 23, Friday

Nicolopoulos informs me that Secretaries Rogers and Laird are not expected to testify before the committee. The aid bill will be voted on before August 6 (beginning of vacation).

I received a telegram from Plytas asking for my telephone number. I replied and invited him to Toledo.

July 24, Saturday
Letter from Lambrias

I received a letter from Takis Lambrias. Apart from his appreciation for my efforts here, Lambrias raises two new issues: the junta's opening toward the East and the dismal outlook for Greek-Cypriot relations. The full text of the letter is below.

> *General,*
>
> *In my opinion, what is taking place in the United States is of historic importance. Your predictions are unfolding and, most important, this is so largely because of your tireless and inspired actions. I have been following these developments as closely as possible (Makis [Arnaoutis] and I were briefed by Sir Hugh yesterday) and feel the need to put onto paper my enthusiasm and feelings, which, in reality, are an expression of "congratulations" to you personally.*
>
> *The hysteria in Athens—a complex revelation because the government, in its discomfort and in spite of its bluffing, reveals all the characteristics they have been trying to conceal—confirms the importance of the developments over there even if this phase continues to be critical.*

Unfortunately, our communication has mysterious gaps. You must have not received at least two of my letters (three in reality, for I sent one twice), with informational material enclosed. Today's letter I am sending registered and I hope it will have more luck.

It includes:

- *A confidential, but journalistic report from the well informed Economist about the junta's opening towards the East, with a pretty upsetting conclusion, as you will see, not reinforcing our point of view.*
- *Facts about Cyprus; Papadopoulos's infamous threatening letter, which it is possible you may not have. The strange thing is that I was convinced that this "bomb" was leaked by the recipient of the threat himself. But I was in indirect communication with him today; he is adamant and is organizing investigations, believing (or pretending to believe) that the people who leaked the letter must belong to the opposite side.*
- *The Cyprus situation also is extremely critical, requiring painful efforts on our part to somehow find out what really is going on. In today's indirect communication, Makarios appears to trust the Americans and does not believe that they also are involved in the efforts to undermine or remove him. The more responsible observers here think that an open crisis—with the danger of conflict—is imminent, beginning in September.*

That is the news. Other matters and personal matters are, as is natural, in a state of constant melancholy and unsurpassable difficulty. The Greek Report is facing legal as well as economic problems. A libel case was launched against me by the pro-junta writer Kenneth Young, international supporter of the regime, and I am under a judicial injunction. I am now trying to publish another.

I am not writing about Tasca's visit to Rome since you surely have more reliable information. On the subject of the newspaper in the States, as I wrote at length in my earlier letters, I do not believe there are realistic possibilities of responding to such widespread—and only then correct—effort. I have such bitter experience with failed promises and so often have reached tragic dead-ends by specific obligations not being carried through, that I cringe at the thought.

But I do not want to close my letter with personal bitterness. It is true, after all, that recent developments have promoted the rise of a fighting optimism to new heights—and it is with this that I will finish for it is you, after all, who is largely responsible.

With much respect and affection,

P. Lambrias

July 25, Sunday

I received a telephone call last night from Maurice Goldbloom, Secretary of the U.S. Committee for Democracy in Greece, of which Congressman Don Edwards is president. He told me that Oliver Marshall's testimony was of decisive importance and may have tipped the scales.

July 28, Wednesday

Goldbloom tells me that Rep. Wayne Hays (D-Ohio, Chairman of the House Administration Committee) is circulating Marshall's testimony to all members of the House.

July 31, Saturday
Midday with Silva

Lunch with Silva. He said they are preparing a series of measures to apply greater pressure. They plan to use the military. A letter from Nixon to Papadopoulos is now being drafted. I told him that if the momentum were lost now, so would be the case. Now is the time for heavy heavy pressure. Nixon's representative must be responsible for finally settling this matter.

He told me that the Cyprus problem is at a critical stage. Erim is trying his best, but the military wants an immediate solution.

He will arrange a meeting for me with Tasca and he will call me.

He thinks the army is the main leverage for any development. The military in Greece trusts Tsoumbas, who is about to be invited to the U.S. I told him about my letter to Senator Muskie and he told me that Muskie is furious with Andreas Papandreou because he published a letter from Muskie without asking first.

August 3, Tuesday

The House approved the committee resolution against the Junta by 122 to 57. This is of immense importance.

Clifford Hackett, Staff Consultant to the Subcommittee on Europe of the House Committee on Foreign Affairs, telephoned me and told me that Tasca said that public opinion obviously is concerned with restoring freedom in Greece.

Hackett said that Congressman Ford stated in an indirect way that the resolution against aid does not create difficulties for the Administration.

August 4, Wednesday

I receive a letter from Professor George Anastaplo enclosing an announcement informing the American public that the Junta considers him a *persona non grata.*

August 5, Thursday

I arrive in Washington at 7:00 in the evening. From 11:00 that night until 2:00 in the morning with John Nicolopoulos at Hackett's house. Apparently Tasca took a mild position in his testimony before the House Committee on Foreign Affairs. He said that there clearly is a desire for return to normal conditions. He could not answer the question about whether or not the Junta gave permission for flights to Jordan to pass through Greek air space during the Middle East conflict; the impression is that it probably did not. The discussion with Hackett provided nothing more than that Tasca seems to be changing course.

August 6, Friday
Lunch with Tasca

Midday at the State Department for lunch with Tasca and Churchill. I presented an overview of the situation as I see it. Mainly, I stressed that time is being wasted on fruitless experimentation.

The main points Tasca, who had just returned from the White House, told me were:

- The regime must understand that they must implement the 1968 constitution now. They have no other choice;
- They must understand that legal structures must be in operation;
- What will happen if the leaders of this regime disappear or die?;
- The main factor for resolving the situation is Papadopoulos;
- Aid must not be used as a weapon, because Papadopoulos uses it to intensify nationalism;
- Young officers are not used to tradition and do not want the image of the King as does Papadopoulos;
- Senior officers agreed with Papadopoulos and Yeorghalas on the aid issue.

I focussed his attention on the following points:

- Elections held by the Junta are ludicrous, if that is what is meant by "implementing the 1968 constitution";

- Papadopoulos is a factor, but without pressure he will not move toward any resolution;
- Greece belongs to all Greeks, who have been rendered ineffective, not only just the 300;
- To his complaint that some in the opposition make his work difficult, I replied that, if we see movement toward restoring our institutions, we will help you, otherwise, nothing will change.

Nicolopoulos drove me to the airport in the evening. He saw Silva today. He told him that Tasca's position toward me has changed. He no longer considers "Vidalis and Dimitrakopoulos the troublemakers in Washington." He is beginning to understand that there is basic change in the air.

August 7, Saturday
Letter from Panaghiotareas in Kiel

I received the following letter from Pierros Panaghiotareas from Kiel dated August 1, 1971.

> For two days now I have been in Kiel, where with great joy and emotion I met with the other members of the group. We talked at length about the situation in the navy and in detail about organizational issues based on your suggestions.
>
> To begin with, there are no reservations concerning principles, as I had already assured you. Great joy is expressed because, in addition to our enthusiasm and belief in the struggle to free our nation from this heavy tyranny, there is an organizational plan and, most importantly, leadership upon whom we can count and with whom we can fight to the end to achieve our final goal.
>
> The main burden of organizing within the navy will be borne by Commander A. Papadongonas, who is being transferred to the NATO War College in Rome where he will stay for six months.
>
> Of course, Commander Pappas and I will continue the whole effort and you will be kept up to date mainly by me, continuously, as we have discussed. . . .

August 12, Thursday
Discussion with Norstad—Tasca displeased

Meeting with General Norstad in the afternoon. I filled him in on the details of my meetings with Sisco and Tasca. He said that some Americans brought him news from Greece that Tasca has clearly spoken in favor of Papadopoulos's work and referred to the general in critical terms because the general is against the regime that is doing such good work. The general answered them that he is not interested in Tasca's opinion, only his principles. The general, however, took Tasca's testimony before the committee seriously. "There he spoke clearly against the regime and he is not so naïve that he will tell the Senate things he does not want known in Greece. Now, of course, he will have problems when he returns." Continuing, he said that he believes the president will make one more attempt to influence developments. He will give them aid while applying pressure for progress. I told him that a letter from the president to the Junta would play a role. On the basis of his knowledge of the president, the general does not think Nixon will write a letter. This can be done by the Ambassador, who must tell them that time has run out.

I told the general that I was planning to go to Europe in September and would like to see Kissinger before leaving. He agreed to write Kissinger next week even though he believes that the Greek issue is mainly under Roger's jurisdiction. I said it would be good for me to meet with him so he can hear the point of view of a soldier who is not interested in politics but in restoring life to normal. He said he would write. While discussing the King, he repeated his impression that he saw a stable and realistic leader, a true King.

AUGUST 20, FRIDAY

I wrote to Congressman Wayne L. Hays, thanking him warmly for his valuable help toward bringing political freedom to the Greek people:

> You are among the Americans who feel that the price Greece and the Free World are paying to rely on a superficial stability by force for the protection of the strategic interests of Greece and of NATO is too high.
>
> The message from the action of the House was received in Greece with the greatest joy, not because any Greek wants to see the defense posture of the country or of the Alliance weakened or because they seek the interference of our friends in the internal problems of the country. The people of Greece have been expressing through all conceivable means the hope and expectation that the U.S. will demonstrate by deeds and not words alone the disengagement from what seemed to be a position of supporting a regime that, despite more than four years of rule by force, has been unwilling or unable to allow the people to select their government through honest, free elections.

August 21, Saturday

First meeting with Pavlos Ioannides, an employee of the consulate in Chicago.

In Detroit I meet the commercial attaché, Ioannides. The first minute I saw him, I told him he must understand that I will not tell him anything that is not public knowledge because I do not know what his position is and I must make sure what his intentions are.

He told me that his father was in the central intelligence agency (KYP), that he, himself, had served in KYP, that he is disappointed with the agency and has repeatedly voiced his opinion. When I asked him how he got his posting in the consulate, he said that Colonel Nikos Moutousis helped him, they may have wanted to get rid of him or they may even have trusted him.

I told him that he could send me:

a. Information about relations with the Iron Curtain countries;
b. Information about internal disputes within the junta or the Junta's plans;
c. Names of officers in the police and gendarmerie who would be join action against the junta.

He promised to renew his contacts and let me know. I pointed out to him that many people are beginning to approach us now, not to offer their services but to play a double game.

He told me he is determined to show that he is ready for everything. He believes there is a large number of officers who already have changed their minds.

August 23, Monday

Ioannides called to say that the entire cabinet except Aslanides resigned. He has compiled a list, which he will send me, of officers who dislike the junta.

August 25, Wednesday

A cabinet reshuffling is expected. I get in touch with Silva. He agrees that pressure has led to some agitation. Markezinis is not in Greece. Averof probably will not participate in Papadopoulos's games. We do not know if those politicians who have collaborated with Papadopoulos will give in.

August 27, Friday

The dictatorship cabinet has taken its new form and, fortunately, does not include any politician.

I get in touch with Silva and Churchill. They believe that Papadopoulos's position is getting stronger. I told them it is just a reshuffle in preparation for possible elections, with the general secretaries in the countryside to oversee things.

August 31, Tuesday

I express my bitterness about AHEPA's stance to the archbishop.

I write the archbishop and express my bitterness about AHEPA's support of the regime.

Recent Information from Greece

September 4, Saturday

Meeting with Eleni Vlachou. She will remain in the U.S. for some time. She told me that Karamanlis is against aid—it is a political tool—and that he now proposes that NATO be used apply pressure on the junta. Mitsotakis is asking if it would help if a group of politicians were to come to Washington.

We discussed overall developments and the need to begin shifting the pressure to inside Greece. She asked me if it would be useful to visit Agnew, and I said, "undoubtedly." We went over my schedule in London and Europe, and agreed to stay in touch.

September 7, Tuesday

Couloumbis returned from Greece. On the telephone he was optimistic because the politicians in Greece have begun to work together but dismayed because Papadopoulos's position is getting stronger.

September 9, Thursday

In his testimony before the Proxmire committee, Secretary Rogers urges the Senate to restore aid to Greece. [Senator William Proxmire, D Wisconsin, was Chairman of the Senate Finance Committee.]

September 14, Tuesday

Senator Pell telephoned. He met the King in Copenhagen and had dinner with him. Pell saw a mature person, responsible, exceptional. The King said he would like to come for the sailing races only if he would see Nixon. Pell discussed this with Sisco who, in a very friendly tone, said that the time is not right.

September 17, Friday
New meeting with Sisco

I was at the State Dept. at 11:45 A.M. Churchill and I went to Davies's office. I told him,

> We have reached a critical point. The two goals of having democracy in Greece and Greece participating in NATO cannot easily be distinguished. And we have reached the point where two branches of your government are both destroying the overall goal. The legislature emphasizes the political side, destroying the strategy, and the executive branch emphasizes the strategy, destroying the political side. The result is the self-destruction of U.S. policy and objectives. Coordination is need, the two sides need to agree and work toward common goals. When that happens, then the president can say, not, "I am providing aid because it is in the interest of the U.S. and NATO," but, "I am providing aid because NATO is an alliance seeking to protect democracies, because Greece is the birthplace of democracy, because the Greek people have the experience, because the armed forces are the protectors of the freedom of the Greek people. For these reasons I share the concerns of Congress and am providing aid now in the hope that this will help the Greek people solve their political problems."

Davies paid careful attention and said, "Do you mean we should put greater emphasis on the political side? What else can we do in terms of pressure, general?"

"Use General Goodpaster, as I have suggested many times," I answered. "He should go and tell them, 'this is the end.' Nixon should send a special envoy to investigate basic facts and report the results. That envoy should go to Greece, visit the King, Karamanlis, and the other politicians."

Davies said, "We appreciate new ideas about how we can influence the situation without making matters worse. Ambassador Tasca is looking for ways to extricate us from the present dead-end, with political leaders in Greece and with Mavros recently. He saw the King, and tried to see Karamanlis."

Davies asked me if I could assess the prime minister's intentions with the recent cabinet reshuffle. I replied, "I know Papadopoulos personally from working together with him a long time ago in the army. Papadopoulos believes that Greece is not a proper country for democracy, even though from time to time he says otherwise for political reasons. Papadopoulos is a realist and will not budge from his position if he sees that the pressure is not serious or constant."

He was agreeing to this when the door opened and Sisco entered. He said, "General, I am sorry I was not here. You have spoken with Rodger, but I would like to hear your opinion on the main point."

I repeated the basic point, for Nixon to make a political proposal. He agreed fully, saying, "It is a change of emphasis and I agree."

"He also could say," he added, "that the present government should move ahead as it has promised on so many occasions. Do you agree?"

"Certainly," I told him.

"General, you must know that my door is always open and I am at your service. You are the only one I trust, for your judgment, discretion, and selflessness. We are glad that you come see us."

I thanked him and bid them both good-bye. As I was leaving, Churchill said: "Your presentation made an impression. I am grateful to you for helping us."

I have heard the same, many times. But I will persist because I must keep reminding them of the situation and their duty.

Visit to Europe

SEPTEMBER 21, TUESDAY
Meeting with Karamanlis and Mitsotakis in Paris

I met Mitsotakis at his home. His position is that Kanellopoulos is blocking Karamanlis being put forward as a point of leverage.

In the afternoon I meet Karamanlis. He agrees that the Americans have a problem. His best solution is that a transitional government be formed to prepare the country for elections. The other solution would be free elections, in which he will stand and win by a landslide. He is in good spirits but would like things to begin in Greece.

I stressed that the current shift is the last chance for the Greeks to take action. Dinner at his house with Mitsotakis and Delipetros.

The need for action in Greece is repeated.

SEPTEMBER 22, WEDNESDAY
In Rome with the King

At noon I again met with Karamanlis, and we discussed his two solutions again. I asked him what he thought should be done if the junta dethrones the King. He replied that this is unlikely because the Americans and the British would not let it happen.

My relationship with Sisco impressed him.

Mitsotakis drove me to the airport. He insisted that Kanellopoulos must take a stand and believes that the King should promote moves in this direction.

I arrived in Rome that night. I telephoned the King and he asked if we could meet right after I checked into the hotel.

At 11:00 PM I arrived at the King's house.

He told me that Nixon had sent him a very complimentary letter thanking him for the telegram about his daughter's wedding. The Ambassador [Tasca] had asked his opinion about aid, and the King replied that he agrees "with the aid as long as there is a condition attached to it—the country's return to normal life." That pleased Nixon a great deal.

Tasca requested that an announcement be prepared saying, "he visited the King in Rome while on vacation." The King replied to the American ambassador in Rome, who was handling this issue, "If Mr. Tasca thinks that the King of Greece identifies himself with the Coliseum and the Tomb of the Unknown Soldier he has not understood what all this is about, and it would be better if the visit did not to take place." They were forced to change the announcement.

He showed me a letter from his friend Buchanan, written in August, saying that he saw Kissinger, who told him that the King "will return to Greece in 1972." The King answered Buchanan and asked him to get in touch with me. He also had a letter from the politician John Kerry of Massachusetts, who is ready to take action for restoring democracy. He gave me Kerry's address so I can get in touch with him.

I told the King about my meetings with Sisco and Karamanlis and ended by saying that he must use his influence now so they will move in Greece toward shaping a specific solution. The King agreed. Time had passed, it was one o'clock in the morning. I asked if we could stop now and talk tomorrow.

SEPTEMBER 23, THURSDAY
Continuing discussion with the King

I met with the King again in the morning. I suggested we discuss measures to counter any move Papadopoulos might take against him. He does not consider such a move likely; does not think a referendum would be a solution. I tell him that at some stage he will have to generate support that will enable him to face difficulties, and that support can come only from the people. He agrees but believes that caution is necessary in terms of time and conditions.

I saw Captain Soulis in the afternoon. He sees the idea within the armed forces that we are moving toward implementing the constitution.

In the evening, the King and I discuss relations with Cyprus. Makarios would very much like the King to visit Cyprus. He even told the King he should have gone there after December 13, 1967.

He asked me to make a presentation of the entire situation the next day in Papagos's presence, to help him understand the assessment in depth.

September 24, Friday
Appeal to the armed forces

I present an assessment of the situation for Leonidas Papagos in the King's presence. The basic thoughts of today's presentation are the developments in Europe and the United States, which are very slow but steady; the Nixon administration is approaching the King; Congress is moving toward a more stable and practical position (curtailing aid); and the general fatigue evident in Greece from the dictatorship being prolonged.

The main line of the assessment is that serious steps must be taken within Greece to condemn the regime, echoing what is heard outside the country, and speeding up whatever steps can be taken for returning the country to normal. All this activity can take the form of prominent, well-known Greeks who have been silent until now, making measured and calm public expressions of concern and specific recommendations for returning to parliamentary rule.

These expressions of concern and recommendations must be directed toward the armed forces, the only factor in today's public life that can influence developments.

Papagos listened attentively, and concluded, "Wouldn't it be better if some people came from Greece and heard this directly from the general? Personal contact is so alive."

We discuss this and come to the conclusion that it would be better for Papagos to go to Greece and show them this presentation in writing.

The King calls Karamanlis and asks if he agrees with my proposals and if he believes that the King himself must make a stand. Karamanlis replies that he cannot get involved in a personal matter.

The King turns to us and says, "There is no other solution," and decides to send Papagos to Athens.

We drew up the following text after our discussion:

> To the Armed Forces,
>
> For approximately half a decade the armed forces have denied the Greek people their responsibility for their nation's fate.
>
> Denying the Greek people their political freedom places the armed

forces in direct conflict with the people, chokes the nation's strength, harms the country's defenses, suspends the development and progress of Greek society, and dangerously weakens Greece's international position, especially within the free world and NATO.

Even one more day denying the Greek people their responsibility makes the problems and the nation's difficulties worse, while crucial questions accumulate in the souls of young Greeks, into whose hands the responsible and modern custody of the nation's problems must be placed as soon as possible. We are fully aware of the historic responsibility all of us bear as we struggle for the nation's future.

We call upon the armed forces to become reconciled with the people.

We call upon the armed forces to prove by their actions that they trust the judgment and maturity of the Greek people.

We call upon the armed forces to lead the country to normal conditions, restoring responsibility to the Greek people, which can be achieved without disturbing the country's peace and order.

We call upon the armed forces to take immediate, concrete steps towards establishing a transitional national government that will create the conditions for completely free elections within a specific period of time. We recommend that the authority for establishing the transitional government be entrusted to Mr. Konstantinos Karamanlis. It is self-evident that these steps must be submitted for approval to His Royal Majesty the King, who should be invited to carry out all the duties of his office.

We believe that the initiative by the armed forces for restoring responsibility to the Greek people will be a historic milestone replacing the nation's agony with the security of progress and well-being. This can be achieved only by reconciliation between the people, with their responsibility fully restored, and the national armed forces, guardians of the country's integrity. This reconciliation will avert the approaching national disaster.

During these critical times all of us, the armed forces and the people, must band together, a united and powerful Greece filled with loyalty to the Greek heritage of responsible democracy and the dignity of the Greek people.

Let the actions of all be guided by the love the Greek people have for Greece and the knowledge that national unity is the only demand the nation makes of us.

We expect the armed forces to choose the road of saving the nation by decisively contributing to restoring responsibility to the Greek people, which also will lead automatically to the responsible Greek presence, today non-existent, within the free world's family of nations and the overall international environment.

- Political leaders
- Former members of parliament
- Former prime ministers
- Former chiefs of the armed forces and generals
- Former presidents of the Supreme Court and judges
- University professors
- Academicians
- Young scientists
- Ideally all of the above, but at least the politicians and military
- Complete the effort and publicity during October

Papagos took this text with him to Greece.

September 29, Wednesday
Back to London

Dinner with Sir Hugh Greene. He was pleased with NATO's parliamentary assembly, where we won by 46 votes to 12 with 9 abstaining. Based on the meetings he has had, he believes that the Senate cannot pass a stricter resolution.

September 30, Thursday

The King calls to say that Papagos is leaving within the next couple of days and asked me what I think about Agnew's visit. I said, "It is a double-edged sword, it may prove to be good. A lot will depend upon you, in Teheran."

October 1, Friday

I telephoned Mitsotakis. I told him that things have started going well, and he told me that Tasca visited Karamanlis, who is pleased.

Before I left my hotel, the King called. I told him about the Tasca-Karamanlis meeting, of which he had not heard. He told me that the American military attaché in Rome came to see him and told him that Angelis keeps repeating what he had told him in the past, that "the King's stance can be favorable, neutral, or unfavorable to the regime. Up to now, it has been none of these." The King answered, "Athens shows no intention of understanding the problems."

October 2, Saturday
Letter from the Archbishop

At home I found a letter from the Archbishop dated September 23. It is an answer to my letter about AHEPA:

Dear Mr. Vidalis,

I share your resentment of certain American citizens of Greek ancestry who subscribe to the policy of division. The Archdiocese is doing what it can (and there is not much it can do in the political sector) to discourage involvement that is not advantageous to the present or future of Hellenism in America. The subject is very delicate and great attention is necessary, but it is also very serious and demands being handled with prudence, neither of which you lack.

With wishes and regards,

Archbishop Iakovos of America

Vice President Agnew visits Greece

October 4, Monday

I write to Sisco about the vice president. I also write to Buchanan about Agnew.

Senator Pell calls to tell me that Senator Hartke submitted a resolution to the Fulbright committee for cutting off aid, which was turned down 5-4. He then proposed that the president be requested to report annually on the progress toward returning to normal political life in Greece, but, after discussion, this proposal was turned down. He believes that the Hays amendment will be approved by Congress and asked for my opinion. I told him this is enough to bring psychological results, since nothing else is possible at the moment. I asked Pell to arrange for Saxbe to use the material I had sent Pell. He said he would do so.

I telephoned Moose, who believes that the Congressional resolution will pass.

October 6, Wednesday

I telephoned Hackett. He said that the State Department and Tasca requested that Agnew not visit Greece.

October 8, Friday

The Archbishop called. He is leaving for Iran. He will meet with the King and told me that Agnew considers the first part of his trip to Teheran and his meeting with the King more important than the visit to Greece. He asked if I had read today's *New York Times.* I had not. We agreed to talk again after his return on October 19. I got the *New York Times* article. Hovey wrote it exactly as we had agreed.

I telephoned Moose. He will inform Senator Fulbright about the announcements from Athens concerning diplomats communicating with politicians. He told me that the committee had not yet reached a conclusion, but it will next week. He is not worried, it will pass as we have discussed and agreed.

Saturday, October 9
In Chicago

We left for Chicago. At two we arrived at Professor Anastaplo's house. He was invited by an advisor to the Joint Chiefs of Staff to present them an assessment of the situation. I stressed to him how critical this phase is, that it requires the greatest amount of pressure possible or it will lead to the U.S. submitting to the junta's terms. He told me he would write an article on Greece for the *Encyclopedia Britannica.*

October 10, Sunday

I called Buchanan in the morning. He sent a copy of my letter to Kissinger. He trusts that Agnew will not be swayed, although the vice president is in a very difficult position. I told him I do not share Kissinger's optimism about elections in 1972 and we must discuss the issue. He will call back tomorrow if he has news.

October 11, Monday
Preparations for the Teheran meeting
Results of Papagos's trip.

Buchanan called. He talked with Kissinger today, who said that everything in Iran has been planned on a military timetable by the Iranian authorities and only the Shah can arrange for a meeting between Agnew and the King.

The King called in the afternoon. I told him that I had been in touch with Sisco and Kissinger through Buchanan. My impression is that there may be pressure from Agnew upon the regime, but it will not be made public. I told him that I asked for four things: a meeting between Agnew and the King, a meeting between Agnew and Kanellopoulos, a formal declaration that the policy is the return to normal order, and that NATO is not just a defensive alliance.

I suggested to the King to try to arrange the meeting through the Shah, and ask Agnew to see Kanellopoulos. He added, "Mavros as well," and I said, "Yes." I also suggested he tell Agnew of the need for a public statement on the American policy for the return to normal order, and to stress the political importance of NATO.

He then passed me over to Papagos, who was back from Greece where he had gone to motivate the politicians and others on the basis of the September 24 text. Papagos saw Mavros in Athens and presented the situation to him. Mavros agreed with the general principle, but said that Kanellopoulos had to agree as well and he had to talk to his own people. Papagos, however, saw him as willing. He did not show him the text. Then he saw Kanellopoulos, who said that he, too, thinks this is needed and believes that the time to move ahead has come. Whether or not Karamanlis is accepted is a matter for the Center Party. He has no objection.

Papagos spoke with Georgios Rallis as well, who told him they should change the text. He does not think they should address the armed forces, and he would send Papakonstantinou to Karamanlis to ask him what he will do if they do what is asked of them.

Unfortunately, so much time has gone by and we have suffered so much, but still we have not understood that the armed forces is the only direction from which change can come. Rallis does not think we should address the armed forces but does not make any alternative suggestion.

Papagos finished by saying that they were all impressed by my assessment, that they see the proposal in a positive light, and that he found them more willing than he expected. He does not think they will go forward as quickly as we would like, but they will move by sending Papakonstantinou to Karamanlis. He explained to them that the King accepted the general's proposal as correct; he supports it and leaves them to their own judgment for the final form.

The King asked me what I think of their reaction. I answered, "Better than I expected, even though I did not like Rallis's position." He told me that Papagos briefed Karamanlis, who said, "What do they want, to bargain?"

I also told the King that the pressure will continue, a Greek position must be formed, and he should see Agnew with the Shah's intervention. He told me to call Karamanlis and again tell him my point of view. I promised I would.

I told the King that Archbishop Iakovos also will go Teheran and will meet him there.

I called Karamanlis and told him that the reaction to Papagos's visit was positive in the sense that it indirectly showed that in Athens they see the junta as weakening and his prestige as getting stronger. It is now necessary to step up the effort we had discussed. The person who comes to you must have specific instructions. This is our last effort. "Agreed, general, but what are we going to do? Bargain?" "This is not about bargaining, it is about making our positions clear," I told him. "If the envoy comes I will do my best to help the King and the situation," he replied. Then he asked me about Agnew. My information is that the pressure he will exert will be discreet, not public. The discussion ended with a repeat of the assertion, "I will do my best."

I telephoned the King and told him of the conversation. I asked him to ask the archbishop to help me. He said, "With all my heart." He told me he would ask the Shah to arrange his meeting with Agnew. He thanked me and said he will call me from there, if need be.

October 20, Wednesday

Richard Moose told me that the Senate debate will be held next week, that there is no essential change in attitudes, that Agnew's trip will affect our case positively, and that he thinks the administration will not try to change what is about to happen in the Senate.

October 21, Thursday
Incident at the Tasca party in Athens

Pavlos Ioannides called to say that Tom Pappas had a dinner party for Agnew to which he had invited Pattakos and Makarezos. The State Department obliged him to retract the invitations, which he did angrily.

According to Ioannides, at the Tasca party, Mrs. Koutsouris, in Mr. Koutsouris's presence, said to Mrs. Tasca, "Congratulations for the work you are doing in Greece." Mrs. Tasca replied, "Who cares about Greece, we are only interested in the United States. There is fascism here, the situation is tragic, let them do as they please." Koutsouris froze and said, "How can you say that?" "I say it because I am an American and see that this place is miserable."

Koutsouris later told this to Pattakos, Angelis, and Apostolopoulos. They did not react but told him they would take action.

October 23, Saturday

I called Papagos. The King is not in Rome. He told me about the meeting with Agnew. The King requested it, and it took place in the King's tent. It lasted for over an hour. Agnew, obviously influenced by the Greek-Americans, said that he hears many good things, that the regime is interested in order and in NATO. He will try to convince them but will not go to extremes. With Archbishop Iakovos, the King mainly discussed the issue of Greek-Americans.

OCTOBER 28, THURSDAY
In Washington

I arrive in Washington in the evening, at Silva's house. They know nothing. They have not learned what was said either in Teheran or Athens.

He told me that an Agnew aid, who had insisted that Agnew should not go to Greece, ended up changing his mind. Agnew returned to the State Department the documents they had prepared for him and asked them to tell him "what good things this government has done."

Tasca is controlled by the CIA. He is so involved in Greece that a change in the embassy is impossible because the Senate would not approve a new appointment. Silva explains that Sisco is reluctant to see me because he does not know anything and does not want to be in a weak position.

The State Department Shifts Its Position

OCTOBER 29, FRIDAY
Meeting with Sisco

Meeting with Sisco at the State Department.

J. S. How do you see the vice president's visit, general?

O.V. On the surface it looks very bad, but the real ramifications are not known. Since the U.S.A. has not changed its policy, I believe that this trip should have promoted that policy. That is, if your policy for restoring democracy is still in effect.

J. S. Of course, our policy has not changed.

O.V. Do you know that we have incidents of shameless lying by the regime?

J. S. I have not been informed, general.

O.V. While talking to a German magazine about the King, Makarezos said that officers are free as citizens to have an opinion as to whether or not they prefer a King or a president of the republic.

J. S. General, I did not know. But let me tell you. U. S. policy has not changed in that we are pursuing two goals, security and democracy. Our position towards the King has not changed.

O.V. If, Mr. Secretary, we see hostile acts against the King from the regime in the future, these acts will be in opposition to the goals of this policy, they will be aimed at prolonging the dictatorship beneath the cloak of a democracy without a King.

J. S. I agree, general, but I do not expect such a development after everything the Vice President did and the time he spent with the King and the regime. I do not expect such a development. The purpose of the Vice President's trip was to help our policy.

O.V. Mr. Secretary, I am pleased to hear you say this, but if, without upsetting current relations, the King is asked to return and specific requirements for reestablishing democracy have not been laid down, don't you agree that this is not a solution?

J. S. I fully agree. (To Churchill, don't put that on record.) That is, if the King is pressured to submit to the junta (use that phrase) without stipulations about the return to normal order, then his return would be useless.

O.V. I think the average Greek needs some clarification about the purpose of the Vice President's visit to Greece and if the visit indicated a change in American policy. Further statements by the Secretary of State and yourself, confirming earlier statements of "disappointment" (in the lack of progress towards democracy) will establish the feeling in Greece that your policy has not changed. If I see the situation correctly, the Vice President has created personal relations with the leaders of the regime, something that can be useful as a new way to influence the regime.

J. S. General, I saw how careful you were today in handling this issue. I will tell you that our policy is always for the return of democracy. As for tactics, we had to choose between two alternatives for handling this situation. One was to apply pressure upon the regime to the point of confrontation. The other, the one we attempted, was to create a relationship of trust with the regime. This does not mean that we agree with what they are doing—we do not agree. But with quiet, thoughtful, sympathetic encouragement we tried to make the regime confident enough to restore democracy. We went with the second tactical choice, and within this framework the Vice President succeeded perfectly. The psychological climate is restored and the discussions that took place will help the long-term progress of our dual-goal policy. It is easy for someone to make rush judgments about the results of the Vice President's visit, but we must wait and see.

O.V. Mr. Secretary, I am glad for your optimism, which I do not share, even though I wish that it be proven that the Vice President succeeded in get-

> ting solid promises for restoring democracy. Should we now expect specific actions in Athens and here to confirm your optimistic outlook?
>
> J. S. Of course. I want to conclude, general, with a very important statement. The Vice President's discussions with the King and in Greece, regardless of how they are portrayed by the regime and others, already have helped and will further help in achieving our goal. This is quite an important statement I am making to you today.

I thanked him warmly. He said, "Let's stay in touch," and I said good-bye.

With Churchill in his office we discussed Sisco's position. He was pleased because he learned things he didn't know. I took notes from Churchill's notepad. I told him that I forgot to tell Mr. Sisco that when President Nixon is forced to take a stand on the aid resolution, he must clearly confirm that the policy for restoring democracy is in effect. I suggested he tell Mr. Sisco that, and he said he would add it to the record of our meeting.

In continuing my discussion with Churchill, I emphasized that the regime is displaying more and more insolence. I believe, since the regime succeeded in their relations with the Americans, it will now turn toward the other pending problem—the King. The best solution for Papadopoulos would be to force the King to return to Greece on the regime's terms, that is, without power and after legalizing the regime.

As I have repeatedly explained to Sisco, I believe that the King must not return under the regime's terms, without secure guarantees.

I saw Silva for a little while. I told him what happened, and he was surprised.

I was planning to go to lunch then and asked if I had any phone calls. Fortunately, I called Clifford Hackett, who told me that Congressman Benjamin S. Rosenthal was expecting me at 1:30 in the afternoon. I skipped lunch and went right away. Rosenthal asked if his Greek-American secretary, who doesn't agree with him, could be present in the discussion. She came and stayed in his office.

I explained my position. Rosenthal asked if I have said this to the opposition, as I am "very persuasive." I told him only partly. The lady added in the end, "The general gives another view, and I agree."

I thanked Rosenthal and left after learning from Hackett the sad news that the Senate, by 49-31, had not approved the Hays amendment. He was, however, conservatively optimistic because Hays would be relentless in the arbitration.

After lunch I went to Hays's office. He was not there. Colonel Abruzzese had not learned of the defeat. I told him. "They will win this only over Mr. Hays's dead body." He would get in touch with Hays and arrange our meeting.

In the evening, at Couloumbis's house, Stavrou told me that he met a theologian very close to Nixon who met Ieronimos in Greece. When asked about the King, Ieronimos said, "Let him know that I always love him, that I pray and strive for his return." Pyrros arrived and told us that the Senate rejected the aid bill in its entirety. Therefore, the administration's victory this morning on the committee resolution was wasted for the junta because Nixon's problems will multiply now.

I called Silva in the afternoon. He was furious with the vote on the Hays amendment. I told him to calm down and asked him to send me a copy of the *Congressional Record* with this morning's debate.

November 1-15
Confusion in Washington

The confusion in Washington continues. The Senate votes a new aid bill. The House will decide next week. According to Hackett, with whom I talked three times, the House may accept the old bill and they will have to compromise. According to him, it is not impossible for the Hays amendment to be included.

November 16, Tuesday
Meeting with the archbishop

I saw the archbishop at 11:00 in the morning in New York. He told me that the King was not happy with his meeting with Agnew and that Nixon spoke against the junta, saying, "Don't talk to me about them again, they are not to be trusted because they did not keep the 1970 time schedule. Agnew is the voice of his master and he put the pressure on them in Athens. But, again, they will not honor anything." I pressed the subject of Greek-Americans. He finally agreed to invite some to dinner with me for a discussion,

November 17, Wednesday

I telephoned Hackett. The discussion in the House Committee on International Relations is postponed. A meeting in Fraser's office determined the tactics and the Democrat group still has hope for the Hays amendment.

November 18, Thursday
Cabot Lodge to the King

The King called me in the morning. He wanted to know what is happening here and gave me the following information:

a. He asked the archbishop to help me;
b. Cabot Lodge and his wife visited him, after requesting an audience. They stayed for five hours. Cabot Lodge stressed that Nixon is always for the King.
c. "Slowly but surely your actions bring results," the King told me.

Lodge didn't tell the King that he was Nixon's envoy, but it seems that he was. He said he will see him again when he returns in the spring. They probably wanted to put his mind at ease.

I telephoned Hackett in the evening. The House brought the original bill with the Hays amendment back to life. Perhaps they will come back to the text, in spite of the detours.

I received a letter from Pierros Panaghiotareas from Athens, describing progress within the navy for action against the dictatorship.

November 13, 1971

I received your letter dated October 30, 1971, with great pleasure, although I have not received your note confirming receipt of my letter.

The situation is now unfolding as follows: initiation has resumed since my return, with great care and prudence. We are getting organized in the manner we discussed before I left. Even though there are very few of the junta's people in our family, they have all the means at their disposal so things are not easy. Fortunately, they have splintered into a thousand pieces; they fight all the time, leaving a little leeway. In spite of all this we control enough key positions and, mainly, the members of our family (he means the navy) are the best. I am truly proud of this.

I found great opposition here to involvement at this stage of the people in khaki. Unfortunately, there is much hatred, and it saddens me. I am doing everything I can so we can move as we have discussed there.

Our goal is to have 100 family members by December, including the new recruits I brought.

What is missing, as I mentioned there, too, is information about the political aspects of the situation. There is a void here. It would be a blessing if you could do something.

On the other side, here there is no doubt that the dictators are heading towards a government with political figures, then they will determine the governmental structure, and finally move to a Franco-style dictatorship. Apparently, the trio [Papadopoulos, Patakos, Makarezos] is cooperating well now, since the revolutionary committee has been reestablished. The hard liners have suffered some serious blows and are not often seen.

I have heard from two or three different sources that if the King makes any move, he will probably have a car accident.

Our mutual friend [Commander Thanassis Sekeris] has not shown up yet.

You must trust us. I assure you that very serious work is being done in spite of the difficulties.

Waiting for your news.

P.S. The courier of this to N.Y. has been thoroughly checked.

I was glad for the information but am worried by the phrase "Unfortunately, there is much hatred (towards the khaki)." I understand it but it is a negative factor, both in the short and the long term.

November 30, Tuesday
Strange visit by the FBI

Mr. Bradner of the FBI came by the office at 10:00 in the morning. He said, "General, I want to ask you to help us. We have information resistance groups against the Greek regime are collecting funds and getting organized to overthrow the regime. Do you know anything as far as the U.S. is concerned?"

"I do not know that there are any armed resistance groups in the U.S., but there is a great deal of resistance within the U.S. against the regime. Your superiors know my positions."

"Which superiors, general?"

"In the State Department, in the Pentagon, etc."

"Do you know if resistance is being organized in Greece?"

"Many attempts have been made and more will be made in the future. Unless democracy is restored, you will see a new Batista situation transform into a Castro one."

"There is an organization in New York called the Committee for the Reorganization of the Greek Government, do you know it?"

"I have never heard that name. There are many such organizations, some having senators among their members, others professors, but all of them are attempts to influence American public opinion."

"Thank you very much, general, please excuse me for bothering you."

The visit astonished me. It shows how broken up and uncoordinated the American services supposedly looking after the internal security of the country are. Really, how much time and money are lost for no reason.

December 1, Wednesday

I wrote to Sisco about the FBI.

December 2, Thursday

I called Congressman Wayne Hays. He told me that the Hays amendment was included in the bill by arbitration. He is optimistic.

December 3, Friday

It has become known that the arbitrators are moving toward agreement on something like a bill that includes the Hays amendment.

I wrote to Buchanan and to Sisco and send them the *Economist Report*, which I also sent to Norstad.

December 4, Saturday
Briefing Karamanlis

I write to Mitsotakis and Karamanlis. My letter to Karamanlis follows:

> *Mr. President,*
>
> *The issue of aid, which has largely psychological reverberations in Greece, is back to where it was before the Senate adventure. (I am enclosing an article published in a pro-junta Greek-American Boston newspaper showing the role AHEPA played in this.)*
>
> *The Arbitration Committee for the Senate and the House is including the Hays amendment for cutting off aid to Greece unless the president decides otherwise. It is expected, barring any surprises, that this will be the final form of the bill. Nixon will use the discretion the bill allows him and will give the expected limited aid. The main issue is how he will justify his decision.*
>
> *In any case, as I explained during our meeting, unless there is a Greek initiative I predict that we will enter a period during which the dictatorship will be tolerated.*
>
> *Now the immediate issue of the King arises. I am enclosing two documents. I am sure you have your own information. The Greek document comes from responsible observers in Greece. You will notice that some points are the same in both documents. It is possible that under the pressure of a dead-end, the regime will resort to this measure. It will attempt to gain time and increase uncertainty while assuming that it is has guaranteed the absence of opposition.*
>
> *My friends here are NOT worried. I remember that you also do NOT think it possible for this issue to be raised again. I do NOT share the optimism*

of my friends. I know that the insane are ruthless, prepared to do anything in order to prolong their power by force.

I believe that we must be prepared to face that possibility as well.

I hope my fears are exaggerated.

Mobilizing people in Greece is the main issue now, while there is still time. Ioannides is saying: "Let's have another two classes graduate from the Officers' Candidates School first, and then let the Americans or Karamanlis try to throw us out."

I will keep you informed about further developments from this end.

Sincerely yours,

Orestis Vidalis

DECEMBER 13, MONDAY

Four years have passed. How different the situation in the country would be if the King's effort had led to restoring democracy.

One has to wonder if the generals who succumbed to the pressure of their subordinates and did not take action to restore legality are now aware of their historic responsibility in ignoring their oath to the country's constitution and the national interest.

DECEMBER 15, WEDNESDAY
In Washington

During our meeting, Buchanan describes what good friends he is with Nixon and Kissinger. He stresses that he helped Nixon financially and would do so again. I explain the situation to him and stress that Nixon himself must intervene. He told me that Agnew confronted Papadopoulos with the issue of elections and the King. I said that he must convince Nixon to get involved himself. And to use General Goodpaster.

DECEMBER 17, FRIDAY

In Toledo.

Richard Moose telephoned. The bill including the Hays amendment passed in the Senate. Later, I called Hackett. He confirmed this and added that it will be voted on in the House on January 18. Therefore, the president will not have the time to react psychologically.

December 23, Thursday
The United States press

The December 16 editorial in the *Hellenic Chronicle* angered me. It supports the decision taken by the Boston chapter of AHEPA to form a "Committee for Justice in Greece" and then urges the AHEPA national office to support this decision and promote the junta. I write Peter Agris and send a copy to George Vournas, who is a lawyer. The purpose of my letter is to remind the publisher of my position in distinct contrast to his position. I am not doing this in the hope that I will change Agris's mind; I am doing it because supporters of the regime must be presented with things called by their real names, particularly if these supporters are in positions that can influence public opinion. Then, at least, they cannot claim that they do not know what the other side thinks, since the opposing position has been stated clearly and sent to them, personally.

December 23, 1971

Dear Mr. Agris,

Since we last met, I have been reading the Hellenic Chronicle regularly and, believe me, very carefully. I believe that your newspaper fills a genuine need for of the Greek-American community. You are doing an excellent job in showing how successful the members of this community are in their efforts to succeed in the vast, very healthy, but competitive—sometimes to the point of intimidation—American society. I believe, however, that the time has come to give you my honest opinion about the way you are handling the situation in Greece.

I am writing you my views in an attempt to make a positive contribution to your understanding of "Greek reality."

You have not succeeded in disguising your direct, unequivocal support of the junta.

I do not see objectivity.

Obviously, you have not perceived the deeper meaning behind the official American expression of "disappointment" in the lack of progress toward the peaceful restoration of responsible democracy in Greece.

It seems to me that you have not been able to see that the regime has brought itself to a dead-end, clearly shown by using martial law as its only means of survival and indefinitely postponing its only genuine national duty, free elections.

Obviously, you disagree with the State Department, which, very early, back in August of 1969, declared:

"We see a dictatorial government that denies Greek citizens their basic

freedoms. We believe that such a domestic situation does not serve the vital interests of Greece, whose stability in the long run depends upon the free activities of democratic forces. . . ."

You have not been able to understand that responsible Greeks both inside the country and abroad, Greeks who love Greece at least as much as you love America, have been trying to convey this simple, tragic truth to our friends for approximately five years.

You have not been able to understand that the leaders of the junta were not motivated by fear of a communist threat when they began their mutinous plotting as early as 1956, but by their conviction that everywhere the ideals of Greece and the West are collapsing, and this heritage was too great a weight for them to bear. They prolong their rule out of, for them, a natural desire to be rid of this weight, and they do so by resorting to a doomed over-simplification of a primitive totalitarian system.

Clearly, you have been impressed with the junta's building of roads, factories, and the like with the help of its rich supporters, but have not been able to realize that the regime destroys moral support, creating "Yes men" in a society with a tradition of lively internal debate, thereby impeding the preparation of responsible, free citizens. You ignore the fact that a vast leadership gap is being created, which will have catastrophic consequences in the future.

You seem unable to grasp that the Greek nation is in a freezing compartment now, but someday the old political problems, together with the more serious ones now accumulating, will surface in a way that can be disastrous. Perhaps you have forgotten that Metaxas's dictatorship was followed by civil war.

The roads and factories would have been constructed anyway with the initial growth in the Greek economy, as was the case with other democratic governments after WW II, but at the same time capable young people would have been prepared for leading the nation and would have arisen through democratic procedures.

You may know that early on, in May 1967, the junta offered me a high governmental position, which I declined. I refused the offer then and continue to be completely opposed to the dictatorship because I believe that if this shameful anachronism continues it will, in the long run, lead our country to destruction. In spite of my stance in regard to the regime, however, I hope you have noticed that my overall position has been very careful, even though they revoked my citizenship.

The many of us who oppose the dictatorship cannot allow anyone to insult us by claiming that our opposition is the result of having lost our jobs. We expect the people who disagree with us to be more accurate and have greater respect for our point of view. I do not dispute your right to have whatever opinion you wish, but I do dispute your objectivity, your efforts to belittle those who oppose the regime, and your ability to understanding our national problem in depth. I never really have been able to explain why the Greek-American press, overall, differs so dramatically from the whole of the American press and mass media.

Before I close these thoughts, I wish to remind you that nothing is more permanent than change. Pakistan is the most recent example.

I know that my opinions are very weak compared to the might of the dictatorship in power. In any case, allow me to suggest that the only position I see for a Greek-American newspaper and for Greek-Americans in general is absolute neutrality in the conflict between the people of Greece and the self-appointed dictators. Any other position involves the danger of severing the bond between the people of Greece and the Greek-American community.

After six-months of communication with the Chronicle, the purpose of this open presentation of my feelings is not publication. Its purpose is to inform you as a responsible American that we must be very careful when, in public, we are dealing with the fate of a nation, such as Greece.

My best wishes to Mrs. Agris and yourself for a happy new year.

Sincerely yours,

Orestis Vidalis

In this letter to Agris, I wrote, "I never really have been able to explain why the Greek-American press, overall, differs so dramatically from the whole of the American press and mass media." I must justify this impression. First, I must point out that there have been some exceptions in the Greek-American press, the best example being the New York *National Herald* (*Ethnikos Kyrix*). As a whole, with very few exceptions, however, all the American press has been against the Greek dictatorship and American policy, in editorials and in persistently describing everything throughout the years of the Greek drama.

Large newspapers, such as the *New York Times* and the *Washington Post*, and newspapers from large and small cities continuously pointed out the flawed policy of the American administration toward Greece. Now, after all these years have passed and this story is being written, it would not be an exaggeration to say that someone could write the history of the Greek dictatorship based on the editorials in large American newspapers. As an example, I mention that the *New York Times* published the following number of editorials against American policy in Greece:

13 in 1969
9 in 1970
8 in 1971

9 in 1972
18 in 1973
4 in 1974 until March

It must be stressed that editorials express the official position of the newspapers on matters of general importance.

The subject of an editorial, which is a essay drawing upon information, reports, and signed articles, is chosen with great care by the editorial staff and management of the newspaper. Most of the *New York Times* editorials mentioned above are accompanied by a large number of correspondents' reports and signed articles that have been published in this newspaper very often. This is the same with almost all American newspapers, large or small. The exception, unfortunately, is the Greek-American press.

In addition to editorials and other articles on the Greek dictatorship, the American press devoted considerable space to publishing telling cartoons that continuously ridiculed American policy and the Greek dictatorship.

December 27, Monday

I received a card from Archbishop Iakovos. "Dear General, winters will pass. May 1972 be SPRING."

December 31, Friday

1971 ended today. Another year, the fourth, of dictatorship in Greece. Much happened in 1971, but we are far from the end of this national adventure. A vicious circle continues. Inside the country everyone expects everything from the outside. Those outside the country cannot overturn the dictatorship unless there is effective movement inside. As long as this balance between the expectations of the two is maintained, both psychologically and substantially, the vicious circle continues to determine the fate of Greece. Certainly, the dictatorship is being worn down and knows so better than any of us, but the more the wear and tear continues, the more the dictatorship will take ruthless steps to stay in power. Until when?

CHAPTER 5

1972

We Have Reached the Fifth Year of Expatriation
The Junta Moves against the King

JANUARY 2, SUNDAY
Trip to Michigan

Trip to Birmingham, Michigan, to visit Athanasios Alexiou. Alexiou is President of the Society for Democracy in Greece. He used to work for the Public Power Corporation in Greece (ΔΕΗ), was laid off by the dictatorship, and now works with Edison in Detroit. He is pessimistic and thinks that the Junta will drag on. He is well informed, tried to form an organization to work against the Junta, but failed. He believes that Andreas Papandreou's positions are untimely. He is willing and ready to work for two purposes, 1) ousting the Junta and, 2) freedom of speech for the Greek people, which he will respect.

JANUARY 6, THURSDAY

I give my best wishes to John Nicolopoulos for his name day. He tells me he will visit Papandreou on Saturday. I tell him that this man, who seems to be blessed with superior intellectual capabilities, has not understood Greek reality because he has lived abroad for so long and has had unfortunate personal experiences. Unfortunately, his present tactics are inconsistent with the fundamental national goal of wearing down and eliminating the dictatorship.

JANUARY 8, SATURDAY
AHEPA's Junta preferences again

I received a letter from George Vournas in reply to my letter to him, with of a copy of his letter to Peter Agris, publisher of the *Hellenic Chronicle*, enclosed. In his letter to Agris, Vournas writes,

> Allow me to say that your editorial is based on the erroneous supposition that AHEPA supports slavery over freedom, supports Papadopoulos, a tyrant, over self-determination. . . . Obviously you are referring to decisions—taken in accordance with instructions by President Sam Nakis—that were mailed to members of Congress. . . .

Recently it has been discovered that these "decisions" represent nothing more than their author's imagination. They were never approved by the National Assembly.

January 10, Monday
Nicolopoulos's meeting with Papandreou

I telephone John Nicolopoulos. He gives me the main points of his meeting with Andreas Papandreou, which lasted six-and-a-half hours.

a. He did not voice any objections about the King. He believes, however, that the King's popularity has decreased. Nicolopoulos replied that the position Papandreou had expressed that the King would return to Greece from Rome had not been borne out.
b. Nicolopoulos spoke to him about me and he appeared interested.
c. He received a cable yesterday saying that a floating radio station broadcasting to Greece has begun operating.
d. He has information that the junta is financing neo-fascists in Italy.
e. He said that he had made strong statements in Germany against the prohibition of the Democratic Union.

John Nicolopoulos will remain in touch.

January 23, Sunday
To Indiana

Matina and I leave for Lafayette, Indiana, to meet with Pavlos Lykoudis. Lykoudis is among the leaders of the Ad Hoc Committee for the Restoration of Democracy in Greece, based in Indiana.

Lykoudis is working systematically, he has formed a group. They met in Cincinnati in November. In April they will meet in Chicago to try to persuade Democratic Party candidates to make statements about Greece.

He is optimistic that they will move forward, since there are issues. He suggested that I not wear myself out with Greek-American community problems but should remain the bearer of ideas from Greece. When I was back in Toledo, Lykoudis telephoned me at 1:00 AM to say he heard that discussions are under way for establishing an American naval base in Greece. He mobilized his people right away and they sent telegrams to Fulbright during the night.

January 25, Tuesday
The Hays amendment is again at center stage

The House approved the aid bill, with the Hays amendment, by 203 to 179.

January 27, Thursday
My fears about Buchanan's position

I write Sisco about the need for the president to make a statement about the aid.

I telephone Buchanan. He tells me he met with the royal couple during the King of Denmark's funeral, and they had a long talk. Buchanan suggested to the King that he return to Greece and try to restore the situation from there, telling the King that he must not insist upon his conditions. According to Buchanan, the King told him that he does not see any indication that the dictatorship wishes to discuss his conditions, and he will not return unless they are accepted.

I am afraid that Buchanan's suggestion that the King return unconditionally, may, in fact, be reflecting the American administration's desire to rid themselves of the inconvenience of the King and strengthen the junta. I record this fear without having anything specific on which to base it, but as a thought that has been bothering me ever since Norstad's and Eisenhower's refusals to act as centers of psychological pressure upon the dictatorship and as an internal reminder to watch the administration's behavior closely for indications that would either confirm or eliminate this suspicion.

I received a letter from Commander Sekeris from Kiel. He writes that the Junta is preparing to dethrone the King. He also writes about disagreements within the Junta, about the progress of the secret preparations within the navy, and requests political instructions. The main points of Sekeris's letter are below.

Dear Mr. Vidalis,

A few days ago I had some news from our friend in Greece, who wanted me to inform you of the following:

A. News of general interest
Some time ago there was a meeting of army intelligence staff officers serving in major army units, all of them fundamental supporters of the "revolution." Intelligence officers from the navy and air force also were present as observers. After protracted discussion they agreed upon the following:

1. Within the first six months of 1972 the King must be accused of:
   a. Masterminding December 13

b. Creating the Cyprus crisis
c. Being absent from his duties for four years.

2. *Based on the above accusations, he should renounce his office without any constitutional change.*
3. *Pavlos [his infant son] should assume [royal] responsibilities with a three-person regency, in accordance with the constitution.*

According to unconfirmed sources, at first Papadopoulos agreed to the above and the order was given for the propaganda against the King to begin in the press and on radio/television. In any case, before replacing the King he wants to take a series of other steps, the most important of which are replacing the head of the joint chiefs of staff and the three commanders of the armed forces during the May evaluations. . . .

With a few exceptions, all of the navy is against the present regime. The few exceptions, representatives of the "revolution," are falling out among themselves because, in general, officers no longer follow orders from higher ranking officers. The result is that these few are falling apart, even if at first they had some power. . . . Therefore, there is optimism in the navy. Ramrod is pretty strong. The most virtuous and capable officers have been initiated. Our friend does not think that this phase should continue for the time being. . . . Also, the best-suited initiates have been charged with drawing up a plan of action. The best plans will be sent to see which one will be chosen. Another group has been charged with gathering information about international and domestic political developments. Your friend asks for your feedback and support on this point. There are no contacts with the army and air force. Our friend in Italy seems to have developed some contact with the air force. When he returns to Greece next month he will strengthen this connection and, perhaps, broaden it to include others. Care is being taken so that the officer assignments next May are made in accordance with our needs. In general, an effort is being made for the navy to be at the best possible level as of August, by which time something must have been scheduled to happen because continued postponements discourage even the most enthusiastic.*

Many questions arise about possible unpleasant developments in the future, such as, for example, what should they do if the King is removed from the throne or if the dictators discover what is happening and are about to take drastic measures.

In general, this is the news from Greece. I met with my brother the other day, who told me about his meeting with our friend in Italy. He is optimistic and hopes to help with preparations when he returns to Greece. My brother also very much would like to meet you in Brussels to exchange information. If you are planning a trip to Europe, please let me know so a meeting could be arranged, a meeting that could be very productive.

Also, in your next letter please let me know if you have received my last letter to you, which was mailed in the beginning of December if my memory serves me correctly, and in which I confirmed having received the attached documents.

Respectfully,

Sekeris

February 11, Friday
News from the King

Arnaoutis came to the house in the evening. The news from Greece is pretty much the same. He made three significant points on behalf of the King:

Either Heath or Hume (he does not know which) told the King that Nixon prefers the King but will not offend the "current government" because they have done all that he has asked.

The French minister (who went to Greece) and Debrè told the King in Copenhagen that, according to Pompidou, in Athens they will insist on the return of the King and democracy. Debrè asked him what he feels about Karamanlis, and the King replied that he is the only successful one, and capable of renewing his success. Debrè asked the King if he agrees that the results of the Athens visit be announced through Karamanlis and, of course, the King agreed.

Kyprianou told the King that they had learned that the Greeks, Turks, and Americans had' signed an agreement, essentially, on dividing Cyprus. As he was leaving, with tears in his eyes, he said, "I do not know if I will see you again." The King advised Makarios to go see Nixon.

February 25, Friday

Theotokis called. According to reliable sources, Papadopoulos has been invited to Washington, he has accepted and will come after April 21; also, he is planning, after making certain changes, to appoint a regent.

He said that Papadopoulos has fallen in relation to Makarios and that the Americans had blessed the division [of Cyprus].

Congressional Hearings on Home-Port Facilities for the Navy in Greece

February 29, Tuesday
Preparations begin

I get in touch with Hackett. He has sent me the State Department document. They maintain that there is no anti-American sentiment in Greece.

Hackett will send them new questions. Next week the subcommittee will hear testimony from members of the administration only.

March 1, Wednesday

I met with General Norstad in the afternoon for quite a while. I told him about the King's worries. I told him it would be dangerous if the issue were to be raised now, after the Russian statement opposing American home-porting in Piraeus. And I suggested that he should try to have President Nixon send a message to the King on March 25.

March 7, Tuesday
Collaboration with Yeorgios Rallis

In the afternoon I leave for Washington.

I see G. Rallis in the evening.

Rallis said that he would try to convince Karamanlis to return to Greece.

Taking the opportunity, I explained to him that I never received the message he had sent on the night of April 21, 1967 to the 3rd Army Corps.

March 8, Wednesday
Testimonies by Rallis and Papaspyrou

Breakfast with G. Rallis before going to the House hearings. Undersecretary Davies sees me in the hearing room and comes over to shake hands. Davies's testimony is a mixture of abhorrence of the dictatorship and the inability to take any positive steps.

Rallis and Papaspyrou testify. The situation becomes tense after they read their prepared statements. Congressman Frelinghuysen, a supporter of the pro-dictatorship policy, becomes extremely aggressive. Rallis is upset. A recess is called. The atmosphere improves when the hearings reconvene.

March 10, Friday

Rallis and Papaspyrou met with Sisco. Silva tells me there was a warm welcome. They spoke well. I ask Silva for a copy of the Agnew statements; he did not know about them. Sismanides is pleased with the visit.

March 17, Friday

I received an invitation from the House of Representatives to testify during the hearings on April 13, 1972

March 22, Wednesday

Norstad's secretary calls and reads me Hillenbrand's answer. "Thank you for your letter of March 2 and for reminding me to send greetings to King Constantine. The intention is to send a presidential message of best wishes to the Greek people through King Constantine."

March 29, Wednesday

The National Public Radio telephones me and asks if I would be willing to speak in response to Ambassador Vassilis Vitsaxis, who will talk about the "government's" successes. I told them I would do so gladly. The program will be recorded on April 14 so it can be broadcast on April 21.

April 13, Thursday
Testimony before Congress

We are in Congress at 1:30 in the afternoon. I am not worried but have the feeling that in a short while I will be alone, obliged to face the good faith and bad faith of opposing interests. I am inspired by the goal. I feel that my voice is the voice of millions of Greeks. The presence of Matina, Efthymios, and our friends gives me courage. All of them are both confident and apprehensive. They remember the attacks on Rallis and Papaspyrou and don't look forward to the same thing being repeated. I sit in the waiting room while Destounis is giving his testimony. They call me to come up at 2:40 PM, and soon I am in the chamber. Destounis is being attacked by congressmen and replies with lies. I watch the military attaché, Colonel Floros Astrinides, while Congressman Buchanan speaks about the need for elections. Astrinides nods his head in agreement. He must be in a tragic position. Soon, almost without thanking Destounis, they call me.

I begin my testimony in a strong voice. The whole procedure was not difficult, but it was not easy, either. Everybody tells me it was a good presentation, but I say it could have been better.

As a baptism of fire in a foreign environment it wasn't bad.

Everybody congratulated me at the end. Congressman Frelinghuysen, who had the toughest questions since he supports the government's policy, approached me and said, "Our military is naïve. I am afraid we have put one more anti-democratic regime in place." I explain that I would be willing to discuss this with him, if he wishes. Congressman. Buchanan shakes my hand very firmly and expresses his admiration.

The embassy people have disappeared. On the way out, Hackett introduces me to a man from the Russian embassy who congratulates me because, "even though he has followed many hearings, he had never before seen a military man with such political judgment and ease." Hackett asks him, "Would you like to have generals like General Vidalis?" and the Russian replies, "I cannot imagine you do not believe that you also wish you had generals like the general."

We left. I was tired. I gave much of myself in this effort. Maybe it is because I feel the circumstances are tragic when a Greek officer is forced to ask foreigners, even though they are friends, to help rid his country of an infection caused by other Greek officers.

We were quite satisfied by a very productive day.

April 14, Friday

After lunch I went to the National Public Radio Corporation offices to record my interview, which will be broadcast together with Ambassador Vitsaxis's interview on April 21.

April 26, Wednesday
Meeting between Papandreou and Sismanides

I telephoned Sismanides and asked him to give a copy of my testimony to NBC, and he told me that the NBC headquarters are in New York. At the same time he said he met Andreas Papandreou with Margaret present. Telis Sismanides told Papandreou that it is not a good time to touch on the issue of the King, that Karamanlis must be supported, and that he must meet with me. Papandreou replied with very flattering words about me—"he is wise and greatly respected," he told Sismanides—and stressed how impressed he was with my testimony before Congress. As for the King, he referred to the past, ending by saying, "What must be done if the Greek people don't want him?" About Karamanlis he said that he is great, but does not do anything. He agreed to write Sismanides about how a meeting between us could be arranged.

Action for New Approaches after the Hearings

May 11, Thursday

The tape from the April 21 radio show arrived. It is awful; they cut 4/5 of my interview.

June 21, Wednesday
Pavlos Tzermias refers to my statement

Huart sends me the article with a note, "Congratulations, you made the S.R. Swiss Review of World Affairs." The article is by Pavlos Tzermias, who concludes with my statement, "A Greece with a Western orientation would be a drawback for the Soviet strategy. Moscow prefers to see Greece governed as it is today, since it derives both short-term and long-range advantages from it."

June 22, Thursday

It has been announced that Secretary of State Rogers will visit Greece. Couloumbis asked me if they should react. I told him it is not necessary.

June 28, Wednesday

I telephoned Hackett. He expects, as he was informed by the State Department, Rogers to make a positive statement on July 4 in Athens. The date is not accidental. It has been selected.

The Democrats Give Us Ideological Support

July 4, Tuesday
Rogers in Athens

Secretary Rogers is in Athens today. Kanellopoulos and Mavros made statements that American policy toward the regime must change; otherwise the Rogers visit is not a friendly gesture toward Greece. A national holiday for the Americans today and Rogers "chose" to be in Athens.

July 6, Thursday

At two in the morning, Georgios Rallis woke us up, telephoning from Athens. He called to say that the politicians did not attend Tasca's reception for Rogers, that Sisco stayed in Greece for about five hours after Rogers left and tried to see Kanellopoulos and Mavros, but they did not agree to his conditions. Sisco did not want to go to their homes and insisted they meet on neutral ground. They refused.

July 11, Tuesday
McGovern is the Democratic candidate

McGovern wins the nomination. In my files, I found an announcement McGovern had sent me at the beginning of his campaign. This first document includes the sentence, "We must stop supporting military tyrants everywhere, including Pakistan and Greece. The continuing support of such regimes by the Nixon administration is scandalous."

July 12, Wednesday

The government press in Athens is talking about a new phase. Perhaps Nixon will apply pressure for change or promise of change to face his domestic opponents.

July 20, Thursday

Nicolopoulos telephoned. He met with Pollis. She doubts that help from senators and congressmen will be effective. She prefers the private sector to be involved. He told me that AHEPA sent a letter to the Democrats criticizing their decision to recommend sanctions against the Greek Junta.

July 25, Tuesday

The Senate passed an amendment to the aid bill that includes a provision requiring the Vietnam War to be ended in four months. The Republicans were furious, voted against the entire bill, so we start all over again.

July 26, Wednesday

I telephoned Hackett. The Sub-committee on Europe of the House Committee on Foreign Affairs approved the aid bill with the paragraph for ending participation in the Viet Nam war. The paragraph on Greece was not included.

July 29, Saturday

Pollis called in the evening. She heard that Christopher of California will send letters to many Greek-Americans opposing McGovern's position on the Greek issue.

Also, she heard from Oklahoma, but could not confirm, that McGovern changed his position on the Greek issue.

TUESDAY, AUGUST 8
Politicians in Greece are for McGovern

Makrias from the *National Herald* telephoned. He had been visiting Athens and, as Marketos had asked him to do, he called to tell me that the politicians are planning to make a statement in support of McGovern. They want it to be published in the *New York Times* and Marketos is willing to cover part of the cost. He is sure that the new AHEPA president is anti-junta and for democracy.

I told him I would help pay for the publication and asked him to give me the address of the new AHEPA president, Dr. Michael Spirtos.

AUGUST 9, WEDNESDAY

I called Senator Nick Petris in California. He said that Spirtos had agreed with him when, at an AHEPA speech a few months ago, Petris had spoken in public against the junta. He will try to reestablish contact. He said that Christopher is speaking publicly in favor of the junta and against McGovern.

Communication with Europe, Greece, and Collaborators in the United States

SEPTEMBER 6, WEDNESDAY
The Herald publishes discussion from the *Congressional Record.*

The *Herald* published yesterday a synopsis of my testimony at the House hearings. It was published with the following introduction.

> The issue of home-port facilities in Greece for the Sixth Fleet already is one of the issues in the pre-election campaign for the presidency, particularly after the formal American association of this issue with defending Israel. In its columns the *National Herald* is publishing the official record, recently made public, of the testimony by General Orestis Vidalis, who has been living in the United States since November, 1968, before the House Committee on Foreign Affairs. After making his statement, he was questioned.
>
> Mr. ROSENTHAL. General, as a senior military officer in Greece after the 1967 coup, what was your relationship to the officers who led the revolt? Did they force you out?

General VIDALIS. They didn't force me out; on the contrary, 15 days after the coup they offered me a very high government position—a position comparable to Undersecretary of State—which I refused.

Mr. ROSENTHAL. Why did you refuse that position?

General VIDALIS. I feel that Greece has had enough of military intervention in politics and it is high time we change this pattern, which has brought nothing but disasters to our country.

Mr. ROSENTHAL. During the previous testimony this afternoon, Mr. Buchanan characterized the regime as a mutinous. Do you agree with that characterization?

General VIDALIS. I agree with the congressman for two reasons. The first is that those who rule the country today began their preparations a full decade before 1967, at a time Greece was in the middle of a bright and successful period. The second is that, if the purpose were only to deal with an impending threat to the country, their intervention should have lasted one, two, or three years. Now we are in the fifth year and there is no end in sight.

Mr. FRELINGHUYSEN. We are as disappointed as you in the fact that the hopes that the Americans have expressed, and that the Greeks have expressed to Americans, have not materialized. I refer to the return of the parliamentary process to Greece. But what can we do to avoid this criticism that you are leveling against us today?

General VIDALIS. Sir, there are three factors for any course of action. One is the policy, the second is the determination to implement this policy, and the third is the means. What is lacking is public evidence of your determination to take the steps needed to move toward your political objective. On the other hand, there is abundant evidence that you are quite determined to provide everything needed to reach your security objective.

Mr. BUCHANAN. Do I understand correctly, general, that it is not so much that you disapprove of the home-porting per se but that you feel we must find a way to make clear the strength of the American conviction to see a return to free elections in Greece?

General VIDALIS. A small item related to the comfort of U.S. Navy personnel at this time, unfortunately, reinforces the tremendous difference in emphasis between the political and security objectives of our countries. As long as this policy continues, our return to democratic institutions will be blocked.

Mr. BUCHANAN. General, I rather agree with the gentleman from New Jersey about your political abilities and hope the day will soon come when you can return to Greece and assume public office.

General VIDALIS. I appreciate your kindness.

Mr. BUCHANAN. I firmly believe what I said.

General VIDALIS. I realize that, sir, but I must state publicly that my purpose is only to assist my country. I am not concerned with what I will do when Greece will be free to enjoy the blessing of free institutions along with the rest of the Atlantic community. But until that time I will continue fighting to show that, after 150 years of our national life we, the soldiers, should remain faithful to our mission and not be involved with politics.

Mr. BUCHANAN. That is highly honorable position, in my judgment.

General VIDALIS. I would like to see one American or one NATO general or admiral visit Greece and say that Greece is part of NATO, but NATO exists to protect our civilization, not just the real estate.

Mr. FRELINGHUYSEN. Would the Greek people understand what such a statement means?

General VIDALIS. Oh, yes, sir. Absolutely. I am disturbed and saddened that the dictatorship has distorted the image of modern Greece, downgrading our people to the point that even our best friends question the ability of the Greek people to understand the meaning of our Western civilization.

Mr. FRASER. General, I want to commend you on your statement. I think what is lacking around the world is an international commitment to support governments based on the sovereignty of the people. We have, in my judgment, much too much temporizing. I am old enough to remember the descriptions of Italy and Germany before World War II, how the trains there were running on time and how everything was going well. The only thing that had been destroyed was democracy, and, of course, the whole world became involved in terrible conflict. I believe that such threats to the international community can be avoided only by people standing up and speaking out clearly.

My own opinion, which coincides with yours, is that there are many ways the United States could make these principles much clearer both to the existing regime and, in particular, to the Greek people. I think one of the tragedies of our relationship is the Greek people again and again are reminded of the U.S. government's embrace of the present regime. I would hope that the commitment that NATO represents to defend free institutions might be made real in U.S. policies. . . . I want to say I admire the position you take and what you stand for and I hope that the policies of our government could be made to reflect this nation's own basic values. This is, after all, what you are suggesting we ought to do.

General VIDALIS. Thank you.

Mr. ROSENTHAL. General, I, too, want to join with Mr. Frazer and my other colleagues and thank you and express my deep gratitude for your thoroughly enlightening views and reporting. . . . I want to commend you for being a man of extraordinarily high principles. I, personally, am very impressed with a man who held the high position you held in the Greek army and your association with NATO, that you have been willing to express views critical of the present regime. I know how difficult that is for someone who has been in government service or has been associated with the government, but I think, as Mr. Frazer has said quite eloquently, that the world will not survive long unless men of principle are willing to sacrifice their own ambitions and speak out in defense of principles.

General VIDALIS. Thank you very much.

September 23, Saturday

Tasca's testimony before the Subcommittee on Europe, House Committee on Foreign Affairs (behind closed doors), is a big issue in the Athenian press. I received the following brief letter from Konstantinos Karamanlis.

September 14, 1972

Dear Mr. Vidalis,

Thank you for keeping me informed. I agree with your assessment, which I also reached some time ago.

It is not strange that the Americans place their own interests before Greek freedom. What is strange is that they do not understand that the two can coexist.

Friendly regards,

Konstantinos Karamanlis

October 12, Thursday

Arnaoutis telephoned to say that the American embassy in Athens sent a report to Washington stressing the need for Angelis to replace Papadopoulos and his entourage. They are waiting for an answer and look forward to all this having been accomplished by Christmas.

In London they are expecting me and everything has been arranged. He made sure to tell me that the information about the report from the American embassy in Athens is confidential and should not be made public.

October 17, Tuesday
Discussion with Norstad

General Norstad asked to see me in the afternoon. He asked me to convey his respects to the King and his greetings to Karamanlis. He very much wants to know what Karamanlis's thoughts are. He thinks the home-porting agreement is ridiculous, that Secretary Laird is inflexible and incapable of understanding the wider picture. He believes that the regime has blackmailed the American government because, unfortunately, the administration has out too much stress on the military issue. "I would cut aid, not publicly, but I would tell them that unless they implement the constitution, I will cut off support. After the elections Rockefeller may be Secretary of State. Right now, any action is unthinkable, but the situation will be different later. The president has been reluctant to get involved with the Greek issue up to now, but he will be influenced by his need for an election victory. Agnew has surrendered to the regime." He wonders why General Goodpaster, who is intelligent, did not react to the home-porting issue. Perhaps he cannot act decisively because of his serious heart condition.

I asked him if he plans a trip to Europe. He said that he has not made his plans yet but may travel toward the end of the year, in which case he will let the King know and see if he could be given an audience. Communication between him and the King had been suspended after Cabot Lodge's trip. "I miscalculated," he said. "I thought Cabot would get fully involved after his visit with the King, but it did not happen, for unknown reasons. The general did not want to get involved, but he will ask to see the King now."

October 18, Wednesday
In New York

Ted Bondas telephoned me in the morning from Detroit. He asked if I wanted to meet Senator McGovern and have breakfast with him. He said he would call me this evening at the New York Hilton for a meeting with McGovern in New York.

New Discussions with the State Department in View of Worsening Developments.

Friday, October 20
Meeting with Sisco in Washington and my letter on ideology

I left for Washington and the State Department. Sisco saw me right away. A summary of our conversation is below:

Vidalis: I hope you are pleased to see that I am not struggling for this cause out of personal interest—because I know there is mutual respect—but out of concern for Greece. I mean, I hope you are pleased as a responsible American, because if we stop being interested there will never be a satisfactory alternative solution.

Sisco: I fully agree, general. I am very glad to see you. But can you tell me, please, where you find the time, since you have a full-time, responsible position in your company?

Vidalis: From 6:00 PM until midnight every day, Mr. Secretary. Five to six hours of continuous study and reflection on the Greek issue are adequate. Enthusiasm and faith in our cause, in spite of disappointments, take care of everything.

Sisco: How do you see the situation, general?

Vidalis: It is getting worse in all sectors. Three factors hold the junta in place, or seem to: the army, the business community, and the Americans, especially your military. Recently, all three of these factors made their displeasure known. You are aware of a movement of officers that shook the junta's foundations and cracked its unity a short while ago, and Papadopoulos took no measures against these officers. I suppose you have been informed that these officers probably are expressing their lack of patience with the "parenthesis" being prolonged, even though some of them were active supporters at the beginning.

Sisco: What is your opinion about Angelis, general?

Vidalis: As an officer, he is honest, diligent, and able. Politically, he is a fanatic supporter of the extreme right. As a leader, he is indecisive. He does not have the courage or decisiveness needed in moments when fundamental differences must be expressed to whoever is in power. He can be swayed. It is dangerous to count on him for any length of time. I very much doubt that he has many followers. In general, I would not base any hope for a solution on him.

At this point, Secretary Rogers telephoned, and Sisco left the room to speak with him. Davies came in and asked if I had read the Tasca testimony, the one labeled "secret" that was not secret. I said, "Of course."

Davies: What impressed you?

Vidalis: The fact that a specific alternative solution was mentioned for the first time. Your ambassador, certainly, is not voicing his own opinions.

Davies: Obviously, he is expressing something the U.S. much wants very much. We hope that the attention paid to his testimony in the Greek press did not harm the process of finding an alternative solution.

Vidalis: It did not harm it in the short run. If, however, the discussion drags on without action or positive results, it will harm the process in the long run. What I mean is that any formal statement of a position, such as Tasca's, not made within the framework of a plan for a realistic solution, only clarifies personal preferences.

Davies: When Secretary Rogers said to AHEPA that the Greeks must decide, some in Greece interpreted it as the green light for all factors, including the army, to exert their influence on how the situation develops. How do you interpret it?

Vidalis: My interpretation is: You are washing your hands of the issue for domestic political reasons. No sensible person can interpret the AHEPA speech as a green light for two reasons:

a. The army must have clear and simple proof that you do not want the parenthesis to continue. Every day, the army is fed the slogan that you support the dictatorship. Papadopoulos tells them and Papandreou confirms it.
b. The regime's security network is so tight that it cannot be weakened through such indirect, ambivalent, Delphic statements.

Mr. Secretary, we should have learned after six years that the issue cannot be solved by wishful thinking, expressions of preferences, and vague statements. It will be solved only when the President of the United States decides to solve it and sends you or Mr. Sisco or a personal representative to tell the regime that this is the end. This must be done with a plan and a schedule for specific actions to be taken later. If this does not happen, soon both you and Greece will have to deal with one of several different tragic ways in which the free will of the Greek people is oppressed.

Internationally, the situation is changing. I have written down my views on the very important issue of ideological conflict, which will continue undiminished in this new era of our coexistence with communist powers. Please, if he does not return, give Mr. Sisco this letter.

Davies: Of course, gladly.

At that moment, Sisco came back into the room.

Sisco: Please excuse me a thousand times. Unfortunately, I am not the master of my time.

Davies: We were having a very interesting conversation, and the general has not finished.

Vidalis: The two other factors, the business community, particularly Tom Pappas and Onassis, are expressing their worries and, finally, the Americans are expressing their worries openly and in private. Sulzberger is clear.

Davies: The prime minister's concern is obvious. We have noticed considerable nervousness lately.

Sisco: What do you think the relations now are between the regime and the King?

Vidalis: We must make clear what we mean by the word "regime." Papadopoulos is different from the others. In general, the regime is is following a policy of alternating between threats and caresses. I don't know exactly what they are thinking today. In any case, as I have been saying for some time now, the one clear fact is that they have reached a dead-end. They are not moving forward and they cannot go back, but they have to do something. They alternate between threats and cold acquiescence so, in a moment of crisis, they can choose whichever of these tactics they believe will be most to their advantage. All the other actors in this drama must have a clear and well-defined position so the regime will know exactly what is in store for them when they choose which steps to take.

Davies: How do you interpret the way the Greek press responded to the King's statements from Verona? Our consul in Thessaloniki sent us a cable with assessments published in *Ellinikos Vorras* written by foreign correspondents about how the subject was presented. They believe it was a trial balloon from Athens. The title was, "The King accepts the constitution."

Vidalis: I do not know the exact text nor the reasons behind it. But it is interesting that it was published in *Ellinikos Vorras*, which usually is a pro-government newspaper. At the same time, I know that *Estia* has written about a referendum. Therefore, in this case, too, we have a two-pronged tactic. I will learn more on the subject when I am in Europe.

Sisco: You know our position on the subject, nothing has changed.

Vidalis: I am glad, but prolonging this uncertainty does not help anyone. Of course, my visit here today is not to make suggestions about something immediate. Everything must be postponed for after the elections.

Davies: We will be glad to discuss your views then, after your return, and, of course, we are interested in the views of His Majesty and Mr. Karamanlis.

Vidalis: I want to remind you gentlemen, of what I asked Mr. Sisco last time; to persuade President Nixon, in connection with providing American aid to Greece, to speak of the need to return to democracy. What I meant then and repeat today is that you put too much emphasis on the military aspect. After the elections we will find ourselves in completely new circumstances. Relations with the communist countries have changed, Viet Nam will end, the Middle East has calmed down at the big power level, and emphasis on the military aspect will continue to lessen. In Greece, the six-year emphasis on the military factor has led to today's dead end, polarization, anti-Americanism and, unfortunately for Greece and the future, changes unfavorable for the internal structure of our society. After the elections, the Pentagon must stop having the primary role in Greece. The main effort should be undertaken by the State Department after making a new assessment and then acting decisively, with emphasis on the political dimension. My letter may contribute to this.

Davies: We have asked Tasca to come here for a reevaluation before the holidays.

Sisco: You know, general, how much we value your opinions. Although today's discussion has no immediate practical purpose, it has been very interesting. General, I wish you a good trip to Europe, and, please, let us meet with you again.

Vidalis: Get in touch with me after the elections, when you have time in your schedule, and we will make a useful assessment.

Davies: You know how much we value your opinion.

Vidalis: Some people are recommending to Mr. Karamanlis that he return to Greece. What do you think?

Davies: I have not studied the matter, but it probably would be the loss of an asset, if there were no results.

Vidalis: That is my opinion too. In terms of time, it must be placed within the framework of a general plan to promote a solution. Of course, the American side must be prepared to support it or initiate it.

Sisco-Davies: Let's leave that for our next meeting. Have a good trip.

Below is the letter I had prepared for my meeting with Sisco and gave to Davies.

The Honorable Joseph J. Sisco
Assistant Secretary
Department of State
2201 "C" Street, N. W.
Washington, D.C. 20520
October 19, 1972

Dear Mr. Secretary,

I thought it would be useful to put into writing some of my thoughts about the critical issue of ideology.

The new era of relationship between the U.S and the Communist powers will inevitably lead to a new psychological climate around the world.

So far, Communism has been contained primarily with alliances and military means. In the process, in our exaltation of pragmatism, the Western world has been singularly unmindful of ideology. Anti-communism has been used as an ideological substitute.

During the new era of coexistence with Communism, inevitably the military considerations will have to retreat and the struggle between our world and Communism will be transferred into the ideological field. Communism has been very clear from its conception of "coexistence" that their ideological struggle will continue indefinitely. We have every reason to believe that they will not retreat from this thesis.

Whether Communism will be successful in the long run in their ideological competition with the West depends on many internal and external factors. Primarily, the outcome will he judged by the strength of our societies and our faith in the Western way of life.

Anti-communism, which served the West during the era of military emphasis, is not going to be sufficient to face the agonizing problems of a new environment of coexistence in peace—a peace imposed by technology—where the key issue will be the nature *of peace for the nations and the people around the world. Peace, where dictatorships of the right or left are emerging every day as the pattern of life throughout the world, is not going to be a promising era for mankind.*

Anti-communism in this new era will be negative, defensive, and regressive. The West needs an ideology to fill the vacuum. This ideology might be the strongest weapon of the West as the new era, with all its complications, will unfold.

We do not have to invent a new ideology. We have it. It is Democracy; refined and improved to meet the realities of our technological progress. The question is to revitalize it and use it in a realistic and forceful way.

The area which is ready to be the recipient of this new emphasis in ideology is NATO. President Nixon in April, 1969, stated on the occasion of the 20th anniversary of NATO, the following:

> *NATO means more than arms, troop levels, consultative bodies, treaty commitments. All of these are necessary. But what makes them relevant to the future is what the alliance stands for. To discover what this Western Alliance means today, we have to reach back not across two decades but through the centuries, to the very roots of the Western experience.*
>
> *When we do, we find that we touch a set of elemental ideals, eloquent in their simplicity, majestic in their humanity; ideals of decency and justice, and liberty, and respect for the rights of our fellow men. Simple, yes; and to us, they seem obvious. But our forebears struggled for centuries to win them, and in our own lifetimes we have had to fight to defend them.*
>
> *These ideals are what NATO was created to protect. It is to these, on this proud anniversary, that we are privileged to consecrate the alliance anew. These ideals—and the firmness of our dedication to them—give NATO's concept its nobility and NATO's backbone its steel.*

Time has come or will soon come to translate this eloquent statement of faith into realistic programs of action.

May I suggest that the President of the United States is the only free world leader who can take such an initiative of long-range nature and impact.

May I also suggest as a first program in such a broader strategy the following:

a) *Establishment under the sponsorship of the President of the U.S. of an International Institute for Democratic Studies in Athens, Greece, honoring the birthplace of Democracy.*
b) *Invitation of all democratic nations to contribute to this project and thereby commit themselves to the moral responsibility for the perpetual preservation and further improvement of the democratic process throughout the world.*

This presupposes the existence of a Democratic government in Greece. The offer and the challenge are great for Greece and the world, so this could be used as new leverage with the present regime.

I suggest such an American position will gradually change the overall climate of negative anti-communist attitudes to forceful ideological goals of the societies around the world. It will have immediate impact in Greece since this project will protect Greece at least as much as the defense assistance; will serve to reestablish in the eyes of the Greek people the seriously eroded credibility and faith in this country; and will associate Greece, the birthplace of Democracy, with an international forum for improving Democratic institutions throughout the world

Sincerely yours,

Orestis Vidalis

After the State Department I visited Wiley T. Buchanan, who is close to Nixon and is acquainted with the King. He is angry with McGovern. He saw Tom Pappas yesterday and told him that he is harming the president by supporting the junta and that he heard unfavorable comments about him. He believes that McGovern is rising. He asked me to convey his respects to the King and agreed with me that if Nixon gets reelected, he must solve the problem. I said, "Why do you say, 'if he is reelected?' Do you doubt it?" "I don't doubt it," he answered, "but it is a tough race and is getting tougher every day."

OCTOBER 21, SATURDAY
Greek generals are willing to sign

I called General Frontistis. He asked me to tell Karamanlis that he sees a huge turn against the regime, together with a continuing lack of interest in taking specific action. Admiral Engolfopoulos and Generals Pipilis, Tsolakas, and he, himself, are willing to sign a generals' statement. He sees a big change in General Gikas, who believes in Karamanlis. Kanellopoulos is disappointed by the break up of the Center Party and his inability to bridge their differences.

Meetings in Europe

OCTOBER 24, TUESDAY
Meeting with Kostas Fetsis

Geneva. Brigadier General Kostas Fetsis telephoned in the evening. I went to the hotel. We talked for a while. He belongs to General Tzannetis's organization. They are organized into small teams. Members: Vardoulakis, Peridis,

Thomopoulos, Koumanakos, Engolfopoulos. Fetsis cooperates with Peridis. He has Zisiou with him. Tzannetis asked me if I will agree to cooperate with them; if I can send information to them exclusively and they will do the same with me. I told them of course, gladly.

The situation, as Fetsis described it to me, is as follows:

- The army is disintegrating
- The navy is with us
- The air force is with us but with some reservations
- There are friendly enclaves in the army
- Tzanetis has taken the initiative to convince the politicians to take a united position. His third attempt is close to success. The issue of the King is still delicate; they believe it will be bypassed.

Eleven generals have signed.

I filled him in on my discussion with Frontistis, that Tsolakas, Engolfopoulos, Pipilis, and Frontistis have signed and that Gikas's position has changed.

October 25, Wednesday

I spent the day with Kostas Fetsis. He told me about Cyprus. Grivas went there giving the impression that he would solve the Greek problem through Cyprus. The fanatics, however, got the upper hand and turned him against Makarios. Karousos is appealing to come back. They are asking Grivas for clarifications, which he gives. They consider Grivas's presence to the advantage of Makarios, who can use it as a point of pressure in negotiations. They suggest that I do all I can to bring Makarios and Grivas into communication. I told them that as long as Grivas is against Makarios, there is nothing I can do. Maybe I can influence Makarios, if they could influence Grivas. The King's statements made a good impression in Greece.

General Stamatis Skliros is talking against the Junta. Zagorianakos may be suitable for use. I suggested caution.

I stressed the great need for a plan of action in depth. The generals should speak out the first month, then the politicians, then the intelligentsia, and so on. An atmosphere of pressure should be maintained.

We should not expect any decisive development without pressure from inside the country. He told me about the army wanting Karamanlis to return. The prerequisites of internal mobilization and American assistance must be secured.

October 26, Thursday
Meeting with Aristeides Kalantzakos

Theotokis and I picked up Aristeides Kalantzakos from the airport. The briefing started at Theotokis's house. Speaking for Kanellopoulos, Kalantzakos said that he is worried because the left wants elections now, while the Center Party is divided. Kanellopoulos did not take a stand on the issue of the King and his feelings are against the Karamanlis solution. Mainly, he does not want to recognize the Constitution of 1968, leaving this act of junta legitimization as his legacy.

Kalantzakos then said that some people from ERE and some from the Center Union suggested that a bi-lateral committee be established to stir up the still waters within the framework of parties. He read us a draft for a statute, which has these main points:

- The people are indifferent
- The armed forces are friendly
- The King is necessary
- Karamanlis can be utilized
- Recognition of the 1968 constitution
- The goal is transition to normal life and not returning to the conditions of April 20 and 21.

Spyros Theotokis became furious when he herd that recognition of the 1968 constitution was included and attacked Kalantzakos harshly. Kalantzakos said, "I came to be enlightened and to enlighten. Nothing is irrevocable." I tried to calm the situation so we could reach a conclusion and told Theotokis, "It is important to listen to the opinions of the younger ones who are struggling as much inside the country at least as much as we are on the outside."

I asked Kalantzakos how many are in his group and how long they have been working together. He said there are about 25 at the top with many more at the base. They were formed two years ago. I asked him if they think that Papadopoulos now has difficulties. He nodded yes. I then said, "Is it possible that you are giving him a way out, by which I mean that your thinking is a result of fear caused by the long oppression and is not correct as a starting point for negotiations? Maybe you should have as a starting point a transitional government that will not participate in the elections?" He agreed.

He then told us that Sulzberger met in Tasca's office with Hatzipetros, Tsoumbas, Averof, and Athanasiades and told them they must believe that the only solution is Karamanlis.

October 27, Friday
Further meetings in Lausanne

In the morning I gave them my assessment of the American position. Spyros Theotokis was insulted when I talked about the politicians being inept. We came to the subject of today and I told them that now is a time for re-evaluation. I concluded that we need:

a. A change of attitude, from defensive to offensive
b. Toughening of our negotiating position
c. The people's pot must come to a boil
d. Skillful infiltration of the armed forces

Theotokis asked if promoting the Karamanlis-King solution would result in the King being dethroned. I told them that if the people reach the boiling stage and the armed forces already have been infiltrated, Papadopoulos's position would be so weak that such a development would be unlikely, but could not be excluded. I left in the afternoon. I warmly bid them both goodbye.

In London in the evening. Arnaoutis told me that Brigadier General Ioannides's officers who had turned against Papadopoulos were arrested. There is an orgy of (corruption.) A CIA report paints the situation in very dark colors. He also said that there is a chance that strong action may be taken against some prominent individuals. The navy is in excellent condition. The army is in a horrible state, but this can be reversed if the situation returns to normal. He talked about officers being unhappy because of the steady flow of information about corruption.

October 30, Monday
Meeting with the King

I arrive at Claridge's at 10:30 AM Meeting with the King. I brief the King on the general situation, in particular about) the McGovern-Nixon presidential race. I told him about the Iakovos—Papademas discussion about Makarios. I read my report on the Sisco-Davies discussion. I told him about my meeting with Buchanan and my discussions with Fetsis and Kalantzakos. We postponed a general evaluation for tomorrow. The King told me that last week had had met with the American ambassador, who told him that the American policy toward Greece is being reviewed and that both Tasca and Sisco will be removed because it is thought that they have failed. The ambassador also told the King that he will go to Washington and, when the King asked if he believes he should raise with Nixon the issue of inviting the King to visit U.S., he answered, "Of course, not only do I think so, but it is imperative and I will do it because I know that the administration is completely unhappy with the way things are going in Greece."

October 31, Tuesday

With the King in the morning. I gave him a full review of the last four years and concluded that Papadopoulos is weaker; the King is stronger, and the King's stance must be tougher. The goal cannot be implementation of the 1968 constitution because submission to Papadopoulos means a loss of prestige, with dangerous consequences in the future. The left will be waiting to take revenge for both the Metaxas and Papadopoulos regimes because they believe both regimes were put in power by the right. The King agreed that circumstances have changed, but said that the hard-liners still can create problems. I told him that Papadopoulos is using this as a threat, but when he realizes that Nixon wants an "end," he will then subdue the hard-liners for their own good, so they do not disappear. Unless they want to take on the Americans, in which case the game changes fundamentally.

He then told me that Angelis will visit him on November 13. During our discussion I stressed that he must not compromise with the junta. Two years ago there may have been no other solution, but toughness is needed now. He told me to call him after I meet with Karamanlis. I said good-bye and left.

Later, I had dinner with Plytas. He told me he went to Greece by yacht. He does not expect a dynamic solution. He asked me to write for a newspaper he publishes in Athens, *Nea Demokratia*—a request from his journalists. I told him that I have written enough, but he can get excerpts from the hearings or my BBC interview.

He asked if the newspaper could circulate in the U.S. I said I will raise the issue with the appropriate organization and asked if he has someone on the payroll to gather and process material from the U.S. for the Greek press. He answered, "yes."

I left for the hotel at 10:00 PM. Takis Lambrias gave me the BBC questions, on which I worked until midnight, when I telephoned Takis to read him my answers. He was enthusiastic, making suggestions on only two points.

November 1, Wednesday
BBC interview

I was at the BBC at 9:00 in the morning. We taped the interview. They were enthusiastic.

November 2, Thursday
Meeting with Karamanlis in Paris

Paris. I met with Karamanlis at 12:30 PM. He had invited me for lunch. I explained how I see the situation developing. He was impressed by the sequences. His clearly stated positions are:

a. He considers that a strong transitional government is needed for six months to a year. This government will restore order in the country, will clear the atmosphere, and prepare the political forces to go to the people.
b. He does not believe he should go to Greece because he would be useless there without the necessary conditions having been established.
c. The American review of the situation will be greatly influenced by developments inside Greece. Two years ago he had suggested activities that were harmless but of decisive importance.
d. He will get in touch with two friends in Greece to renew the effort because he believes we now are facing a critical situation.
e. He thinks that participation by the generals is important. He had received a letter from Gikas saying that things have reached an impasse. He will write back to encourage the generals to move ahead.
f. When the issue of the King arose, he had notified the politicians to threaten—by leaking information—that they would transform the regime's referendum into a political referendum against the Junta. They did not do it. But he does not see any threat against the King now.
g. He did not consider the King's Verona statements necessary and believes

   they were weak on the point that the King refers to wise men, etc., and not to the people's elected representatives. (This reminds me of the comment along the same lines that I made to Papagos. His answer was that this way the junta could not react).
h. He believes the Americans can influence events in the following ways:
   1. Psychological preparation as, for example, Sulzberger's articles.
   2. Secret message from Nixon to Papadopoulos that the parenthesis must end.
   3. Use NATO. Military officers first, followed by the Council of NATO Member States, or both at the same time.
   4. He will propose more detailed steps when he is asked to provide them.

We talked until 4:00 PM.

November 3, Friday
Meeting with General Levendis

I arrived in Geneva. Spyros Theotokis was waiting for me. We took a taxi to the house where General Levendis is a guest. Spyros dropped me off and returned an hour later. Levendis gave me a document that he had also given to Karamanlis. He thinks no one is doing anything. When he returns he plans to try to motivate them to action. I suggested that the officers should be concerned with the situation and stressed that he should try to have them sign a declaration. He was impressed by my testimony before Congress and made favorable comments. He made plans to meet Theotokis on Tuesday.

November 4, Saturday
The transcript of my BBC interview

I arrived in Washington. I gave Silva an overview of my impressions. He said that Papadopoulos is ill, that officers in the Army War College [Thessaloniki] and the National Defense School [Athens] are discussing the situation openly. Angelis does not inspire confidence. He will arrange with Sisco for us to meet without the pressure of time and he will let me know. He agrees that it is possible that things might happen now. He considers Nixon's reelection to be a sure thing.

We arrived in Toledo in the evening. Matina was moved when she heard the BBC interview.

November 6, Monday

Among other things, I found at home McGovern's statement on OXI Day.

November 7, Tuesday

Election day. Nixon won by a landslide, but his party did not do well in the Senate and the House. His victory is crushing. McGovern, beaten, talked about how his ideas will prevail in the future.

November 8, Wednesday

I call the office of Senator Pell. He won his state by 55%-45%. I send him a telegram and a letter. I also write a congratulatory letter to Congressman John Brademas.

November 10, Friday

I called Arnaoutis and asked him to relay the following to the King:

- The situation in the Senate has improved and the House remains the same. Nixon beat McGovern but the Democratic Party won over the Republicans.
- Nixon is tightening the government administration and has asked for a reduction in the number of federal employees by 1,500. No decision about Greece should be expected within this year. Initiatives will be postponed for months.
- Information about the junta's deterioration is being confirmed from everywhere. Angelis is considered weak.
- I believe that King should maintain a firm stance when he talks with Angelis. He should stress the future dangers for the nation and the army if this situation continues, and he should call upon the regime to face up to their responsibilities.

When I asked if the King had sent a congratulatory message to Nixon, Arnaoutis answered, "Of course, separately," probably meaning, but without making this clear, that Papadopoulos was going to send one as well.

November 17, Friday

Theotokis called early in the morning. He had received my letter about my upcoming trip to Washington and wanted to give me the latest information from Athens that "my ex-colleagues are moving to oust Papadopoulos, support Angelis, have the King return, and accept the 1968 constitution." I asked how reliable this information is and he replied, "reliable source."

November 18, Saturday
A long and interesting discussion with General Vernon Walters

In Washington, Vernon Walters picked me up with his car and we drove to his house in Fort Meyer, an army base outside the city. We greeted each other very warmly. It has been about 15 years since we both were serving in NATO's Standing Group at the Pentagon in Washington. Today, Walters is Deputy Director of the CIA. I report our discussion below as accurately as possible:

> V.W. I remember, Orestis, the effort you were making at the university then. All of us wondered how you managed with all the work at the Pentagon and the family.

> O.V. It really was a major effort back then. I remember, Dick, in June of 1956 when my service at the Standing Group was coming to an end and I

asked the General Staff for six months of leave without pay. The Greek representative, General Yerogiannopoulos, received a cable from Athens on the last day of September saying that my request had not been approved and I should return home. I told him that I was not going back home, I would finish the university even if they placed me on temporary suspension or I had to resign. My stance bent the General Staff's resistance and they assigned me for three months with the Greek delegation with full pay. That is how I managed to finish my thesis and get my Master's degree.

V.W. A higher power, Orestis, which seems to have the ability to connect individuals with greater purposes, arranges all this. I have been following you during this long period of turbulence and controversy and I must tell you that I and many others admire you because you succeeded in overcoming everything, you came here and adapted perfectly in a new country, in a new job, while your heart remains in Greece.

O.V. Thank you, Dick. It seems that man is armed by the higher power to deal with even the most difficult situations and move ahead.

V.W. Not all men, Orestis. The great will of God is not so generous. How is the family?

He had met Matina but did now know our son, Efthymios. I told him about Matina's superior spirit on December 13, 1967, the offer from Heyden at Anatolia College in Thessaloniki to take Efthymios into boarding school on scholarship, how we left with the help of Webel and Norstad, and of Efthymios's progress in school. When I told him that Efthymios was valedictorian of his class, was accepted at Harvard, Princeton, Cornell, and Williams, and that he is attending Harvard, he stopped the car. We had just entered Fort Meyer. He said, "This is unbelievable. I am very happy today, indeed." He added that he very much wanted to meet Efthymios. We arrived at his house. We were silent for a while in the small living room. He broke the silence.

V.W. Orestis, I am very glad that we are going to talk together today. There are some things I want to tell you and then we can talk and see what we can do. First, however, please tell me how you see developments since you came to the United States.

O.V. Before Tasca left for his posting in Greece I had dinner with him at the Metropolitan Club. It was just the two of us that evening. We spent two hours in polite disagreement. He was telling me that the policy of evolution will pay off and that it is the only credible option, and I was telling him that the policy of pressure and "few allocations with immediate tradeoffs" would bring results. I did not convince him and he did not convince me. As we were leaving he escorted me to the door and said, "General, I want to make clear to you that I consider my mission critical and of utmost importance. If, when the time comes for me to leave Greece, the country is still under a dictatorship, then I will consider both my mission and my career a failure."

"Mr. Ambassador," I replied, "it is with great joy that I hear your statement. I am completely satisfied with your goal, but if you follow the policy you described, you will fail. I hope from the bottom of my heart that I am proven wrong."

That is how Tasca and I parted back then. He did what he said and failed; Papadopoulos received everything from the Nixon administration, kept none of his promises, and led the country, NATO, and himself to a dead-end. During these four years, the Nixon administration fully supported Papadopoulos, sacrificing a great deal, even American prestige and respect in the eyes of the Greek people. During these four years, instead of taking advantage of your support and also keeping his promises, he blackmailed you and extended the police state, believing and announcing all the time that "I hold the Americans in my pocket."

V.W. Orestis, I assume you already know that it is more than obvious that Papadopoulos's position has been seriously eroded. What we are now trying to do is avoid having another Papadopoulos for another four years and we believe, Orestis, that the situation is very delicate. I always believed that Italy is in this mess because they did away with the monarchy. I imagine you know that the president considers the King a great asset. And the position of the King in Europe is very good. He is greatly respected. What stops many of my people is the fear of going from Papadopoulos to a Papandreou situation. Do you know, Orestis, that Papandreou personally attacked me even though I have not been in Greece for 11 years? It is not that any one has—or could have—objections if Papandreou were to come to power later through the democratic process. Right now, though, he disrupts the opposition forces and—in a negative sense—serves as an excuse to prolong the presence of Papadopoulos in the political scene.

O.V. Dick, you mentioned the King. I want to tell you that I had never been to the palace in the past and had no role in politics. But the King took a historic political decision on December 13, 1967. He proved that he is the only Greek leader willing to sacrifice everything to honor his oath as the main protector of the Greek constitution. It is not the King's fault that December 13 did not succeed. It is the fault of all of us who did not implement his political decision on the ground.

The King's decision is of historic value. This is what we must protect; this is what we must use. The most critical phase Dick, will be the epilogue to this drama. If the King is forced to return to Greece with less power, then nothing is gained and no one's interests are served. The country will march toward a worse crisis that will erupt powerfully, with the public on the front line. There is a great deal of pain, a great deal of bitterness, and if the epilogue is not the correct one then there will be a great deal of revenge.

V.W. Orestis, the King cannot return weakened. The King is a huge asset, as I said. Another asset, Orestis, is Karamanlis, and the third asset is you.

O.V. Dick, I thank you for your esteem. I am just trying to offer whatever I can to my country during these strange times. To you I can say that not only the future of Greece is at stake in this situation, but the future of Greek-American relations as well. If we don't lead the way, then chaos will come, from which neither Greece nor the Western world will gain.

V.W. My esteem for you is not new, but now it has expanded to many others as well. But please, Orestis, tell me what do you think we can do now, in this delicate phase.

O.V. Sulzberger's articles were very good. They were thought to have been "dictated."

V.W. That is how it is. I met with Sulzberger a little while ago, before the articles were written. And, of course, you know that he had written articles taking the opposite line some years ago.

O.V. Of course, I know that. Therefore, since these articles were suggested, the momentum must continue. More messages like that should be sent out. Dick, I knew our discussion would reach the point of specific suggestions, so I have prepared a report that includes the main points of initiatives you can take to speed up the developments. First notice the title, "U.S. Initiatives and Actions in the Framework of NATO."

Below is the report I had prepared and given to Walters during our discussion: [Translated back into English from the printed Greek text.]

U.S. Initiatives and Actions within the Framework of NATO

I. Policy

The Alliance is being damaged politically and militarily by the continued military dictatorship in Greece. Every effort must be made for democratic institutions to be reinstated. This policy is in the interest of Greece, NATO, and the western world.

II. Psychological Preparation

1. Unofficial expression of concern based on the above:
   a. Former NATO commanders such as Generals Norstad, Lemnitzer, etc.
   b. Conservative leaders such as senators and congressmen or individuals known in Greece such as Professor Eisenhower, Senator Scott, Representative Ford, and well-known Greek Americans such as Archbishop Iakovos, etc.
2. Special case

Reply from President Nixon to King Constantine's letter congratulating him on his re-election. Message of appreciation for the King's dedication to the Western Alliance (Verona speech) and expression of hope that the King will resume his responsibilities.

III. Secret Preparation

1. NATO Military Leaders
   Expressing the above policy (I) during their discussions with the regime in clear language that cannot be misinterpreted.
2. New Greek ambassador to the U.S.A. (General Sorokos)
   During the formal presentation of credentials he should hear from the president a clear formulation of the same policy and of the need for the regime to begin talks with King Constantine about the resumption of democratic procedures.
3. Inviting King Constantine to meet with the president for secret talks. At the same time the U.S. should communicate with other Greek leaders capable of playing a role during the transition period and seek their advice. Mr. Karamanlis, whose popular support is unquestionable today, must be the first whom the American side should meet.
4. NATO Council
   Secret discussions with the major NATO nations securing their support for the official statement based on the above policy (I) during the meeting of ministers at the council. It probably should include a proposal of a specific program such as the attached.*

   Insistence that the regime must take steps to enable the country to return to democratic procedures.
5. Special Presidential Representative
   A special representative will assist a smooth transition from the present regime to a transitional government, sworn into office by the King, that will lead to elections within a specific time period (for example, one year).

IV. Re-establishing Normal United States Relations with the People of Greece

Visit by the President to Greece when the King will be there.

American initiatives taking place within the NATO framework will have the following advantages:

a. The United States does not appear as interfering in domestic political affairs—although, of course, now you are interfering by providing assistance and support to the dictatorship.
b. Apply pressure to the regime from many directions (military, political, state, and Alliance)
c. Make the Alliance, on which Papadopoulos depends, an institution that condemns him and his position in the army will be shaken.
d. It is within the framework of NATO, then, that a policy decision by President Nixon must be taken. This policy is expressed in paragraph I of this text, without which nothing will happen

V.W. I follow you, Orestis, and agree one hundred percent.

O.V. The initiatives and actions must be separated into open and secret. The open ones are designed to influence nonadministration circles, that is the armed forces in general and the public.

V.W. Of course, there must be more Sulzberger-type actions so one can build on them.

O.V. Please, read the report and we can discuss it afterwards.

He read it through without interruption. When he finished he looked at me and said,

V.W. You are greater than I thought, Orestis. Your concept and tactics are excellent. I will be at the White House on Monday.

We started discussing each point in detail.

V.W. Add Grunter to the generals. Eisenhower is the president of a university and he can address the ideological aspect of having a dictatorship within NATO. For an answer from the President to the King I must hurry, maybe one already has been sent. What, exactly, did the King say in Verona about NATO?

I had the transcript with me and read two lines from it. He asked for it and I gave it to him.

V.W. In discussing the principles of NATO, all our people in Greece can stress democratic values. I am afraid that Goodpaster will be hesitant.

O.V. Why, Dick, when that is the policy and when the quality of the armed forces is at stake?

V.W. I don't know if he will do it. But I much like your idea about the NATO council and the participation of other countries. I agree that the discussions should be positive. If you had said, "Throw Greece out of NATO," I would have said, "No," since that would allow the regime to boost their patriotic pretensions with marches and the like, and we would have no results.

O.V. My suggestion is one that allows President Nixon to do something original. I believe that emphasizing the ideological foundation of the Western world is necessary, and this particular suggestion may help.

V.W. Orestis, I read this with great attention. I fully agree. I will see how the others react.

O.V. The last of my secret recommendations is the solution. The junta abolished its own constitution and immediate elections under any government would be disastrous. The only solution, therefore, is a transitional government appointed by the King to restore normal conditions and lead to elections.

V.W. I fully agree with you, but to get there everything else has to be done first. If not, we will have to see how we will get there.

O.V. Of course, but we will not get there if we don't have the target in mind and if, in the meantime, we in Greece do not destroy what you are trying to do—if, in fact, you are trying to do something—here.

V.W. Orestis, if you mean that our people are helping the regime politically you are not well informed. Tasca already is clear in his reports about the regime eroding. Everybody fears that chaos will break out. It is now obvious that the situation is ripe for a correct, alternative solution. If you were to recommend Papandreou to me as a solution, I would say, "Of course not." The whole solution, as you describe it, is in our thinking. But you have outlined the whole in a pretty attractive way—that is how I see it.

O.V. You mentioned Papandreou. I tell you there is no such danger right now, not even an issue. The more time passes, however, the more chaos and irregular solutions become likely.

V.W. I imagine you agree that there must be an initiative from the army with all this.

O.V. What do you mean? Angelis?

V.W. I don't know if Angelis is strong now, but the way things are in the army, that is, the way the military's faith in Papadopoulos has eroded, it is possible for Angelis to play a role.

O.V. Do you see something immediately pressing, something that requires immediate action?

V.W. Nothing except the erosion of Papadopoulos's position; the military now regard him as a politician.

O.V. Dick, how this drama ends is of great importance. The King must return only as the main factor in movement towards democracy.

V.W. Of course. Submission does not serve anyone.

New Meeting with Sisco
Crucial Letter to Panaghiotis Kanellopoulos and a Report to General Tzannetis

NOVEMBER 29, WEDNESDAY

I left at 8:00 o'clock in the morning for the office. At 9:00 I rented a car for Detroit and at 11:15 I left for Washington with a small delay.

I was at the State Department at 2:20 in the afternoon. I met with Churchill, whom I had not seen for some time. Silva was on leave. Together we went to Sisco's office. He asked Churchill to stay.

J.S. I hope they will leave us alone for a while, general, because I want to hear what you have to say. What is the news from Europe?

O.V. The situation in Greece continues to deteriorate. The officers are beginning to see the dead end. A little at a time they feel the weight on the shoulders, they hear about the corruption, they see the Greek people facing them with hostility, and they worry. At the same time they see that nothing bothers the regime and, in particular, they see that aid from you is continuing unabated.

J.S. Has Papadopoulos increased his influence in the army? Or maybe he has not been able to move even in that direction?

O.V. He now has less support than he had in the beginning. Most army officers are unhappy. Now they see him as one more small-time politician.

J.S. Do you, perhaps, believe that any uprising is imminent? I ask because I do not see one.

O.V. I do not see any imminent uprising, and for an uprising to occur constant pressure is needed from here. You must understand that, with his promise to hold elections, Papadopoulos is buying time, giving the impression that he is moving towards elections to please the Americans, showing that he has the Americans in his pocket, while all the time not making any move whatsoever toward real change. Most of all, he wants to project the idea that the United States supports him. This is the tragedy; he is turning the Greek people against the United States and against NATO.

J.S. I do not know, certainly, how he presents our relations. What I do know is that while we were in Athens, the secretary and I, we made it absolutely clear that this situation cannot go on. And I know the regime was not pleased by our visit.

O.V. I am glad to hear it, but the general impression about the visit is quite the opposite.

J.S. The secretary's statement at the airport should have been correctly interpreted by public opinion and the opposition.

O.V. Public opinion was encouraged only by Tasca's testimony and the Sulzberger articles, and I believe that will be the case with today's *Newsweek.*

J.S. It was excellent, don't you think, general?

O.V. Very interesting, indeed. But it is not enough. For four years all kinds of aid has been given to the junta. For four years most official voices of the administration have talked about the return to democracy. I have put together a report that is very interesting. None of it is my own; it consists entirely of quotations, reports, statements, or your own records. The Greeks know that for four years you have held the hope out to them that you would help democratic developments. Of course, there are those who believe that you never wanted the regime to change. This document reflects your efforts, and your failures. Please, read it. Going back to the immediate past is useful for the future.

J.S. Thank you, I will read it. But tell me now, what do you and the people you talk with in Europe think we can do?

O.V. Two authorities can solve the matter in a very short time. The President of the United States and NATO. I will repeat the views we have discussed in the past, but I believe it useful to keep stressing them. The NATO countries were, up to now, interested in more general issues, but now that Viet Nam is coming to an end and the relations with Russia and China are evening out, they can shift their attention to the Greek problem. The strategic argument shaping relations with a dictatorial regime no longer is so persuasive. NATO can play an important role in Greece's return to the right path. Most of the NATO member countries also are member countries of the EEC and they have expressed their opposition to the Athens regime. Pressure from NATO would be multinational, economic, military, and political. Even more important is that a NATO intervention would affect the officer corps.

There are many ways NATO can act. Instead of being discouraged by the U.S., countries raising their voices against the Greek regime should be encouraged and U.S. representatives should encourage others to join their ranks against the dictatorship. Perhaps the Secretary of State could ask retired NATO officers, such as General Lemnitzer, to influence NATO in the correct direction.

After this effort is under way, pressure the regime during forthcoming NATO Council meetings on the grounds that NATO cannot tolerate the dictatorship any longer. Then comes the president's turn.

The president can, for example, send you as his representative to tell the gentlemen in Athens that the will of NATO cannot be ignored.

J.S. I know your thinking and agree that now the strategic factor is less important and the emphasis is on the political dimension. This is what makes NATO intervention possible now, while it was not possible during the past four years. Your thinking is well grounded. What do you think, George (Churchill)? Do you have any questions for the general?

G.C. No, it is clear.

J.S. Let me think about it.

O.V. And, of course, there must be psychological preparation. Articles like Sulzberger's and *Newsweek*'s are effective, but a sustained barrage is necessary. Maybe Secretary Rogers can whisper into the ear of former NATO commanders to make statements, can whisper to Archbishop Iakovos to make statements. Even more important, in the New Year messages between the King and the President, the President should point out the King's strong support of the Atlantic Alliance.

J.S. How can he say that? Do we have something new?

O.V. We have the speech in Verona.

J.S. (to Churchill) Do we have it?

G.C. Of course.

J.S. Please give it to me.

O.V. I have told you before and I repeat it now. The period for study and coincidental activities is over. Detailed scheduling of specific actions by NATO and the U.S. is needed. Inertia will result in all of us, the so-called conservative opponents of the dictatorship, being neutralized, thereby reinforcing the complete polarization of the two extremes.

J.S. It has always been like that.

O.V. In any case, you have so much experience in being blackmailed by dictators, that you have even paid in blood.

J.S. Yes.

O.V. I know that the administration's new term has not begun and time is needed to take action, but I stress that the initiative should be taken away from the Athens regime and placed in the hands of those who can exert decisive influence, that is, NATO and the U.S.A. Time, consideration, and scheduling are needed. But decisiveness, most of all.

J.S. Let me think about it. Change is necessary, but what change?

O.V. I understand that you have no answer today, but this indecision must not go on. I thank you for your time.

At the end, Sisco asked me what I thought about the home-porting facilities. The question was off the immediate subject of our discussion. I answered that I had expressed my opinion formally and publicly.

O.V. I believe you have placed the cart before the horse. Throughout Greece the demand is for the U.S. to separate itself from the regime, yet your navy wants bases. Had you given precedence to the restoration of democracy, then the bases would be a logical extension of our cooperation. Now the bases are hated because they are considered an extension of the dictatorship.

J.S. You mean you have no objections to the home-porting?

O.V. I told you, as an official or unofficial Greek, I would have no objections if home-porting came after and not before our national problem was solved.

J.S. You see, almost an hour went by without interruptions. Thank you, general.

I left with Churchill and went to his office. He asked me about Sorokos, who is arriving tomorrow. I said, "He must understand from the first minute that he has a big problem, and not be allowed to convince you to stop the pressure. Instead, he must relay your pressure to Athens. If you follow the present tactic of friendly persuasion you will render Sorokos useless. He must understand that he arrived at a time when he will not be taking, but giving."

December 4, Monday

Rallis telephoned from Athens. He asked me to write Kanellopoulos to accept the Karamanlis solution. Everything is ready except for that. I promised. I also asked him to tell Kanellopoulos that we spoke on the phone and I am appealing to him to lead the Karamanlis move.

December 6, Wednesday

I send a letter to Walters. I write to the King and send him a copy of the letter to Walters. Nixon replied to Karamanlis.

December 7, Thursday

I telephone Silva and ask him to send me a copy of the Nixon letter to Karamanlis. He said that a different letter was sent to the King; he will send me both. Pyrros sent me the list of senators after the elections. There is improvement.

December 13, 1972, Wednesday

Anniversary of December 13, 1967. Five years have passed. The King's action is starting to be justified in the hearts of many without being able to explain why it failed.

Marketos telephoned to say he has someone to take the letter to Kanellopoulos. I sent it to New York by registered mail. I never sent a copy of this letter (below) to Karamanlis and, even today, so many years later, I doubt that he ever learned of this.

Toledo, December 13, 1972

Mr. President,

I know of your struggles, difficulties, disappointments, and national concerns.

I am certain you know how much I respect you. Great turmoil has brought us close. Today our common struggle and the same national vision unites us. I believe this bond gives me the right, I mean, generates the obligation, to address this appeal to you.

Why today and what is the appeal?

Crucial and decisive moments are coming. The next few months will determine further developments. Most of the junta's supporters here are turning against it. On the other hand, others who call themselves realists insist that even though the regime is untrustworthy, dishonest, and corrupt, it is still solid because it is based on three factors:

- *The absence of a specific realistic solution that can be cultivated and ripen in the minds of all.*
- *The armed forces, still considered the supporters of the regime.*
- *The apathy of the Greeks, even though it is obvious that the people detest the regime.*

The number of people opposed to the dictatorship is growing.. It's supporters are in a difficult, but not desperate position. Disagreements between the two different factions within the regime will continue until February or March, when the formal policy will be clarified. Unfortunately, experience teaches us that sentiments, ideologies, and even future dangers are ignored when direct pressure that can seriously upset the present, even undesirable, balance, is applied.

The regime knows its internal weaknesses better that anyone, it knows that the armed forces are uneasy, and, primarily, it knows that the American position is being re-evaluated with the possibility of unknown future decisions. In this phase it is the regime that is trying with public shows such the Acropolis Advisory Group, the Five-year Plan, and Papadopoulos's trip to the U.S.A. to maintain the terror by presenting long-term plans—meaning long-term servitude—while apparently enjoying American support. The regime considers that if the low morale of the Greek people continues, thereby blocking any serious psychological initiatives against it from within the country, it will succeed in having the United States postpone any decisions detrimental to it. The absence of any serious activity inside the country strengthens the regime's supporters here and makes it impossible for the Senate to undertake any new initiative helpful to our cause.

Up to now, the regime's public shows have generated laughter and denials. But the serious lack of activity is noted on "the other side of the hill."

The conclusion of my evaluation right now is that a counterattack is needed despite the difficulties. The two first initiatives in my appeal to you would have great effect at this point.

First: Under your and Mr. Mavros's leadership there should be a procla-

mation that the country demands a transitional government under Mr. Karamanlis, the return of the King, and elections within a set time period.

Second: A declaration by the generals, former chiefs of staff of the armed forces, that continuing the present situation places the nation in extreme danger.

The clear positioning of the political, world under its leadership in Greece, and the generals' declaration will become new, valuable factors. And if, with proper preparation, other more general expressions of support for the above-mentioned positions follow, then we will have a completely new climate.

I do not think I need expand on the reasoning for such steps because I am convinced you know the reasons full well. Without hesitation, I suggest that right now there is no other realistic and generally accepted solution, as I believe that there is no individual other than you with the stature needed for this solution and to counterattack.

I hope I have been convincing in this necessarily short space. I hope you will accept my appeal and make the counterattack a reality. The moral victory will be exclusively yours.

While the New Year is beginning, together with the warmest wishes from the three of us to Mrs. Kanellopoulos and yourself—Efthymios is quite proud when he hears your name mentioned at Harvard—I wish that you will overcome the difficulties and lead the country to where your Greek soul wishes it to be.

Yours,

Orestis Vidalis

December 21, Thursday

Silva sent me copies of the Nixon telegrams to the King and Karamanlis. Both are irrelevant to the situation. He thanks them both for their congratulations on his reelection and adds that he "looks forward to cooperating with all nations for the enforcement of world peace."

December 31, Sunday

1972 is over. A year of struggle, hard work, successes, and many disappointments.

The main successes are:

- Keeping the issue alive in the U.S.
- Maintaining satisfactory communications with the opposition in Greece.

- Because of the reaction of the Greek people and outside pressure, the regime is starting to show signs of fatigue, but no dramatic developments can be foreseen yet.

The disappointments are:

- The need to cultivate a climate of resistance among officers on active duty has not been understood even by the politicians.
- With few exceptions, there is no obvious resistance against the dictatorship from most of the intellectual world.
- The need for politicians of all political shades to come together and draw up a common plan to damage the dictatorship has not been understood.
- Neither the King's nor Karamanlis's value has been put to proper use.
- The politicians have made no serious attempt to influence the Western world, especially the U.S., against the dictatorship.
- Most Greek-Americans either support the regime or are indifferent.

In spite of all this, our campaign against the junta will continue unabated, with much greater chances for success now than ever before in the past.

My personal contribution will continue from a position of strength and stability in Owens Corning, which has proven to be a wonderful base. With health, therefore, and perseverance, God willing, 1973 will be happier.

CHAPTER 6

1973

1973—A New Year Dawns

JANUARY 7, SUNDAY

Allamanis discovered that Nixon did not receive Pattakos, even though he met with the Turkish Defense Minister and the former Foreign Minister of the Philippines. Pattakos did see Agnew, who however, did not go to the embassy.

I spoke with Dick Walters and thanked him because Nixon did not meet with Pattakos. I also told him about the affair in London where Laurence Olivier, in the presence of the Queen and with funerary music in the background, read a letter from a political prisoner in Greece. The British and Greek press made a major issue of this.

JANUARY 8, MONDAY

I called Papademas, who told me how things were in Washington. He discovered that under American pressure the regime will proceed with a veneer of democratic measures, such as elections for lower level institutions, etc. He also found out that they have written off the King.

JANUARY 9, TUESDAY
Regular communication with George Rallis begins

Rallis called me to say that the *Vradini* newspaper will publish a very strong article of his and would I please see that it gets distributed.

JANUARY 14, SUNDAY

I spoke with Silva on the telephone. He has learned from unconfirmed sources that Papadopoulos is thinking of declining American aid. Silva's explanation is that Papadopoulos wants to stir up a patriotic storm to cover the extremely difficult position he is in. I will talk to Silva tomorrow to confirm this report.

January 16, Tuesday

Marketos called. The Junta announced that it has no need for American aid. We will meet Thursday evening.

January 17, Wednesday
in New York

I was surprised and saddened to read in today's *National Herald* the telegraph from N. Angelis in Athens referring to the *Apoyevmatini* newspaper, which reports that Archibishop Iakovos made laudatory remarks at a dinner held by Greek-Americans in honor of Pattakos.

During dessert, Archibishop Iakovos spoke warmly, extolling the patriotism of Mr. Pattakos and asking him to convey to the Greek people, the government, and the prime minister the heartfelt greetings and admiration with which the Greek-American community follows the work being carried out in Greece.

I wrote the following brief note to the Archbishop.

Your Reverence,

How is it possible for the insane people in Athens not to become insolent when they hear about the "admiration with which the Greek-American community follows the work being carried out in Greece." I am wondering.

Yours,

Orestis Vidalis

January 19, Friday

Had lunch with Graham Hovey of the New York Times. An article of his will appear on Monday. He also told me that he will write an editorial on Greece within the next two or three weeks.

January 21, Sunday

Spyros Theotokis called. He was in London and our people there are terrified by the aid issue. They think, as does the King, that it indicates collusion by Nixon. Tomorrow he will go to Rome. I told him that I do not see collusion and that the King needs to be tougher.

January 24, Wednesday

Received letter from Archbishop Iakovos on 19.1.73 in response to my letter of 17.1.73.

Dear Mr. Vidalis,

The comments about "admiration" are indeed to be admired. If one of those present was questioned maybe they would provide you with more accurate information.

With much love
The Archbishop

January 25, Thursday

Spoke with Couloumbis. He was pleased with the Allamanis—Saunders meeting where he raised the idea that Kissinger visit Karamanlis and the King. Saunders spoke of two problems. The Nixon problem of not intervening in a foreign country's internal affairs, and a strategic problem. Couloumbis will send me a summary of the meeting.

I telephoned Allamanis. He agrees with me about what has to be done.

I phoned Sismanidis to say that I would accept to meet with Andreas Papandreou anywhere away from his headquarters at any time, though preferably over a weekend.

January 30, Tuesday
First contact with the Peridis connection

Today I read in the Athenian press that the new Greek Communist Party of the interior [not oriented toward Moscow] accepts the King and will not raise the issue of pulling Greece out of NATO. If this is accurate, the people who hold this position not only are fervent supporters of democracy, but realists as well. Late last night Makreas, who introduced himself as a pilot with Olympic Airways, called from Kansas City. He wants to meet with me. I told him to come to Detroit. He'll call on Wednesday.

Petros Koumandouras called in the evening to say that the Washington group is going ahead this time and the first meeting will be on February 24 at the Cosmos Club. Couloumbis, Nicolopoulos, Sismanidis and Dimopoulos had gathered at his place and decided to organize a dinner at the Cosmos Club on March 24 at which I am to be the keynote speaker. I told him that this pleased me very much and asked which language would be more appropriate. He said that only English can be effective.

I asked him to consider expanding into Chicago.

January 31, Wednesday

I wrote to Saunders and thanked him for meeting with Allamanis and Couloumbis. I also received the summary from Couloumbis about the meeting:

Dear General, *January 27, 1973*

A few words to describe the meeting Allamanis and I had with Mr. Kissinger's aide, Mr. Al Saunders.

Mr. Allamanis developed his historical views and I translated. His main points concerning the present situation were:

1. *Papadopoulos has lost control of the junta.*
2. *The United States has alienated the Greek people by embracing the regime (i.e., visits by Agnew, Laird, Rogers, Stans).*
3. *The present unstable situation can slip beyond the control of the Western alliance.*
4. *Government: The United States must push for the Karamanlis "solution." First: At least 80% of the population will support Karamanlis. Second: He is trusted by 90% of the officers on active duty and by all of the security forces. Third: Karamanlis will maintain a pro-Western and pro-NATO policy because this is of essential interest for the Greek people.*
5. *The White House must study the Greek issue and not allow the Greek folder to gather dust.*
6. *In general, it would be useful if the United States would show that it does not support the Greek regime. Specifically, Mr. Allamanis proposed that Kissinger meet with either the King or Karamanlis.*

The meeting lasted for an hour and a quarter. Saunders's responses can be summarized as follows:

1. *I concur with your analysis of the situation.*
2. *We are constantly studying the Greek issue because we have two problems about it.*
   a) *The ability of the United States to intervene in Greece (and elsewhere) has been seriously curtailed in comparison with the past. Peoples, especially friendly peoples, must shape their political futures on their own.*
   b) *The United States has vital interests in Greece and the eastern Mediterranean. It must, therefore, maintain relations with the Greek government of the day, regardless of its political hue. How effective will the measures Mr. Allamanis proposes be? What dangers do they hold? The United States does not support the present regime any more or less than yesterday's or tomorrow's.*

Mr. Allamanis told him that Papadopoulos cannot turn toward Moscow because Greek officers, who are 100% pro-Western, would "virtually arrest him."

Saunders impressed me. He was polite and he liked to talk, unlike so many Americans who only listen. We left after Allamanis requested that his greetings be conveyed to Nixon and Kissinger.

Efforts to Establish Formal Communication between AHEPA and the King

FEBRUARY 3, SATURDAY

Krasas telephoned to say that Spirtos will go to Greece to give Papadopoulos a commemorative medal from AHEPA. He had found out that this was an old decision. I told him that I had written to Spirtos that we should meet. Krasas talked with Spirtos and found him sympathetic to our cause but said that there was nothing he could do. I had a long conversation with Krasas. I told him that sporadic actions do not bring results. "Struggle" is required. The Junta will remain oblivious unless pressure from Greece-Washington-Europe is brought to bear. Later I called Krasas and told him to phone Spirtos and tell him that if he wanted at least to appear neutral he should give something similar to the King.

Colonel George Konteas (Greek Air Force, ret., initial code name: Makreas) arrived at Detroit airport at 3:00 in the afternoon. He does not know a great deal and is desperately pessimistic. He believes that no one is doing anything. We discussed:

a. The need for exchanging information.
b. An article being written about the Spirtos visit for the Greek-Americans.
c. They need to realize that a "counterattack" is necessary.
d. The navy is in an excellent position but they will not join unless progress with the organization can be guaranteed.

FEBRUARY 4, SUNDAY

Konteas left with Matina for Detroit at 10:00 in the morning. He was pretty upset but seemed to have taken heart. We will see what he can do.

At 12:30 PM we had the three-way conference call, Krasas-Spirtos-Vidalis. After the introduction we told Spirtos that he should go to Rome, after giving AHEPA's medal to the Greeks, to give the same medal to the King. Spirtos said that he would do so. He said that he found the idea excellent but he did not have an extra medal. Krasas undertook to find one. I stressed the damage done to Greece and America by the dictatorship continuing in power. We agreed to meet in Youngstown, Ohio. Krasas will see him in New York on Thursday. I then called Krasas and advised him not to tell anyone. He said that he had told Nicolopoulos.

He undertook to call Arnaoutis to make sure that the King would be in Rome on Thursday after next and would telephone me with the answer. I hope we can make this meeting happen. It would be a step forward.

February 5, Monday

I wrote to the King about Spirtos. Doctor Mike Spirtos is now Supreme President of AHEPA and is going to Greece in that capacity.

Krasas called. He had spoken with Arnaoutis, who was very pleased. Arnaoutis will relay the conversation to the King who, however, is leaving for Germany. We agreed that on Thursday Krasas should submit to Spirtos a draft telegram for Spirtos to send to the King. Krasas will telephone Arnaoutis on Thursday.

Krasas called again in the evening. He said that after many mishaps the medal will be ready at noon on Thursday and delivered to Spirtos at the airport. He also said that he had spoken with Mitsotakis about opening an office in Washington. I gave him the text for the telegram.

Later in the evening Petris called. He said that he had received my letter and had spoken with Spirtos, who immediately said that I had called him and that we would meet in Youngstown on the 24th. Spirtos said that he would be giving the medal to the people of Greece. That he did not mention the visit to the King could simply be caution or it could signify a retreat on his part. Petris also said that he would be coming to Toledo between the 20th and the 22nd.

February 6, Tuesday
We discover the resistance icon of the Virgin Mary

I called Krasas and told him of the Petris—Spirtos discussion and expressed my concerns. At first he said he would call Spirtos to tell him the medal would be ready but then he changed his mind and asked me to do it, giving me all the necessary phone numbers. In the afternoon I phoned Spirtos. I told him that the medal would be ready and Krasas would give it to him at the airport. "Excellent. I am facing tremendous resistance but I will go. I will tell the politicians in Athens that I will go to Rome." We will meet in Youngstown.

Received a letter from Zisiou in the evening in which he railed against the big shots in Athens and the Americans. He sent a note based on which we opened the icon of the Virgin we had received long ago. Inside was another image dedicated to me; on the one side it had the inscription: "The free besieged in the prisons and army camps of Greece to the bravest fighter in the struggle to render the Greeks responsible in their own house, General Orestis Vidalis. He who thinks freely, thinks well. . . ." On the other side was the "oath of the resistance."

At 9:15 PM I called Arnaoutis to ask him to tell the King that I suggest that he be in Rome on Thursday, February 15, in order to meet with Spirtos, who was facing nearly intolerable pressure. Arnaoutis said that the King was committed to an official invitation to Germany and would then go to Denmark.

February 7, Wednesday

Arnaoutis phoned. He had spoken with the King, who said he could see Spirtos in Saint Moritz, where he will be a guest of the Shah.

February 8, Thursday

Krasas called in the evening. Spirtos signed the telegram to the King. He was very pleased. The telegram is below:

> To his Royal Highness
> King of the Hellenes
> Constantine
> 13 Via Porta Latina
> Rome—Italy February 7, 1973
>
> *It is our pleasure and honor to inform his Highness that AHEPA, on the occasion of the fiftieth anniversary of its founding, wishes to express its fraternal solidarity with all the Greek people by bestowing a special gold medal on his Highness. Consequently, we beg the staff of his Royal Highness to inform us of the proper arrangements.*
>
> *Doctor Michael Spirtos*
> *Supreme President*

Nicolopoulos went to the Mint in Philadelphia to pick up the medal. The Mint had been advised by people unknown to us not to give us the medal, but after some delay they were instructed to do so. Spirtos said the pressures were intolerable.

February 9, Friday

I leave for Washington, where I was met by Krasas. We went to the Cosmos Club and then to his hotel, where we had dinner and talked. He had spoken with Karamanlis on the telephone about Spirtos. I do not like it. His initiatives tend to the spectacular, so I explained my "low profile" philosophy.

February 10, Saturday
Meeting with Vernon (Dick) Walters

Dick Walters picked me up from the Cosmos Club at 10:00 in the morning and we drove to his house. On the way, he spoke about Cyprus and how he supports Makarios and disagrees with Grivas. Makarios, he believes, is supported by the people.

The main points of our conversation at the house were:

> V.W.: The situation has deteriorated but is not yet past the point of no return. Direct intervention by us applying spectacular pressure would be counterproductive because it would drive the Greeks to a patriotic outburst against us.
>
> O.V.: Yes, but no progress is being made.
>
> V.W.: But there is progress. Papadopoulos has not managed to create a party or organization of his own. No dictator has survived without support from an organization. His personal dominance will fall apart.
>
> O.V.: Yes, but then everything will fall apart with him. There is a huge amount of anti-American hatred.
>
> V.W.: I don't agree. You must know that we are constantly applying pressure. The vice president, Rogers, and everyone are applying relentless pressure.
>
> O.V.: Yes, but Athens ignores it because the people are silenced by the catchphrase that you support the regime.
>
> V.W.: That is ridiculous. Why would we support a personal regime that will fall? But we cannot just go in and throw them out.
>
> O.V.: Then you must make your displeasure known through other means. That is what I came to tell you. You could ask Professor Eisenhower or General Norstad or someone else to lead a private campaign to restore democracy in Greece.
>
> V.W.: That is good, worth discussing. I will look into it.
>
> O.V.: In addition, if AHEPA were to invite the King to come here he should meet with President Nixon. That would be an indirect message.
>
> V.W.: That, also, is a good idea. I will look into it.
>
> O.V.: Third, you could congratulate AHEPA's president, who is going to visit both Greece and the King. AHEPA is a critical factor.

I showed him the icon. He was dumbfounded. I told him that if there is no progress we will have a civil war. He answered, "I don't think so." He said he would look into my three suggestions and get back to me.

FEBRUARY 12, MONDAY

I called Arnaoutis and told him to tell the King that I had seen Dick Walters, who considers AHEPA important.

FEBRUARY 17, SATURDAY
Student unrest in Athens

I called Arnaoutis in the evening. He told me that Spirtos's visit went very well. Apparently he told the King that it was the best part of his entire trip. He also said that Tasca told him that no one supports the regime. The King characterized Spirtos as a dynamic person and told him that if he needed anything he should get in touch with me.

Arnaoutis also said that the student unrest was growing and that some generals, including Tzannetis and Vardoulakis, made statements to the effect that military service is an honor and not a punishment.

Close Cooperation Begins with Konstantinos Mitsotakis—AHEPA Announcement of the Visit with the King

FEBRUARY 19, MONDAY
Communication with Konstantinos Mitsotakis

Return to Toledo. Letter from Mitsotakis, saying that he will come to the U.S. The letter is below:

> Paris, February 15, 1973
>
> *Dear Orestis,*
>
> *Stelios Allamanis gave me your news and a copy of your detailed open letter of January 13 about our national problem. I fully agree with your assessments and conclusions, unfortunately I must tell you at the start that the domestic front is not helping and may not help until this is over. Despite all of our desperate efforts, they remain bogged down, unable to overcome their personal weaknesses and petty partisan concerns. Stelios's trip to Athens has sparked off a new effort, but, again, I am doubtful about the results.*
>
> *On the other hand, student unrest is spreading—everyone is supportive, there is even some coordination on this issue—and the economic situation is deteriorating rapidly. Inflation is soaring and will get worse with the recent devaluation of the drachma against the dollar.*
>
> *Judging from the information reaching us, there is little to hope for from the American side and our position here in Europe seems to be worsening as*

well. At least our position is strong in Germany after Willy Brandt's election and in the Common Market after the changes at the Commission. Personally, I am convinced that internationally and domestically, conditions are favorable for our forces to mobilize, if this is well prepared and well organized. The junta, basically, is rotten and discredited even among the military corps. Karamanlis is well and is operating systematically and consistently. His popular support is higher than ever, though opposition from politicians—especially Kanellopoulos—is also more intense and outspoken than ever. Karamanlis is not considering now, nor has he ever considered, going to the United States, despite the invitations he has received, and I think that he is correct in this, given the present situation. I, on the other hand, have decided on my own initiative to come in early March for three weeks. The purpose of my trip is to convey views, investigate intentions, and restore direct contact with our friends struggling there. I expect to arrive in New York between March 6 and 8. I have not made a detailed schedule, though I will spend several days in Washington. Before I leave I will communicate our friends here and in Athens, with whom I am always in close contact.

Please write me your views on all the above. You may inform our friends there about my trip, though I will write to as many as I can myself. I will ask everyone for advice and assistance so I will be able to do as much as possible.

One more thing. After Granitsas's trip I have spoken on the telephone with Krasas, who spoke warmly and at length about you, saying that he is working with you. I remember him from long ago but haven't heard anything about him for the last six years. Please let me know in confidence what you think about him.

With friendly regards.

Yours,

K. Mitsotakis

P.S. Please respond quickly.

February 20, Tuesday

Konteas called, from Canada. He met with Peridis for an hour and told me the following news:

They are sending me a report on the army (they will send the same report to the King and to Karamanlis), they are not ready to link up with the navy movement, it is difficult to open more fronts and they do not think the navy is ready. They don't think that Lambrakis will raise the issue of the monarchy; the chiefs are scared and hesitant. The four-star generals, to be followed by others, will continue to speak out in order to keep the student unrest from being exploited. I am advised to be careful with Sorokos, what I say on the telephone, and the tone of my letters because they are read by others as well. They took no action against Spirtos because he did not make any statements. I asked him if he knew that Spirtos had visited the King and he did not. I told him to tell them and that I would meet him on Saturday.

Sir Hugh Greene called from New York. We discussed matters in general and agreed that we would talk again before he left for Europe.

I wrote the following letter to Mitsotakis:

Dear Kosta,

Thank you for your letter.

It will be a great pleasure to see you and talk with you.

I will arrange for you to meet with Sisco between March 12 and 17. As for the rest, we'll play it by ear.

Krasas helped me immeasurably with Spirtos. His sudden appearance, however, and the ease with which he moves raise doubts and discomfort.

I am proceeding with him cautiously and without haste, accepting his offers of assistance without commitment until I can ensure that he works harmoniously with everyone and, of course, until the doubts are dispelled. I am optimistic that he will prove to be a valuable colleague, but be careful in the meantime. The struggle is unconventional, requiring patience, wisdom, and careful handling to promote unity.

In the next few days I will meet with Spirtos in Ohio—AHEPA's president—who returned charmed from his meeting with the King. He may prove to be decisively useful.

Everything, however, depends on activity in Greece. Without disagreeing with your pessimistic view, I am doing everything I can to make people there aware that they should have no illusions about salvation coming from outside.

These words were hurried to get the letter off to you. Perhaps it would be a good idea for you to begin your visit here in Toledo. It would give us great pleasure if you would be our guest and we could discuss the whole situation at leisure. Consider arriving here on Saturday, March 10, and you could leave for Washington on Sunday.

My greetings to Mrs. Mitsotakis.

Friendly regards,

Orestis Vidalis

I also wrote to the King and sent a few words to Peridis.

February 21, Wednesday

I called Silva and told him about Spirtos meeting the King. He told me that Spirtos will go to Washington on March 31. I asked him to request a meeting from Sisco for Mitsotakis during the second week of March. He will call me.

February 24, Saturday
First meeting with Dr. Spirtos

We left in the morning for Youngstown, Ohio. Matina drove. Krasas expounded his views during the drive.

I clarified my positions:

1. There is no division into phases. Short-term goals (Nixon) coexist with long-term ones (resistance in Greece and the Greek-Americans.) I do not allow myself to set time limits. It is a difficult and unconventional struggle.
2. The struggle must be pursued patiently and should be led by Greek-Americans—in particular elected politicians—and possibly AHEPA.
3. The effort to form a committee of Americans will continue.
4. Kanellopoulos and Mavros represent and express the political world in Greece and their contribution is essential. For Karamanlis to become active there must be broad-based resistance in Greece and calls for him to step in as a national solution.
5. I chose this path; it was not imposed on me. I am not interested in any political aspect, just in the national problem. That is what I have been doing for the past four and a half years. There is one common goal for which we can all work together.
6. Personal contact will continue. Some things will remain secret.

We arrived at Youngstown, and I called Spirtos. He was holding a news conference and would then come by our room. We went down for lunch and returned to the room where Spirtos met us a short while later.

I asked him how the trip had gone.He began by saying that he arrived in Athens on Friday. They were met by Papaloukas. The next day he saw Pattakos, who told him, "democracy has major flaws, it distracts the people and is not appropriate for Greece. Dictatorship is a living condition."

With Papadopoulos he discussed children's holiday camps and the draft as it applied to Greek-Americans. Papadopoulos considered their greatest problem to be the King. The regime tried to learn if he would visit the King. Spirtos also met with Tasca, the American ambassador, who already knew that he would visit the King.

In Cyprus, Makarios impressed him. In Istanbul he asked the Turkish governor to allow Iakovos to visit the patriarchate and to permit repairs to its facilities. On both subjects the governor seemed positive.

Spirtos told us that he had had a half-hour private conversation with the King, who is interested in visiting the U.S.A. He found the King mature. Spirtos's entourage was enthusiastic about the King, with whom they had dinner.

Spirtos told me that Manesiotis and William P. Tsaffaras did not agree with the visit. "Now that it has taken place," I asked, "do you believe that it was the right thing to do?" "Certainly," he answered. "I wanted to do it for a long time but it had not occurred to us. I am pleased now. In Greece the people are against the regime, which does not want to budge."

Then, for an hour, I explained the situation to him. I told him that we are faced with new conditions, that the policy of friendly persuasion has failed, that anti-Americanism is rising, that our society has lost cohesion, and that the people are fed up.

"Few people take historic initiatives. People do not often have the chance to work on something of historic importance. Right now, you have that chance. When it is lost, you will lose your leadership advantage," I emphasized.

The conversation brought out national feelings. I told him that people cannot live without institutions and he replied, "Tasca tells me the same thing."

I then asked him if he was prepared to undertake initiatives. If so, then he should ask to see President Nixon to tell him that the Greeks refuse to accept the dictatorship, that anti-Americanism is rising steadily, and that AHEPA will invite the King to visit the United States and Nixon should see him. "What does inviting the King entail? Are there financial and other obligations?" "No, no obligations, financial or otherwise. It simply means organizing six or seven opportunities for the King to meet with the community at large venues, at AHEPA gatherings, churches, etc. A meeting with President Nixon is a necessary prerequisite."

He took notes and said that he would call Silva at home to discuss with him what needs to be done to request a meeting with the president.

I told him that, if he thought it would be useful, I would address a closed meeting of the Supreme Lodge. He answered that it might be useful, but first he has to discuss with them the subject of the King's visit and move that forward. I reiterated that, if and when my presence would be useful, I would be happy to do it.

Finally, I said that, in order to publicize his visit with the King, he should sign a press release I had prepared. He read it, corrected some points that were too harsh, and agreed for it to be released. I gave him my phone numbers and he left, escorted by Krasas. When Krasas returned, he said, "that was like an electric shock for Spirtos, but you ought to take something to calm you down sometimes because that was very intense."

We drove back to Toledo in the evening.

February 25, Sunday

Yesterday, the *New York Times* published the editorial about the students that Hovey and I had discussed a few days earlier. The main points of the article follow:

> Strikes and demonstrations by thousands of university students have generated one of the most serious challenges to Greece's military dictatorship since it overthrew the legal government nearly six years ago. Democratic political leaders and professors have given outspoken support to student demands for restoration of academic freedom and university autonomy and for a stronger student voice in academic policy.
>
> Retired officers of high rank, who object to making military service a punishment rather than a duty, have joined the students in protesting a decree that empowers the government to revoke student draft deferment even for minor offenses. This resentment against making the Army a "jail," as a group of retired generals put it, is believed to be shared by many officers on active duty. . . .
>
> It is tragic in this evolving situation that many Greeks, including the officer corps, believe that the United States wants to keep Colonel Papadopoulos in power. This belief has been strongly fortified by the White House decision to allow the Navy to establish a home-port in Athens.
>
> The Nixon Administration is said to be having second thoughts about its policy toward Greece and it is reported that the National Security Council may review it. Such a re-examination cannot come too soon for the sake of long-run Greek-American relations as well as for the best interests of each country.

February 26, Monday

I called Couloumbis and Granitsas and urged them to support Spirtos. I also wrote Karamanlis.

February 27, Tuesday
AHEPA Press release

I called Andrew Brocles to send a letter to Spirtos. Marketos published the full text of Spirtos's press release today: [Translated back into English from the printed Greek text.]

1922-1972, 50th Aniversary

ORDER OF AHEPA
THE AMERICAN HELLENIC EDUCATIONAL PROGRESSIVE ASSOCIATION
Founded July 26, 1922 in Atlanta, Georgia

Youngstown, Ohio, February 24, 1973
Press Release:

Announcement by Dr. Michael Spirtos
Supreme President

The Supreme President of AHEPA has just returned from a trip to Europe, including visits to Athens, Nicosia, the Ecumenical Patriarchate in Constantinople, and King Constantine II of All Greeks.

At this point I would like to confirm that AHEPA is a non-political and non-partisan brotherhood, which expresses the ideals of the community of Americans of Greek descent.

This community, of which the social spirit has recently been praised by President Nixon himself, has steadily supported the stated policy of the United States government in the field of international relations.

One stated policy of particular interest to all Americans of Greek descent is the wish of the United States to see Greece return to democratic rule as soon as possible.

The present Greek government also has expressed its desire for the reestablishment of democracy in Greece both through public statements and privately to Ambassador Henry Tasca.

For all the above reasons, I can only express my disappointment that I have not seen any real movement towards constitutional rule during the current year. I consider it my duty, as an American and as a member of AHEPA, to speak in support of the democratic ideal and call upon all fellow Greeks in positions of leadership, to rise to the level of political maturity demanded by sacred Greek tradition concerning our participation in the community.

Senator Nicholas Petris (CA) sent this telegram to Dr. Spirtos:

Congratulations on your decision to include in your trip a visit to King Constantine and your courageous and eloquent statement to the *Washington Post* on the need to publicly support democratic principles. Rest assured of my full support and my will to act similarly.

Tomorrow the *National Herald* will publish a photograph of the President of AHEPA with the King.

March 5, Monday

Discussions with the *National Herald* and the press in Athens over AHEPA's invitation to the King.

AHEPA announced that they have not invited the King "officially."

March 6, Tuesday
Communication with George Rallis

George Rallis called from Athens to say that four tanks are guarding the Medical School.

Krasas called to say that two Greek-American congressmen sent a telegram to Spirtos.

I read in the *Athènes Presse Libre* (owned by the distinguished journalist Richard Someritis) that two students, Maria Vasilopoulou and M. Gratzias, died of their wounds. No word of it from Athens.

Couloumbis told me that he sees concern within the junta over Spirtos.

I received a copy of a letter sent by Nikos Stavrou to Secretary of State Rogers. It was dated February 28 and co-signed by sixteen university professors.

March 8, Thursday

I received a long letter from Arnaoutis. Lower ranking officers are turning against Papadopoulos. The regime is facing a dead-end and Papadopoulos will do something to distract public opinion. The CIA people know what is going on and are very active in the army, but they cannot find a leader. He mentioned the Spirtos meeting with the King. Pattakos wrote a memo to Papadopoulos telling him that things are not going well.

March 9, Friday
The Mitsotakis couple in our home in Toledo

The Mitsotakis couple arrived at our house at 5:05 P.M.

Mitsotakis and I were left alone in my study. I told him that we should discuss Greece and Europe tonight and leave America for tomorrow. I said that he should lead the discussion of the first two and I would lead the discussion about the U.S.

> K.M.: The situation in Greece, after the student unrest and the bad economic developments, is unfavorable for Papadopoulos. People are beginning to criticize the regime openly. Kanellopoulos, primarily, but also Mavros, have blocked the Karamanlis solution.

> Europe, except for the Common Market, has come to terms with the regime and feels that Karamanlis now wants an elected rather than a transitional government.

When he finished, I showed him my letter to Kanellopoulos, and told him that I had appealed to everyone to promote a solution based on Karamanlis and the King.

> O.V.: Unfortunately, Kostas, we have two supreme leaders. This is our fate. Karamanlis must realize that we have not reached the point of elections, where we would have a political solution. We are still in a national crisis that he is not helping us overcome. If he does not help, he is slowing things down. We do not know if we ever will reach a solution and, if we do, whether or not his name will still have any appeal among the young.
>
> K.M.: Orestis, we must be realistic. We cannot get Karamanlis to move.
>
> O.V.: Then he should leave us alone and not complain. You must understand and tell him on my behalf that, while up to now I did not think that he should speak out, now the time has come for him to help shape the psychological climate in the armed forces, the people, and the young. Unless he is in secret negotiations with Papadopoulos about which I don't know.
>
> C.M.: The Americans must help him, Orestis.
>
> O.V.: Why should the Americans help him, when he has done nothing? The other day Wayne Hays asked if Karamanlis were still interested. Tell him that he must make an announcement, that after six years the nation is in extreme crisis, with students "punished" with the draft, the Church under assault from within and without, the government not daring to keep the promises it made regarding its own constitution. He should propose the immediate restoration of the King and the formation of a national salvation government composed of people the nation—the armed forces and the people—can trust to take us back to normal.
>
> K.M.: That is what I came for. I will see him and tell him.

March 10, Saturday

In the morning we continued talking. I described the past and present in America. I spoke to him about Archbishop Iakovos, about Sorokos, Marketos, and the *National Herald*. He did not believe that anyone would be interested in buying the *National Herald*.

I told him at length about Sorokos. I explained that my letters to Sorokos were, essentially, directed to the regime. I said that I don't consider this correspondence to be a discussion between two people but, instead, a way of challenging arguments that are, basically, the junta's positions. I told him that Sisco will not be able to see him and that he will meet with Davies instead. When he asked if it would be advisable to see Lagoudakis or Couloumbis, I said, "Of course." I also recommended that he speak with as many Greek-American congressmen, including Republicans, as possible.

March 12, Monday

I called Mitsotakis. He had met with Silva, who told him it would be extremely good if AHEPA invited the King and his family to visit America and be received at the White House. Spirtos should not ask permission, but should simply inform the administration that he had invited the King. This is precisely the scenario we have in mind.

Mitsotakis said he wants to meet before he leaves, and I told him I would go to New York. Marketos said that Spirtos sent a letter of thanks to Papadopoulos, expressing his wish or hope that he will lead the country to democracy.

March 13, Tuesday

I called Spirtos. He will wait until the 30th to deal with the Supreme Lodge. He will hold a closed session in order to be completely frank with them. He has received 30 letters and telegrams. Mantzoros's article, published in Chicago, annoyed him. "Do you think," he asked, "that it would be a good idea to invite Papadopoulos at the same time as the King? Krasas proposed the idea to me."

"No, I disagree completely. No purpose would be served and you should forget about it."

"All right, general, I won't raise the issue."

Brademas's assistant called and said that the congressman sent a congratulatory letter to Spirtos and will post me a copy. With the exception of Sarbanes, he is not having much luck with the other congressmen.

March 17, Saturday

I wrote Brademas about March 25 (Greek Independence Day) to rouse the Greek-American congressmen.

I received a report from Peridis about the army, mailed by Konteas from Australia.

March 18, Sunday

Spirtos called. Mantzoros in Chicago had attacked him. Spirtos said he would sue and asked me to give him the names of some lawyers to work with his. I said I would get back to him.

He also said that he wrote a piece on AHEPA's charter for the *AHEPAN* magazine. I said that was excellent. He will send me a catalogue of the names and addresses of the members of the Supreme Lodge. I called Parry and asked him to recommend some lawyers. He will call back in the morning.

March 19, Monday
Report on the armed forces

I wrote Karamanlis and the King and sent them the Tzannetis reports. I told both of them that they need to break their silence. The letter to Karamanlis is below:

Mr. President *March 19, 1973*

Yesterday I received a copy of a report on the armed forces written by General Tzannetis's group, which I am forwarding to you and the King only. No one else has received a copy.

The data for 1972 were not ready. When they have been processed they will be sent us as an appendix.

The report's main conclusion is that there will be change within the officer corps only when there is a basic change in the overall climate.

Mr. Mitsotakis will tell you in detail of his visit here.

I wish only to submit that, in view of the student unrest, in view of army service being transformed into a form of punishment, and in view of the concerns expressed by official circles here, it is necessary for you to outflank those in Greece and announce a message of national salvation on April 21.

It is easier for you to take such an initiative than it is for the King.

In order to assist developments in Greece and here, you must break your silence.

I am fully aware of the significance of this suggestion, which I have avoided making so far, but I am deeply convinced that the time has come for you to participate actively, regardless of what is done or not done inside Greece.

Yours truly,

Orestis Vidalis

March 21, Wednesday
New York. Discussion with Mitsotakis and a meeting with Archbishop Iakovos

In the morning I saw Mitsotakis, who came to the hotel. I repeated that it is time for Karamanlis to take center stage. He told me that many people in Washington told him complimentary things about me. Both Davies at the State Department and Pell told them that Sisco says, "General Vidalis is the only Greek with whom we speak responsibly."

We agreed that Mitsotakis should apply pressure on Karamanlis.

At 1:00 in the afternoon. I saw Norstad. A general discussion. He did not understand the significance of the student unrest, though he was well informed. I asked him to try again to get me to see Kissinger and he promised to write to him. [Demonstration by University of Athens students at the downtown law school building.]

At six I went to see the archbishop. Effusive as always. I told him about the student unrest the previous day. He seemed pleased with the students and said that Papadopoulos feels that he has lost on the education issue. He said that Papadopoulos is under great pressure and, since he is intelligent, he will not want to go to extremes. I told him that I was not so sure and added that the denouement is the most important phase of the drama and everyone with influence must apply pressure for a smooth transfer.

I said that the King was pleased with Spirtos's visit and saw it as the first gesture by the Greek-Americans toward returning the situation to normal. I also said that it would displease the King—as it would the rest of us—if Spirtos were not supported.

The archbishop was not complimentary about the AHEPA leadership. He said that Ploumides and Manesiotis were thinking of taking steps to remove Spirtos, that many had opposed his election because they knew he was not pro-junta, and that they did not want him to damage relations with the regime because of their investments in Greece. "If he were to telephone me I would tell him that he did well to visit the King and I would back him up. Otherwise, though, I cannot interfere. What might be interesting would be for me to invite all the Greek-American congressmen for a meal and have you present."

"Yes, that would be very good. But as for Spirtos, you realize, now that he has seen the King, that any action against him would also be an action against the King, which would strengthen the junta."

"Certainly. If he calls me I will back him up."

I got home around 11:30 at night. I read only Panaghiotareas's letter from Athens. It was in code and genuinely optimistic:

Dear Uncle Alexander,[1] *March 5, 1973*

It has been a long time since I have written to you to say how fondly I remember you and that you are always in my thoughts.

These days I am very happy because the little house I told you about is ready and I hope to inaugurate it as summer approaches.[2]

As you know, it was built with a great deal of effort, difficulties, and worries. Thank God, however, everything has gone well. If my good uncles in America did not tease me all the time, saying they would help me and then changing their minds, everything would have been better.[3]

I would invite you to the house-warming party now but we have not yet decided the exact date.[4] *In fact, please send me your telephone number so I can call you when everything is ready.*

Things here are wonderful. The lousy students tried to do something but, they were beaten up and so shut up.

The only bad thing is that prices have gone way up and it is hard to make ends meet with my salary.

That's all for now.

Much love,

Pierros

March 22, Thursday

I called Spirtos and told him that he should not consider the archbishop as being pro-junta—though we cannot expect him to make any public announcements—and that if he called Iakovos he could expect support. He thanked me and said that he would call the archbishop tomorrow and let me know how it goes.

March 26, Monday

Received a letter from Peridis. The generals' effort failed. They backed off at the last moment and, it seems, they will propose something to . . . Papadopoulos. I also received a long letter from Konteas through Thailand. Great confusion. Andreas, the King, are all mixed up.

[1]Code for Orestis Vidalis.
[2]Code for navy action plan.
[3]Code for U.S. position toward the junta.
[4]Code for execution date of the navy plan.

MARCH 27, TUESDAY
Letter to Panaghiotareas

Today I sent this letter to Pierros Panaghiotareas:

My dearest nephew,[5] *March 26, 1973*

Belated thanks for your kind Christmas and New Year wishes. May you and your family have a productive and happy 1973.

I was most pleased to receive your letter of March 5. I was very happy to learn that you think your new house will be ready soon. You know I am impatient to help you finish the house and I am ready to do anything I can. I would, however, like to get some idea of the design of the house so I can visualize what kind of house you are building. Remember the three-room design we discussed? Were you able to include the other two rooms[6] *or were you obliged to build the house around your original room?*

I hope you can forgive me these silly questions, but I do want to help you, if you need my help, so that when you decide to move everything will be ready and complete for you to have a comfortable life after you move in.

Please, if you find the time, tell me about all this as soon as possible. Is there any chance your architect[7] *can make a trip abroad? That would be the perfect way to satisfy my curiosity.*

We heard about your students and the press here is supporting your young people to the full. We may not know much about the political situation there but the reality of injured students at the university or drafted into the army for supporting academic freedom always provokes sympathy and support from my countrymen, at least from those who have the time and inclination to care about their fellow human beings. Of course, how we feel about your students is not important. What is important is how you, the people of Greece, feel about all this.

I really hope we will stay in touch. Greetings and best wishes to the whole family and thank you for keeping me informed about your progress.

I cannot wait to learn more about your new house and, naturally, want to come see it at the right time.

Sincerely yours,
Alexander[8]

P.S. My telephone number is about to change. I will send you the new one as soon as I get it.

[5]Code for Pierros Panaghiotareas
[6]Code for the army and air force, apart from the navy.
[7]Code for sending a contact for direct communications.
[8]Code for Orestis Vidalis.

Uprising by Athens University Law School Students Begins —Information from Greece—

MARCH 28, WEDNESDAY

Nixon and the King exchanged telegrams (Greek Independence Day).

I spoke with Spirtos, who was pleased with the discussion. I asked him how he felt in light of the upcoming Supreme Lodge meeting. He said that a high-ranking AHEPA member had come to see him. Spirtos had shown this man all the correspondence—letters and telegrams he had received—and told him he was considering inviting the King, to which the other man did not object. The man read the letters and telegrams one by one and asked if Spirtos had requested that they be sent, to which Spirtos replied that he knew none of the writers other than Vournas. His visitor was impressed, and told him to repeat all this for Supreme Lodge. Spirtos is expecting the President of AHEPA Canada, who will help him. He was clearly optimistic.

Athens University Law School Leads Uprising

Georgios Konteas, a former air force officer and my contact with General Peridis, who had been passing on information and messages from Greece by telephone, began organizing our communication into reports he writes and mails from various countries he visits.

The first such report, dated March 18, 1973, arrived from Thailand today:

> Destroy after reading because, as you will see, it contains sensitive information.
>
> Before I left Athens, about a week ago, I had a long conversation with Mr. Peridis in which we discussed many vitally important subjects. He asked me to transmit to you the following about the situation in Athens:
>
> 1. Students. The movement's direction and control includes us as well. The leadership includes professors as well as students. Fortunately, many professors are working with us. Their spirits are roused and the unrest will continue.
> 2. Polytechnic. The Polytechnic Senate resigned. Its resignation was not accepted, though the Senate is insisting on it. No other decisions have been taken by either side. It is not yet known who ordered the police to invade the grounds and treat the students so violently. The conjecture is that the order was given by a police hardliner named Babalis, but this has not been confirmed.
> 3. University: During the events, 3,000 students (confirmed number)

were surrounded in the Law School, not 450 as Papadopoulos falsely claimed or 1,000 as the papers said. The number 3,000 was issued officially by the university's deans. (And an item of my own, from a reliable source. The students found a large number of butcher's knives in the law school bathrooms. Apparently, these were placed there by provocateurs, members of the security police, for the dissident students to use so there would be serious injuries, thereby justifying the police move into the building.)

4. Political positions of Athens University professors. At this point 55 professors are against the junta and 70 in favor. Most of those in favor were appointed recently and arbitrarily by the junta, not through regular faculty procedures.
5. University of Thessaloniki. Similar unrest occurred there at the same time. Eight students were arrested. Their families have had no news of them for a week.
6. In general. Our side thinks that a good job was done (personally, I disagree; I think much more could have been accomplished.)
7. The declaration from the four-star generals is ready. After much effort they managed to collect . . . 12 (!) signatures, including that of Mr. Frontistis. They are already having trouble publicizing it because the newspapers are afraid to carry it. I pointed out the BBC—Deutsche Welle route, which then would allow the papers to publish it without risk. Mr. Peridis did not tell me what they have finally decided to do.
8. Along the same lines, a declaration by more than a hundred high-ranking retired officers from all service branches is being prepared to follow. I told Mr. Peridis that something like this would be a grave error on our part. On the one hand, the declaration will bring no positive results (as it did not for Messers Tzannetis and Peridis, which passed unnoticed and allowed Papadopoulos to make the cheap shot, "here everyone is entitled to their opinion, don't we have democracy?") On the other hand, these people are very useful, we are going to need them to do a great number of things, and it is not right to neutralize them in this way and throw them into the lion's den. Mr. Peridis said that he would pass on my objections upstairs. I do not know what the "Demogerontocracy" will finally decide.

   The time for interminable discussions is over. The latest events show that the fruit is almost ripe enough to drop. We must—if we do not want to leave the initiative to the communists—act, and we must act quickly and correctly. At the end of the day it is shameful for professionals like us to let the students take all the risks. . . .
9. Other matters.

- I mailed the famous "report on the situation in the armed forces, etc." from Sydney. I hope you already have received it. From the quick glance I had of it, I did not find it that good. I think that it needs solid editing before being forwarded, because, besides being badly translated, it has many other flaws.
- Despite what we have experienced, we remain careless. The report contained a handwritten note . . . . You understand that, in the unlikely event of my capture, they would have immediately caught everybody else because ESA has handwriting samples of all high-ranking retired officers.

Respectfully,

Leonidas

March 30, Friday
AHEPA decided to invite the King

Spanoudis came by in the afternoon. He had seen Panourgias and Peridis. He told me that Panourghias was wondering if it might be worth trying an anti-American strategy. Spanoudis was very well informed. I told him to tell Peridis that:

a. We must promote the Karamanlis-King solution or some other solution.
b. We must penetrate the army.
c. The report was received and forwarded, but it is out of date and inaccurate as far as the other two service branches are concerned.
d. There is no money for the press. Without a visible political solution, the situation will not change.
e. Nixon does not want Papadopoulos, but he won't oust him by force.

We ate at the Sylvania club.

At one in the morning, Spirtos called to say: "After a heated discussion we voted, six to one, to invite the King if the State Department raises no objections."

I told him not to ask for permission but simply to inform the State Department of their intentions, and he agreed.

I told Spanoudis immediately, with the warning that he was to tell only Peridis about it.

March 31, Saturday

I called Silva and asked him to guide Spirtos. He should examine whether or not Spirtos should give them a letter informing them of AHEPA's decision. A delicate matter. "I'll see what I can do," Silva said.

Late at night I spoke with Spirtos and suggested, in order to help him out, that he should not raise the issue of the King's visit with Nixon and Rogers but just inform them that AHEPA has invited the King. "Agreed," he said, "that's how I'll do it."

April 1, Sunday

A calm day. Efthymios told me that his fellow students at Harvard disagree with me on three points: the issue of the King; the issue of the Americans, whom they consider responsible; and the social system. They prefer socialism.

April 2, Monday
Four generals *send letter to Papadopoulos*

Konteas called. Generals Frontistis, Pipilis, Seiradakis and Sakellariou sent a letter to Papadopoulos fifteen days ago. If he does not respond, they will publish it in the press, whereupon the others will follow.

He also said that the newspaper *Ethnos* (Nation) will be published again, this time as a weekly. They need help with subscriptions to *Vradini*, *Christianiki*, and *Ethnos*. He asked me to send him addresses for them to send promotional material. I told him that Spirtos is very good. The student unrest has quieted but will break out again. I said that we must meet next time, and he agreed.

April 3, Tuesday

I called Spirtos in California:

> M.S. General, I am sorry I haven't had time to call you. You were right about the bureaucrats. I spoke bluntly with Davies. I told him that I had held an open house in Athens and everyone under 65 is against the regime.
>
> Please, general, ask Silva to tell you how it went. But Marketos is out of his mind. He collared me at AHEPA's office and asked me about the King, in front of everyone, particularly in front of Liber. I told him I couldn't tell him, it was an executive meeting. Liber told Sorokos and Silva that what I say is the opinion of only one man. I asked Silva if I could use that and he said, "you sure can." When I went to the AHEPA office, I said to Liber, "You

can say anything you want to Sorokos but with representatives of the administration you have to be careful. If you want to divide AHEPA, I'll provide you documentation showing whether or not I am alone."

Liber went pale and was thrown off balance. But, general, Davies suggested that I write Papadopoulos directly, not through the embassy, and say that we are going to invite the King. It would be good to see his reaction.

O.V. Doctor, I disagree totally. Davies wants to avoid responsibility, he wants to make the decision of an American organization subject to Papadopoulos's approval; the thought alone is outrageous.

M.S. OK, general, I won't do it. Forget it.

O.V. When do you expect the answer, Doctor?

M.S. Soon. If they don't call me by Friday when I leave for Canada, I'll call them. General, I respect you and you have my full confidence.

O.V. Thank you. I know your position and my aim is for you to have results.

M.S. Premature disclosure would be disastrous.

O.V. I agree completely and am following what we agreed to the letter.

M.S. I know that and I appreciate it.

O.V. We'll stay in touch.

April 5, Thursday

I called Dick Walters in the morning and I told him about AHEPA. He did not know it. He said: "This is a very constructive move. I'll do what needs to be done immediately. I'll let you know."

April 6, Friday

The King called from London at 6:30 AM. He had received my letter and was pleased. I then told him that Kissinger told Potamianos that the King did not do well on December 13.

Spirtos called later. He asked if I could write three texts for him for public appearances. I asked what he wants the themes to be. "Greek culture throughout the world—The congruity between Greek and American values—American manifest destiny," he said.

April 11, Wednesday
Problems with the royal invitation

Theotokis called in the afternoon. He said that he will forward my ideas along with his own suggestions because he disagrees that we can expect a solution from within Greece, through his contact with Kanellopoulos. I told him that things are in such a mess here that if there is no pressure from Greece, we can expect nothing.

- But my dear Orestis, you know we disagree and have disagreed for a long time. Don't these gentlemen know that they have made a shambles of our country?
- Spyros, you know what has happened and is happening, but we must be realists.
- OK, I will forward it to Athens along with my own views.

In the evening Dr. Trifyllis called to say that AHEPA is in an uproar over Spirtos's visit to the King and the he, himself, does not think that AHEPA can invite the King. "I asked the Church and I received the same answer, although not from the archbishop himself. You see, general, AHEPA is not a political organization and it does not want to get involved."

"Doctor, thank you for the information. AHEPA is involved, one way or the other. This fact fuels hatred against Greek-Americans and Americans, and if they don't change their attitude and behavior the basic relationship between Greece and the U.S. will be changed for the worse."

April 17, Tuesday
Letter from Mitsotakis

I received the following letter from Kostas Mitsotakis.

> *My dear Orestis,* *Paris, April 10, 1973*
>
> *I am writing this having just finished my round of European contacts. Of course, I saw Karamanlis often and at length after I returned. I visited the King in London last Saturday and communicated with those back home. Basically, I conveyed my impressions and strongly stressed the need to take action, without which nothing can happen. I have not yet made any public statement and if I do I will tone it down, but in my private meetings with everyone I was very blunt and forceful.*
>
> *I do not yet have results. Karamanlis is fully aware of the problem and is not wrong in his evaluations, but he has not yet decided on a course of action. The King seemed more mature than ever and willing, as always, but he is waiting for the politicians to make the first move. In Athens there was one—*

significant in my view—development. Kanellopoulos moved decisively and sincerely toward Karamanlis, but he has not yet broken the opposition of the leading figures remaining in the Center Party.

I will inform you of any new developments here without delay, but I do not expect anything before Easter.

The student unrest continues and the arrests have provoked strong reactions in Europe. The Tsatsos arrest is poisoning the junta's relations with West Germany.

The King seemed determined not to accept the invitation to the U.S. unless he is guaranteed to see Nixon. He is not prepared to take a calculated risk. Karamanlis agrees with this. My own position is the opposite.

Information is constantly coming in from Athens about unease in the army and moves made by Makarezos and Ioannidis on their own behalf. They are positioning themselves as the heirs of Papadopoulos, of whom it is said that he does not control the units in around Athens. The Americans are still active. The word is that they are increasing their influence within the army's leadership. Rumors also are rife that the CIA, which is always furiously active, is preparing a change and that their station chief recently went to Washington and got the green light. For many, unfortunately, this is comforting. The moves within the army, however, are a serious matter.

On my return I found a telegram from Gratsos, who had lost your telephone number. I called him and gave him both. Last Monday he called—twice, actually, because he did not find me the first time—to say that despite the high regard in which they hold you, they have avoided seeing you intentionally, but are active for our cause both in the White House and the American Legion. I think you must communicate with Gratsos (C. Gratsos—888 7th Ave., 18th floor, tel. 48990900 or 2593409.) He has been honest with us and can be very useful. I have enclosed the note as he gave it to me for Senator Waggener (he specified that he is of Carolina) and Speller.

From the King I learned out that the signs from Kissinger are not good. Please let me know the result. The packages have already been sent to Greece and we will visit Opropoulos, with whom we have spoken over the phone.

Please write your news and I will keep you regularly informed from here.

Please convey our warmest greetings from Marika and me to Matina as well, and as our thanks for your hospitality in Toledo. We were very happy to see you even if only briefly.

Let us hope that our next meeting will be in Greece.

With much affection,

Yours,

Konstantinos Mitsotakis

Public Expression of Opposition to the Regime

APRIL 18, WEDNESDAY
Letter from former Chiefs of the Army General Staff and the Greek General Staff

Today the *New York Times* published an editorial about the generals. I called Hovey and thanked him.

In the editorial entitled "Warning to the Colonels," the *New York Times* wrote:

> Greece's military dictatorship has received a stern rebuke and an admonition to return the country to democratic rule from an unexpected but significant source. Four retired generals who have held the highest positions in the Greek armed forces have warned Premier Papadopoulos that his regime is "no longer permissible," and called upon him to "create immediately" the conditions for a return to "free democratic institutions."

After describing the generals' service records, the paper continued,

> Their letter expressed concern that continuation of military rule would turn Greeks against the armed forces and the United States.
>
> "Rightly or wrongly," it said, "the people feel that the United States supports a regime which grew out of a coup d'etat and which fails to respect the moral and ideological principles of NATO."

The article concluded,

> It will be interesting to see whether Colonel Papadopoulos can reject so easily the warning of four of the most respected officers to serve Greece's armed forces in recent years.

APRIL 23, MONDAY
Karamanlis statement

I heard that Karamanlis issued an important statement.

I called Silva and told him the latest about Karamanlis and that Kanellopoulos, Mavros, Zighdis, Papaspyrou, and Stefanopoulos all made statements backing Karamanlis. I asked him to keep an eye out for possible negative reactions, which he should report to Sisco. He said that Sisco was in Teheran.

Rallis called from Athens and said that Karamanlis's statement had created a general stir. I told him that what is needed now is support from all the other politicians. He said that, apart from Markezinis, everyone else (Kanellopoulos, Mavros, Zighdis, Papaspyrou, Stefanopoulos) had come out in support, and the intellectuals and officers (Frontistis, etc.) will follow.

I received a letter from Lambrias dated April 21 containing Karamanlis's statement in Greek in full and a summary in English.

April 24, Tuesday
New briefing from Peridis via Konteas

Today the second report from Peridis's contact, Y. Konteas, came in from Thailand, dated April 13, 1973. He conveyed the following:

For your information:

1. Here they insist that your information is incorrect about the readiness of the piece you told me over the phone. They say that if something like that existed, they would be the first to know. Mr. Peridis wonders whether your information may be coming from a lower ranking officer (technical) who had served in Washington. If, indeed, your information is from such a source, then, surely, it is hugely overblown. (He means the information conveyed by Panaghiotareas.)
2. There have been no developments as a result of the letter from the four-star generals. The five will meet in a few days to take decisions. The rest are waiting (and years have passed waiting). In any case, the general may publish the letter in the press if they do not get an answer.[9]
3. As for the two sections of the report with which you do not agree, they were prepared by experts in both services who are considered here to be the best informed. They do not agree that the situation here is better than has been described.
4. Students. The unrest has and will continue to come in surges. Activity continues despite the occasional surface calm. Fifteen days ago, the ESA [Greek Military Police] called in Tzannetis, Vardoulakis and Erselman for interrogation about the student unrest. They were asked questions, many of them close to the mark. Apparently, the surveillance network is excellent. In the end, they were not held. They were reminded that the old file is still open (threats). They were cautioned and released. In general, the ESA behaved decently and within the bounds of propriety.
5. The *Ethnos* will be re-issued in a few days as a weekly, though not with that name. Instead, it will be called *Sthenos* (Vigor). You see, the news-

[9]His information is dated. The letter already had been published at this time.

paper was ruined financially; it owes money to everyone and could not be published under its old name. Please help them get subscribers.

6. Addresses of prominent people. It is thought that sending such things as printed material, petitions, and protests from here would be more effective than sending them from there, which is why the addresses were requested. Anyway, it's up to you.

I left for New York in the afternoon.

April 25, Wednesday
Meeting with Gratsos of the Onassis Group

At 2:00 in the afternoon, I met with Gratsos of the Onassis Group in his office. The discussion lasted about an hour, with him attacking the junta. He had told Onassis that we would meet today, and Onassis sent his greetings and the message that he is prepared to help Karamanlis's effort. He considers Karamanlis's effort excellent because now there will be a specific solution. Onassis is very strongly against the junta. I will be told, sometime when I am in New York, when to meet with Onassis. He will use Waggener, whom he will ask to support the Karamanlis position and he, himself will work on Nixon. I insisted that he do whatever he can immediately.

I wrote to Mitsotakis and drew his attention to the new effort by Nixon and Kissinger on European-American relations. I stressed the need to influence the governments of Europe as much as possible to include the principle of democratic government in the new charter governing American-European relations.

Cherter of *Time* magazine called to ask about Karamanlis's statement. I told him that its value lies in providing an alternative solution, laying down the psychological foundation and, coming after the student unrest and the generals' letter, clearly expressing the desire of the Greeks to be rid of the dictatorship. He asked what the King will do and I said that I did not know. He said that some opinion in Washington maintains that the hardliners will prevail. I replied that the regime's supporters have used this excuse to justify their inaction for six years. He gave me his telephone number, in case I want anything from him.

I left for Toledo in the evening.

At home I found a copy of Spirtos's letter to Davies: [Translated back into English from the printed Greek text.]

Mister Rodger P. Davies
Assistant Secretary of State
Near East and South Asian Affairs
Department of State
2201 C Street N.W.
Washington D.C. 20520

Order of AHEPA
The American Hellenic
Educational Progressive Assn.
Supreme Lodge
Headquarters
1422 K Street, N.W.
Washington, D.C. 20005

April 20, 1973

Dear Mr. Davies,

Further to our conversation of Monday, April 2, 1973, referring to the decision taken by the Supreme Lodge of AHEPA relating to the invitation to be submitted to King Constantine of Greece, according to your proposal this thought would be discussed with the executive staff (of the State Department.)

I was under the impression that your office would inform me about the results of this proposal of yours. To date I have received no information and the Supreme Lodge of AHEPA is anxious to learn the next steps that must be taken now.

I hope to have your news in the very near future.

Yours truly,
M. S. Spirtos, M.D.
Supreme President AHEPA

April 26, Thursday

I wrote the King and sent him a copy of Spirtos's letter.

Efthymios called in the afternoon to say that a large number of Harvard professors have sided with the students in Greece. They are preparing an open letter to be sent to Greek newspapers.

Spirtos called in the evening. Davies had responded to his letter and he read me the reply. Davies said that they are not against a private visit but they do not want any official involvement. We agreed to discuss it on Tuesday. Davies's answer was as follows: [Translated back into English from the printed Greek text.]

Dr. Michael N. Spirtos
Supreme President AHEPA
6850 Van Nuys Boulevard
Suite 152
Van Nuys, California 91405

Department of State
Washington D.C. 20520

Dear Dr. Spirtos, *April 9, 1973*

Following your visit I spoke unofficially with my colleagues at the State Department and other interested services about AHEPA's proposal to invite King Constantine to visit the United States. While certainly there is no obstacle to stop AHEPA extending such an invitation and while His Majesty will be broadly welcomed in a private visit by his many American friends, we agreed that it would be inappropriate for the Government of the United States to answer a hypothetical question about the official reception King Constantine might receive if he chose to come here. However, the restrictions I mentioned during our conversation must, obviously, be taken into consideration.

Thank you again, Dr. Spirtos, for the time you gave to share with us your impressions from your trip.

I am looking forward to a new meeting with you.

Sincerely yours,

Rodger P. Davies
Assistant Secretary of State
Near East and South Asian Affairs

April 27, Friday

The *New York Times* today published the article I discussed with Hovey on Tuesday, April 24, entitled "The Karamanlis Solution." The article described Karamanlis as the most capable Greek prime minister of the postwar period.

Visit to California

May 1, Tuesday

I arrived in Los Angeles just after noon, local time, and called Spirtos. Around 6:00 in the evening we left for his house. We discussed his prospects for reelection in August. At first he was adamant that he would not run because of the great financial sacrifice entailed and because he thought he could not win. I asked if he knew Judge Manos. He answered that Manos is excellent but he was not aware of his views on the junta. So I told him that years ago I had met Manos over a meal with a couple of my friends in Toledo. During the meal he showed that he was strongly opposed to the junta. "Even if they are gods I don't want them because they are a dictatorship," I quoted him to Spirtos, who was very pleased with this information. "If I had known this, things would already be much better. I'll call him tomorrow. If we can form a team together we can really do something good," Spirtos said. During dinner he remarked that with a team he would make the financial sacrifice because they could do very good work, implying that with Manos's help he might be reelected.

We then spoke of the Davies document. I asked him if it was in answer to his letter and he said no, the two crossed in the mail. Davies sent him a second letter with a copy of the first when he received Spirtos's letter. He thought that Davies did not discuss the subject with the White House. Spirtos was thinking of distributing the letter to all members of the Supreme Lodge and asking them if they agree to invite the King on those terms.

I told him that this might not be the best solution. Since Davies was not definite, we should clear the matter up with Nixon directly. I suggested that he write Nixon, telling him that he has returned from Greece, Cyprus, etc. and considers it his duty to brief the president about his impressions. During the meeting he should tell the president that the Supreme Lodge has decided by six votes to one to invite the King to take part in AHEPA activities and to ask Nixon if the King's program could include a visit with the president. Spirtos lit up at this idea, as if he had discovered America. "I'll write him Thursday because tomorrow I'll leave at 5:00 in the morning. This way is better because then everyone will fall in line." He was obviously thrilled with the idea of meeting Nixon.

At 8:00 PM we left for the AHEPA conference.

Spirtos's people swept the [local] elections. At 10:30 P.M. they asked me to speak to them, which I did, briefly. I told them, "What you did tonight, electing your representatives, is illegal in Greece." I spoke of Spirtos's initiative to make AHEPA the foundation of Greek culture around the globe, about the distance I had kept from AHEPA in the past, and how my happiness with Spirtos's initiatives had given me the opportunity to regain contact.

May 3, Thursday

Nick Petris arranges for me to meet supporters and opponents of the junta in his house

In the evening, a meeting at Nick Petris's house with supporters of the regime. Zisis just got back from Greece. Concerned about his many investments, he was anxious about the economic situation. He admitted that the junta is incapable of changing, the situation necessarily will come to an end, but nobody is providing them any guarantees that investors will not be hurt. He asked me this five times. I gave him the stock answer that they must understand that before any clarification they must prove that they have decided to close the parenthesis. I told him that Karamanlis has spoken of avoiding retributions.

Judge Vavouris repeatedly insisted that he was not for the dictatorship, that the affair must end, though he maintained that it had been necessary because of the threat of communism. The rest listened carefully, especially when I stressed that "nations cannot live without institutions, without continuity, without preparing future leaders." A recently elected local congressman who had never shown any interest before was all ears now.

May 4, Friday

Nick Petris picked me up from the hotel at 5:30 in the afternoon.

Around 8:00 PM the opponents of the regime began arriving. Professor Newman was first. This gathering was also very interesting, mainly because the followers of Andreas Papandreou present heard me speak of a national crisis—not a political one—that requires everyone to come together not to promote individuals but to promote the position, "Enough is enough, the Greeks must regain their sovereignty." Professor Newman asked if I agree that international observers should be present for elections. I told him that I favor a transitional government composed of people trusted by all sides. If the transitional government is accepted and supported by all parties, foreigners would not be needed. If, on the other hand, the result of the elections is likely to be disputed, then by all means, bring in the observers.

During the discussion I said: "You are wasting your time with committees. The only way is to penetrate AHEPA and support Spirtos." This idea was greeted enthusiastically.

I told Nick Petris that I could see no other solution but to channel his energies through AHEPA in support of Spirtos. He fully accepted this and will work on it.

May 5, Saturday
Visit with Mayor Christopher of San Francisco

At 11:00 AM we went to Mayor Christopher's office. He told us that he just returned from Greece. He asked Papadopoulos the same question he had asked two years before, "When are you going to hold elections?" He asked the question in front of the entire group from the California Chamber of Commerce. Papadopoulos answered, "I will hold elections when the conditions are right. I will not give notice because it is not wise to let my enemies know what I am thinking." Before they left, Papadopoulos said something that Christopher found significant, "Soon I will announce surprising measures."

> C. I waited for April 21 since the meeting had been held a week earlier, because I had interpreted "soon" as "immediately." Nothing happened. I told Papadopoulos that it must end, that this situation cannot go on. It really is a complex situation, general, and I don't want to divide the Greek community as the Venizelists and Royalists did back then. What do you think I can do?
>
> O.V. Mr. Mayor, you should go see Nixon and Agnew and tell them to change tactics.
>
> C. Before I left for Greece, Agnew told he that he was upset with the situation and that Papadopoulos lost the case when he did not hold elections in 1970. I asked Agnew if I could say this to Papadopoulos, and he said "yes," so I did.

Nick Petris interjected, "Why don't you tell the Greeks here what you have said to us today, Mr. Mayor?"

> C. I agree with the general, it is better to speak with Nixon and Agnew now. I will let six months go by, and you can put this in your diary, and if Papadopoulos does nothing, as the general believes, I will write him a letter, one of the ones I know how to write when people deceive me, and I'll ask you, Senator, to come read it. Put it in your diary, six months from April 15.

He showed us out, saying that he would go to Washington to speak with Nixon and Agnew.

Declining Support for the Junta

May 7, Monday
Kissinger evasive

Norstad's secretary, Mary King, called. At last the general received an answer to the letter he sent Kissinger. The reply thanked the general and said, "while aware that a meeting with Vidalis would be highly interesting, my schedule is so overloaded that a meeting is not possible at present." I thanked Mary. Kissinger is avoiding me.

May 16, Wednesday

Nikos Stavrou called late at night. He said that the officers coming to the U.S. for training are trying to undermine the junta. He will try to verify this and will ask me for help.

Later, around midnight, Konteas called from Canada. Androutsopoulos, Tasca, and Pappas met at Filiatra in Messinia, and Androutsopoulos resigned afterwards. The rumor that he resigned because they did not give him the governorship of the Bank of Greece is not true. Tsoukalas resigned over the action taken against *Vradini* and the other newspapers. Thirty-two top officers will soon sign a statement similar to the one made by the chiefs. The position is hardening and, according to him, we are heading for the creation of a government in exile. Pesmazoglou is being held in isolation and will be tried before a military court. Konteas asked if the twins [Karamanlis and the King] had support and I answered, "certainly." I stressed that they must keep in mind that Watergate has paralyzed everything. I also told him that I had heard that Makarezos would come to the United States unofficially on his way back from China and Japan.

May 22, Tuesday
Statement signed by 34 generals

Rallis called. Apparently the appeals courts will confirm the seizures, obliging them to prosecute the author—Karamanlis—and the newspapers, unless there is an amnesty for the press. He said that the new issue of *Politika Themata* was out, with the statement made by the 34 generals. I told him that the situation here was very confused but was to the disadvantage of the regime's supporters.

The statement and the names of the high-ranking officers from all three of the armed services are below:

> We, the undersigned retired officers, ascertain and declare that:
>
> The recent highly important statement by former prime minister Konstantinos Karamanlis, the memorandum by the Honorary Chiefs of the General Staff, as well as the repeated declarations made by almost all other prominent individuals and political leaders in our country, lead to one fundamental national conclusion: The vast majority of Greeks, of every political persuasion, already are united in their fervent desire to regain their political freedoms and move as fast as possible towards the rule of law and the establishment of democratic institutions. As do almost all Greeks, we, also, salute this hopeful fact of national unity as being of the greatest importance, providing a sound foundation for the procedures required to fulfill this pan-Hellenic yearning.

Lieutenant Generals: Matalas, K.; Papageorgopoulos, K. (former Field Army Commander); Tzannetis, S. (former Army Inspector General); Leventis, G. (former Army Inspector General); Kollias, K. (former Field Army Commander); Tsichlis, G.; Thomopoulos, P.; Peridis, G.; Vardoulakis, A.

Major Generals: Koumanakos, G.; Bechrakis, D.; Mantzos, K.; Martzoukos, H.; Zalachoris, N.; Papadopoulos, D.; Panourgias, P.; Harvalakis, T.; Miliarakis, A.; Petropouleas, M.; Iliakopoulos, S.; Fetsis, K.; Papadopoulos, K.

Brigadiers: Erselman, A.; Bouras, A.; Papakonstantinou, K.; Kazalakis, A.; Vavaroutsos, E.; Bloutsos, A.

Vice Admiral: Spanidis, A. (former Deputy Chief of the General Staffs)

Rear Admiral: Rozakis, A. (former Chief of Naval Operations)

Commodore: Stavridis, M.

Lieutenant General: Diamantopoulos, S. (former Chief of the Tactical Air Force)

Major Generals: Hatziioannou, E., Kokkas, K.

Athens, May 1973

MAY 24, THURSDAY
News of arrests in the navy

The first item on the morning news was from Greece. "Two admirals have been arrested for planning to take three warships from which they would issue an ultimatum to the government to resign and to incite the armed forces to mutiny." What could have happened? I fear that they have been betrayed.

Later I found out from Makrias that one of the admirals was Engolfopoulos. They announced that it was only a very few officers, influenced by statements made by "royalist" officers outside country. Much emotion among our circles. Again, general disappointment.

The *Velos* Disobeys Athens and Reaches Italy

MAY 25, FRIDAY

Branco called in the afternoon to say that the destroyer *Velos*, after declaring that it refuses to obey orders from Athens, left NATO exercises and went to Fiumicino near Rome.

In the evening I called Arnaoutis. He said that the commander of the *Velos* is Captain N. Pappas. I said we must take great care with the situation and the crew.

May 26, Saturday
Concern over the fate of the Velos's *commander and crew*

There is concern that Andreotti might extradite Pappas and his crew, who are requesting political asylum.

I phoned the King and told him of these concerns. He said that the issue had been settled 30 minutes earlier (it was 1:00 PM Toledo time). Pappas and 30 members of the crew, officers and NCO's, received permission to enter Italy under political asylum. Pappas would not leave the ship until, after three hours of negotiations with the ambassador, he received assurances that the sailors would not be punished when they returned. I said that we are faced with the armed forces becoming completely fractured and he must move with great care. He replied that Karamanlis proposed that he make no statement and that he, Karamanlis, would make a statement tomorrow after a few points not yet clear become clarified. The information now at hand is that tanks have occupied the airports, the fleet's home port has been occupied by marines, and the army is in an uproar. The King will telephone the Queen of England and the Shah of Iran that evening to apply as much pressure as possible on Nixon to promote the Karamanlis solution. He asked me to do the same with Dick Walters and Sisco.

I called Walters. We had not spoken in a while. I said that I understood from the news reports why he had not called me. He said, "We have progress despite the bad news of the moment. Papadopoulos's position has been weakened more than it ever has been before and the uproar inside the armed forces is huge. Between loyalty to Papadopoulos and loyalty to the unity of the armed forces, the officers will choose loyalty to the unity of the armed forces. I told the King about Walters's views on Papadopoulos and the unrest inside the armed forces. The King asked me to explain to Walters and Sisco the need for the great powers to apply pressure now.

I called Stavrou, who said that he learned that Tasca had asked Makarezos to come to the U.S. on his way back from Japan and that he is expected on June 6.

May 27, Sunday
Captain Pappas interviewed

The King called. I told him that on Tuesday Walters will speak in favor of the Karamanlis solution with Nixon. I also told him about the *New York Times* and he immediately said that I should tell the editor that Pappas gave two interviews, one to the press and the other on television, in which he said,

> We did not ask to see the King either before or after our arrival. We are not royalists or politically involved. We are Greek officers who can no longer tolerate military rule of our homeland. We support NATO and in these critical hours are appealing to a NATO country.

I asked if they are being taken care of, and the King said they are being taken care of very well in a hotel outside Rome. The Italians want to move them somewhere farther from Rome. At the moment they do not need money, but they will later. He also said that the commanders of every naval vessel have been arrested along with air force officers. No concrete information about northern Greece is available. That the regime has not made an official announcement means that it is facing something serious. I told him that I would go to Washington.

May 28, Monday

I called Arnaoutis. He said that Athens announced that 35 officers had been arrested in addition to Engolfopoulos, Minaios, Rozakis, and Konofaos. The plan had been to go to Syros and then blockade northern Greece. Apparently, the attempt was on a much larger scale than had originally been thought. The announcement was made by the Ministry of Defense and not by the government.

At this point I must note my intense disappointment that, despite the preparations we had begun with Panaghiotareas and the other officers who knew of the original plan about the navy's attempt (see April 22, 1971), no one informed me that the navy was going to make such an attempt.[10]

May 29 Tuesday
Walters feels that Papadopoulos's power is diminishing

I left for Washington in the afternoon. At 4:30 PM Walters came to the Cosmos Club. In general, he was not worried about developments in Greece and

[10]Later, in 1985, in the book *To kinima tou Naftikou* (May 1973) Nikos Papadimitriou wrote: "The diplomat G. Sekeris, the officers' sole 'political advisor' . . . visited his brother, Lieutenant Commander A. Sekeris, in Kielo. Together they reviewed developments in Greece and discussed certain organizational matters about the attempt and making political contacts, while maintaining contact with the cashiered Brigadier O. Vidalis, formerly Chief of Staff of the Third Army Corps, who had gone abroad and was trying to organize resistance cells against the military regime. Mr. O. Vidalis, a capable and experienced officer—G. Sekeris reveals—had prepared a suitable staff plan, which, had it been properly organized and executed, had the potential and the likelihood of success. Naval officers in the first cell, however, rejected it as being too army-like. . . . (page 161)

said that Papadopoulos had never been weaker. Both the Karamanlis alternative and the fractured unity of the armed forces were major negative developments for Papadopoulos. He never had expected such developments so soon, and he does not think Papadopoulos will dare touch the issue of the King. If he does, it will be an act of desperation that must be dealt with head on by Karamanlis, the King, and the others. They (the Americans) are doing what they can, in private. The feeling is that Papadopoulos would use public intervention against the Americans and freedom. I said that I disagreed about this because the Greeks already are against the Americans.

Senator Jackson Mobilized

May 30, Wednesday
First meeting with Senator Jackson

In the morning the King, who knew I was to meet with Sisco, called to say that the American ambassador in Rome, Volpe, told him "it is not in the best interest of His Majesty to meet with the ambassador." The King met with the deputy, told him what he had to say, and added that "when the Greeks hear of the American government position and the stance taken by the ambassador they will become aware of the collusion." He asked to see the ambassador and he told me to tell all this to Sisco when I see him.

Pyrros called to say that he had arranged for me to telephone Jackson's assistant. I called and was told to be there at 1:30 in the afternoon to meet the senator.

I went to Jackson's office. I explained the situation, stressing that the armed forces are ineffective and that there certainly is no desire to move toward democracy. The result is that our institutions have been dismantled and we have a tragic situation in Greece.

His reaction was completely positive. "What can we do?" he asked. "The administration must move decisively and tell Papadopoulos that you have given him everything and he has done nothing." He found this appropriate and added that Kissinger must take action. Then I told him that a statement from him would be particularly significant. He promised to make one. I stayed until 2:00 PM.

I went to see Sisco. As always, he greeted me warmly. "Unfortunately," I told him, "again we see each other in difficult circumstances." Then I described the situation, how the two-pronged policy of friendly persuasion in favor of democracy while providing everything for security had led nowhere. Now we have reached the point where we have neither a democracy nor an operational armed forces. Papadopoulos cannot reestablish the armed forces, only a democratic government can do that. Sisco repeated the last two points, that the armed forces are ineffective and that they cannot be repaired by the regime.

We discussed the issue of the King. Sisco did not know if the junta had taken a decision or if it would do so in the future, but he would talk to people and weigh the pros and cons of a referendum.

> S.: What is your opinion?
>
> O.V.: It is impossible to hold a free referendum. It will lead us to worse complications. No one will accept the result. If it is actually free, then there is no chance that the junta could win.
>
> S.: What will happen, general, if things stay as they are?
>
> O.V.: Pressure will continue, reaction will continue, and at some point there will be an explosion. There is no possibility of reversing the situation.
>
> S.: What should we do, general?
>
> O.V.: Send a representative to tell Papadopoulos that it's over. Or indicate that you want the Karamanlis—King solution. Invite the King to the U.S. But how can such an indication be effective when your ambassador in Rome avoids the King?
>
> S.: General, I have to tell you that we studied the matter in depth and did not want to give the impression that we or the King had anything to do with the navy's attempt. We believed this stance was in the best interests of the King and of the U.S.A.
>
> O.V.: You are more afraid than you need to be. The junta has been blackmailing you for six years and your reactions are passive. Confidence in America is evaporating.

After Sisco I went to see Pell. He thinks that the King must visit the U.S., without necessarily seeing the president. What the president will tell him is unimportant, nor does he need to see him.

He told me the spirit of resistance had gone down over the last two years because all the Greek-Americans talk in favor of the regime in Athens. "They do not know and they do not observe," I said. He asked me what to do. I replied that he should insist with Sisco that they do something, since, up to now, they have failed completely.

I left for New York.

MAY 31, THURSDAY
Attempt to finance Pappas's group

At 10:30 I met Gratsos in his office. He spoke of the "navy's childishness," so I explained how hard it is to take collective action under a dictatorship. I also told him how the navy's action brought the situation in the armed forces to the surface. The regime reacted by returning to the issue of the King. I asked for his help on two matters: to see Agnew and promote the Karamanlis solution and, second, to help the captain and crew of the *Velos*. I said that I understand it must be in secret, but it must be done. He promised to speak with Onassis and get back to me.

In the afternoon, I met with Oikonomidis and Anastaplo. The latter revealed himself as a fanatical follower of the King. He has been working with Kennedy to get Nixon to invite the King officially and then try to overthrow the regime from the inside. They are, he said, waiting for one of Papadopoulos's people to come over for aid, and they will use him as a means for change. He was very emphatic and I was very reserved. He said that I would see that it was more than talk and soon I would meet the entire team. He asked me to keep the meeting and the conversation secret.

Very interesting revelation, but I doubt that it will succeed. I hope I am wrong.

The Junta Begins to Move toward Change in the Form of Government

JUNE 1, FRIDAY
Efthymios and I meet with the archbishop

I left for Boston, where I arrived at midday. As soon as I saw Efthymios he said, "We have news. Papadopoulos has declared the establishment of a republic and the abolishment of the monarchy, with a referendum on these decisions in two months and elections in 1974." I was taken aback. I called Matina, who said that Dimitris Antoniou had rung and said the same thing, adding that the marches in Athens had stopped.

I called Arnaoutis, who was crushed. I told him that the struggle begins now.

I also called the King. He said that he was preparing a declaration. He passed me on to Papagos, who gave me the main lines, repudiation, explanation for his silence, denial that he participated in the navy's attempt and praise for it, no fear of a referendum so long as it is free.

Efthymios and I left to see the archbishop, whom we met in his office. I told him that it was time to speak out. He was clearly shaken. He asked for Agnew on the phone but the vice president was not in. He then asked for Brademas and Sarbanes but they were not in either. We stayed for quite a while. I told him to call the King. He told me privately later that Agnew called him. Agnew told him that he had not been informed yet and the archbishop should wait for Agnew to inform him. We agreed that I would call him on Sunday for the archbishop to tell me.

June 2, Saturday

I called Makrias and read him the text of a statement on the junta's decision to change the form of government.

He read Karamanlis's statement, which said the following after the regime announced its intention to change the form of government:

> With today's arbitrary decision by the government in Athens, the national crisis in Greece has reached new heights. Obviously, the government took this dramatic step to divert the attention of the Greek people from recent events, above all, from the acute political problem the country is facing. Greece's problem right now is not whether or not it is a constitutional monarchy, but the restoration of rule by the people.
>
> I pointed out precisely this problem in my last statement, recommending, in order to avoid violent developments, the search for a peaceful and measured solution.
>
> I believe, therefore, that the government declared the establishment of a republic in order to prolong the dictatorship, decorating itself with elections and referenda. Clearly, it believes that all this will simplify its problem, and does not understand that this is making the problem more complex and acute.
>
> It is well known that the government used the navy's tragedy as a pretext for its new coup, involving in this the name of the King and my own name.
>
> I categorically declare that reference in the government's announcement to the King and to me is completely inaccurate. If I had encouraged this attempt in any way I would have had the courage and the moral duty to confirm it.

I called Mitsotakis. Everyone issued statements, even the followers of Koligiannis, except for Andreas. He also said that four deputy chiefs of staff resigned. They consider the Americans responsible.

June 3, Sunday
The King's declaration

The *New York Times* carried the King's statement and details about the departure of the four generals on the front page.

I called Walters. He said, "I told you. He has a long way to go between now and the 29th of July. You should keep alive the farcical nature of the whole thing. I do not want to perpetuate Papadopoulos. Did you see the four generals? There will be movement." I replied: "Dick, I do not trust anybody in the administration. I only trust you."

I called Pyrros. Sixty-five congressmen have signed the congressman's letter. I asked him to send the letter to the King, which he will do. He told me about Fulbright's letter to Rogers and its similarity with the congressmen's letter.

I called Iakovos in Boston. He had heard the King saying, "it is not a matter of constitutional monarchy or constitutional republic; it is a matter of democracy." I asked him if he had seen the full text of the King's declaration and he had not. I told him that the King accepts a referendum but only if held by a transitional government with a free press and all political prisoners released. Iakovos will call me after he speaks with Agnew.

I called Buchanan, but he was not in. He called me later from Texas. I told him that the administration's policy has failed terribly. He tried to excuse them because of Vietnam and Watergate. I said that if Tasca had been replaced by someone substantial, the situation would have been solved long ago. He promised to see Kissinger and Nixon and call me.

Yesterday, I spoke with Spirtos on the telephone. He had not sent the letter to Nixon and did not know what to do. I told him that the King remains the King until the Greeks decide in free elections. Therefore, nothing has changed and he should proceed with the original plan. At the moment it does not matter if he sees Nixon or not.

June 4, Monday

Rallis called. He said that none of the statements was published by the press in Athens and that applications for membership in EPOK can be found in banks and the offices of public utilities.[11] I told him about the letters written by the congressmen and Fulbright, and we agreed to stay in regular contact.

I wrote to Jackson's assistant, Munroe. I called Dimitrakopoulos and told

[11]EPOK (Greek Cultural Movement). Its founders included people who had been members of junta governments. The *Vradini* newspaper wondered openly how under a regime forbidding any kind of political activity, the government approved the charter of a clearly political organization.

him about EPOK. He called back to say that UPI etc. had sent instructions that the subject should be looked into. He also said that the junta had warned that politicians and parties from the past could not participate in the elections.

Pyrros called to say that the letter had been signed by 80 congressmen. The *National Herald* published my statement today:

> The Greek nation is being tested. The homeland is in turmoil. The time has come for the Greeks of America to take a clear position on the tragedy of Greece.
>
> Greece's young people led the way in expressing their concern for the future.
>
> Politicians, some officers, and the people sided with former Prime Minister Karamanlis in calling for the King to be restored and a government of national salvation to be formed.
>
> Our armed forces, in the attempt to avoid civil war, were mortally wounded.
>
> Our heroic navy is no more.
>
> Our unbeatable air force is under guard by the dictatorship's mercenaries. The army, divided between praetorians and prisoners, is being subjected to the greatest trial. In the midst of these momentous and tragic developments, the "song and dance" about a so-called change of scenery and elevating the dictator to president of the "republic" are acts of desperation, clearly moves to prolong the dictatorship.
>
> The Greek people know that King Constantine has been and still is the first fighter for restoring democracy to our country.
>
> Those who trusted in the dictatorship's honesty or its promises should consider the responsibilities they bear in regard to Greece and America.
>
> The Church, organizations, and all Greeks should raise their voices and thunder that they no longer accept the dictatorship or its decisions.
>
> The Greeks of America and around the world will recognize only the decisions of the Greek people, freely expressed, in a climate of freedom and not under martial law, in an atmosphere where there is a free press and not prisons, in an environment where the Greeks freely can take decisions about the future of their nation.
>
> Until then, King Constantine is and will be honored as the symbol of the unity of all the Greeks, against the most brutal of dictatorships.

June 5, Tuesday

The King called in the afternoon. I told him that his declaration was well received among both Greeks and non-Greeks. It was especially appreciated that he did not inveigh against foreigners. He spoke of the issue of recognition. The Americans will wait for the referendum. ABC will interview him on Sunday. I should call him as soon as I hear it.

I telephoned Pell about the issue of recognition and told him that for political and psychological reasons it should be delayed. He said that he had spoken with and written to Rogers, and I told him about the congressmen's letter, of which he had not been aware.

I telephoned Dimitrakopoulos. I told him that recognition would be delayed until the referendum and that Papadopoulos considers that Watergate has completely disrupted America. He should tell this to Fulbright and urge him to prove that they are not in a state of disarray.

June 6, Wednesday
Letter from Petris—spirit of victory

On June 3, I had given Nick Petris the news and asked him to mobilize the west coast. I received a moving letter from him today: [Translated back into English from the printed Greek text.]

Nicholas C. Petris
11th Senatorial District
Senate
California Legislature

June 3, 1973

Dear Orestis,

Your phone call this morning was like the arrival of the runner from Marathon—greetings!

Though the message was not one of victory, it is definitely the beginning.

Greece today is moving, the promise of clean air is powerful and clear. If the people of Greece receive the information—if they know of the King's acceptance of the challenge (referendum) and his demand for genuinely free elections—and the identical demand by all political parties—they will emphatically respond with a vote against the dictatorship.

Can we dare to dream that the doors of a Free Greece will open soon? Oh how our hearts jump for that happy event. Perhaps we can go back to Greece, meet you there to celebrate the Resurrection. All honors are due to you for your courage, your penetrating vision, your leadership. You are writing a proud chapter in Greek history—alone, exiled—without the support of the Philike Hetairia.

Yours truly,
Nikos

I telephoned Iakovos, who had just spoken with the King. The King was moved. The archbishop told him that he had notified the patriarchate to delay recognition and not stop the *Polychronio* [a prayer for the good health and fortunes of the monarch]. The King agreed that a statement from Iakovos was not advisable but that at least other prominent people should support the King. Iakovos told me that he would do whatever he could.

Konteas called from London to say that their head no longer exists, but the body is unharmed. They are able to make a move similar to that taken by the *Velos*, but they need support, not a refugee camp.

June 7, Thursday

I spoke with the King, who said that he would be on ABC's *Issues and Answers* on Sunday.

June 9, Saturday
Arrests because of the navy's move

I went to the office and called Couloumbis and Stavrou. I asked Couloumbis to write down the main points of the meeting with Davies.

The minutes of the meeting between the professors and Rodger Davies:

> Meeting between the Assistant Secretary of State Rodger Davies and Professors Couloumbis and Stavrou on Friday, June 8, 1973 from 3 PM to 4:05 PM.
>
> A. Rodger Davies
>
> I. Evaluation
> Following the events with the students and what occurred within the armed forces, it is clear that instability (upheaval and violence) will increase in the country unless representative government returns to Greece. Recent events confirm that Papadopoulos's position is weakening. Papadopoulos has two choices: 1) He can continue to exercise dictatorial power. 2) He can follow the national trend towards representative government. I hope he chooses the latter.
>
> II. Recognition
> We—our legal advisors—are studying the problem. We are not in a hurry to finish the study. We are, however, continuing our daily contacts with the Greek government.
>
> III. General policy
> An overall reassessment of American policy towards Greece is now being undertaken.

The long-term interests of Greece and the United States are best served by a democratic and representative government in Greece. Only the Greeks, however, can be responsible for these developments. Democracy cannot be imposed from the outside.

B. The professors' proposals

I. Specifics
Recall the American Ambassador for consultations. The president or the Secretary of State should answer questions in a news conference and clearly express the view that the Greek people must be allowed to express their will freely in open elections and a referendum.

Perhaps the U.S. Navy's home-porting arrangements should be delayed.

II. General
It must be realized that neither the referendum nor the elections will be considered legitimate (and thereby allow conditions in Greece to return to normal) unless the united political forces of Greece freely participate in them. These political forces include: a) outside Greece, the King, Mr. Karamanlis and the people around them, and, b) within Greece, Messers Kanellopoulos, Mavros, Zighdis, and all the other political leaders and prisoners, such as Mr. Pesmazoglou. In 1947 the United States lost the support of the left in Greece and then, between 1965 and 1967, the support of the center-left, and since 1967 they have been steadily losing the center-right as a result of American support for Papadopoulos's regime. If the U.S. loses the support of the center-right, then American interests will depend solely on Papadopoulos and his subordinates.

The U.S. ought to be concerned about the balance of power between Greece and Turkey needed for maintaining stability in NATO. With the Greek armed forces weakened by political divisions, Turkey could be tempted into adventures with negative consequences for both Greece and Turkey, as well as for NATO and the U.S. America must be ready to deal with the prospect of a European move to expel Greece from NATO, unless a genuine compromise can be reached leading to unity in the armed forces.

C. Assistant Secretary Davies's response

He prefers to keep the American ambassador at his post in Athens.

As for an announcement by the president, he took note of the suggestion without commitment.

As for the navy's home-porting arrangements, he took note and said that home-porting is necessary to reduce costs and improve conditions for navy personnel. Alternatives, however, are being examined. On the need for a genuine referendum, he took note and made no commitment.

On the subject of Turkey, he said, "Yes, we should be concerned. We are examining the situation." About NATO he said, "We would not be surprised if Papadopoulos pulls Greece out of NATO as he did with the Council of Europe."

In general, our influence in Greece is limited these days even though we are in communication, especially through the pentagon, with the Greeks, who are particularly sensitive about internal affairs. The latest example was a request by the Secretary of State to the Greek authorities to accept high level legal advisors, which was rejected without explanation."

The King called, as we had agreed.

O.V.: How are you, your Majesty?

K.C.: I am well but they are driving me mad with interviews. Your news first, general.

O.V.: I have seen the text of your interview. I like the aggressive spirit and the optimism, but I'll have to see it on television first before I give you my final reaction.

K.C.: When can you give me your impressions? I want your views first and then the general impact.

O.V.: I will call you at 9 AM your time. Your Majesty, at the first chance you get you should thank Congress, the press, and the people of the United States. I have arranged for the *National Herald* to publish the full text on Monday morning. Radio stations in New York and Chicago and ABC television have announced that they will broadcast it. I have notified my people in many states. There will be full coverage. The State Department informs me that they are not in a hurry to grant recognition to the new situation, they are reviewing their policy, and they see Papadopoulos's action as an act of weakness. I am sending you the minutes. Your Majesty, the Kousoulas text, which Arnaoutis sent me long ago, must be made public.

K.C.: I will talk with him tonight and let you know. Iakovos called. He said he's on my side, he won't stop the *Polychronio* without instructions from the patriarchate and he is working to delay recognition. I thanked him and told him how moved I was by his sentiments.

O.V.: Your Majesty, I think that we need a great deal of domestic turbulence.

K.C.: It will be done.

Around 10:30 PM Konteas called and said:

- They have arrested Fetsis and the Tzannetis group has dissolved.
- They knew about the navy's move but told him nothing.
- On Thursday, June 3, they arrested the following air force officers: Colonel Kokkinidas, Commander of Andravida air base, Major N. Stappas, Operations Officer of Angchialos air base and Captain Apostolakis of Souda air base.
- The chief of the air force, Mitsainas asked to handle the interrogations himself and was cashiered.
- Der Spiegel has published the names of naval officers being tortured, such as Troupakis.
- The people, expecting upheaval and unrest, have been withdrawing their deposits. Makarezos announced that deposits would not be frozen.
- They are facing problems with hard currency. They need 15 million dollars to pay for tanks purchased from France and cannot produce it.

I told him that the Americans are in no hurry to grant recognition, they are reviewing their policy in depth, and think that Papadopoulos is acting from a position of weakness.

June 10, Sunday

The main editorial in the *New York Times* was entitled "Constantine as Symbol."

We went to Friedman's, family friends in Toledo, Ohio, to listen to the broadcast. It was very good. I called Couloumbis, who liked the aggressive and optimistic tone. He would have preferred it if the King had spoken more about the Greeks and less about himself but it was very good. The King telephoned. I told him that the aggressiveness made it very good. I would have suggested that he add that the aid was exploited for political reasons and to thank congress, the press and the people. I read him an excerpt from the *New York Times* editorial and he enjoyed it. I told him about the arrests of the air force officers and the rest of the news from Greece.

June 11, Monday

Rallis called. The junta is proposing having Papadopoulos become president as a solution. A new announcement will be made by the politicians, who are united as never before. Also, in Brussels the Americans are expending an enormous amount of energy trying to torpedo opposition to the Athens regime in NATO.

Oikonomidis called to say that Anastaplo is in Washington. They insisted on international supervision for the forthcoming referendum. I told him that there is no point in international observers unless the prerequisites for freedom are established before the referendum.

I received a letter dated June 6 from Jack Maury confidentially informing me that he discussed with the Secretary of Defense the "unfortunate behavior of some of our officers (American) who helped the 'Colonels' promote the impression that they enjoy the full support of Washington." He also wrote, "Dick Walters also drew attention to this issue and I hope that it had an effect. At least Secretary Jim Schlesinger, who is a man of action, will see that his instructions are followed."

June 12, Tuesday

Letter from A. Pollis—the junta published notes on the preparations for December 13

I received a letter, unfavorable to the King, from A. Pollis:

> *Dear Orestis,* *8 June 1973*
>
> *I think that before I talk about Pappas I should make my political position clear. I am not a monarchist and I do not wish to work for the return of the King to Greece. I will use all the legal arguments against ending the monarchy, all the arguments against the referendum, but only because eliminating the monarchy is a move on Papadopoulos's part to strengthen himself further.*
>
> *I realize that there is a movement to establish an international commission to supervise the referendum. My own view is that it is dangerous. If such a commission ever were to be set up and the Greeks were to accept it (most unlikely) they might realize that the majority of Greeks couldn't care less about the monarchy. In New York, ordinary Greeks (not the elite whom Constantine represents) who are anti-junta, at the same time refuse to be concerned about the monarchy.*
>
> *Along the same lines I think it would be wrong for Pappas to present himself as a monarchist. I think Pappas should be strictly neutral—he should speak about the destruction of the effectiveness of the Greek armed forces,*

about the extensive opposition to Papadopoulos among officers, etc.—but not in favor of the King.

One comment I have heard from many Greeks is that Constantine said nothing against Papadopoulos until he was deposed and Papadopoulos took away his annual salary. A poor man cannot help but feel this way. I need not comment on Frederiki.

I see no need for Pappas to come here immediately just because there will be a referendum—There is nothing he can do about the referendum one way or another. He certainly is not going to convince the U.S to depose Papadopoulos before the referendum.

I think he should come at a time when he could be most effective in the cause of Greek freedom. This means when enough meetings have been arranged with individuals about the Greek issue. He should come when the House Foreign Affairs Committee is holding its hearings on Greece (no date has yet been set) and when arrangements have been made for him to see key people in the Defense Department. I have a contact—I don't remember his exact rank, but he teaches at Fort Leavenworth every year—who can make arrangements for Pappas to meet with some top people in the Pentagon. I think it would be better for the request to come from him rather than from any of us who are so closely identified with the Greek issue. It would take up to, but not beyond, the middle of July to make these arrangements for Pappas.

Incidentally, I have learned that all the Greek officers who left the Velos and are in Italy are in dire need of money. I'm passing on the following information to you because I was asked to keep Pappas's bank account in mind.

Nikos Pappas
Conto Numero 41/01922/18
Banco di Sicilia
Agencia Numero 2
Piazza Barberini 23
Roma, Italia

With best wishes,

Adamantia

Dr. Addy Pollis
54 West 16th st.
New York, New York 10011

The King called and said Athens is claiming that the King was preparing a coup and a new dictatorship to be installed on December 13.

June 13, Wednesday
The King's reply and my letter to Pollis

The King called in the morning and read his statement rebutting the charges about his dictatorial tendencies:

June 13, 1973
Statement by His Majesty the King

An official government source in Athens published, for obvious reasons, some information that is totally without foundation. I am, therefore, obliged to make the following statement:

The claims about my so-called discussion with the men who led the coup are the product of a sick imagination. At no time and under no circumstances have I ever expressed support for any kind of dictatorial regime in Greece. My opposition to the revolution has been common knowledge since the first moment of its existence. Proof of this is the fact that I did not sign the order imposing martial law on April 21, 1967, as the revolution falsely claimed. Furthermore, no Constitutional Act introduced by the revolutionary government bears my signature.

As for their claims to have discovered notes indicating that, had my action of December 13, 1967 succeeded, I intended to abolish the freedoms of the Greek people, I state that I am not aware of any such notes and that the whole claim is unworthy even of denial. What I had in mind for the future political development of Greece had been expressed, in general terms, in my announcement to the Greek people on December 13, 1967. I fought and I continue to fight for the restoration of the freedoms of the Greek people because I believe that the Greek people are among the most mature in Europe and sufficiently capable of enjoying the benefits of a democratic system.

I am aware that in coming days a broad campaign will be launched against me, using all means available. I also understand that under the shadow of the imposed dictatorship, there is no way for the truth to reach the Greek people or for anyone to express opposition. I am counting, in any case, on the judgment and good sense of the Greek people to understand this most recent effort to deceive them.

I also wish to declare that I am not disposed to answer any further slanderous accusations, which reflect solely on those who utter them.

I wrote to Pollis, replying to her letter about the King, Pappas, etc.:

Toledo, June 13, 1973

Dear Adamantia,

Thank you for your letter of June 8.

I appreciate your wish to make your political position clear. I also wish, once more, to make my position clear. I have always maintained that the sole objective during the current crisis is to assist the people of Greece to decide what they finally want to have as a government and a constitution.

The issue of the King has divided the anti-junta people in the past, and if no collective effort has been possible against the junta it is primarily because of the different positions concerning the King.

At this moment, however, the situation is very clearly defined for the following reasons:

a) The regime considered the King their primary enemy and, therefore, felt that their one last hope for remaining in power was to depose him.
b) All political leaders (with the exception of Papandreou) including Melina, Theodorakis, Georgios Mangakis, and Georgos Mylonas have spoken against the junta's action and hold the position that there will be time for a free choice about the constitution after the Greek people are free.
c) The King, himself, has clearly stated that he wants a referendum if the people are free to decide on this issue. Under these circumstances, being for or against the King is not an issue now. The issue has always been and is now so even more clearly, for the anti-junta forces to unite against the dictatorship and accept as a fact that the people of Greece will finally decide on the issues of the constitution, the King, and the government.

If we do honestly devote ourselves to this goal and all anti-junta forces, including the King himself, proceed as one united force in seeking freedom for the people of Greece, then we can accomplish a great deal. If, on the other hand, we stress the conflict between supporters and opponents of the monarchy, then we simply are playing Papadopoulos's game.

This is all I wanted to say on that issue.

Now, as far as Pappas is concerned, I fully agree with you that Pappas should take the position of a soldier concerned about the effectiveness of the armed forces being destroyed and the people's lack of freedom.

He should come here when the House Foreign Affairs Committee holds hearings and when arrangements have been made for his visit to have the greatest effect in this country (U.S.A.). It seems to me that it would be particularly effective if your contacts could lead to an invitation for him.

I am aware of Pappas's problems. I talked with him the first day he arrived in Rome. I am doing my best to get them financial assistance.

Finally, I agree with you that establishing an international commission to supervise the referendum, which is going to be rigged anyway, is totally undesirable now.

Adamantia, I hope I have answered the questions you raised.

We know each other well enough to realize that what is needed now, more than ever before, is collective action.

Thank you again for your letter.

With best wishes,

O. E. Vidalis

June 14, Thursday

I called Sterling Munroe, Senator Jackson's assistant, who told me that the senator issued a statement yesterday. He read me some passages from the press release, about which I was enthusiastic. I thanked him warmly.

I called the King, told him about Jackson's statement and read it to him.

He had information from Karamanlis that not much would happen at NATO. Also, Secretary General Luns said that the Greek naval officers are not being tortured.

June 15, Friday

I received Jackson's statement.

Senator Jackson is one of the most respected people in the Senate. His opinions and actions are always well-thought out, the result of lengthy consideration. Everything the senator says is taken very seriously by the administration, any administration, Democratic or Republican. The senator kept the promise he made to me during our meeting on May 30.

As soon as his statement reached me, I wrote the following letter to Senator Jackson:

Dear Senator Jackson *June 15, 1973*

I wish to express my most sincere thanks and my deepest appreciation for your excellent statement. It has already created a sensation in all responsible circles.

I am sure the message will be an extremely encouraging sign for the people of Greece, who are faced with the perspective of at least another seven years of the same oppressive mockery of government or violence. I wish the "Voice of America" could transmit it in Greece, in addition to the European radio stations that have already transmitted it.

Your statement is by far the best presentation of the problem and the most realistic approach to solve it I have ever seen. It definitely can become the framework for concrete, further action from both the Senate and the Administration.

I personally think the dictatorship gambled in the belief that there will be no reaction from this country because of the "Watergate paralysis." If follow-up activities occur as a result of your very strong position, both by the Senate and the Administration, the dictatorship will realize that they miscalculated.

The dictatorship is now primarily involved in a campaign to demoralize the people of Greece, implying it had the green light from Washington to proceed to their last madness.

What is needed now is for the Greek people to get two definite messages: a) that this country did not give the green light for what has happened, and b) this country—Senate and Administration (including the Pentagon)—will show a determination to secure at least your minimum recommendation, i.e., "genuinely open and unrigged popular referendum."

In view of this critical situation, I urge you to do your best so that your minimum recommendation is persistently implemented, particularly by the Administration.

Sincerely yours,

O. E. Vidalis

P.S. A "genuinely open and unrigged popular referendum" means no martial law, a free press, free expression of all positions by opponents of the dictatorship, and establishment of a transitional neutral government to guarantee a totally free vote, abstention of the police or military from intervening in the vote, an honest recording and reporting of the results of the vote.

The archbishop, whom I called, told me that Brademas and Sarbanes are working on nonrecognition. I said that this was very important. The greater the delay the higher the morale of Athenians and Greeks in general.

Movement in the U.S. for a Free Referendum. Jackson, Petris, Iakovos, Pell, and Many Others Concerned

June 18, Monday

I wrote Nick Petris and sent him Jackson's statement. In the letter I stressed:

Now is the time to act at least on the main issue touched upon by the senator when he said, "We must insist upon a genuinely open and unrigged popular referendum on the recent decree abolishing the monarchy." This is the minimum demonstration of some progress.

I know that the mass media, the press, the police, and the special security forces are involved in the worst brain washing operation in Greece to get the Greeks to say "Yes" to an unopposed ballot (Papadopoulos-Angelis), saying that martial law will be lifted "if the referendum is positive" (for the regime).

Now is the time to do your best. Try to convince that mayor we met to do something.

Try to convince everyone to write Senator Jackson to thank him for his statement and urge him to insist that his proposals be implemented in full.

The King called. He said that Tsibidaros asked to interview him for the *National Herald,* and he asked for my opinion. I told him unreservedly to accept because the *Herald* is performing a national service. He said that Karamanlis spoke, urging the Greeks to vote "No" and that the junta has changed completely. The main factor is Ioannidis. Papadopoulos seems to be a hostage. Our officers are being tortured. He asked if I had any news and I said no.

Spirtos sent me a copy of his letter asking to see President Nixon.

June 21, Thursday

I called Hovey. They have prepared an editorial, to be published by Sunday, which refers to Jackson's statement.

I called Nick Petris. He said that 54 California state legislators signed his letter to the president urging him to reexamine the Greek problem.

June 23, Saturday
Letter to Nixon

I called Nick Petris and asked him to mobilize his people in support of Senator Jackson's effort. He sent me the text of the letter to Nixon:

Honorable Richard M. Nixon
President of the United States
White House
Washington D.C.

Nicholas Petris
California Legislature
Senate

Dear Mr. President, *June 19, 1973*

We respectfully urge you to review your policy of recognition of the military junta in the light of current developments in Greece.

The dictator has proclaimed abolition of the monarchy abolished and establishment of a "republic" with himself as president. These decisions he will submit to the people for ratification on July 29, 1973.

The question is not whether Greece should have a monarchy or whether Papadopoulos should be president.

The question is whether the people of Greece are entitled to choose their own government in an atmosphere of freedom.

We contend that the people of Greece are entitled to determine their own destiny. They have the right to conduct genuinely free elections, with all political viewpoints represented, with a free press and all the conditions necessary to ensure freedom of choice.

The conditions for free elections do not exist in Greece today:

1. *Martial law still prevails in all the major population centers, especially Athens and Thessaloniki;*
2. *No opposition candidates for the office of president are permitted;*
3. *No political parties are permitted to hold meetings, or rallies, or appeal to the public in any way;*
4. *No public expression of support for the monarchy is permitted;*
5. *The traditional safety mechanism of a caretaker government (normally run by non-partisan persons) to rule during the election period will not be used;*
6. *Political prisoners are still in jail, or in exile within Greece, or under house arrest.*

Mr. President, when full diplomatic recognition was restored and military aid resumed to Greece heavy emphasis was placed in public statements by the Department of State and our Ambassador to Greece on the promises made by the junta to return quickly to representative government.

Those promises were made to the Greek people and to the American government.

In view of the obvious flagrant disregard of these promises, our government should review its own position relations with respect to the military dictatorship, and withdraw recognition until the conditions are fulfilled.

Otherwise, we will once again find ourselves in the position of giving recognition, aid and comfort to a self-appointed government reinforced by a phony election.

The people of Greece deserve more than this from our country which so often professes a belief in democracy and assumes leadership of the "freedom loving countries" of the world under the banner of self-determination for all peoples.

Very truly yours,

Nicholas C. Petris

The names and signatures of 54 California state senators and congressmen follow.

Peridis sent me a letter full of fighting spirit.

The King called. He liked Jackson's letter and texts. He asked when Spirtos would see Nixon. I told him that, because of Leonid Brezhnev's visit, he has received no answer and does not yet know, but he should hear next week. The King asked what Spirtos would say, that he should tell Nixon that the situation is completely out of control, that Nixon must be tougher on the issue, and that Nixon should invite the King.

He then told me that a new ship had tried to escape from Greece, there was a struggle with the marines, and the director of the 2nd bureau (intelligence) of the air force was arrested, though he had been considered a junta supporter. This information had not yet been confirmed. I thanked him for calling.

I received the following letter from Iakovos about the *Polychronio* and the King:

> The Archbishop
> of North and South America
> Iakovos
>
> *My Dear General,* *June 20, 1973*
>
> *I am sorry (as I have already written where it was needed) that, according to a Patriarchal Letter, received two days ago, the Polychronio will no longer be chanted.*
>
> *I hope that God shall grant that the remaining strength of our people will not be crushed and that he for whom I and many others will not stop praying will stand strong, straight, and unbending in spiritual endurance.*
>
> *For the Lord we will walk through flames.*
>
> *†Iakovos of America*

June 25, Monday

I telephoned Pell. He announced that the Senate had approved his amendment by 45 votes to 41. Senator Jackson, who expressed himself enthusiastically about General Norstad and myself, helped a great deal. I thanked him warmly.

June 26, Tuesday

I spoke with Gratsios and told him of the Senate's decision. He said that he had heard that airmen had been arrested and that he had telephoned London and found out that the ship-owners are at last against the regime. "I told them repeatedly," Gratsios said, "that the junta would nationalize everything, but they wouldn't listen." Onassis will be in Paris soon and will coordinate aid for Pappas and then call me. I told him that I would write Onassis to ask Joe Waggener Jr. to support the Senate proposal.

JUNE 28, THURSDAY
Senator Jackson's remarks to the Senate

Jackson sent me the minutes of the June 25 Senate session. He spoke highly of Norstad and myself without mentioning our names.

Senator Jackson's remarks to the U.S. Senate and the discussion that followed, on June 25, 1973,[12] are below:

> I have been following with growing concern the developments in Greece. Over a period of time now we have been reassured by our Government and the Greek Government that some real progress would be made toward returning to normalcy. Every time a promise has been made, we find that repression continues.
>
> What I am concerned about relates to the ability of Greece to discharge its responsibilities to NATO. One can talk all that one wants to talk about the internal situation in a country being its own business. However, the facts are, Mr. President, that the internal situation in Greece has deteriorated each month and each year as a result of this regime.
>
> Mr. President, some very thoughtful people who follow the goings on in NATO—some outstanding officers and professional soldiers who have only one concern, and that is the security of Western Europe and the Mediterranean area—have expressed their continuing concern about the developments in Greece.
>
> I can say to the Senate that one very high ranking, retired officer who served overseas in connection with a NATO assignment has conveyed to me his deep concern about the events in Greece. As a result of the latest defection of naval officers, we have a situation now in which the ability of the Greek Government to make a viable contribution to its NATO commitment is in serious question.
>
> Mr. President, I am pleased to cosponsor the amendment of the distinguished Senator from Rhode Island (Mr. Pell) in an effort to see if we cannot jar some sense into the leadership of Greece. My concern runs directly to the ability of the Greek Government to fulfill its commitment to NATO. The course that government is following at this time, with all the

[12] U.S. Congressional Record 6/25/1973, p. S 11925

> repression that is evidenced there, is disgraceful. So I would hope that the Senate would express its deep concern about the developments in Greece by agreeing to the pending amendment.

Senator Pastore asked Jackson if he thought the proposed measure might force Greece to withdraw from NATO. Senator Jackson replied,

> Not at all. On the contrary, it is an effort to nudge the Greek Government to make a viable contribution to NATO. I point out that I have talked with a former high ranking Greek officer who has left and is now with an American company. This is a very responsible, sober, and sensible man. He is a moderate individual. That man informed me—and he has kept current with all that is going on in Greece—that the military competence of the Greek Government is a hollow shell. The last development concerning the Greek Navy was the straw that broke the camel's back.
>
> The deep concern comes from people who want to see to it that Greece is capable of making a real contribution to NATO.

Hackett called to say that the Foreign Relations Committee was evenly divided, thirteen to thirteen, and therefore the bill must go to arbitration.

He also said that Congressman Frelinghuysen (a long-standing supporter of the junta) said that they must warn the junta and that he had sent a letter to Papadopoulos.

JUNE 29, FRIDAY
The archbishop sent a strong letter to Rogers

Rallis called. He had heard about the Senate, but Rogers's remarks had made a bad impression in Greece. He said that a popular campaign committee had been formed by nonpolitical figures, that *Politika Themata* will become a daily to help the other two papers, *Vradini* and *To Vima*, and that it needs journalists.

I telephoned the archbishop. He said that he had written a very strong letter to Rogers. He sent copies to the King and me.

JULY 3, TUESDAY

Dimitrakopoulos called and read me the testimony by the new director of the CIA, Colby. Answering a question from Symington about a *New York Times* article, Colby said, "The CIA did not engineer the 1967 coup but we could not conclusively answer whether or not Greek president designate George Papadopoulos was ever on the CIA payroll. We worked with him from time to time in his official capacity."

Averof and Garoufalias were arrested today. Averof for "writing the navy's proclamation to the Greek people" and Garoufalias for "giving three million [drachmas] to the officers' families."

July 7, Saturday
Iakovos's letter to Rogers

I received a copy of Iakovos's letter to Rogers. It is very good:

> *The Honorable General Orestis E. Vidalis*
> *Toledo, Ohio*
>
> *July 3, 1973*
>
> *My dear general,*
>
> *Thank you for your letter and the photocopy of the minutes. I have enclosed a photocopy of my letter and I hope it will not be long before there is greater wisdom and a more honorable treatment of our "situation," as well as of every other unacceptable trend or situation.*
>
> *Through fire for the Lord*
>
> *Archbishop † Iakovos of America*

His letter to Rogers is below:

> PERSONAL
>
> *Dear Mr. Secretary,* *June 29, 1973*
>
> *On the eve of my departure for Greece where I will officiate at the Memorial Service marking the First Anniversary of the passing of the late Patriarch Athinagoras I, I come to you with a very special concern. I have never addressed such a letter to you, nor would I have done so now, were it not for the statement made by you two days ago pertaining to the official policy of our Country, towards Greece.*
>
> *This statement on the tyrannical situation in Greece contradicts both our political philosophy and the interests of our country, which interests should lie with the people, and not in the hands of the leaders who form an unacceptable, self-imposed and self-perpetuating oligarchy.*
>
> *Under the present situation, the people of Greece are not free to choose their political leaders, nor are they free to chart their own course of political destiny. Our present "hands off" policy is not one which is consistent with the global interests and concerns of our Country. The abolition of the monarchy and the establishment of a military democracy is not "internal" nor is it the*

personal matter of the self-imposed dictators of Greece. Greece, the cradle of democracy, where the rights and the dignity of man first saw light, deserves both our respect and our concern.

My motivation in addressing this letter to you, Mr. Secretary, is purely American, purely Christian and purely moral, for as a clergyman, I must at all times, stand for the freedom and the dignity of the God-made Man.

Sincerely,

Iakovos, Archbishop

The Honorable William Rogers
Secretary of State
The State Department
Washington D.C.

July 8, Sunday

I received a letter from Zisiou with, as usual, much current information on the situation. In this letter of 6/30/73 he informed me that someone from my immediate environment is relaying precise details of my activities. I have had such clues in the past but have never been able to identify a suspect.

July 9, Monday

Rallis called. Copies of *Politika Themata* are running out. "EVERYBODY VOTE NO" is on the cover. He wants prominent journalists.

July 12, Thursday
Meetings with Congressmen Hays and Frelinghuysen

At 9:45 AM I met with Congressman Wayne Hays. He was in Greece five weeks ago and asked to see Papadopoulos, who at first was reluctant but relented in the end. Papadopoulos said that he would move towards democracy. Hays expressed the fear that his visit may have accelerated the dethronement of the King, who is the most popular Greek if there is a popular Greek. In the villages he saw apathy, which I explained was not apathy but lack of trust, fear, and hatred that cannot be expressed otherwise. I asked him to support a proposal similar to the one made by the Senate, and he said he would but that Nixon would change it. I told him that the relationship between Congress and Nixon has changed, and I drew his attention to the need for immediate action in order to bolster morale during the referendum. He promised to do everything he could.

At noon I saw Congressman Frelinghuysen. Very polite, he admitted they have been blackmailed. He had written to Papadopoulos but not received a reply. The committee is in agreement to do something but they cannot agree on the wording. I told him that he should take the lead himself to bypass any difficulties. "I have not seen the Senate text," he said. "General, you're right. You are putting me to work, but I'll do it. If I change my position it will pass." I thanked him and we left together, he on his way to vote.

July 13, Friday

I received a letter from Congressman Paul Sarbanes, dated July 6, 1973: [Translated back into English from the printed Greek text.]

> *As you know, recently I and other members of the House of Representatives wrote to the president expressing our concerns over continuing developments in Greece. I am aware of your own concerns about the situation and would like to thank you for the excellent leadership you have exercised on this most interesting issue.*

I telephoned Spirtos, who said that Liber was furious about the text for the AHEPA convention. He said it would break up the organization, but Spirtos was adamant. He read me his report, which was caustic. We discussed the issue of inviting the King. Manesiotis is no longer reacting much, but he will ask if Makarios will come and, if not, then he will turn his full attention to the King. I told him the invitation must be announced by the 20th or the 25th in order to have any effect on the referendum. As for his future candidacy, many want him to run for a second term. He finds that his opponents don't have a case. If they ask him to, he will stay on.

July 16, Monday

The King called. The French government barred the broadcast of his declaration in Greek but the BBC and Cologne will broadcast it. He will send me the text by registered letter. Venizelos announced that he had not communicated with either the King or Karamanlis. I told him about the hearings in the House and my contacts with congressmen.

Dimitrakopoulos called to say that the hearings were overwhelmingly against the pentagon.

JULY 17, TUESDAY
Karamanlis statement

Lambrias sent me the Karamanlis text in English.

JULY 19, THURSDAY

I telephoned Hackett, who said that the bill is proceeding without the Senate amendment and, therefore, will have to go to arbitration.

Rallis called. Terrorism is continuing but public sentiment is 90% NO. He fears that they will rig the results.

AHEPA Invites the King to Attend the Convention and, Eventually, the King Declines

JULY 20, FRIDAY

Spirtos called. He had sounded out four and only one was against inviting the King. He asked me if he should proceed so the King could be invited before the 29th of the month. I said that I would have an answer for him tomorrow.

JULY 21, SATURDAY

I telephoned the King and told him that Spirtos wants to invite him to the AHEPA Convention on August 23 in Florida. He asked if Spirtos would run and I said this was not yet certain but that his accepting the invitation clearly would facilitate matters.

He asked to be allowed to think it over and would give me an answer tomorrow afternoon.

I called Spirtos and told him that he would have his answer tomorrow. There is no longer a question of Washington. If the King comes he will go directly to Florida. I asked if Agnew would attend and he said no, though Yatron and Sarbanes would. I asked him how he saw the climate. "The great majority, even those who are against the monarchy, will be glad to see the King," he answered.

JULY 23, MONDAY

I telephoned Spirtos, who said that of the nine, eight were in favor and one against.

The King called and said that the BBC and Paris broadcast an excerpt of his declaration, in his own voice, while German radio broadcast the whole thing but not in his own voice.

I told the King that *Newsweek* had an article. He asked about the AHEPA Convention. I said that eight were in favor and one against. He said he would answer in the morning. He wanted to ask Karamanlis as well.

Pyrros called to say that he had seen Silva, who told him the administration is worried that something might happen. Kissinger wrote a stern warning to Tasca and is in favor of toughening their stance against the Colonels. They estimate that 70 to 80% of the Greeks will vote NO. I relayed all this to the King.

July 24, Tuesday
The King accepts AHEPA's invitation

I spoke with the King. He had not telephoned because he had not found Karamanlis to get his opinion. He proposed asking Iakovos and drew attention to the risk of organized disturbances. I told him that relations between Iakovos and AHEPA were not at their best and gave him the archbishop's phone number.

The King called later and said that Iakovos agrees and that I can, therefore, notify Spirtos to proceed.

Iakovos had tried to reach me so I called him and we spoke. He said that the State Department will release his letter and strong statement on Thursday or Friday. The *New York Times* had contacted him and asked about it. He said he is prepared for all the consequences, but he clearly was not at ease. I told him that the Greeks would stand by him, things have changed. He asked me to send a copy of his letter to the King.

I telephoned Buchanan and told him that I had sent him the King's text and that now was the time for the administration to make a statement about the referendum.

The King told me that he had fully briefed the Shah, who would meet with Nixon today.

July 25, Wednesday

Spirtos telephoned. He sent the telegram. He had had an intense discussion with Manesiotis, whom he had told that he had invited the King.

The King called and said that Papadopoulos may make a speech tomorrow and that they had released some navy people, including Engolfopoulos and Minaios.

Pyrros telephoned and said that Silva had told him, "If Papadopoulos makes it to Sunday, he has a 50% chance of continuing, but his chances of making it to Sunday are less than 50%."

July 26, Thursday
Difficulties begin with the King's visit

I telephoned Spirtos and asked him to call me as soon as he gets the telegram. Late in the afternoon, it still had not arrived. I called the King, who said that he had sent it at 8:00 AM Rome time.

Late at night Spirtos telephoned and said that the King had sent it to Washington. The Washington people with the Supreme President of the Board of Trustees sent a telegram to the King asking him to cancel his acceptance.

I asked him, "What does this mean? Who did this?" He said that he had spoken with the members of the Supreme Lodge and everyone held firm to their positions. I said, "Then send a telegram thanking the King for accepting the invitation with the signatures of all the members who agreed with the invitation." "I'll do it immediately," he responded.

At two in the morning I called the King. I told him what had happened and suggested that Papagos send a telegram to AHEPA-Washington telling them to forward the telegram to the elected president and the members of the Supreme Lodge. I told the King that all this happened because the AHEPA representative in Washington is an appointed functionary who belongs to Sorokos. Had the telegram been sent to Spirtos's address, none of this would have happened. But it does not matter because the Washington people do not represent anyone. I assured him that if I detected any trouble I would inform him immediately. I also said that Spirtos would send him a telegram thanking him for his acceptance of the invitation, signed by all those who approved the invitation.

July 27, Friday

I called Spirtos and told him that the King received the telegram, unsigned, what his answer was, and that the Queen also would be coming. And I said that he should move swiftly to send a press release to AP, UPI, etc.

I telephoned Rallis. He said that he had given an interview, everyone will vote NO, and that they fear that the printers may go on strike for two days. I told him about Iakovos and AHEPA's invitation to the King. He was very pleased.

July 28, Saturday

The King telephoned. I asked him if he had heard of the *Washington Post* article about Tasca railing against the junta. He had heard of it on the radio and asked if Tasca had acted on his own. I told him that, as far as I know, Tasca would not do such a thing without approval.

July 29, Sunday

The junta manages to win the referendum in Greece

The referendum was held. The results released were over 80% in the countryside and 55% in the capital in favor of the junta.

Spirtos called to say that, in the end, the people who were preparing a reaction did not hold their meeting. I told him to give Brademas the task of preparing the King's reception and general care.

July 30, Monday

On the behalf of the Parliamentary Defense Committee for the Restoration of Democratic Legality, Panaghiotis Kanellopoulos today made the following statement:

> No people on earth would freely vote to such an extent in favor of those holding power. And I did not imagine that there would be Greeks who would present the Greek people in such a light.
>
> The announced results of the referendum are completely contrary to the real will of our proud people. I reject the validity of these results because I respect my fellow citizens. Nor can I accept that the only free Greeks are those who live in large cities—where the regime was forced to reveal something, although not accurately, of the percentage of NO votes—or that the inhabitants of the countryside are not just as free and proud, perhaps more so, than the inhabitants of large cities.

August 1, Wednesday

The King telephoned in the morning. I said that I had sent him everything he needed for his speech, that Iakovos needed psychological support, and that the King should call him. He asked if the junta could block his arrival at the AHEPA convention. I said that to date I had no signs that they could. He said he had given an interview to Canadian television in both Greek and English. The interviewer had asked him if he, personally, had any indication that the vote was rigged.

He telephoned again in the evening to say that he had learned that Spirtos's opponents were going to publish a telegram in Athens saying, "Spirtos does not have the right to invite the King." He asked if Spirtos could publish the telegrams.

I telephoned Spirtos. He said that he had the majority of the Supreme Council and was not going to back down. We discussed the matter of the invitations and he said he saw no reason not to send them. I told him that in view of the reaction against him and to avoid his opponents being able to say that the invitations were not accepted, it was my belief that it would be better not to send invitations except to all the Greek-American congressmen. He agreed. He had not yet spoken with Sarbanes.

AUGUST 2, THURSDAY

Spirtos telephoned and said that Terzis sent a telegram to the King telling him not to come. He found this out from the *Washington Star*, which had called to ask about it. Spirtos explained to them that he had a ten to three majority in the elected board of directors and that the King is an international celebrity.

AUGUST 5, SUNDAY

The King called at 7:00 AM He had received the telegram from Terzis. We agreed that he should forward it to Spirtos. In October he will come to the U.S. and stay with a friend of his who will invite various prominent people for dinner. In addition to Spirtos and myself, should he invite the archbishop, he asked and I said, "Certainly."

I telephoned Spirtos. He said that the Greek consulates were calling Greek-Americans and urging them to send telegrams against the King's presence at the AHEPA Convention. He will call the State Department to see what can be done about it because, as an American, he cannot tolerate interference by the Greeks in American internal affairs.

AUGUST 7, TUESDAY
The King's visit is cancelled

I telephoned Spirtos, who said that pressure was mounting furiously. I asked if he feared the invitation would be withdrawn. He said certainly not by him, but he does not know what the others will do. I then said that I will recommend that the King say that he will not come. Spirtos did not object and seemed relieved.

I telephoned the King and told him that Norstad was trying to arrange an invitation to Eisenhower's university [Johns Hopkins], but that he thought he needed to ensure that Rogers and Nixon meet with the King. The King responded that he was not interested in that. It would be enough to speak with the senators. I then told him about the need to cancel his visit here because I foresaw trouble and a possible withdrawal of the invitation. I suggested that he send the following telegram: "I was informed elements outside the AHEPA are trying to divide your organization, misinterpreting the meaning of my presence at your national convention. Since I highly value the unity within the AHEPA, I regret to inform you that the Queen and I will not be able to attend your convention. I express my best wishes to you personally, to the Supreme Lodge, and to the members of the AHEPA for a most successful convention and a bright future for your organization."

The King was upset. He asked if all this had been expected and I said no. He asked what Spirtos said. I said he agrees with my suggestion. I insisted that, in view of future plans, he must postpone the trip. He will give me his answer tomorrow morning.

August 8, Wednesday

I telephoned Spirtos in the afternoon and asked him for his predictions. He said that he had received three telegrams withdrawing support for inviting the King and that the Supreme Lodge would meet on Saturday to discuss the issue.

I called the King and told him that Spirtos has lost the support of the Supreme Lodge and begged him to send the telegram in the morning. He said that he had tried to find Iakovos, but without luck.

August 9, Thursday

At 7:00 AM California time I telephoned Spirtos. He thought that it would be advisable for the King to come but not speak. His mere presence would impress. I told him that no change to the initial invitation would be acceptable by the King and neither would I propose it.

Around noon the King called to say that he had received a handwritten letter on plain paper, not archbishopric stationery, from Iakovos saying that he would be in Geneva attending the Council of Churches and that certain matters had arisen making it necessary for the King to cancel his visit. The King sent the telegram to California.

Around 5:00 in the afternoon Spirtos called to say that he had received the telegram, which he read to me along with the reply he had prepared.

So this phase of the adventure ended today.

August 13, Monday

Charges filed against politicians, generals, and myself over the navy

Makrias called to say that they have filed charges against Karamanlis, Rallis, Tzannetis, Peridis, and Vidalis because of the navy revolt.

August 15, Wednesday

I received a letter from M. Theodorakis in Paris containing his statement on Karamanlis's latest announcement.

August 16, Thursday

We received newspapers from Athens. *To Vima* carried the indictment summoning me to be interrogated about the navy's move. It mentions that Fetsis met me in Switzerland where I told him about the navy plans. The indictment does not show that Panaghiotareas [who had been arrested] revealed the documents.

August 19, Sunday

I received a letter from Zisiou sending me a copy of the August 14, 1973 *Vradini* with a piece about the navy's move.

> Charges, which under current law carry sentences of 10 to 20 years imprisonment and the loss of political rights for 2 to 10 years, have been filed against:
>
> 1. Sixty-nine officers and citizens for the celebrated navy case, to be tried by the Athens Special Court Martial.
> 2. Konstantinos Karamanlis, former Prime Minister, Konstantinos Papakonstantinou, Georgios Rallis and E. Kefalogiannis, former ministers, Nikitas Venizelos, former M.P., S. Tzannetis, Lieutenant General (ret.), Georgios Peridis, Lieutenant General (cashiered), Orestis Vidalis, Brigadier (cashiered), Rozakis, Rear Admiral (ret.) and others have been summoned to regular interrogation for the same case—following the filing of criminal charges against them—before the Court Reporter of the Athens Special Court-Martial.

Marketos called in the afternoon to say that he had heard Papadopoulos proclaiming a general amnesty domestically. He asked me what it meant.

I responded: "It is a good maneuver to gain time, avoid the trial about the navy, and demonstrate magnanimity. It changes nothing. Things will change only when the Greeks are freed and can judge and decide for themselves about their own institutions."

AUGUST 21, TUESDAY
Spirtos in trouble at AHEPA convention

Yesterday, the Department of State issued the following press release on developments in Greece: [Translated back into English from the printed Greek text.]

> We have consistently urged the Greek Government to return the country to a political system that ensures political freedoms and guarantees the participation of the Greek people. In this connection, we note the statement by President Papadopoulos that political freedoms will be restored and free elections will take place in 1974. As friends and allies of Greece, we welcome all measures leading to the restoration of political normalcy in that country.

I telephoned Spirtos in the morning. He had had only 20 minutes of sleep. He told me that a battle was going on over the text in the convention brochure. He was obviously tired. The attack against him had been very strong. The text printed in the brochure for AHEPA's 51st convention (19—25 August) follows:

> M. N. SPIRTOS, M. D.
> SUPREME PRESIDENT
> ORDER OF AHEPA
>
> *OUR HISTORICAL DUTY*
>
> We convene today on this our 51st Anniversary with the basic objects of our beloved Order in jeopardy. We are facing a historical challenge to examine candidly our responsibilities.
>
> We are the direct link between the people of Hellas and the people of the United States of America. The single most important ideological tie between the two cultures and people is the concept of freedom and dignity of the individual.
>
> Today the people of Hellas are deprived of the voice in determining their institutions. Our task as a link is in jeopardy. We who cherish liberty as a blessing in this great country of ours and as a most valuable possession, cannot allow ourselves to forget what the late President John F. Kennedy said:
>
> "If men and women are in chains anywhere in the world then freedom is endangered everywhere."
>
> It is our mission dictated by our own AHEPA Constitution to oppose tyranny and oppression. It is our obligation to be irreconcilable enemies of all forms of totalitarianism and its different disguises.

Our brothers in Hellas are not free. If we are to maintain our identity and our personality as true AHEPANS, we cannot afford to close our eyes to the denial of freedom in Hellas. As honest Americans dedicated to preserve our own dignity and our own self-respect, we must arouse the people of this country to the goal of restoring the freedom of the Hellenes.

The lessons of the past six years urge me to warn my fellow AHEPANS against complacency and false promises.

If we do not act decisively now, in 1976 we will run the risk of celebrating the 200th anniversary of our land, the land of the free, while freedom will still be suppressed in its birthplace, our beloved Hellas.

Assisting the Hellenes in restoring their freedom is NOT politics. It is a sacred obligation of all of us to the land where our freedom was born.

Fellow AHEPANS, it was my duty, at these historical moments, as your elected representative to be candid. It is now your responsibility to reflect and meet the greatest challenge we have ever faced throughout the history of our great organization.

Fraternally,

M. N. Spirtos, M.D.
Supreme President
Order of AHEPA

AUGUST 23
Text added to the AHEPA issue

The junta's agents in AHEPA manage to keep the brochure from being circulated. In order to overcome the crisis and the unbearable pressure so that the brochure could be released with the above text, Spirtos agreed to the addition of an insert containing Secretary Roger's answer to reporters with the following addition:

> The above statement by the Secretary of State was received following the publication of the Supreme President's message.
>
> This statement satisfies your Supreme President that definitive progress is being made to realize the principles I declared in my message.
>
> M. N. Spirtos, M.D.
> Supreme President

Kissinger Became Secretary of State.

AUGUST 27, MONDAY

The King telephoned. He asked if I have news. I told him that Sorokos did not attend the AHEPA convention after all and that Spirtos was sorely tried. The decision not to come was the right one. A supporter of the junta, but not fanatic, from Spirtos's party won the election. I spoke with General Norstad, who thinks that Kissinger's appointment is a significant development and he wants to speak with him because he thinks there must be a meeting between Kissinger and the King. He will let me know. The King did not think they would see him and that if a meeting cannot be arranged he should come here even if he doesn't see them. I will contact him if I have any news. I told him I was leaving for Washington.

I went to Washington and met with Pyrros, Couloumbis, and Nicolopoulos in the evening.

Couloumbis had seen Churchill, who told him that they are trying to keep their distance from Papadopoulos but cannot because of the moves toward liberalization he is taking.

We discussed Kissinger with Pyrros and the new secretary's efforts to approach Congress. We agreed that he should sound out Moose and, through him, Fulbright in order to prepare the ground for a discussion with and favorable response from Kissinger.

Efforts Continue without Pause

AUGUST 28, TUESDAY
Discussion with Walters

In the afternoon, I met with Dick Walters, who came to my hotel. He was pleased because he had been able to prove that the CIA had not been involved in Watergate. He told me that Papadopoulos had won himself some breathing space in the short term but he would face trouble in the long term. He stressed that the most important thing was the army's stance.

I told him that the army's stance is influenced by the stance taken by NATO and Nixon. Now that Kissinger is assuming new duties it is time for him to announce that in NATO they feel that the Greeks should be free to shape their own institutions and elect their own governments.

"I agree that something must be done between inaction and upheaval. I'll see Kissinger and see what can be done." I told him it would be good to anticipate the Senate's questions with a favorable statement. I also said that another change would be for the administration to be free to meet with and talk with any and all Greeks.

Finally, it would be a tragedy if Nixon went to Greece. "That will not happen. Personally I am against all travel to Europe but I don't know if they will listen to me."

I said that the Greek problem could be solved more easily by the Nixon administration than by a Democratic one. He agreed and added, "As he solved the Chinese and Soviet problems, which could not have been handled by the Democrats who would have been considered fellow travelers. Just as the Democrats have an easier time solving the problem of domestic order." He promised to do something. We shall see.

AUGUST 31, FRIDAY
The White House responds to Petris

Nick Petris sent me a copy of the White House response to the letter sent by California Senators and Representatives: [Translated back into English from the printed Greek text.]

White House Washington August 21, 1973

Dear Mr. Petris,

On behalf of the president I would like to thank you for your letter co-signed by members of the Senate and House of Representatives of California referring to American policy towards Greece.

An essential element of American policy towards Greece has been the maintenance of close relations concerning mutual security, both bilaterally and in connection with NATO, which the two countries have enjoyed for two decades. At the same time, since the 1967 coup, we have recognized that the long-term stability of Greece and, therefore, the long-term mutual security interests of Greece and the United States would seem to be better served by a political system that provides governments chosen by the people.

While we have avoided interfering in the internal affairs of Greece we have steadily shown our support for the stated intentions of the Greek government to return the country to a parliamentary system.

In the contemporary world we have diplomatic, trade, and other relations with many countries that have a variety of political systems. This fact reflects the increasing awareness that relations between two countries are—and should be—broader and more durable than the relations and transactions between governments.

Relations between the United States and Greece have been maintained for many years with successive Greek governments.

As you know, the various elements composing our foreign policy are constantly being reviewed. We are following developments in Greece closely and, naturally, are studying them seriously.

In relation to the issue you mention, U.S. military aid to Greece, I believe you may be interested to know that in January of this year the Greek government announced its decision to decline American military aid as of January 1, 1973. However, in accordance with our administration's evaluation that Greece still needs some aid to carry the financial burden of defense in order to fulfill its substantial role in NATO effectively, Greece will still have access to the arrangements (we have) for military sales and credits.

Thank you for sharing your thoughts with the president.

Sincerely,

Ronald L. Elliot
Special Assistant to the President
To the Honorable Nicholas C. Petris
State Capitol, Room 3082
Sacramento, California 95814

September 4, Tuesday

Spirtos called. He told me that his position was received and supported much more strongly than he had expected. Kofinas had proposed that the Supreme Lodge send two telegrams in favor of Papadopoulos and Sorokos, but this was rejected. According to Spirtos, the Supreme Lodge is opposed to the junta. I asked him about Tsafaras's position. "It is good," he said. "He will do nothing in favor of the junta."

September 9, Sunday

The King telephoned and said that he is concerned about what the politicians will do about the Markezinis prospect and the possible measures. If they abstain they will achieve nothing, as history has shown. If they participate, it means recognition. I told him that this is a matter of tactics. What is important is unity among Kanellopoulos, Mavros, Pesmazoglou, and Stratos. If there is unity, any decision will carry weight.

He told me that the people in London were getting ready to return. The news saddened me. "They are tired, general, and want to go back."

"Do you know if Markezinis will meet with Karamanlis?"

"Karamanlis is in Italy, general. He will stay for another ten days. But even if he were in Paris, I don't think that Karamanlis would meet with Markezinis."

"That is good news, Your Majesty, if it's true."

September 10, Monday
Discussion with Norstad

I telephoned Norstad and told him that because of the natural delay, despite the fact that our friend (the King) would like to meet his friends (Kissinger, Nixon) and because our friend has to schedule his movements, he proposes either that we ignore the official meetings and hold only private ones or that the visit be postponed to February or March, giving him (Norstad) enough time to consult and arrange the matter.

The general responded, "Thank you especially for calling. I have not written Kissinger because I am afraid the letter might be overlooked now that he is abroad. I tried to reach him by telephone but it proved impossible, he cannot be found anywhere. I much prefer the second option because I want the King to enjoy recognition on his visit to America. I know that I can achieve this."

"Perhaps it will not be possible in view of the relations between the King and the regime?"

"I want to try because I do not think the King should come without official recognition. If I do not succeed, then we can plan for the private visit. Please convey my respects to the King and my warm affection."

I thanked him and called the King, telling him about the discussion. He asked if I thought that Norstad could succeed. I answered positively and said, "In any case he wants to try because he does not think you should come here without your presence being officially recognized." The King told me to plan either for the first ten days in February or the second half of March. He asked if the general could telephone him. Norstad had told him that he is afraid of transatlantic telephone calls. I have not told the King that Norstad and I communicate by telephone.

"Please convey to him that his support in these times is good for our morale, though I am afraid that he will not achieve anything because the way they are going, Nixon and the CIA will lose Greece forever." He thanked me and I said that I would write.

September 14, Friday
Mitsotakis in Greece

I called Couloumbis. He said that they telephoned Mitsotakis on Thursday evening. Mitsotakis told them that he would return to Greece; Karamanlis had agreed; Karamanlis himself would not return at this point; Mitsotakis did not know what he would do if he encountered Markezinis; and the King's stock was down. When Couloumbis asked what they should do, Mitsotakis said, "You must continue as if nothing has changed."

I telephoned Rallis. He said that for the first time he had seen a serving officer, a former follower of Papadopoulos, who was furious with Papadopoulos, saying, "We did not carry out the revolution so that he could become boss." I told him that there were a thousand fanatics in favor of Papadopoulos, another thousand fanatically opposed to him, and the rest were indifferent or not inclined to act. If we had unity behind Karamanlis, they would help as well. The King must be patient, Rallis responded, because the young do not want him. I replied that only unity among the politicians and the creation of a breach between Papadopoulos and the armed forces could be decisive.

"You," Rallis said, "are considered a fanatic royalist and Mitsotakis is seen as opposed to the Centrists, therefore your freedom of action is curtailed." "What are you considered?" I asked. "I don't understand that stuff, nor does it interest me. What interest me are unity and a possible approach to the armed forces. You know this from everything that I have done. Supporting any solution promoted by the dictatorship would legitimize a political aberration and I will never agree to that."

"I will go to Paris for ten days," Rallis said, "because Karamanlis is not moved by a shorter visit. I will see the King. I telephoned Claridge's but he was not there. I must see him now, he's alone." I replied, "He is terribly alone and needs much support." "I know," Rallis answered.

September 22, Saturday
The generals have problems of their own

I am in Boston. General Frontistis came to the hotel around 11:00 AM. He described the difficulties they had getting the text signed. Seiradakis was attacked by the former Centrist generals, particularly by Petropoulos. They applied pressure on Chatziprodromos, Vlachos, and Argyropoulos, who had initially signed but then withdrew their signatures.

Petropoulos and the rest maintained that Papadopoulos is gunning for the King and Karamanlis and, therefore, it is correct that they should not cause him trouble now.

Gikas did not sign, saying, "that they must move to reveal the rampant corruption." He was working with Stametelopoulos. Yennimatas maintained that they must move to overthrow the junta with the army, without saying how. After Pipilis signed the letter to Papadopoulos, he was put under such pressure that he balked at publication. At a reception Pipilis had met Angelis, who attacked him viciously, but in the end he agreed to publication and since then has behaved impeccably.

Frontistis believes that the King's case has been forgotten.

SEPTEMBER 27, THURSDAY
The charges against me at the court martial

Today I received a copy of the ruling in my court martial. The case was tried on June 22, 1973. The judges were:

Evgenios Karachalios, Reserve Judicial Counsel II, President
Panaghiotis Dimas, Lieutenant Colonel, Artillery
Vassilis Mavromitros, Lieutenant Colonel, Artillery
Grigoris Paraskevopoulos, Lieutenant Colonel, Artillery
Nikolaos Nikolaidis, Reserve Judicial Counsel III
Deputy Judge Advocate—standing in for the Judge Advocate—was Evangelos Fioratos, reserve assistant Judicial Counsel I.

The Judge Advocate proposed a not guilty verdict on the charges filed and the court found me not guilty by 3 votes to 2.

The charges included that, "in the U.S.A. from March 1969 to June 1970 he did commit acts incompatible with his status a Greek citizen and against the interests of Greece."

The "anti-national activities" for which I was charged were based on specific acts relating to public statements I made in the United States. The specific acts forming the basis for the charges leading to my court-martial, as published in the court's decision, follow:

Specific acts
in decision number 51/1973 by
the Special Athens Court Martial
of Brigadier General Orestis E. Vidalis:

a. On March 30, 1969, for the anniversary of Greek Independence, in the Greek Orthodox Church in the city of Toledo in the state of Ohio, he gave a speech on "the future of Greece" in which he studiously and very carefully spoke against the present situation in Greece.
b. In April of 1970 he had published in the American newspaper *National Herald* and in the American periodical *Greek Report* an article on the 150th anniversary of Greek independence in which he dropped pretenses and ceased to be diplomatic, standing clearly against the present situation in Greece. The content is anarchist and anti-national, such as "And we have reached 1970. The regime is nothing new—

unfortunately it is a sad repetition, the supremacy through violence of extremism opposing measure. It is a method that has been tried many times before and has always failed, not just in preventing the repetition of a new aberration, but even in preventing the tragic national adventures to which it usually leads. The regime is an anachronism because for three years it has been condescending towards the Greeks, showing a complete lack of confidence in them. It feeds on their humiliation. . . . The regime is an anachronism because it has not solved a single problem from the past. All problems are in the deep freezer while new and complex difficulties are born out of institutional decay, the persecution and ruin of our best and brightest, and the spreading of irresponsibility throughout the entire country. The regime is an anachronism because it offers the young nothing but emptiness, uncertainty, and insecurity. . . . It (the regime) uplifts and rewards opportunism, ignorance, flattery, subservience, denunciation, and base instincts. . . . The regime is enslavement of the people in a police state. . . . The sacrifice of prominent Greek citizens, the persecution of the best officers . . . the resistance of the people which forces the police state to ever greater severity . . . . those who believe that the regime can evolve and become a healthy political entity are either opportunists or are unaware that of its own free will the regime will never abandon the monologue because it is incapable of dealing with the difficulties of dialogue. . . . Renewal cannot be expected of the regime, merely a continuation of the rule of violence. . . . let us all unite behind the single aim of "restoring responsibility to the Greek people."

c. In May of 1970, in statements to the newspaper *The Christian Science Monitor* he characterized the present regime as misguided and stated that it is experimenting catastrophically at the expense of the nation. He stated that the present regime rewards opportunism, aimlessness, flattery, obsequiousness, and treachery.

d. On June 8, 1970 he sent to Robert L. F. Sikes, member of the U.S. House of Representatives for Florida, a letter in which he condemned the regime in Greece and distorted developments in Greece for the sole purpose of defaming the country abroad, the content being anti-national, such as "The mutiny of the Colonels is a form of violence . . . obviously, you are unaware that the Greeks are not running their country. You overlook the fact that the country is run by a very small minority who does nothing else but humiliate the proud people of Greece. . . . The people of Greece are frustrated, confused, and alienated from all those who support or tolerate a dictatorship that exists only through its sole weapon, Martial Law. I can assure you that your statement has

> made the dictatorship very happy, but it has made the Greeks extremely unhappy and more confused. It certainly has reduced the confidence of the Greek people in the U.S.A. . . . Dictatorships of the kind we have in Greece do nothing but directly assist Communism." He also sent copies of the above letter to another twenty-one (21) members of the U.S. House of Representatives.

September 30, Sunday
Discussion with Norstad

I called Norstad and told him it would be good to schedule the King's visit for the first ten days of February. "That works for me as well because I'll be going to Europe later," he said. I asked if the King could have an answer by the end of November so he can arrange his schedule. "Certainly, I will definitely have an answer by then."

October 4, Thursday
The Greek press on our return

We received newspapers. On September 29 *Vradini* had a full-page article titled, "Who's coming and who's not." It mentions Mitsotakis, Opropoulos, Theodorakis, Mangkakis, Vidalis, Plytas, Papandreou, Mylonas, Vlachou, Kokkas and Mercouri. The section on me begins "The army's intellectual. He was dubbed this for his extensive education. . . ."

Matina could not help herself and called Efthymios while I was at the airport to tell him about it and he said, "Tell the intellectual to start writing."

October 8, Monday

Spirtos called as soon as he got back from Washington. There had been a meeting of the Supreme Lodge. They had attacked the president because he had sent a telegram to Papadopoulos on behalf of the Supreme Lodge. Sorokos hosted a reception in honor of the Supreme Lodge to which he invited all former AHEPA presidents except Vournas and Spirtos. They protested and Charles [George Charles, legal advisor to the Greek embassy in Washington during the junta years] told them that he had special instructions from Sorokos. Then some, such as the priest, returned the invitation, saying, "If you did not invite the former presidents because they do not support your dictatorship then I am returning the invitation because I am much more opposed."

October 10, Wednesday
Agnew resigns—Markezinis prime minister

Agnew resigned.

Markezinis was appointed prime minister and sworn in yesterday. In his statements he said nothing new. He spoke of free elections.

October 14, Sunday
Meeting with Theodorakis and Farandouri

We arrived in Milwaukee. In the evening we went to a Theodorakis concert. A large crowd. Maria Farandouri was very good. At the end of the concert Matina and I went backstage to meet Theodorakis and Farandouri. One of his people told him I was there. He turned toward us and briefly left the crowd that had surrounded him asking for autographs. We greeted each other warmly. This was our first meeting.

"I saw your son," he said.

"He told us," we replied.

"What are you going to do?" I asked him. "Will you go back to Greece?"

"I will," he answered. "I will start all over again for the third time."

"I won't go because nothing has changed," I answered.

"I have to go, I have my music, which will help me continue the resistance."

Matina handed him a copy of his book *To Chreos* (The Obligation), which Rounis had bought her at the entrance, for a dedication. Theodorakis said, "Eh, no, it is not I who should write a dedication to you, when it is you who have taught us about obligation," and he swiftly but thoughtfully wrote, "To Mr. and Mrs. Vidalis, with a thousand Greek wishes. Mikis Theodorakis." He was surrounded by a crowd. We bade our farewells and left.

October 31, Wednesday

I arrived in Washington and met with Pell. He told me the situation is good in Greece following the amnesty. I told him nothing has changed. They were forced to cancel the navy trial and declare the amnesty because it was difficult and dangerous case for them to pursue.

We spoke of the King. He knew that the King would come to the U.S. in February. He told me that the members who would draft the aid bill finally had been selected and he showed me the list.

The Polytechnic a Resistance Milestone

NOVEMBER 15, THURSDAY

The radio reported this morning that 2,000 students have occupied the Polytechnic and are broadcasting to Athenians on a jury-rigged transmitter.

NOVEMBER 16, FRIDAY

A critical day. The students organized demonstrations outside the Polytechnic and clashed with police. In the evening tanks appeared in the streets of Athens. Shots were heard throughout the city. Rumors speak of many dead.

NOVEMBER 17, SATURDAY

I phoned Walters. His information was current but he stressed the anti-American aspect of the disturbances. I told him that they should have expected it.

I called Spirtos, who knew what was going on. He will try to do what I asked of him, to send telegrams to Nixon, Kissinger, and Fulbright.

That night tanks broke down the entrance gate of the Polytechnic. Shots were fired. People were killed and there were hundreds of injured.

Martial law was declared and a curfew imposed after 4:00 PM.

A large demonstration in Omonia Square was broken up after three hours of clashes by the police using tear gas fired from helicopters. There were many injured.

NOVEMBER 19, MONDAY

Buchanan called and asked if the disturbances were caused by leftists. I denied it categorically and told him to get Kissinger moving.

NOVEMBER 20, TUESDAY

Dimitris Antoniou and Zisiou called in the morning. We were cut off. All they had time to say was that the word is being spread that the disturbances are being directed by the left, specifically from Moscow. It is a lie.

I told them about the demonstrations and the position taken by the press here. I also told them that high-ranking officials here had told me the same thing about Moscow involvement and that I had scolded them.

I phoned Petris and gave him the latest details. He said that he sent Fulbright a telegram that 200 were killed and that it was shameful American weapons were being used against Greeks. He will try to motivate others. I let him know that Spirtos is also active.

Nicolopoulos heard from someone inside the embassy that 12 officers had demanded that Papadopoulos resign. I said that I had no such information.

A news report said that Kanellopoulos, Mavros, and Zighdis were under house arrest.

Papadopoulos Overthrown by Ioannidis

November 25, Sunday
Awakened at 4:00 A.M.

A telephone call from Arnaoutis woke us at 4:00 in the morning. He said, "There has been a coup in Greece. Papadopoulos was overthrown. Gizikis took over as President of the Republic. Martial law is still in effect, a curfew was imposed, and the likely prime minister is said to be Androutsopoulos." I asked, "What is Gizikis?" and he answered, "A member of the junta." "I will inform you first, to see what you can do from there and, if you have any news, contact the King directly at Claridge's."

Shaken by the news, I called Marketos immediately. I told him that Gizikis, also a military man, had taken over and closed with the comment that, regardless of what happens, the fact that Papadopoulos fell is a victory for the students and for the entire resistance because the myth of invincibility has been shattered. Then I called Dimitrakopoulos and woke him up, in turn. The news took him by surprise, he was pleased with Papadopoulos's fall. I said our position must be one of anticipation and very, very cautious optimism.

Silva called and said that he is insisting at the State Department that they must now actively support Karamanlis and the King.

I telephoned the King in London at Claridge's in the late afternoon. I told him that Walter's group had informed me that this coup had been planned to take place months ago. I added, "The radio stations here are reporting on Gizikis's royalist sentiments and that he met with you a long time ago. He answered, "Here in Europe the radio stations are saying the same thing, though not about a meeting and certainly there never was such a meeting. I asked him what he knew about the constitution being suspended and he answered, "What can I know, this man was sworn in as President of the Republic. Now, which constitution he abolished, I don't know." I said, "From the American side we have no indications because it is Sunday and because of the general disarray in Washington caused by Watergate. The only thing they have done is that they have State Department employees monitoring the situation round the clock." He asked me to inform him if I heard anything new.

On the way back from the airport, I heard Andreas Papandreou on the radio saying, "the CIA engineered the coup against Papadopoulos."

The fact that Papadopoulos was deposed was important because it destroyed the myth of invincibility and raised the morale of the resistance while at the same time making the dictatorship's supporters abroad much more circumspect. It is still far too early to see what will develop. On the one hand, the fanatic torturer Ioannidis and, on the other, Latsoudis, K. Rallis, Triantafyllakos, and Tsarmaklis form quite a heterogeneous group. Because one cannot count on moderates prevailing and, therefore, on reconciliation between the army and the people and a return to normal conditions, I believe that all means of bringing the greatest amount of pressure to bear must be used as soon as possible.

I phoned Pell at home. He had heard the news and said, "I don't see that we can do anything at once. We must see how matters develop and then see what we can do." I told him the new group consists of two teams and external pressure can help the moderates in their internal conflict with the hardliners. One available option would be to revisit the June amendment together with Senator Jackson and, if possible, Senator Percy and others. I also said that I thought it would useful for him to coordinate with Senator Fulbright to launch a general campaign. He replied, "You are right, immediate pressure to strengthen the moderates is a good thought and I will see what I can do."

November 26
Discussion with Spirtos

Doctor Spirtos called in the morning. He asked for my opinion of the situation. Briefly, I told him that I will consider it a continuation of the previous situation until it is proven otherwise. He asked me if I agreed with Andreas Papandreou's evaluation, which he had heard, and I said no. I did add, however, that the U.S. administration is largely responsible for developments because it helped the dictatorship in all the ways that it did. Now is the time for maximum activity and pressure, I told him. He said he would call the president and members of AHEPA to try to motivate them to act. I recommended that he also see what he can do in California.

Schecter of *Time* magazine also called and asked for my opinion on the situation for an article he was writing. I described Gizikis, Ioannidis, and the mediocrity of the entire group forming the new government; that they are unable to turn Papadopoulos's failure into success.

I telephoned Professor Kafatos and said that maximum pressure is needed. Specifically, I urged that he lead an effort by Harvard professors to appeal to Kissinger asking him to change U.S. policy from supporting the dictatorship to a policy of disengagement. He fully agreed, and asked if the students should send letters about the junta to senators and representatives, and I fully agreed. I suggested that they target senators Fulbright, Pell, Jackson, Scott, and representatives, including Ford.

November 28, Wednesday

Comparing the two protagonists. Talk at American University

I left for Washington in the afternoon. Nicolopoulos and Couloumbis met me at the airport. Nicolopoulos, in particular, insisted that I go to a meeting at American University. I accepted without enthusiasm, mainly so I would not discourage them.

Various people spoke. Pyrros tried to get the people attending from the State Department and the CIA to enter the discussion, but they did not open their mouths while I was there.

We were there at least an hour, maybe more, when Nicolopoulos asked me to tell the audience my thoughts about the situation and the people involved.

I asked to come forward so I could see the audience and said, approximately, this:

> Your professors, essentially, kidnapped me when I arrived at the airport, but I thank them because they gave me the opportunity to follow the discussion and your concerns. Everybody's imagination is working these days, generating impressions and beliefs about the people and the future. I will try to present an issue that I believe is of special importance in interpreting these events. Specifically, I am referring to the difference between the situation in Greece in April 1967 and the situation today.
>
> Then, following long psychological preparation, a climate had been created of the failure of democracy to contain the supposed communist threat, a climate of distrust towards politicians who were seen as corrupt.
>
> Then, the economy was booming because of measures enacted by previous governments.
>
> Then, the armed forces were united, homogeneous and, unfortunately, gave the impression that they participated in and supported the coup in April 1967 as one.
>
> Then, our young people were quiet, untroubled, and took their lead from the general population in passively tolerating the regime.
>
> Then, finally, the dictator had been preparing the ground for his coup for at least a decade, and was brilliant in using blackmail and intrigue.

> These conditions, and, in particular, the catchphrase that he would heal the nation and restore democracy, gave him plenty of time and scope to act.
>
> Today, in contrast, the new dictatorship has not inherited a failed democracy but the bankruptcy of dictatorship.
>
> Today, the people are not apathetic but furious and deeply scarred emotionally by seven years of deceit.
>
> Today, the economy is in terrible condition, with inflation the second highest in the world.
>
> Today, our young people are not merely troubled. They realize that the nation is being led from bad to worse but are showing their heroism and self-sacrifice in the effort to regain their political and academic freedom.
>
> Today, the armed forces are fractured, with no esprit de corps, no coherence, and no fighting ability.
>
> Today, the Greeks hate our allies who supported and support the dictatorship to protect their secondary interests.
>
> Today, Europe has cut Greece off and is refusing to accept the country into the European Community.
>
> This comparison of then and today leads me to the following realistic conclusion. There is no chance that the new group can transform the utter failure of the first dictatorship into success. It is not possible because the problems are huge and the new group has neither the brains nor the experience that would enable it to deal with current conditions. If the new group insists on the same strategy followed by their predecessors, they will complete the ruin of Greece.
>
> These thoughts should be considered by our allies, who must draw their own conclusions about their own strategy from here on out, for the protection, naturally, of their own interests.

I apologized for not being able to stay longer. Before I left, I stressed the importance of the student uprising, which is one of the few comforting developments for the future of our country because it proves that our young people have realized that they must solve the problems that we elders have not been able to solve for 150 years.

In the morning before I left for Toledo, Buchanan telephoned and read me a letter he sent Kissinger, telling him that the situation is tragic despite the students being released (of which I had not previously heard) and asking Kissinger to send someone influential, such as General Norstad, as the new ambassador to use his influence for restoring democracy.

November 29, Thursday
Meetings in Congress

Jack Maury came to the hotel at 2:00 in he afternoon. He told me that the day before he had testified before the Rosenthal committee in closed session. Maury denied Papandreou's claim that the CIA was behind the latest coup. He added that the situation is fluid and there had been discussion about the possibility of recalling the ambassador and the chief of the military mission. He, personally, thought it inadvisable to proceed with implementing the Sixth Fleet home-porting agreement.

I asked him if he knew how many had died at the Polytechnic and if he were aware of any impending action on the part of the U.S. administration. He said he did not know the number but would find out and call me. Later, he did call and said that the number they confirmed to him was thirteen. I said that I did not accept the accuracy of that number and that either the intelligence services were misinformed or were deceiving us. As for any impending American actions, he said he knew nothing and that everything depends on Kissinger.

I left the hotel and went to Congress. I saw Jim Pyrros, who had nothing new. He drove me to Jackson's office.

I saw Munroe, Jackson's principal aide, for half an hour. I explained the situation, noting that there is a brief window of opportunity for everyone. For the junta to change its tactics, which, unfortunately, can only happen under pressure. For the administration, if it realizes that it has a few seconds to salvage America's reputation and interests in Greece, and for Congress to play a decisive role this time. I told him that now is the time for Senator Jackson to take a public stand again and to try to influence Kissinger in private. He promised to brief Jackson.

Then I went to Pell's office. His personal assistant was expecting me to lead me to the small office that Pell uses for some of his meetings. On the way, the aide told me that Pell, Jackson, and Percy submitted a separate bill suspending aid to Greece. He gave me a copy of the bill and a long text of the submittal statement. After this the meeting in Pell's office was very brief, I thanked him warmly for acting so quickly after our telephone conversation and said that it was particularly pleasing that the bill was co-signed by Jackson and Percy. He said that was not correct; only Jackson co-signed the bill and not Percy.

At 6:00 in the evening Philip Cook of *Newsweek* magazine came by. We discussed the situation. I outlined my thoughts as I have been expressing them these days, insisting on the inability of the new team to transform Papadopoulos's failure into success, the division into various opposing groups, and the intense anti-Americanism among the Greeks. I briefed him on the Pell-Jackson bill, of which he had not been aware. He asked if I wanted him to write something about me after our discussion and I categorically told him NO, to not mention my name but use the conversation for background purposes..

NOVEMBER 30, FRIDAY
New efforts in the Senate. Meeting with Davies

I saw Churchill, and he introduced me to his new aide, John G. Day. He told me that, unfortunately, because of today's breakdown in Israeli-Arab talks, Sisco was working with Kissinger to deal with the new complication and I would see Davies instead. We went to Davies's office.

Davies said that two days earlier he was briefing a congressman, telling him that there are only two choices in Greece. Either there will be movement toward more normal political developments or they will be relapse to martial law under Papadopoulos or another group. "I hope," he said, "the congressman does not believe I had knowledge of the new coup, because I didn't."

I replied that there is only one real choice and not two. Any dictatorial regime is doomed to fail in the current Greek climate. Papadopoulos's failure was set because he did not recognize in time the compelling need to lead Greece to normal political conditions.

In my opinion, both Papadopoulos's junta and the leaders of the new coup suffered from the same misunderstanding in believing that Greece's problems were so simple that they could be handled by some 20 or 30 officers. They had no idea how complex the basic problems facing any government are. Papadopoulos managed to extend his grip on power with the help of the Americans. His last effort to restore parliamentary government came far too late and in an atmosphere of distrust.

Davies did not agree that American policy aided Papadopoulos and the discussion digressed for a moment into how Greeks see American policy.

Davies asked me how I see the situation and I said:

O.V.: The country has reached an impasse, together with the regime and the U.S., which helped it. Neither side realized that the solution was to restore normal political life in the country.

D.: Why couldn't we accomplish anything?

O.V.: You did not accomplish anything because you limited yourselves to words and not deeds. Furthermore, you said one thing and did another. I'll give you an example. Former Secretary Laird was on his way to Athens

> to announce the resumption of aid and by chance he ran into King Constantine in Rome. He told the King why he was going to Athens and asked him if he knew about it and what he thought. The King said that he did know about it and his opinion was that, together with the resumption of aid they should have ensured as a quid pro quo a positive step towards democracy. He asked Mr. Laird if something like this had been secured. Laird answered, "Certainly, your Majesty." You see, he said one thing and did another.

Then the discussion turned to the differences between 1967 and 1973. I stressed that the situation today was completely different from 1967 for the following critical reasons:

- In 1967, there was some tolerance for the coup because of the political upheaval that preceded it. Today, there is no such climate. In contrast, the people's patience has been exhausted and they will accept no further prolongation of the dictatorship.
- The economy Papadopoulos inherited was in excellent condition and helped sustain him. The new group, however, is facing high inflation and serious economic difficulties.
- In 1967, there was no youth movement. Today the young have become an avenging force, with ends and means still unknown.
- In 1967, the coup leaders claimed to have saved the country from a parliamentary system that had failed. The 1973 coup took power from a dictatorship that had failed.
- The myth of Papadopoulos's or any dictator's invincibility has been shattered. The new leadership will be much more susceptible to popular pressure or vulnerable to another coup.
- Papadopoulos had been planning the coup for 10 or 12 years and had developed ideas for governing the country. As an individual, Papadopoulos was remarkably intelligent and capable. The present leadership lacks quickness of mind, is in disarray, oversimplifies everything, and is improvising as it goes along.

Davies said, "There were valid grounds for our relationship with the Papadopoulos government. The recent crisis in the Middle East proved how hard it would be to maintain our position in the Eastern Mediterranean without Greek support."

"I recognize," I said, "the importance of your strategic interests in Greece, but they, too, will be threatened if the situation is allowed to go on as it has so far."

Turning the discussion to the need to pressure Ioannidis, I said that the famous two-pronged American policy—protecting the mutual security interests while prodding the regime toward parliamentary government—is starting to fuse into one single need. The need to replace words with deeds, which will have to be expressed by genuinely implementing your policy. If you carry out the policy you will have results in this confused situation, and I stress, "They will alter course in accordance with the obstacles they encounter. If there are no obstacles they will head towards destruction."

As I was getting ready to leave, Sisco came by and said he was sorry for two reasons: first, he had wanted to see me and, second, he wanted to hear my views, which, naturally, Davies will pass on to him.

Day escorted me to the State Department exit. He asked if he could call me as Silva used to do and added that he is certainly at my disposal for anything I want. He also said they had heard from Greece that Ioannidis had said that Karamanlis is 65 years old and out of touch with the reality of contemporary Greece. I replied that if Karamanlis is out of touch for certain reasons, then for completely different ones Ioannidis is also very far from what is happening in Greece, especially among the young.

December 3, Monday

Lambrias called me in the morning at the office. He asked if I could be in Brussels next Monday to take part in an interview arranged by Sir Hugh Greene because of the summit meeting of NATO foreign ministers. I replied that this was impossible, but told him that Greene should use the Pell-Jackson bill and I would send him any material I have that Greene might be able to use.

December 4, Tuesday

I was pleased that Graham Hovey had finished the article, mentioning the Pell-Jackson bill, that was published yesterday in the *New York Times.*

Pyrros phoned and said that he had read the *New York Times*, *Time* and *Newsweek* and realized that I had a hand in all of them. "Your modus operandi is to have your hands everywhere and your fingerprints nowhere," he told me.

December 6, Thursday

I wrote Congressman Hays, sending him the Pell-Jackson material and asking him to lead a similar effort in the House.

I wrote to Brademas and asked him to lead an effort with the Greek-American community.

I left for Boston.

December 7, Friday
Meeting with Professor Kafatos

Efthymios and I went to see Professor Kafatos. He had set some of his students to prepare material on the Pell-Jackson bill to be distributed to churches on Sunday.

When the three of us were left alone in his office I said, "If you have a hand in the Committee for Activity Against the Dictatorship, my warmest congratulations." He replied, "Certainly, but now we need to create a staff to maintain the activity." I told him that the next steps I see are, first, broadening the committee and forming regional chapters. I gave him the names of Nick Petris, Spirtos, Lykoudis, Anastaplo, and Petros Koumandouras. He thought the idea of regional chapters was excellent and we agreed that I would telephone him the addresses of the five the next day.

I then told him that it would be useful to establish a four page monthly newsletter to be distributed nationwide. Also, he should send a letter from the existing committee to all members of the House and Senate Committees on Foreign Relations and Armed Forces. Finally, I told him to send a personal letter to Fulbright. All of these letters to support the Pell-Jackson bill.

He said that they were thinking of sending the announcement of the committee to all senators and representatives. Finally, he said that they were thinking of getting an hour on a Boston radio station.

I said that all the activity in Boston is good but what is important is to expand the committee across America so that the local chapters can engage in local activity while the central organization directs activity on the national level. I drew his attention to the point about not involving Greek names, such as mine or Papandreou's for fear of politicizing the effort and perhaps dragging it toward partisanship.

He said that he had undertaken to teach at the University of Athens for six months and what did I think. "As things stand," I replied, "your presence now in Athens would be good but not necessary. Instead, your presence here to direct the effort you have started is absolutely necessary. When the dictatorship is gone, then your presence in Greece will be valuable." He and Efthymios talked about how he could be helped, and Efthymios told him that there are enough people among whom the work can be divided, so that the burden will not be too heavy on any one person.

December 8, Saturday

I telephoned Pyrros, who said that a new book by Sulzberger is out that I must buy because it contains much that I need to know that is being written about, such as Norstad's visit to the King in December 1971. "You should probably be called Greece's Kissinger, in constant motion, trying everything," he said.

December 9, Sunday

Marketos phoned. The announcement about Sorokos leaving has been released and he asked my opinion of Tzounis. I told him Tzounis is better than good, he is excellent.

Petrakos and Pollis called. They said the situation in Greece has left them at a loss, they never expected it to turn out this way.

Pollis also said that they have a videotape of the scenes at the Polytechnic and will broadcast it tonight. I asked her to send me a copy.

December 10, Monday

I called Efthymios. He said the distribution of the Pell-Jackson texts to the churches yesterday was well received and some people handed over their business cards, offering their help if necessary. One old man said to him, "Greece is giving the light today." He reminded me to send the newspapers to Kafatos and I mailed them to Efthymios to pass them on to him. He also said he wrote Zisiou.

I phoned Anastaplo, who will meet me at Newark airport tomorrow afternoon so we can talk before I go into New York. I called Nicolopoulos, who said that Churchill was given a leave of absence, interpreted as a transfer away from the Greek Desk at the State Department.

Someritis's newssheet, which arrived today, said that Papadopoulos had decided to withdraw and had sent three high-ranking officers to Paris to offer Karamanlis the leadership a few days before the Ioannidis coup. According to sources, these officers never arrived in Paris.

December 11, Tuesday
Meeting with Anastaplo

I arrived in New York in the afternoon. Anastaplo met me and we sat down to eat at a restaurant. He said that Kennedy had been about to take a stand on the situation in Greece at a public meeting but backed down at the last moment. He also said that the Americans are not behind Ioannidis and Kissinger will have harsh words for the Greek representative at the NATO

Council. I said that I, too, did not think that the Americans were behind this latest change but that did not absolve them from their responsibilities for the breakdown of everything in Greece. He said the Americans feared that allowing elections would give the communists 30% of the vote and, accordingly, they do not know what to do. I said that if they do nothing then they certainly will lead the people to bloodshed and communism. He asked what I thought they should do. I said that: a) the alarm must be sounded in the Greek-American community. Its awakening would have a decisive effect on both Washington and Athens. The junta could not invoke the argument "No interference in our internal affairs." b) Congress must be supported (he had not heard of the Pell-Jackson bill). c) Fulbright, in particular, must try to influence Kissinger.

He said my view of the Greek-Americans was correct. It would be easy to gather two thousand signatures on an open letter to Nixon to be sent to Congress as well. He will do it after he asks to be released from some commitments. I did not insist he tell me what commitments, but I did press him to do it if he could.

December 12, Wednesday
Meeting with Marketos and the archbishop

In the morning I met Marketos. He said that Makarezos spoke to a German newspaper and concluded that he recommended a Karamanlis solution.

Then we went to see the archbishop together.

The archbishop told us that Maliotis had telephoned with good news from Greece. I asked what he meant by "good" and he said Vardinoyiannis and other Cretans telephoned Maliotis with an optimistic prospect. He then said that he thought that the Americans were behind the change because they were displeased with Papadopoulos and Markezinis, who had denied them use of the airfields.[13] Indeed, the archbishop said so to Louros and gave him a note saying so for Louros to pass on to Karamanlis.

Iakovos added that he had information that officers shot each other at the Polytechnic and in Peristeri because some of them refused to turn their weapons against students and others insisted that orders be followed. He had been in Pittsburgh. When the liturgy was over, a young woman who had been

[13]In an interview with *Kathimerini* on February 21, 1993, Markezinis maintained that he was not "overthrown by the Polytechnic but by Kissinger, . . . A week before he had asked me to give them bases for operations in Crete, because he believed that the war in Israel would flare up again. I didn't want to have anything to do with that. I wanted to keep us out of it." In the end, with the concurrence of Papadopoulos, he replied to the Americans "diplomatically but negatively."

born here but lived in Greece stayed behind. She approached him and said that she had been at the Polytechnic, there were more than a hundred dead, and she asked what the Greek-Americans were doing. He replied that the Greek-Americans cannot change things. He had given himself until December 10 to take a stand, after clarifying in his own mind what the situation is.

Marketos then spoke to Iakovos, reminding him that in May 1967 the Archidocesan Council had adopted a position indirectly criticizing the regime and that this had made things easier for the press at the time.

A new decision from the Hieratic Council is needed now more than ever because the position the archbishop took in his letter to Rogers must be underscored and strengthened, Marketos said. A clear stance on the part of the Church will influence the Greek-Americans, and that will have an effect on Washington.

Marketos did not agree with the archbishop that the Americans created the new regime. None of his information or indications pointed in that direction. He asked Iakovos to issue a message for Christmas or the New Year and the archbishop said he would write two, one for Christmas and one for the New Year.

I told the archbishop about my meeting at the State Department with Davies and, briefly, with Sisco, who had agreed with my analysis and conclusion that the present group cannot turn Papadopoulos's profound failure into success.

"I don't agree, in spite of Papadopoulos's possibly negative position regarding American use of the airfields, that the Americans caused the change," I said, "because this change has created a fluid, uncertain, and unstable situation, as the Americans themselves attest, so it is not logical to accept that they would replace the familiar, to them, factor of Papadopoulos with the present unknown factors."

"I also don't agree with the view," I continued, "that the Greek-Americans have no effect. All these years various administration officials have literally tortured me with the argument that the Greek-Americans favor the regime. All those, such as Roger Davies, who say that they have no effect, are saying so to discourage you from initiatives that could mobilize the Greek-Americans because they do not want to be bothered."

"The Church in general," I went on, "has always played an important role at critical moments. Damaskinos, for example, assumed the titanic task of leading the transitional government in 1944. Today the nation is going through the greatest crisis in its history and the Greeks, who in 1973 proved in every way—the navy, the Chiefs of Staff, the fake referendum, the Polytechnic, workers, young people, the press, the politicians—that they will not compromise with the dictatorship, would be much encouraged if the free part of Hellenism living in this country would now, at least now, demonstrate active involvement. The time has come for your Reverence to undertake the difficult yet historic task to awaken the Greeks of America. This must happen now that the junta is divided, does not know where to go, and will be forced to give in when it faces pressure from all directions indicating that it has reached a dead-end."

He listened to me carefully and said that both he and the Council will follow through.

DECEMBER 13, FRIDAY
Letter to Karamanlis

I wrote to Karamanlis that I met with Iakovos and that I do not agree with his view that the Americans created the new situation. I also said that I would be in Paris on January 14 for us to meet. The letter follows:

> December 13, 1973
>
> *Mr. President*
>
> *Yesterday Babis Marketos and I visited the archbishop. He told us that the Americans caused the latest change and, in fact, had sent you a brief note to that effect with Mr. Louros.*
>
> *I explained to him that my information and evaluations contradict this theory. I pointed out that the Americans and the administration itself are breaking down—I attach a related weekly report addressing the corporate world (a conservative publication)—Kissinger does not play with uncertain solutions, Ioannidis's succession ensures nothing for the Americans because they know that the present group—meager and powerless to realize the extent of the problems—is incapable of transforming Papadopoulos's flagrant failure into success.*
>
> *I explained to him that, according to my information, there are two factions or tendencies, the fanatics of violence—Ioannidis, etc.—and the moderate generals and others who disagree and are pursuing a Karamanlis national government.*
>
> *Without specific information, nonetheless I am convinced that the Americans can or could—at this stage—support a Karamanlis solution, seeing it with relief and elation were it to materialize.*
>
> *Marketos agreed with me. Iakovos accepted my thinking and agreed to consider what he can do personally to contribute to the application of psychological pressure, both openly and behind the scenes. I will be in Paris on Monday, January 14 and would very much like to meet with you that evening.*

Best wishes for the holidays. I hope that 1974 will be a happy year for the homeland.

Yours truly,

Orestis Vidalis

December 14, Friday
Discussion with Moose

I telephoned Couloumbis, who said that he had lunch with Nicolopoulos and Day and that Day had told them of Ioannidis backing away from the initial joint decision they all made and of the fluidity of the situation. Couloumbis told me that Moose asked him for information to support the Pell bill in the Senate.

I called Moose and he said that Fulbright asked him to prepare a statement and to promote the Pell bill.

The committee will decide next week if they will table the bill as is or attach it as an amendment to the Israeli aid bill.

Moose asked me to give my views on the situation and I explained the internal structure and the differences among the members of the new regime, the extremely difficult conditions they have to face, and their inability to transform failure into success. I told him of Makarezos's statement, of which he had not heard, and he asked me how to respond to the administration's three points:

a. That American pressure will only cause the hardliners to react fanatically,
b. That the armed forces are fulfilling their obligations, and
c. That Greece is necessary for the Middle East.

I said that the first argument has been used for 7 years. The hardliners understand only harsh language and the moderates, seeing the impasse growing from the pressure being applied from all sides, will be equipped with arguments to lead the country toward a government of national salvation. It is an argument used by those who have been formulating policy to date, who do not want to rock the boat. As for the second, whoever maintains that the Greek armed forces are an effective organization today is lying through his teeth. They are hiding their objective of maintaining control of the area while remaining indifferent to the quality of the armed forces. When the navy revolts against the army, when the air force is deprived of fuel and its air bases are guarded by army troops, and when the army is run by a hierarchy separate from the natural and proper chain of command, then we do not have armed forces with any noteworthy fighting ability.

On the Middle East, despite the aid delivered to the dictatorship, it did nothing more than what any Greek government would have done. In an Israeli-Arab conflict in which the Middle East was in danger of Russian penetration, Greece would be powerless to help because at sea the navy is disintegrating and on land the army and air force are in no position to deal with a serious attack.

December 18, Tuesday

I received a letter from Wayne Hays saying that the Pell bill has no chance of passing in the House as is. Its only chance is as an amendment to the Israeli aid bill.

Moose telephoned and said the Pell bill passed in the committee despite rabid resistance from Senator Hugh Scott (R. PA) and was sent to the full Senate with one amendment proposed by Senator Jacob K. Javits (R. NY). I said that I attached great importance to the discussion we had a few days ago to convince Senator J. William Fulbright (D. AR), Chairman of the Senate Foreign Relations Committee, to handle the issue of the need to change American policy through direct contact and discussion with Kissinger.

I sent a letter to Spirtos urging him to lead a campaign to support the Pell-Jackson bill.

December 24, Monday

I received a letter from Pell. He sent me copies of the committee's report and the latest draft of the bill, asking me to do everything I can to support it.

December 26, Wednesday

I phoned Brockles, as he had requested. He wanted to tell me that he is completely disappointed with the Greek-Americans and thinks we should turn to the American Jews. I told him I had sent him the Fulbright committee report and asked him to approach senators to support the Pell-Jackson bill. The question of the Jews is complex, where it can be used to good effect it is worth pursuing, but a more general campaign is not possible.

December 31, Monday

Couloumbis called Matina and wished us all the best. I called him back and recommended that they lobby senators to support the Pell-Jackson bill. I suggested that they try to influence senators who had voted against us last time as well as our main supporters to again take a clear and categorical stance.

I phoned Dimopoulos and told him, too, to lobby the Senate. He said he knew the Republican senator for Colorado, Peter H. Dominick. I told him that he had voted against us last time, which Dimopoulos had not known.

Here ends 1973. The year of blood. This new element, added to the pain, bitterness, hatred, and lack of freedom will play a decisive role in the year that begins tomorrow.

CHAPTER 7

1974

1974—Seventh Year of Dictatorship

JANUARY 7, MONDAY

Norstad sent me a personal and confidential file containing a note from Mary King stating that the letter attached to the note was sent by registered mail to the general from a Paul Kiritsy, 75 Warren Street, Southbridge Mass. The letter, dated December 18, 1973, was from Wing Commander Koniotakis to Norstad. In it he blamed the Palace for everything that happened while wishing the general well and thanking him for his interest during Koniotakis's four years of suffering in prison and exile and for the general's correct position on the Greek problem.

JANUARY 11, FRIDAY

Discussion with Hackett and a long exchange of views with the Assistant Secretary of State

Washington. Cliff Hackett met me at the hotel and we had lunch together. He told me that he and Congressman Fraser were about to go to Greece. They were pleasantly surprised when Morgan, Chairman of the House Foreign Relations Committee, approved the trip. They have not yet notified the State Department for fear of a reaction from the administration, Tasca, or Athens. They are thinking of giving just two days notice before they go in order not to leave anyone time to react because they really want to go.

He asked me whom they should see.

Then he asked me what I know about Ioannidis. I said that Ioannidis was a fanatic proponent of violence, small in spirit, uneducated, an honest man but, in general, completely incapable of understanding and dealing with the nation's complex problems. I also said that the ruling group is divided into those who want the violence to continue and those want movement toward normal conditions.

The only policy that can be effective today is pressure from all directions to highlight the full extent of the problems and broaden the rupture between the two factions.

He asked if the army has an effect upon Greek society and I replied that, unfortunately, the Greek army has become a foreign body hated by society as a whole. Greece today is under domestic occupation and the only thing that Greek society wants is to find a way and an opportunity to get rid of the shackles applied by the army. Cliff Hackett then asked, "What would you do if you were an American and could affect policy?" I replied that first, in view of the failure of the policy followed over the last 7 years, I would clearly define the policy that should apply in the future. This new policy, in my opinion, must be "unconstrained by any support for the dictatorship combined with a promise to support Greece across the board should normal democratic life be restored." I said the two prongs of this policy would create a crack within the ranks of the junta while at the same time strengthening the supporters of normalization, enabling the Greeks to see Americans in another light. "After determining the policy," I went on, "a schedule of steps implementing the policy must be drawn up. Examples of such steps are not extending home-porting facilities to the aircraft carrier, suspending aid, as the Pell-Jackson bill allows. Stop the high-profile visits. No financial help in the form of loans or other assistance, all of which would have to be capped with a clear announcement of the American position in public, or at least in private to begin with."

Then I went to the State Department where I was received by Day, who led me directly to Assistant Secretary Rodger Davies's office.

I told Davies that I was less interested in the present than deeply concerned about the future of Greece. What interested me about the present was that the people of Greece consider three entities responsible for the present Greek drama and they hate all three: the army, the capitalists, and the Americans. The result of this popular displeasure, I fear, will lead to the opposite pole, that is, to totalitarianism of the left.

The Soviet Union, of course, was closely following the present situation and would exploit a turn toward the far left unless things changed. The Soviets have proven to be masters of patience.

Davies told me that the thought I had put to him during my last visit, that there are two factions, has been confirmed by developments, but they do not discern intense competition within the junta. One thing that concerns him is that some officers are coming forward who see relations with America as bilateral, not within the NATO framework. They demand a very great deal from American while forgetting that in the recent war in the Middle East the United States handled all its needs on its own, with no help from anyone else. These people forget, therefore, that America does not need other powers as much as other powers need America.

I said that there always were such officers, used by Papadopoulos to blackmail the Americans. Now Ioannidis is using them to keep up the blackmail.

These people have no awareness of the complexity of the problems and understand no language other than direct pressure.

Davies then told me confidentially that Tasca would be recalled next month on leave.

"At that point the issue will be reexamined because, really, the situation occupies and worries us although our policy remains that Greece's internal problem is a problem for the Greeks."

I told him this theory (that it is a matter for the Greeks) convinces no one because how is it possible for the unarmed Greek people to solve the problem from inside while they are facing the American-armed junta? Do not forget, I said, that all institutions in Greece were destroyed and nothing was created to replace them, with the result that it is completely impossible to tell what will happen next. I said the situation will get worse if the workers come back from Germany and if tourism drops in the summer.

He agreed, and said that Turkey is facing similar problems. He added that Ioannidis is deceiving himself if he thinks he can improve the situation by replacing Androutsopoulos—which is being discussed—with someone else. We know that he has offered government posts to former members of parliament from the ERE and the Center Union, but they replied that they did not want any involvement.

Then he said, "We would very much like to know, if possible, what His Majesty the King and Mr. Karamanlis are thinking." I replied that, after I meet with them, I will see if there is any subject about which there could be a useful discussion of their views and will tell him after I return.

I told Davies that I recognize that the U.S. is facing tremendous problems and officials do not have time to devote to the Greek issue. He replied that that is not correct and that, as long as there is an issue, time can be found, such as now that Tasca will return.

After the meeting with Davies I went to see Day in his office. We continued the discussion. He said the issue of the army concerned him seriously because he thinks the influence exercised by the hardliners is serious. He does not agree with those who say that America can do nothing, but he could not predict what the results would be if America were to intervene.

He then told me some confidential things about Karamanlis.

> First, he is particularly esteemed at all levels of the administration for his successful term as prime minister, his popularity, and his influence over the army.
>
> Second, Mr. Karamanlis must know that the rumors that the CIA intervened and overthrew Papadopoulos are fantasies.

Third, Ioannidis recently has begun talking about Karamanlis, adding, however, that Karamanlis is old and far removed from Greek reality.

I then went to Dimitrakopoulos. I learned nothing new. He insisted that the Karamanlis solution must be supported. I said I agreed with him but it is unrealistic to expect Kissinger to come out trumpeting the Karamanlis solution. What we must do is convince Fulbright to use all of his influence on Kissinger in favor of abandoning support for the dictatorship while, at the same time, promising to strengthen a democratic Greece.

New Trip to Europe

January 12, Saturday
First stop, London

I arrived in England. Arnaoutis was waiting for me at the airport. En route into London he said that the situation in Greece is horrible, fluid, the Chiefs of Staff are in favor of the Karamanlis solution, while Ioannidis and his flunkeys are in favor of continuing the dictatorship.

These days in Athens, according to Arnaoutis, Papadopoulos is saying, "Call Karamanlis to come because otherwise Greece will be destroyed." He thinks the likely outcomes are the street, with unknown consequences, or a group of soldiers will take over and lead the country back to normal conditions.

In the evening I went to the Karrasess'. Maria Rolfe was there as well. Kostas Karras, a very careful analyst, succinctly put the main characteristics of the present situation. My synopsis:

a. In contrast with June there is a distinct decrease in the King's standing because of his inactivity. He told me that he had repeatedly asked Arnaoutis to arrange a meeting with the King but nothing happened.
b. There is intense disquiet among financial circles, though it is not expected to become action.
c. The students intend to continue, knowing that they contributed to Papadopoulos's fall.
d. The communist party, especially the Russian section, with money and organization, have shown and will show serious activities to exploit the prevailing climate and the disorientation among the young.
e. In the army, Ioannidis's faction wants to continue the situation indefinitely and the generals' faction wants to return to normal life through Karamanlis. Some other younger officers are leaning toward a

Yugoslav-type, essentially socialist, regime, not the Qaddafi model. They would turn against big capital while leaving small private property alone.

f. He cannot rule out an agreement between the latter group of officers and the students, which would create an entirely new situation.
g. He sees three scenarios:
    1. Ioannidis prevails, guaranteeing reaction by the students and an unknown stance by the rest of the military. In this case the influence of the Moscow-backed faction of the communist party will be very significant.
    2. Action by the followers of the Yugoslav model.
    3. Action by the moderate elements in the military along with the political world to restore normal conditions.

He was very clear in his belief that the student movement was fully supported by the people and the next time the same thing happens the uprising will be general.

What I want to note from my meetings today is the difference of opinion between Arnaoutis and Karras. Arnaoutis told me that the King's standing has clearly improved over the last 20 days while Karras says that the King's standing is at its nadir.

Karras clearly is intensely concerned while Arnaoutis is not.

I fully share Karras's concerns.

January 13, Sunday

In the afternoon I met with Sir Hugh Greene, Peter Thompson, and Professor Strauss, who is Greek and not English, as I had first thought.

They explained to me what happened at the NATO council, that is, that Van der Stoel was very active this past year, that the Belgian and Italian ministers indirectly referred to the Greek issue, and the Dutch, Norwegian, and Danish ministers took a clear stand on the Greek issue. In the summer, when NATO will hold a summit marking its 25th anniversary, they will act again.

I asked Greene to send letters to congressmen stressing the differences between the situation in 1967 and today and concluding that the situation is fluid and unstable.

Then I met with Eleni Vlachou. She was very optimistic because of Papadopoulos's fall. She clearly felt that the issue of the parliamentary monarchy is finished and that Karamanlis probably will play a role.

January 14, Monday
Meetings with the King and Karamanlis

At 10:30 PM I went to Claridge's, where I met with the King. He greeted me very warmly and soon the queen came in, just to greet me, and left. I expanded on the situation from the American side and told him that he must agree that there no longer is any point in his coming to the U.S. He fully agreed.

I told him about my latest meeting with Davies.

Then I noted that, beyond the problems of the present, I was concerned about the problems of the future, especially in view of the attitudes and psychology of our young people. Specifically, I mentioned the case of the Greek students at Harvard, who asked to meet with me after many months and only after I helped them pass on their messages during the events of the Polytechnic, which I relayed to Lambrias at night. The young cannot accept the concept of a hereditary monarch. If the monarchy is accepted at all, it will be only as the guarantor of democracy and popular sovereignty in Greece. Common acceptance of this role will require great effort and, certainly, silence does not help.

He listened carefully and said nothing to show his disagreement. Then he gave me his latest news:

a. Connally, the former governor of Texas, asked to see him and he received him at Claridge's. The meeting lasted two and a half hours. Connally was completely uninformed. He was stunned by what the King had to say about the position of the American administration and promised to involve himself with the matter immediately.
b. In October, an American ambassador, whom he did not name, visited him and asked him, "What can we do, Your Majesty, to make Papadopoulos go?" He answered that he cannot tell them what to do since they have been supporting him up to now.
c. He met with the Foreign Minister of the United Kingdom last October, who had distressing news. The King told him that the situation is chaotic and everybody ought to be very concerned because anything was possible, including the worst, Ioannidis's appearance on the stage. On November 26, the minister called him and, among other things, asked, "Are you a prophet, Your Majesty?"
d. During the events of the Polytechnic, he had prepared a statement. He discussed it with Karamanlis and they agreed that Karamanlis would make a statement first and then the King would make his. Later, Karamanlis notified him that he had changed his mind, and so the King cancelled his own statement.

e. In October he had gone to Paris with the queen to meet with the Queen of Iran. He invited Karamanlis, who came to his hotel. The discussed the elections and agreed that a single united democratic front should be formed to prepare for the elections. This united front would withdraw at the last minute if there was any sign that Papadopoulos was preparing to tamper with the results. He urged Karamanlis to go to Greece to lead the front.
f. He confided in me that Karamanlis had had a lengthy meeting with Kissinger last summer.

Then I told him that I believe he should not link every thing he does and says with what Karamanlis will or will not do. I said it seems as if we have two sovereigns at this stage. I particularly noted that he must stand with the young, regardless of what Karamanlis does. I asked if he was planning on doing anything now, and he answered, "No, because I am closely following what is brewing inside the army."

He also said that Tasca let him know that the Americans would raise no objection if he were to go to Greece by whatever means, but, also, that they would not do anything to help him return. At the same time, Tasca told him that he no longer saw Karamanlis returning.

We agreed to telephone each other so that we can meet in Zurich after my meeting with Karamanlis.

I left London and went to Paris. As soon as I checked into the hotel, I left and went straight to Karamanlis.

He asked how I saw the situation in America. I said that under Markezinis we were sidelined. Everybody thought or pretended that we were headed for real elections. After all, that is what the Americans wanted, to get rid of the Greek headache. At this point, he interrupted and said something that surprised me, that the politicians in Greece rushed things and pressed prematurely and more than they should have, sweeping along the students and resulting in the events of November and the bloodshed.

I said that the Greek politicians had no choice because they should not provide the junta with historical justification.

Continuing my description of the situation in America, I told him about my meeting with Davies, Marketos's excellent work, the Pell-Jackson bill, and concluded that no one can expect help from the American administration. In view of this situation and because no one can expect progress from the dictatorship's initiatives, that is, from Ioannidis, I said that I thought he ought to repeat his positions.

"In April of 1973, I clearly stated my position," he said, "but, beyond that, prominent people know in detail what I believe, that is, that there must be a transitional government that will draft a constitution, impose some order upon the army, give some time for new political forces to arise, and this government can lead to normal conditions within eight to nine months."

I replied that what prominent people know must also be known by the public. At this point he needs to address himself to the army as a whole, describe its responsibilities, identify exactly why the nation is going through the greatest crisis in its history, and outline the method he believes will lead the country to normal life. A new clarification of his position would create problems within the junta, improve the morale of the Greek people, and affect foreigners as well.

"Many people overestimate my powers," he replied. "I will think over what you say, but when I act, I always want a result."

I responded that it is neither necessary not possible to always have a direct result. An indirect result, such as motivating those officers who want normal conditions to act, can be desirable, even valuable.

He has done it before, he replied, but no officer ever resigned.

No one will resign, I countered, for many well-known reasons. That is not the purpose and, in any case, things are very different now. I stressed the seriousness of the problem with the young, who are both my hope and my concern.

He said he agreed and that normal conditions can be restored only through the process he outlined.

I answered that I completely agree, but that he must declare this now, in order to silence those who say, "Karamanlis is in contact with the new junta," or "Karamanlis is a dictator," or Karamanlis is sick and not involved." I mentioned specific instances when these things have been said. "The politicians and the resistance in Greece," he responded, "those who took a bomb and moved it from one house to another and call themselves heroes, have no understanding of what must be done."

"That is another reason to repeat your position," I said.

"These resistance types," he went on, "have no contact with reality. Mangakis was where you are sitting, telling me that, unknowingly, he transported one of these bombs in a suitcase. And he described the dangers of the resistance. So then I told him, 'All of you talk of the resistance and none of you speak of the officers like Vidalis, Vardoulakis, and others who risked everything, even their lives, so that the Greeks might be free.' Mangakis agreed."

He asked if the King had information from Greece and I told him that he knows that even Papadopoulos was talking about Karamanlis coming back. That he, too, is concerned about the young, and that he told me in confidence of a new personal problem, that the new junta wants to take back the Tatoi estate as well.

I also told him that the State Department wanted me to relay the following to him:

a. The people who overthrew Papadopoulos, including Ioannidis, had agreed to invite Karamanlis to form a transitional government and that Ioannidis abrogated the agreement after November 25.
b. All circles of the American government hold Karamanlis in high esteem.
c. Ioannidis recently has begun talking about Karamanlis, adding, however, that Karamanlis is old and out of touch with contemporary Greek reality.

He said he could confirm the first because he knew that two officers had been selected on November 25 and were preparing to travel to Paris. This never happened. He added that I should tell the Americans, who had placed such trust in the Markezinis solution, that, "I had completely reliable information that Papadopoulos and Markezinis had agreed that, if I contested the elections and conditions were right for me to win, they would find a pretext to cancel the elections."

Before I left I repeated that it is necessary for him to clarify his position one more time because the people in power today lack strength of mind and do not realize how crucial the moment is; they are surrounded by flatterers and opportunists.

January 19, Saturday

I went to Zurich and met with the King in the VIP lounge where I told him about my discussion with Karamanlis.

January 20, Sunday

Peridis woke us. I asked him first about our connection. He said he is not travelling to America but would call me from somewhere else. He told me he sent a long letter to Toledo on the 7th, but I have not yet received it.

I asked if they are in contact with the army, and he said they are concentrating their efforts on that now and it is easier than it used to be. He said the new junta was spreading the rumor that they have been in touch with Karamanlis and had his terms. I said that I discerned nothing of the sort during my meeting with him.

Then I asked what feelings there are about the King and he said it was good but that someone needs to convince him to speak. They had been expecting a statement for the New Year but nothing. Silence is harmful.

January 26, Saturday

Back in Toledo. Found Peridis's letter and two depressing ones from my sister.

January 29, Tuesday

Left for Washington.

January 30, Wednesday

Met with Pyrros in the morning. We called Fraser to arrange for me to see him but he came to Pyrros's office, and we met briefly. He said the situation is desperate, the Greeks believe the Americans can have a decisive effect but he was disappointed with the capabilities of the American embassy. I said the only practical way to achieve results was to convince Fulbright to involve himself personally with the Greek issue and apply pressure on Kissinger.

In the afternoon I met with Davies instead of Sisco. I repeated my impressions and the general disappointment in Europe with American inactivity, which is synonymous with supporting the junta. I laid out the situation in Greece and the position of those who oppose the regime concerning the restoration of normal conditions.

While there is still time, I said, sending a high profile American as a special representative of the president would be of decisive importance today, if he relayed to Gizikis and Bonanos the president's deep concern over the situation and how it is harming the effectiveness of the army and Greek-American security interests. I stressed that the United States was overestimating Ioannidis's strength and underestimating their own ability to affect developments in Greece.

"This thought," Davies said, "comes at a very good time because we are preparing a political briefing for the Secretary and we will include your thoughts among the other proposals." At the end, Davies thanked me for the visit and will relay my views to the top echelons of the department. He repeated his bureaucratic phrase, "don't expect anything," saying, " the American government does not intend to get involved in changing the political systems of other countries."

I know that Kissinger was informed of the conversation and signed the telegram to the American embassy in Athens containing a detailed description of my meeting with Davies.

I returned to Toledo.

News from Greece

FEBRUARY 4, MONDAY

Rallis telephoned from Athens. He said he would send me a letter, and he asked me to examine the subject as soon as I receive it and write back. I promised I would do so immediately. He said Tasca will hold a reception, now that things are tighter, and has invited them, and they do not know what to do. I said that during this period of American indecision they should go. The situation here is, in general, desperate concerning the Greek issue; the administration is concerned but inert. The Americans attach great importance to Ioannidis's strength, perhaps to justify their inactivity.

FEBRUARY 5, TUESDAY
Peridis's evaluation of the current situation

I arrived in Washington last night and met Hackett in his office this morning. He described everything he saw in Greece and gave me a letter Peridis handed him with the instruction that he should be careful with it because it is dynamite. Peridis's letter follows:

> Before discussion with your friends. A synopsis. Continuing what I wrote to the Karno address.[1]
>
> 1. Brig. Karayannis Efthymios—Brig. Vlangopoulos—Lieut. Col. Pilichos M.—Col. Ioannidis (cat—not Paraskevas)—Lamboulis—Chronaios (KET—Armor Training Center)—Boukouvalas—Loukoutos—Chrysos—Xiros, etc. wth Ioannidis. Steiakakis, Perdikis, Lalaouinis, Bonotis, Spanos, Papayeorgiou (all colonels or lieutenant colonels) the other group.
> 2. Constant daily confrontations among the big guys [Galatsanos—Papanikolaou (Air Force) best] at present little expected. Not entirely decorative, had managed to prepare something of their own as initiates before 25 Nov. Must, therefore, have something independent.
> 3. At present Ioannidis in control though he has enough trouble with his own people. Unless he has started playing the Papadopoulos violin, "I want to but the others won't let me." Possible.
> 4. I believe his philosophy must be close to the Turkish model. No proof. From what I remember. Harshly anti-monarchist. He wanted "the King dead. Not injured." Introverted type, austere, honest (until proof

[1]Code words: Lakis = Karamanlis, Anna = King, Sam = U.S.A., Leonidas = Connection between Peridis and Vidalis, Gakis = Peridis.

of the opposite)—not eloquent—missing from Christeas's movement. May be in touch with him now (indications)—drinker—asexual—likes to act from behind the scenes.

5. Many signs they are planning high-profile trials of various followers of Papadopoulos (Balop., Aslan., Karydas, etc.) to muddy the waters or gain time (possibly also Makarezos, the KYP [Central Information Service] is collecting material on him). It is said they were in touch with Lakis, who set terms but it is not yet time . . . perhaps continued deceit.
6. Anna must be more active and not just behind the scenes. We were all expecting a message for New Year's. Out of sight (or hearing . . .) out of mind!
7. They are spreading (Ioannidis said at a New Year's speech to officers and troops that young people under 45 are needed—even he is not suitable, he says) that Lakis is too old but also that he is physically incapable (he steps here and goes somewhere else).
8. Ten days age they had a gathering of 400 (ranking from second lieutenants to colonels) at Elefsina air base (evaluation: commissars conference!) Think of it! Even second lieutenants now! It is said that even the NCO's have their own organization. Stress sad state and consequences to Sam.
9. We expect and hope that, after the Middle East is solved, we will rise as a priority on Sam's list. They should not underestimate the campus or that anything can occur. Great risk that others will control it. In any case, they are preparing differently now from what we hear.
10. We are well, working on a variety of things. We are attempting deeper penetration in the old family. The pulse is there, the feelings are cold. What they have been reduced to is shameful. They want out. Totally unable to communicate among each other because of close surveillance, terrorism, etc.
11. We are seeking the "catalyst" that would give the moderates the opportunity to act. If something like the failed May attempt happened now it would be a catalyst. Another is the campus.
12. From now on Leonidas will be calling you from Europe where I have started doing business.
13. Is there any way to organize a printing and distribution center in Europe for mailing informative unsuspected material directly to members of the old family? Look into it.

Kisses,

Gakis

Fraser and Hackett met with about 45 people covering the entire political spectrum in Greece. Mavros was the most optimistic of them, only because he considered Papadopoulos's fall decisive and his successors incapable of handling the complex problems. Not even Mavros, however, was able to point to specific developments to justify optimism. Everyone is expecting an explosion. Everyone agrees that the situation cannot hold, the junta is divided, all problems are in the deep freeze and—worst of all—they do not have the brains to understand how critical the situation is.

Hackett was preparing the report and, after Fraser sees it and makes additions, it will be printed and distributed to the committee and beyond.

He asked me what I thought they could do and I repeated what I had already told Frazer, that is, to convince Fulbright to involve himself personally and pressure Kissinger.

Then I saw Jim Pyrros. Completely out of the blue in his effort to help as much as possible, he told me that he would arrange for me to meet with the Chairman of the House Armed Forces Committee.

Interesting Meeting with Day

Then I met Day and we went out to lunch. It was our first meeting not preceding or following a meeting with his superiors.

In the beginning, he showed me a telegram from Tasca informing the State Department that the hearing of my appeal to the Council of State [analogous to the Supreme Court] over the loss of my citizenship had been postponed. I thanked him and said I was aware of it.

Then he said they had information that some officers in Larissa tried to move against the regime last week. Nothing came of it, but it did force Ioannidis to go to Larissa.

He also said that a rumor was circulating in Thessaloniki that Androutsopoulos would leave and General Frontistis would replace him as prime minister. I asked if he knew where Frontistis was, and he said no. I said he is in Boston, and I may meet with him soon. After asking me not to reveal the source, himself, he told me that they had decided not to proceed with the second phase of home-porting, that is, the aircraft carrier and other vessels. There will be no announcement, and if they are asked, they will say that it cannot be done for technical reasons.

I asked what was the significance of Tasca's reception for the politicians when he had held one just a few days ago when Fraser was there. He had not heard of the new reception. I told him I had urged those who asked me to attend the reception without being sure I was right. "You did very well for two reasons," he said, "a) because since November 25 Tasca is clearly an enemy of the regime and, b) because American policy is under review at this moment."

During the discussion I told him that they had left may things unused, such as the Greek-Americans, and I recommended he get in touch with Marketos. He praised the *National Herald*, which he reads on a daily basis and which has full coverage of the situation, something no newspaper from Greece can give him.

I returned to Toledo in the evening.

FEBRUARY 6, WEDNESDAY

I called Marketos in the morning. He said he had seen Iakovos, who had just returned from a three-day trip to Greece. Iakovos had not been invited but went to see his deeply ill brother. Since he was there, he asked to see Ioannidis and Gizikis. Ioannidis did not even bother to answer. Gizikis telephoned him without, however, asking to see him.

Marketos told the archbishop of his plan to visit Nixon and Iakovos agreed that they should go together.

I wrote to Karamanlis, repeating what I had told him in Paris, that he must speak out:

Mr. President *February 6, 1974*

Yesterday I returned from Washington. It was my second visit since my return from Europe.

I think I should inform you of the following:

- *a. Tasca is deeply concerned. He keeps on describing the situation in dark colors, adding that he is essentially powerless to influence developments.*
- *b. The Nixon administration has decided to cancel the second phase of homeporting, that is, the use of our ports for the aircraft carrier, etc. They will not announce it and, if asked, will attribute it to technical difficulties.*
- *c. They maintain that Androutsopoulos will not last long.*
- *d. They had information that last week officers in Larissa moved against the regime. Nothing came of it. Ioannidis was forced to go to Larissa.*
- *e. The Archbishop went to Athens for three days to see his sick brother. He attempted to see Gizikis and Ioannidis. Gizikis simply phoned him, without expressing any interest in seeing him, and Ioannidis did not even call.*
- *f. Tasca will come to Washington very soon and it is expected that Kissinger will study the situation and proceed with decisions. He is under pressure from the Senate and has promised to formulate a position within the month.*

My information from Greece is discouraging. The economy is getting worse, the young are totally disappointed, the military is divided and spying on itself and everything is so inert that it resembles the deep freeze.

I return to my suggestion that you address yourself to the army, describe the tragic circumstances we are in, and clearly outline the solution. Let Ioannidis say what he wants, perhaps the pressure may become suffocating.

I will keep you informed if I have anything specific from here.

Yours truly,

Orestis Vidalis

February 8, Friday
Rigging the High Court vote on the referendum

I wrote to the King, informing him of the rigging of the High Court vote, as Peridis described it and as Day confirmed when I raised the issue. In a letter dated January 7, 1974, Peridis described what happened.

1.7.74[2]
In the High Court for the referendum (invalid or valid). First vote, 21 invalid, 7 valid. Then pressure. Second vote, 19 invalid, 8 valid, more pressure. Third vote, 15 valid, 13 invalid. The decision was conveyed to the bishop by the main culprit (Kanellakos) unsigned! And then the carrot! Kanellakos President of the High Court, decision signed end September . . .[3]

I ended by pressing the King to make a statement on March 25 and attached a document I had proposed to him in 1973 that he had not used. The text has been altered. I sent the letter by registered mail.

February 9, Saturday

I received a reply from Kennedy to the letter I had sent him and Muskie about the Pell-Jackson bill. In his reply Kennedy wrote,

> I was pleased to hear your views and I share your feelings that all those who are interested must continue their efforts on behalf of freedom in Greece.

[2]Code words: Bishop = Government, carrot = reward

[3]In the republished issue of *Politika Themata* number 7, 5–20 October 1973, is a special 16-page insert titled "Referendum 1973" containing full coverage of the reactions of politicians, legal scholars, and others following the announcement of the results.

February 10, Sunday

Not all is rosy in the Senate. Andrew Brockles of Dallas sent me the reply from Republican Senator John Tower to a letter of his urging him to vote in favor of the Pell-Jackson bill. Tower's response is the complete opposite of Muskie's and Kennedy's position. Tower wrote:

> *Dear Mr. Brockles,*
>
> *I will not support Bill SZ754 for the simple reason that, of all the members of the Atlantic Alliance, Greece is one of the foremost members in fulfilling its security obligations. Greece and Turkey bridge NATO's southern flank and would be valuable in any conflict in the Middle East and Mediterranean. The military aid provided today to Greece is not special aid to maintain the present regime in power because that would happen anyway. The aid provided, however, is essential to ensure the means to deter or repel a communist attack.*
>
> *In the long history of military aid, both Soviet and American, the only lesson that can be drawn is that aid provides the country issuing it relatively little leverage over the internal affairs of the recipient. While I condemn as much as you do the authoritarian behavior of governments, I do not believe that suspending aid will impose change upon this authoritarian behavior, instead it will increase the danger of Greece falling victim to communist adventurism.*

This letter is important because it shows, even now after 7 years of dictatorship, that its supporters are in the grip of anti-communist hysteria and overlook the damage done not just to Greece, for which, perhaps, few people care, but also to the United States, which no longer shines with its former prestige, and to the Atlantic Alliance, which exists to defend the values ignored by the dictatorship's supporters.

Discussions in Boston

February 15, Friday
At Marketos's for Rallis's diary

Marketos said I was right when I told him that Nixon is completely incapable of applying any pressure on Kissinger. Michalis Sotirchos, who is in touch with the White House and with Nixon, confirmed it.

FEBRUARY 17, SUNDAY

I telephoned Mavrogenis in Chicago and told him to begin supporting Democrats with Lykoudis and to make it clear to the Republicans that they are turning against them because of the Greek issue.

I telephoned Spirtos, who said that he is preparing a third party in AHEPA that may begin small but surprises are not out of the question.

FEBRUARY 20, WEDNESDAY
Frelinghuysen in Athens

I telephoned Hackett, who will send me their report in a few days. He knew that Frelinghuysen is in Athens. He told me that these are Frelinghuysen's last undertakings because he will not run again. He added that, as a result of personal communication with him, he knows that was Frelinghuysen was sick and tired of the junta issue. I again stressed the need for Fraser to communicate with Fulbright to get him to intervene personally with Kissinger.

Attention on Greece—Stewings and Movements

FEBRUARY 28, THURSDAY
Fraser-Hackett report

The Fraser-Hackett report on their visit to Greece arrived at home around noon. They proposed two basic actions: a) Not extending the home-porting arrangements with a simultaneous announcement of a clear position against the military dictatorship and, b) posting a new ambassador free of any relationship with the past.

In the afternoon I went to New York. Pollis came to the hotel and we had dinner together at the hotel restaurant. I asked her if she saw any chance of activating the organization in view of the November elections. She spoke of the indifference of the Americans and the difficulty in getting them to unite.

The only one showing any interest is Kulukundis, who will provide funds for an organization office to publicize everything needing to be relayed to Congress or anywhere else. I told her that if she does not expand the organization so that there are representatives from many states, it will be a waste of time. If, however, it succeeds, then the senators and congressmen who favor our cause can help.

March 1, Friday
Discussion at the New York Times *about Roberts visiting Athens*

I went to see Hovey at the *New York Times.* We had not seen each other for some time and, in a way, he tried to justify that he had not dealt with Greece because he had been swamped with other issues. We ate together, and I told him that Fraser's report marked a good opportunity to return to the subject. He said he would as soon as he found some time. I asked if it would be easy to get an editorial of mine published and he said that, although the editor in charge of the editorial page is under the same supervising editor, he is completely independent and the best that Hovey could do is put in a good word. This does not mean that it should not be attempted, because the editorial could be of great interest at the right time. If it does not happen, he will find an opportunity to say something in an editorial despite their policy of not saying "we told you so."

I returned to the hotel where the new representative of the *New York Times* in Athens, Steven V. Roberts, came to see me at 2:00 in the afternoon. He had been head of the Los Angeles bureau and been given awards for his coverage of the student movement in America.

We discussed the situation in Greece for a long time. He said he had heard in Washington that the Karamanlis solution was no longer considered likely. He kept notes and his questions were those of a beginner, confusing the situation in Greece with the situation elsewhere, such as the student unrest in America or Vietnam. I tried to explain that it is a mistake to compare situations because the differences, which always need most attention and thorough knowledge, are what lead to completely different developments.

March 4, Monday

Day called me and said he had met with Anschuetz, who was very pleased with the meeting. They have information that Karamanlis is in touch with Bonanos. They know that Bonanos and Ioannidis have excellent relations and fear that Bonanos is playing a double game. I sent Karamanlis the Fraser report.

March 16, Saturday
Mavros exiled

Dimopoulos called. He had spoken with Mitsotakis, who told him that there is strong consensus among the politicians to harden their stance on two issues, Cyprus and the economy. They will announce that no act or debt will be recognized after democracy is restored. Mavros made a statement or sent a telegram to Wilson on his assumption of his duties and told him that he hopes the Labour Party will take a better stance. Gallagher, the foreign minister, viciously attacked the juntas of Greece and Chile and said that the British fleet was forbidden to appear in Greek waters. According to Dimopoulos they arrested Mavros in Athens and sent him into internal exile.

I phoned Day. He had not heard of Mavros's internal exile. He said they confirmed that Ioannidis was unable to speak to officers in northern Greece and they have observed unusual movement by Bonanos in northern Greece. He said Tasca was coming and he asked me if I want to see him. I said yes but they should notify me well in advance. He also said that the politicians were already in communication with serving officers.

March 18, Monday
Why I will write General Davos

After various—although unconfirmed—reports about events in northern Greece, I decide to write General Davos. My decision is based on the following thoughts:

- For a long time I have believed and I still believe that the armed forces should contribute to or lead the search for an end to the drama. My proposal to the King and the text Papagos brought to Greece are proof of this belief.
- Unfortunately, the politicians then considered that that text should not be addressed to the armed forces. Furthermore, my involvement in the efforts for the navy's move was based on my belief that the drama should be ended by the armed forces. Properly prepared, the armed forces can bring this drama to a successful end and, in doing so, restore some respect in the public mind for our military uniform.
- Papadopoulos's failure and Ioannidis's dominance divided military officers, raising many questions in their minds about the effectiveness of the new dictatorship.
- The upheaval among the young and increasing external pressures will lead thoughtful and moderate officers to consider the responsibilities they will bear if they continue to support a regime of even less ability than the one that failed.
- Davos had served under me and I considered him a moderate man and, primarily, a good soldier.

Pyrros called to say that the State Department announced that they will not send the aircraft carrier, and they were scathing over the junta's stance toward Mavros.

March 22, Friday

I spoke with Munroe and told him that Monday, when Jackson would speak to AHEPA, was a Greek national holiday and the Greek people are not free. I urged him to use this as an introduction to criticize the regime. He answered that the senator, out of respect for his hosts, would choose his words carefully, but he cannot hide his feelings and what he has said before. I thanked him and told him to look at the file, which has my speech in Canton.

Day telephoned and said Tasca would very much like to see me and would like to know if I could be there at 11:00 AM Thursday, March 28. I said I would be there. He also asked if I knew that Zighdis would be in Washington. I replied no.

March 26, Tuesday

Pyrros, Couloumbis, and Nicolopoulos told me that Senator Jackson was wonderful last night at the AHEPA meeting. He was really blunt with them. Their ambassador said nothing and certainly neither did Ford, who was also present. Apparently Jackson indirectly mentioned me.

March 27, Wednesday

I left for Washington.

With Tasca and Zighdis in Washington

March 28, Thursday
Meeting with Tasca

I went to the State Department and saw Day briefly while I was waiting to see Tasca. I asked him what new information they have about Bonanos. He replied that their information was contradictory but he might be flirting with Karamanlis to buy his silence. He said they confirmed that Davos had forbidden Ioannidis from speaking to the officers in Thessaloniki.

Day and I went to the office Tasca was using. Tasca greeted me rather more effusively than usual and began the discussion by saying that on the airplane he had reread my testimony to Congress and found it extremely interesting. I thanked him and said, "Yes, but what next?" "You know Ioannidis," he replied, "and what do you think of him?" "He is fanatic, uneducated, and incapable of understanding the country's problems," I answered, "and his only skill is at using violence through the military police. I do not think that he will try emulating Nasser because he is unqualified."

Tasca praised the Markezinis solution, adding that Papadopoulos would have had to fall after the Markezinis solution was in place but the politicians and others in Greece were convinced that we had to go through this stage as well. In Athens Papadopoulos's fall generated much optimism, which has begun to fade recently. He railed against Zagorianakos because he was caught napping. [Zagorianakos was the junta general in charge of Athens who did nothing to anticipate or prevent Ioannidis removing Papadopoulos from power on November 25, 1973.]

T. The problems facing Ioannidis and the others are immense. However, they are fanatics, do not accept pressure, and their minds are focussed on keeping the regime in power. Unlike Papadopoulos, who did have some, they have no popular support, are primitive, and completely ignorant. They tried to bring in some capable Greeks but no one wants to serve with them.

O.V. Since the policy of "evolution" has failed, obviously something new must be done by the American side. You have been involved for a long time and perhaps new faces and new ideas are needed.

T. "Evolution" did not fail and is continuing. Everyone's attention must turn to the army, which will provide the solution. I know people and things and I believe that the army is the determining factor at this stage.

O.V. Certainly the army is the main factor in a possible solution, but we must not forget that without establishing an appropriate psychological climate and increasing the obstacles before the junta there will be no favorable development.

You have changed the description of your policy from "care for the restoration of democracy" to it being "a case of the political freedom of the Greeks."

T. That came about from Kissinger's appearance before the Senate for his confirmation hearings.

O.V. That is not accurate because, long before, in August 1972, Rogers used the new phrasing at AHEPA's conference.

T. Yes, but at the same time he was giving me instructions to lodge protests with Papadopoulos.

O.V. These protests are known only to him and you, while they should be public knowledge in order to have an effect. At this point I think that change should be in the direction of cutting off any and all support (military, financial, etc) while declaring that aid will resume as soon as democracy is restored.

> T. I do not think that open pressure can help right now, while behind-the-scenes pressure can bring results this year, during which matters will have to develop, for otherwise problems will lead to a complete impasses.

During the discussion he spoke warmly of Zolotas and Averof.

Day and I returned to Day's office, where he said, "I want to tell in confidence these items: First, Tasca will see the president now, at 12:30, right after you. He already has seen the Secretary of State and he is not going to leave Greece. Second, he is in favor of and is working towards a government of national unity. There will, however, be no official announcements. Third, Kissinger very much wants the government of national unity. You can relay this as long as you do not attribute the source."

I thanked him for the information and said, "In the past I never was certain if the statements or information given me by various American officials had anything to do with reality. Now I am pleased because I can see that what you tell me, happens."

Meeting with Ioannis Zighdis

In the evening I went to Fairfax and met for a while with Zighdis and Dimitrakopoulos, who had seen Day and been cheered by what he heard. Zighdis and I went to the Sheraton Hilton hotel for dinner. The main points he made were:

> First. He was in London when Dimitrakopoulos notified him to come and testify. He decided to come despite the probability of retaliation, internal exile to Yaros, or having his citizenship revoked because the situation is critical and maximum pressure had to be brought to bear on the Americans.
>
> Second. The Americans must understand that if they do not help solve the problem quickly they will be faced with Qaddafi types who, for the first time, will have the opportunity to push for neutrality by taking advantage of anti-American sentiment.
>
> Third. Dimitrakopoulos moved fast and compelled him, but Zighdis had not been able to meet high-ranking members of the administration and, therefore, his presence in Washington was not fully exploited.
>
> Fourth. In Greece both Mavros and Kanellopoulos are quite optimistic and are not pressing things. Both have a basic weakness. Kanellopoulos thinks about what Karamanlis will say and Mavros what Papandreou will say.

> Fifth. The army is divided into factions. So far excellent behavior has been demonstrated by Galatsianos, Davos, Sykiotis and Zalachoris, the commander of the armored division of whom many expect much.

He asked if I could help him meet with members of the administration. I told him that we must rule out any chance of communication with Kissinger, but I could look into the possibility of him meeting Schlesinger, the Defense Secretary, and Saunders, Kissinger's aide on the Greek issue.

March 29, Friday

The *Washington Post* reports on Schlesinger's press conference yesterday, in which announced that the plan to home-port the aircraft carrier in Greece has been postponed until there "is greater harmony in our common positions than there is at present." Asked if this decision of the United States is permanent, Schlesinger responded, "That will depend upon the development of Greek affairs."

I telephoned Jack Maury, the new Assistant Secretary of Defense. He asked if I had seen the article in the *Post*. "Certainly," I said, "and I am very pleased." "You know," he said, "there are many who, seeing yesterday's White House announcement naming me Assistant Secretary of Defense and today's announcement by the Secretary about the aircraft carrier, will see your hand in it." "I don't mind," I replied, "although I should not be given the credit for this."

I said that what I wanted to ask of him, as something very useful and an investment in the future, was for him to arrange even a brief meeting between Schlesinger and Zighdis. Zighdis belongs to the *Enosi Kentrou* (Center Union), is clearly in favor of the Atlantic Alliance, and he should not leave America without having spoken with the Secretary. I reminded him that Zighdis had been a minister in George Papandreou's government and is opposed to Andreas Papandreou's positions. Maury promised to take care of it.

April 9, Tuesday

Jim Pyrros called to say that Congressman Frelinghuysen spoke against the regime on April 3. Have things started to change?

Up to now Congressman Frelinghuysen was one of the most fervent supporters of American policy toward Greece and an opponent of those who stand against the dictatorship in Greece. On April 3, 1974 he made statements in the House that are of particular interest. Excerpts from his speech follow:

He said that he visited Greece last February, met with the prime minister, the foreign minister, talked with Ambassador Tasca and members of his staff, and met "unofficially" with a group of former parliamentarians.

> My general impression about the present Greek political scene is one of concern mixed with bad premonitions.
>
> The trusting mood evident during my previous visit in the fall of 1971 has been replaced by a state of uncertainty and adverse restlessness. Precisely in which direction the government of Greece is going is unclear and, in fact, it is difficult to define who directs and controls the government.

Further on, the congressman refers to his previous opposition to actions against the dictatorship.

> What is clear to me now, after recent discussions with Greek and American officials, is that there is no movement—or even the pretense of movement—towards elections or even movement towards political representation within the government's structure. Some promises made immediately after the November coup are no longer discussed.
>
> There are innumerable rumors about internal dissent and the military's internal division into opposing factions, with one group in a dominant position.
>
> In the meantime, there are signs that opposition to the government is spreading, not just among students and intellectuals, as in the past, but also among the previously peace-loving middle class.
>
> There is real danger that resistance among moderate elements of the Greek political scene will increase. This development may be accelerated by the recent arrest of the leader of the Center Union, George Mavros. One wonders what purpose is served by this arbitrary and thoughtless act.

Referring to Kissinger's statements, Congressman Frelinghuysen said,

> Whatever stance the State Department adopts does not prohibit us, as individuals, from pointing out to the leaders of foreign countries the effect developments in their countries have on their relations with the United States and on the conscience of the American people. That was the clear and simple purpose of my remarks today.

April 12, Friday
Athens tries to intimidate Zighdis

Zighdis told me that Papaspyrou telephoned and told him that the *Akropolis* and *Eleftheros Kosmos* newspapers published editorials accusing him of treason because at a time when the Turks are threatening the country, he inveighs against the armed forces.

In Europe for New Discussions

April 15, Monday

I phoned Pyrros and Day about Zighdis. Day was unaware of the campaign against Zighdis and would try to do everything possible. Day said they were having serious difficulties negotiating with the Athens regime over Souda.

I left for London.

April 16, Tuesday
Meeting with the King

I arrived at the hotel around ten in the morning. Ten minutes later the King called. I went to Claridge's and told him of the changes at the State Department. He asked me if I know what Stabler's post is. I said he is now Deputy Assistant Secretary of State for European Affairs. The King knew him from his time in the Rome embassy and considered him extremely well disposed. We had lunch together, and the King said the former member of parliament for Kozani, Michalis Papakonstantinou, had visited him. During his discussion with Papakonstantinou the issue arose of if the King should return with a referendum or without one. Papakonstantinou believes that if he is called, even by the army, the King should return only after a referendum. The King asked for my opinion and, without hesitation, I said that only after a winning a free referendum can he return with authority. "You, yourself, have defined the issue clearly, but beyond that," I added, "I do not think there is any other solution because without popular support the reaction against you will be considerable." He asked that we meet in Geneva with Rallis and Theotokis. He also said he had received a very warm letter from Iakovos.

April 20, Saturday

I arrived in Geneva and went to Mylonas. We spent about an hour together. I told him about the latest American developments, and we both agreed that we could expect a solution only from the army. He said he had seen Karamanlis in March and been disappointed with the meeting. Karamanlis took the position that when elections are announced he would run. Mylonas said to him, "You are going to B, while A has not been solved. How are we going to get to elections?" Karamanlis responded, "A will be solved by others." They also discussed the constitution, over which they disagreed. Karamanlis is in favor of a constitution drafted by a few people while Mylonas wants a constitutional parliament.

April 21, Sunday
Meeting with the King, Theotokis, Rallis, Arnaoutis, and Vidalis

Around noon the King, Theotokis, Rallis, and Arnaoutis arrived at my hotel, the Richemont. We had lunch around 3:00 o'clock. During the discussion, Rallis maintained that Karamanlis should return to Greece. Theotokis, Arnaoutis, and I disagreed. I maintained that returning to Greece would render Karamanlis useless, though I added that if he continues to stay silent he will soon be useless in Paris as well. I stressed that at this moment, with the military divided, the politicians are keeping silent and the people do not know what to think. A clear stand taken by Karamanlis would rock the boat. Theotokis supported the view that Karamanlis should go to America. I agreed with this, provided he does not wait for an invitation before coming.

Rallis, who found himself isolated in his opinion, turned to the King and asked, "Your Majesty, what is your view of this matter on which we disagree?" The King responded, "Mister Karamanlis has a political sense that leads him to nearly instinctive decisions. Therefore, only he can know if it is better to return to Greece or not. What I know and believe is that if he becomes active, he will certainly contribute decisively."

I added then that we do not have a great deal of time for activity of whatever kind. If the hardliners are still in control after June, there will no longer be any point to Karamanlis doing anything.

Because Rallis had previously said that the political world is discredited, the right falling apart, the center without a leader, I reminded them that the *Akropolis*, in its attack against Zighdis, spoke of passion for power. At this stage, we also need a spirit of sacrifice and, perhaps, along with activity in Greece and abroad, it would be useful, on the one hand, if the politicians announced that no one from the old parliament would run in the first elections and, on the other hand, if the generals announced that they had no intention of rejoining the army.

"Who will accept that?" Rallis replied. Theotokis did not agree. I was obliged to add that this gesture is not even a sacrifice because what I am proposing is something over which we do not have power, but it would have considerable psychological effect. Rallis said that he does not disagree, he has already stated as much publicly, but he considers it a practical impossibility to get everyone to agree. The King agreed with me on the need for speed, whatever we do. Rallis will relay our views to Karamanlis, whom he would see for some time in Paris.

April 24, Wednesday

I left for London in the morning and had lunch with the King. He said he had told Rallis in private to stress the need for close cooperation with Karamanlis but had forgotten to ask Rallis to brief him after his meeting with Karamanlis. We discussed nothing new. As he was leaving, he said, "Keep your suitcase packed, just in case."

April 25, Thursday
Discussion about NATO

Thomson, Sir Hugh Greene's aide, came by the hotel in the morning. We discussed the situation in NATO. I drew his attention to the developments that began today in Portugal with the army's move against the dictatorship and asked him to have Greene send a letter to Hayes asking him to launch an initiative in the House in favor of the Pell-Jackson bill, amended, however, to stress that restoration of democracy will lead to the full restoration of aid as well.

Eleni Vlachou held a dinner party in my honor, inviting Mr. and Mrs. Papagou, Mr. and Mrs. D. Horn, Takis Lambrias, Maria Karavia and Arnaoutis. Whether in jest or on purpose, three or four times Vlachou called me "tomorrow's prime minister." At some point we were talking privately and she said I should assume the leadership of the resistance because we had reached a dead end with the absence of any activity. I agreed that the general silence was very unpleasant but our concern should not lead us to exaggeration. Time is crucial; outbursts of self-promotion are not justified nor can the problems be solved by changing leadership responsibilities when the struggle is in full swing.

Return to America
New Efforts with the Administration

April 27, Saturday

New York. Zighdis came by the hotel in the afternoon. I told him my impressions from the trip in general terms, mainly about the silence kept by the politicians and Karamanlis and some speculation by officers. I let him read a copy of my letter to Davos. He told me he feared being arrested when he returns to Greece and that he was angry that he had not been able to meet with any high-ranking American officials.

We had dinner together.

May 1, Wednesday

Washington. I had lunch with Day at the Cosmos Club. He said the State Department had sent a message to the embassy about Zighdis to make it clear to the people in power that the effect upon their relations with the United States would be very unpleasant if they persecute Zighdis for his testimony before the congressional committee. Then he told me that it had been decided that Tasca, on his way back to Greece, should stop in Paris and see Karamanlis. The embassy in Paris got in touch with Karamanlis, but he replied that he was about to leave and it would not be possible to arrange a meeting with Tasca. They repeated the effort, but Karamanlis did not change his initial position. Day, clearly, was irritated.

May 2, Thursday

Report on the stance of some NATO countries toward the Greek dictatorship

I received a letter from Thomson, Sir Hugh Greene's aide, with a copy of Greene's letter to Hayes and the report I requested on European countries.

It should be noted that Greene's letter to Hayes fully reflects the discussion I had with his aide, Peter Thomson, on April 25 in London. It was particularly gratifying that it included the modification I asked them to add to Pell-Jackson bill about full restoration of aid as soon as democracy is restored in Greece.

May 7, Tuesday

I telephoned Zighdis, who had not met with Stabler yesterday and was annoyed with the delay.

I sent a registered letter to Stabler, the Deputy Assistant Secretary for European Affairs, and a report on restoring democracy in Greece through the NATO alliance.

May 12, Sunday

We returned to Toledo in the afternoon. Kostas Karras telephoned and said that many ship-owners were beginning to come round and his mother will give me more information. He relayed the rumor, which he considered unlikely but which he had heard three times, according to which Greece is being pressured to provide the northerners with an outlet to the Mediterranean in the form of a corridor along the Evros River in return for Russian pressure for peace in the Middle East. I said all that is fairy tales and he did not disagree.

I found a letter from Frelinghuysen, a card from Sekeris, and a letter from Arnaoutis dated May 8 telling me that the King spoke to Stabler on the telephone.

Frelinghuysen's letter: [Translated back into English from the printed Greek text.]

Dear Mr. Vidalis,

Thank you for your letter referring to my recent remarks about Greece. I apologize for the delay in responding.

As I mentioned in my remarks on April 3, while I believe that our security interests will be better served if Greece returns to a more popular form of government, our relations with Greece are complex. I assure you that as a member of the House Foreign Relations Committee I will continue the open dialogue between the two governments.

Thank you again for your letter. Please keep writing to me.

Yours truly,

Peter H. B. Frelinghuysen

May 14, Tuesday

Efthymios spent the entire day talking with General Frontistis. He was very pleased.

Dimopoulos telephoned. Athanassiadis of the *Vradini* had sent him a letter containing some questions for Kissinger and a sealed letter from Potamianos for Kissinger. Athanassiadis hoped to have answers to his questions for the June 3 front page.

May 16, Thursday

Dimopoulos telephoned. He and Nicolopoulos met with Day on the *Vradini* matter. Day told them that it was impossible for Kissinger to deal with the matter and was dubious about expecting a public statement from Kissinger. However, he did keep the letter to act on it.

May 17, Friday

I received a letter from Peridis who, after describing the situation as fairly desperate, concluded with the view that he is expecting developments in May or June.

May 23, Thursday

I arrived in Washington yesterday and saw Wells Stabler, the Deputy Assistant Secretary for European Affairs, in the morning. My visit with Stabler was a fairly formal visit marking the transfer of the Greek Desk to the European Affairs Department.

In the afternoon I met with Buchanan. He had telephoned yesterday to tell me that the new Chairman of the Joint Chiefs of Staff, General George Brown, whom he had met at a dinner a few days earlier, criticized the regime and praised the King.

May 24, Friday

I wrote details of my meeting with Stabler to the King:

> May 24, 1974
>
> Stabler received me impeccably. Certainly he told me he was pleased to speak with the King and he thanked me for the letter and the report (NATO).
>
> I told him that I, personally, am pleased that he is assuming his duties now at a time when new faces are necessary to allow a change in policy. I insisted on the moment being crucial and the immediate need for a change in American posture. I recommended the following as the means for change: a) NATO—as the report suggests; b) Allowing Congress to vote to suspend all aid with the simultaneous provision that all aid and grants will resume as soon as democracy is restored; c) The Greek-Americans, who will be meeting in June in Chicago under Iakovos. I said that a whisper from the State Department to Iakovos could lead to a vote against the regime and an appeal for restoring normal conditions promptly; d) Selecting a prominent American, such as General Norstad, to be the president's representative to apply final pressure to restore democracy.
>
> He listened carefully. We then discussed his questions:
>
> a. Assuming that a decision is taken to implement your proposals, what will be their effect in Greece and how can we ensure that we do not come up with an even more hard-line group?
> b. What scenario do you see if there are measures to restore the King, a national unity government?
> c. If relations with America freeze completely, does not the junta have other alternatives?
>
> My positions were familiar. (Synopsis below):

a. America's lax stance to date has permitted the continuation. Carrying on with the old strategy will prolong the situation and lead to the point of intransigence until the Americans are kicked out. A change in the American stance today would strengthen the moderates in the army, change the popular perception against America, help mobilize the currently silent opposition, and lead to a chain reaction of psychological and substantive developments. It would rid us of the mantra griping the army and the people: "Since the Americans are helping them, what can we do?"

   A change in the American and NATO stances also would disarm the far left and its supporters. It would definitively block any future chance of cooperation between Ioannidis's fanatics and those who are neutral in this contest but gripped by anti-American hysteria.

b. The King is the guarantor of normal conditions, stability, and democratic development within the framework of the Western world. If there is a change in the American position, any basic scenario—I cannot predict the initial form—will lead to the appearance of the King as being responsible for the transition to normality. A change in the American stance now could lead to a scenario for normalization. Inaction, continuing support, or additional irresponsible statements such as those made by General Goodpaster will lead to bloodshed and uncertainty.

c. Papadopoulos always blackmailed and succeeded in getting extensions. The new team will do the same. If the French provide them with heavy armaments and you continue to coddle them now, we will have dramatic competition among arms manufacturers and the entire situation will become disappointingly sad. If you take a clear and strict stand within NATO, then the fanatics in Athens will know they cannot blackmail you and the French will be more careful in view of their relations with you and their other NATO partners.

Stabler said he had assumed responsibility for Greece just a few weeks ago and was trying to deepen his understanding, and he thanked me for the discussion, which lasted an hour and a half.

He said we should stay in touch. Before I left, I recapped the following:

a. The method chosen—NATO, Congress, etc.—is of secondary importance. What is of primary importance is taking the political decision, "Change the policy."

b. There is no time for delays. Your predecessors had or found time—claiming that the Constitution of '68 will be implemented or the Markezinis solution. Now the problems are pressing, the junta is incompetent, the young hate everything, and the Alliance is facing a Greco-Turkish crisis—just for domestic reasons.

He agreed and promised to stay in touch.

Day of the Greek Desk, who was present at the discussion, had told me before the meeting that they have information that the French were nearing agreement on providing Greece with Mirage fighters, AMX, and ships in total value far more than American aid, to be paid back in the future from income generated by Greek oil. According to Day, the terms of the deal are very good but they overestimate the oil income and underestimate the amount of time needed to exploit the oil. De Gaulle's people are handling the agreement, but they feel that the new French president will not object because of pressure from industry.

After the discussion with Stabler, Day told me that Kissinger was the main problem. Stabler was very well disposed and wanted the change, as did Lowenstein. Kissinger, however, has not, himself, become involved and is not available to become involved. He does not delegate decisions and has time only for burning issues. They will see what they will do with NATO now that they have to take a position because of the NATO meeting (therefore the usefulness of my report).

France's stance provides the dictatorship another substantial pillar of support, allowing it to blackmail the Americans and thereby continue in power. This automatically raises the question of what all those Greek politicians and others who live in Europe are doing to confront French policy, since France, too, supports the dictatorship for its own interests?

May 25, Saturday

Yesterday, spurred by the Congressional debate during Zighdis's testimony, I wrote to the archbishop urging him to mobilize the Greek-Americans to take a stand on our national issue:

May 24, 1974

Your Reverence,

For years I have tried to stress to you the role that the Greek-Americans could play in the tragedy of our homeland.

You did not agree with the emphasis I placed on this factor.

I tried to explain to you that my friends here used the stance of the Greek-Americans to rebut my arguments about the situation in Greece.

That their excuses were but a put-off does not alter the fact that the Greek-Americans were used negatively.

Recent proof is the debate during Zighdis's testimony. I have noted the relevant excerpts on pages 21 and 22.

I firmly believe—and I will not tire in my efforts—that, as things have developed up to now, the Greek-Americans can and must show their positive presence. The convention in Chicago may be a unique opportunity for the Greek-Americans to take center stage in history and take a stance under your spiritual guidance.

The hours back home are crucial. Relations with Turkey are deteriorating and hatred of America is soaring.

Sincerely yours,

Orestis Vidalis

May 29, Tuesday
Turkish move toward Lesvos

John Day from the State Department called and said that a few hours ago Turkish warships sailed out of the Bosphorus toward the Limnos-Lesvos area, escorting a special oil-exploration vessel. The ships are expected to be in position tomorrow morning, U.S. Eastern Standard time. The Greek armed forces are on alert and the situation is considered very tense. I thanked him for the information and he promised to keep me informed if there are further developments.

When I telephoned the King and told him about the Turkish moves he said that they had been in continuous conference in Athens and he had not known why. He begged me to call him at any time and to ask for the bedroom phone so he could answer it himself if I had anything new.

June 1, Saturday
Letter from the Archbishop

I received an angry letter from the Archbishop, in reply to mine:

The honorable Orestis Vidalis
Toledo, Ohio

Dear Mr. Vidalis *May 29, 1974*

Thank you for your letter of the 24th and the enclosed document. I have a single answer to Mr. Buchanan, Mr. Zighdis and yourself: The Greeks of America are apolitical as far as the issue of Greece is concerned. They are interested in (and offer much to) American political affairs but not to Greek political affairs.

One more thing. If they were interested they could deny Mr. Buchanan an easy negative argument while providing him or his colleagues with another, that the Greek-Americans are untrustworthy because they are more interested in Greek politics.

There was much prejudice against the Greeks (for precisely this reason), just as there was against the Italians and the Japanese. Just as anti-Semitism exists (and is increasing) today.

The American administration (not members of Congress) wants fewer political headaches. Kissinger espouses the principle, "let sleeping dogs lie." I have reason to believe that the vast majority of Congress trusts Kissinger and his political or diplomatic philosophical precepts.

The situation in Greece will not change unless the Greeks of Greece change it. If you have a different opinion, i.e., that the Greeks of American can change it, you do not have me in agreement.

With much respect and warm wishes,

The Archbishop

June 4, Tuesday

I saw Day in the afternoon. He said he would travel to Greece via London, Paris, and Thessaloniki. I told him to see General Tzannetis and to tell Davos that I hold him in high esteem. He said they have information that Britain might raise the question of the Alliance at June's summit meeting. He also said that the bureaucracy has done what it can and now it is a matter of pressing Kissinger.

He considers Norstad and Jackson the right people for this, along with editorials in the *Washington Post* and the *New York Times* and pressure from allies and from inside Greece.

June 6, Thursday

Day telephoned to say that he will not go to Greece after all because Tasca disagreed.

June 9, Sunday
Response to Archbishop Iakovos

I wrote and mailed my response to Iakovos:

Your Reverence, *Sunday, June 9, 1974*

Thank you warmly for your letter of May 29.

It is revealing and highly interesting as an interpretation of the inertia of the Greek-Americans.

Today I feel the need to clarify my positions on two of the issues touched upon:

- *The Greeks of America are apolitical as far as Greece is concerned.*
- *The Greek-Americans cannot change the situation in Greece.*

First, the "issue of Greece" is not political, it is national, it is even humanitarian. It is national because the foundations of the nation are at risk from the continuing disintegration of institutions, the prevention of new leadership arising naturally, the disintegration of the armed forces, making our young useless, etc, etc. It is humanitarian because Greeks are being humiliated, imprisoned, exiled, tortured, and murdered by Greeks.

I have never asked you or any Greek-American to involve himself in Greek politics. I have, however, always believed that the Greek-Americans, properly guided and informed, could externalize approximately the same feelings that led you to your letter to Rogers and to repeat that "the people of Greece are not free to choose their political leaders nor are they free to chart their own course" and "Greece, the cradle of Democracy, where the rights and the dignity of man first saw light, deserves both our respect and our concern."

Clearly you were not indulging in politics with these confidential confessions. Neither were the Washington Post, the New York Times and the rest of the press. Even Senator Jackson and other prominent individuals were not indulging in politics when they expressed their views. They did it because, as Americans, they were bothered by the "sleeping dogs."

On the second issue, I never have claimed that the "Greeks of America can change the situation in Greece." I believed and I still believe that the Greeks of America, simply by making known their humanitarian concerns, could help the Greeks in their agonizing effort to rid themselves of the suffocating embrace of the "national saviors" and those who support them. More than a few Greek-Americans have, for material reasons, supported the mutiny of the few against the many.

In order to mitigate somewhat the perception caused by the scandalous intervention of these people, I believed that the right-minded majority of the Greek-American could appear on the historical stage in the interests of both Greece and America, at least now, and say "that's enough, after seven years of humiliation of Greece and the Greeks, it bothers us as free people, as Americans."

That would impress the souls of the Greeks and Washington. The rest is up to the Greeks in Greece, whose present feelings towards America you know. One of the many reasons for those feelings is the stance of our compatriots here, in America.

With these clarifications out of the way, I want to assure you that I respect your views as you expressed them in your last letter. Because, however, we see the problem from different perspectives, I do NOT intend to call upon your help again on our national issue. I have done what my duty compelled me to do. Perhaps some day I will be accused of a lack of realism in seeking the support of the Greek-Americans, but I will not be accused of inertia.

Sincerely yours,

Orestis Vidalis

Return to Europe

June 11, Tuesday
In Europe again

I arrived in Geneva. Matina telephoned in the afternoon from Ohio. Pell had telephoned her and said that Dimitrakopoulos had asked him to have the Senate Foreign Relations Committee invite Karamanlis. "I cannot," he told Matina, "do anything unless the general tells me to or agrees in some way. Please, if you speak with the general, ask him if he thinks it is appropriate and if the invitation also should be extended to the King."

June 12, Wednesday

I went to Maria Beckett's house. Mitsotakis came straight from the airport. He had seen Karamanlis in Paris. He expects nothing from the politicians in Greece, other than that now they are all trying to influence the army. He urged Karamanlis to launch a serious effort from Paris.

I then went to see Mylonas. I described the situation in America to him in general terms and he said he saw no other solution other than a suitable intervention by the army. Before I left he said to me, "I will confide something in you. Don't you think you should become the Spinola of Greece?" The idea surprised me coming from Mylonas, who went on to ask, "How is your relationship with Kanellopoulos?" "Excellent," I replied. "How is your relationship with Opropoulos?" "Very good." "How is your relationship with officers in Greece?" "Ioannidis's group doesn't want to see anything of me, not even a sketch. The other serving officers, I don't know."

He ended the conversation by saying, "I know that you cannot do anything, but I can." I report the conversation just for the record.

June 17, Monday
Answer from Archbishop Iakovos

Today I received the following response from the archbishop to my letter of the 9th:

> The Honorable
> Orestis Vidalis
> Toledo, Ohio
>
> *Dear Mr. Vidalis* *June 13, 1974*
>
> *I read your somewhat perturbed letter and your hurried conclusion carefully. You know very well my views on the subject as well as my stance on the whole issue and if I consider it national or political.*
>
> *My anguish, my fears, my hopes, and my prayers are known only to me. No one else. Apart from God. I will always act as my conscience dictates in any direction I consider correct.*
>
> *With warm wishes and affection,*
>
> *The Archbishop*
>
> *Iakovos of America*

June 20, Thursday

London. I saw Lambrias in the morning. I told him I need his help to produce a monthly newsletter for military officers, in which I thought that Eleni Vlachou should be involved as well, and he said he would be pleased to help.

I had lunch with the King and told him again of my actions concerning Stabler, Iakovos, and also about Pell's telephone call. I added that I had decided to go to Paris to see Karamanlis for yet another attempt to energize him and see what his intentions are about going to America. He had nothing new.

In the afternoon I saw Eleni Vlachou and told her of the newsletter for officers, and she offered to help and distribute, together with Lambrias.

June 22, Saturday
Meeting in Paris with Karamanlis

I left for Paris and met with Karamanlis from 5:00 to 7:00 PM I told him we can expect nothing from America or the Greek-Americans and it is the last opportunity for him to act. But this time it cannot be another assault like before, that is, issue a statement and expect the dictatorship to fall. This time he must himself work on a serious publication in Greek that Vlachou and Lambrias could then exploit. This time even the ship-owners have decided to help. He agreed with my evaluation, said that I overestimate his powers, but thinks that he must do something for three reasons: a) Because he must not let down those who believe in him. b) Because hope, without which death comes, must be rekindled, and c) Because he feels the need to return to his homeland.

On the points I raised, he thought that an official organization must exist before the newsletter, which can then report on its activities. I fully agreed but added that I felt that time must not be wasted organizing this assault. He asked what the King was doing and if he had any special information. "He is well," I said, "but he does not know anything beyond what is commonly known." I asked Karamanlis if he would be willing to come to America. "The Americans either do not want to understand they have a problem," he replied, "or they do not want to say so. They notified me from their embassy here to see Tasca on his way back to Athens. I asked them if he had instructions from the administration and specific things to discuss, and they replied that the conversation would cover the entire horizon. I replied that I would be on 'a cruise,' because I had warned Tasca, at a previous meeting, to reach specific conclusions and then we could talk. The same is true with America. I won't come and testify before Congress because there is no point. To come just to be seen signifies nothing. I could come to America only if it would lead to a result and if the administration were prepared to discuss specific actions."

June 23, Sunday

England. I went to Ascot, to the house where the King is staying. It was their first day in the house. I told the King about the discussion with Karamanlis, my impression that he probably would do something, and his position on traveling to America. He said he might go to Paris around the end of the month, at which point he would ask to see Karamanlis to apply pressure himself. But the trip is not certain.

I went back to London. Takis Lambrias came to the hotel and I showed him the text I had prepared for the BBC. He liked it and suggested a couple of changes in the wording. Since we did not have time to go to the BBC, we agreed that I should record it on one of Arnaoutis's tape recorders.

The Junta and the Turks Take Aim at Cyprus

JULY 1, MONDAY

I wrote Karamanlis and sent him the report I sent to Stabler at the State Department on formulating a policy based on the Alliance's fundamental principles.

I received a letter from Zisiou. The main points are below:

7/1/74

Here there now are two crucial issues. They may prove fateful for the people in power, but they may have even more tragic consequences on this unfortunate country. One is Cyprus. Makarios's decision to break up the junta's conspiracy on Cyprus (EOKA, National Guard officers, etc.) On this subject, if there is an official break between Makarios and Athens, then we, too, will help reveal the foul way the junta has undermined the national struggle. Obvious reasons compel our silence for the time being. The other is the sudden escalation of tension between Athens and Ankara over the Aegean. Many believe in: a) British instigation in favor of the Turks (see article in Ellinikos Vorras "Oi Sachanakides"). b) American intervention in favor of Athens or Ankara to stoke tensions to increase arms sales (communist version), or to distract attention from political or economic chaos. c) Unilateral Turkish provocation aimed at sharing control over the Aegean. The tensions certainly are worsening the economic chaos (mobilizations, arms purchases, transportation, fuel). The people are unprepared and unwilling for conflict and, perhaps, tired.

The possibility of a shooting war ruled out, but if irrationality prevails, both sides will suffer territorial and material losses (Karagats for Turkey—small island for Greece.) The Aegean Islands have been heavily reinforced. The last purges were against followers of Papadopoulos and a few unwanted wretches. In the army, then, the following factions exist: a) Officers loyal to democratic procedures, without power or cohesion, 45—55%. b) Officers believing in continuing the dictatorship indefinitely—Qaddafi and Ioannidis types—very powerful in the capital, 20%. c) Officers believing in the Turkish model strong in northern Greece but restrained because of infiltration by Ioannidis's informers, 25—35%.

The commissar system has essentially disintegrated within the expeditionary forces (field army, army corps, divisions). Officers can speak freely among themselves without fear of repercussions. The natural hierarchy has been reestablished. Ioannidis's informers are still widespread but have lost their power to do anything but tell tales (ESA members, intelligence staff, and isolated officers). Serious members of the old April 21 guard, people like Peta-

nis, Daskalakis, Tasopoulos, etc, have been discharged. The class of 1947 (colonels to brigadiers) was decimated. Lower ranking officers (captains and majors) are in a sensitive spot, changing their positions because of repression and anxieties, etc. It seems that the army has acquired a mentality of serving the Americans without national feeling (NATO consciousness). The feeling of bitterness among the people for being toyed with strong after the NATO meeting and declarations. The voice of OEV (Vidalis) was heard and welcomed, moved people, and formed the foundation-stone of the decision to struggle. The struggle, heaven help us, is limited to statements. But more is needed for it to develop further, all the things we have said, but, nothing. The most basic thing is needed, encouragement from abroad. Especially from the U.S.A. All that can be done from here are small, sporadic, exhortations. Influencing and energizing the army—the main lever of change—is difficult, requiring a great deal of work and, above all, intense psychological operations. The meat trial and the sentences imposed provided nothing for the people. It simply made the effort to cover up Balopoulos clear. Coolheaded estimates are that the trial was a personal failure for Ioannidis, who tried to stop it so that it would not appear to be a condemnation of April 21 corruption. [Balopoulos, a member of the junta's Revolutionary Council, was involved in a scandal about wholesale distribution of spoiled meat.]

Nonetheless, despite the efforts, the shadow of guilt fell on the Papadopoulos brothers, Pattakos, etc. And it was just one aspect of the scandals.

I see uncle George (Peridis) regularly as well as the other friends.

Before I end this, I believe unshakably that we are living in one of the most crucial and dangerous cycles in our history. May God help us.

I am expecting your letter. Greetings and kisses to all of you.

Kriton[4]

JULY 9, TUESDAY

I wrote Senator Pell:

[4]Code for Kostas Zisiou.

July 9 1974

The Honorable Claiborne Pell
United States Senate
Committee on Foreign Relations
Washington, D. C.

Dear Senator Pell,

The situation in Greece has deteriorated to the point that not only the future of Greece is in jeopardy, but peace in that part of the world is threatened.

Archbishop Makarios officially accused the dictatorship for plotting to overthrow him and establish another dictatorship in Cyprus.

Relations with Turkey are strained to a dangerous point.

Top officials of the Ministry of Foreign Affairs and prominent Greek diplomats have resigned.

In this very critical moment I can only address myself to you in the belief that you will again, as always, assist Greece and NATO.

Attached you will find some thoughts and a proposal I prepared for you.

I urge you to take any action you will judge feasible and appropriate at this time.

Public support of Archbishop Makarios by the U.S. is a first priority issue which should invite the Administration's attention since it is not an internal matter that "the Greek people" can "resolve." Public opinion and all political leaders in Greece strongly support Archbishop Makarios.

With kind regards.

Cordially yours,

Orestis E. Vidalis

July 10, Wednesday

Meeting with Congressman Wayne Hayes in Washington. He will launch an initiative to suspend all aid, including private transactions with companies in Greece. I insisted that he include in his proposals that all forms of aid and support (private and public) will be restored as soon as democracy returns to Greece.

July 14, Sunday
NATO meeting, Ottawa

The NATO meeting in Ottawa reconfirmed the principles upon which the Atlantic Alliance rests.

I took the opportunity to make the following statement, which was broadcast by the BBC and published by the *National Herald* on July 14, 1974. Again I mainly addressed myself to officers:

> The Atlantic Alliance recently renewed its "devotion to the principles of democracy, respect for human rights, justice and social progress."
>
> The signers of the Ottawa declaration expressed the will of the peoples of the Alliance and confirmed the fundamental principles that will govern NATO's life during its second quarter century.
>
> According to the declaration, the Alliance's raison d'être remains "the maintenance of the values composing the heritage of our Western civilization." The security of the NATO area is a means and not an end.
>
> The ideological underpinnings of the Alliance take on primary importance in this period of détente between East and West. If the peoples of the Alliance do not have faith in it serving the ideals of freedom of social progress, then any number of tanks, warplanes, and warships are nothing but useless weight.
>
> Those of us who believe in the worth of the Atlantic Alliance must consider that the Ottawa declaration expresses that which free people expect from an alliance of free nations.
>
> Unfortunately, the sole sour note in this renewal and confirmation of the aims and goals of NATO came from Greece.
>
> The representatives of the current regime were forced by circumstances to avow that they signed the declaration without reservations although they know full well that the people, especially our young, seriously doubt the extent to which the Alliance's declarations will be transformed into actions.
>
> The officers and especially the leadership of the armed forces—as the sole repository of power—assumed the obligation, according to the declaration, "to develop and strengthen the implementation of these principles of democracy and respect for human rights" in Greece.
>
> The officers of the armed forces, but also the political and military leaders of the Alliance, ought to know that, in the common interest, the Ottawa declaration must be ratified by the people of Greece. Without this ratification, the value of the Alliance to Greece and the value of Greece to the Alliance must be considered undefined, uncertain, and in serious doubt.
>
> The people, today silent observers of these developments, should neither overestimate nor underestimate the importance of the Ottawa declaration until the real intentions of all those who assumed its obligations become clear.
>
> It would be wise, however, to keep in mind—following our already bit-

ter experience—that our free institutions will not be restored by foreigners or alliances, who only look after—often cynically—their own interests.

July 15, Monday
Junta launches armed raid against Makarios

I received an express letter from Spyros Theotokis with his first public statement since we started working together against the dictatorship.

Theotokis's statement of 7/9/74:

Statement by the former Greek Minister for Foreign Affairs, Mr. Spyros Theotokis

7/9/74

The president and National Leader has sounded reveille for Hellenism with his historic condemnation against those causing the bloodshed on Cyprus. What he denounces can be neither doubted nor criticized. Instead, it imposes awareness of responsibilities and coming together.

All Greeks, everyone who feels for Hellenism, is obligated to work together against the national dangers Makarios's message points out with such dramatic clarity. For myself, I have no reason to add my own voice. During my long absence from the homeland I have preferred to cover my sadness and worry about everything happening there with silence. Silence, however, whatever reasons may dictate it, cannot stand before a national tragedy, when the fate of a large and living part of Hellenism is at risk.

Having once been partly responsible for the so-called Cyprus problem, I had the unshakable conviction that it could be solved only through political wisdom, avoiding violence from any side at all costs. I followed this conviction of mine with all its consequences. I continue to believe, unshakably, that even hostile antagonism, not just conflict, between Greece and Turkey, NATO members in such a critical part of the world today, can lead to disaster.

The need, however, to keep peace and calm in the eastern Mediterranean, for the benefit of its nations and the entire free world, cannot become a weapon for blackmail or repression. It cannot be invoked by the government in Ankara to promote baseless claims on the Greek seas or on Cyprus, nor by the regime in Athens to justify its illegal existence.

As for the latter especially, which proved its unbearable incompetence in handling foreign affairs, there is only one national policy; that which President Makarios clearly expressed. Those who truly want union between Greece and Cyprus are obliged to ensure and strengthen the island's independence. On the other hand, those who plot and/or tolerate

> the partition of Cyprus forever betray the vision of union, since it is self-evident that parts once separated will never join the national whole.
>
> Real Greeks and Greece's true friends have a sacred obligation at this moment: To respect and defend the independence of the Republic of Cyprus and the standing of its president, who has been freely and repeatedly elected by the people of Cyprus.

The tragedy begins. Cypriot troops commanded by Greek army officers overthrew the government of Cyprus yesterday. There are conflicting reports on the fate of Makarios, following the attack against the Presidential Mansion. Tanks are in the streets of Nicosia.

JULY 16, TUESDAY

Makarios' fate is unknown.

I wrote Doctor Spirtos. I described how the situation had deteriorated and added, "Developments over the last two days in Cyprus prove how right you were in your official statements last year at AHEPA's annual convention." I went on to ask, "I wonder what must happen for the Greek-Americans to raise their voices against this tyranny. Is there any chance now for AHEPA to issue a statement against the intervention in Cyprus?"

JULY 17, WEDNESDAY
Makarios saved

The Atlantic alliance was in session over the Cyprus crisis. It recommended self-restraint.

The dictatorship in Athens described the crisis as an "internal affair of an independent state."

Archbishop Makarios, who was saved, accused the leaders of the Greek military dictatorship for staging the coup and called them "fascists" in a radio address.

In this first broadcast he said, "Greek-Cypriots—you know who is addressing you. You have elected me. I am not dead. I am at your side."

Makarios sought refuge in Malta, with British help, and announced that he would appeal to the United Nations.

In these tragic hours, I felt the need to express what every Greek felt over the treasonous military intervention in Cyprus. My statement, which I sent today to the *National Herald* for publication, is below.

> At this moment of supreme national crisis, restraining the rage felt by every Greek soul over the unpatriotic insanity of the few, I address myself to the right-thinking officers of the armed forces, appealing to their patri-

otism and inviting them to contemplate their responsibilities to the nation.

In November of 1973, the oath breakers of 1967, brought low by time and their illegal acts, were, rightly, overthrown by you, the soldiers.

The question that has remained unanswered since November 25, 1973, is, "Why were they overthrown?" To continue the inflexibility of 1967 or to return the army to its duties, the Greeks to their political responsibilities, and for Greece to regain control over its own affairs?

At this moment, in the souls of the Greeks, the extension of the state of violence to Cyprus confirms the belief that November 25 happened only to continue and expand the intransigence of violence and exclusively serve foreign interests.

While everything is being risked, I continue to believe that Greece can be saved, even at this extreme moment, by right-thinking patriotic officers.

My responsibility, as a Greek citizen who cannot rest before this onrushing national calamity, is to call upon you to take up your responsibilities.

The insanity in Cyprus, which has provoked the outrage of world public opinion, cannot possibly lead to realizing our national desire for Union. It threatens partition, either through bloody conflict or through diplomatic machinations.

Right now the responsibility of the generals and all armed forces officers is to clarify their position against history. You are obliged to tell the nation today, at this moment, if you assume your responsibilities for what is happening and will happen on Cyprus or if you have surrendered the homeland and Cyprus and yourselves to backstage irresponsibility.

In particular, I call upon the generals to contemplate their historical responsibilities because I believe that none of them wishes to go down in history in that category of generals who proved to be frightened servants of their insane subordinates.

History will judge all of us by what we do and what we do not do.

July 18, Thursday
Fears of a Turkish landing

Anxiety over the situation in Cyprus continued. Fears of a Turkish landing were expressed. Apparently Britain, as a guarantor power, washed its hands of the affair. But Kissinger simply recommended self-restraint. In the meantime, I heard from London about the movements of Turkish landing craft and escort vessels from the Turkish coast.

July 19, Friday

In Ankara Sisco[5] met with Ecevit in an effort to avert Turkish intervention.

I phoned Spirtos and we agreed that AHEPA would send the following letter to the President of the United States.

Dear Mr. President,

We have been following the recent events in Cyprus with the gravest concern. We share the anxiety of the U.S. and world public opinion after the Greek military regime's intervention which resulted in the overthrowing the elected government of this independent country.

We fully support the elected President of Cyprus, Archbishop Makarios, in his efforts to restore the independence and the constitutional order in the island.

Time has come for the U. S. government to take, together with the NATO allies, all necessary steps to convince or force the Greek military junta to realize that the U.S. and the free world cannot any more tolerate tyranny in Greece which has evolved into a source of international tension and possibly conflict in that sensitive part of the globe.

The patience of all free men has been exhausted. We expect the U.S. government to lead NATO in restoring our prestige as protector of freedom and rationality around the world.

We urge you personally to lead this effort.

Respectfully,

M. Spirtos, MD

July 20, Saturday
Turkish landing on Cyprus

Turkish forces landed on Cyprus near Kyrenia. Ecevit announced that the decision to intervene was taken at a special government session just before daybreak.

So began, following the treasonous intervention of Athens against Makarios, the Turkish exploitation of the opportunity they had been seeking for years. The Turkish attack signals the beginning of a phase of our history. Who knows when it will end and at what cost to the nation?

I received a letter from Senator Pell, dated July 17, enclosing a letter to Kissinger dated the same day.

The letter to me simply informed me that Senator McGovern has agreed to sign the statement I had discussed with Pell, similar to Hayes's.

[5] In an interview given in July 1993, Sisco described his actions on those days in 1974.

Pell's letter to Kissinger:

United States Senate
Foreign Relations Committee
Washington D.C. WA 201510

The Honorable
Henry A. Kissinger
Secretary of State
Washington D.C.

Dear Henry, *July 17, 1974*

The news of the possible overthrow of the Cypriote government of Archbishop Makarios is a matter of great concern. I know you must be aware of the grave repercussions which this event may have not only in terms of the possible renewal of communal strife on the island but also for the future of Greek-Turkish relations, the position of NATO and wider U.S. interests of the U.S.A. in the eastern Mediterranean.

The overall Greek situation, which has heretofore focused on the internal policies of the junta, has now become an international problem concerning which the United States is justified in seeking a solution. I would, therefore, urge that the Administration review its policy toward Greece in the light of the following factors:

- *The need to contain the present crisis and to restore the situation in Cyprus to its previous balance as promptly as possible.*
- *The need for the United States Government to make clear, both publicly and privately, that we can not condone the conduct of the junta and that the United States disassociates itself from any responsibility for the junta's foreign and domestic policies.*
- *The need to work with other members of NATO to bring the Alliance's influence to bear in support of a return to a representative government for the Greek people and the restoration of responsibility in the conduct of Greek foreign policy.*

Given the current crisis in Cyprus, I believe a new policy toward Greece which can have the wholehearted support of the Congress is of the highest priority.

You may be assured of my support for efforts to achieve such a policy.

Warm regards.

Sincerely,

Claiborne Pell

JULY 21, SUNDAY

Fighting continued on Cyprus despite the unanimous call by the United Nations Security Council for a cease-fire and negotiations among Greece, Turkey, and Great Britain to restore peace and constitutional order on the island.

The junta ordered general mobilization.

These tragic days of July have shaken Greeks everywhere. Archbishop Iakovos appealed to the administration because he felt that "the tragedy of Cyprus is a tragedy for the Greek nation, not merely the tragedy of a single people, those of Cyprus, or a single island, that of Cyprus."

Kissinger's reply to the archbishop was a brush-off, continuing the American administration's cynical handling of the Greek issue through all the years of the dictatorship and highlighting Kissinger's own devious behavior.

JULY 23, TUESDAY
Davos's libelous answer

While the tragedy played on, I received a letter from Davos in Thessaloniki dated July 13, 1974, in reply to my letter of March 25, 1974.

This letter completely shattered my hopes but also the rumors that had circulated about Davos. His letter proved his devotion to the dictatorship, a lack of any concern for his slanderous response, slanderous not just to me but also to all those who individually or collectively took a stance against the dictatorship.

The Junta Self-destructs

JULY 24, WEDNESDAY

The junta succumbed to its crimes. It folded beneath the weight of its treason, beneath its inability to handle the situation it created on Cyprus, beneath the dramatic failure of the mobilization itself. Konstantinos Karamanlis was called upon to deal with the national impasse. He arrived in the early morning hours in the airplane of the President of France. The crowds wildly proclaimed him during his arrival and chanted "Democracy, democracy."

Karamanlis made a brief statement when he arrived: "I am here to contribute with all my strength to the nation's return to normal life."

A tragic period in the life of the nation came to an end. Let us hope that the new period beginning today will justify the struggles and sacrifices made by the Greeks who believed in the people of this country.

July 25, Thursday
Congratulations to the government

I sent congratulatory telegrams to Karamanlis, Mavros, Rallis, Lambrias, and Mylonas.

Senator Pell sent me a letter that Senators Hubert Humphrey, Gale McGee, G. McRowen, and he sent Kissinger on July 18.

The letter proposed:

- Suspending diplomatic recognition of the Nikos Sampson regime.
- Taking all steps possible to ensure peaceful restoration of the Makarios government and the expulsion to Greece of the officers who took part in the coup.
- Full coordination with the Senate Foreign Relations Committee before the administration proceeds with definitive diplomatic moves relating to the crisis in Cyprus and the eastern Mediterranean.

July 27, Saturday

Senator Pell addressed the Senate on July 24 to mark the junta's departure from power.

Pell's remarks bring to mind the man absent from Greece at a time when all Greeks are joyous and relieved because of their release from the dictatorship's shackles. King Constantine is absent from the repatriation and jubilation.

Many felt that the King erred, first, by accepting a referendum and, second, by not returning as soon as the national government was formed.

I counter these thoughts with my belief that the King was right to leave the nature of the republic to the judgment of the Greek people after the preceding upheavals. The King's behavior, starting with December 13, 1967, continuing with his uncompromising stance against the dictatorship all these years, and ending with his waiting for the judgment of the Greeks, proved his faith in democracy and the spirit of sacrifice that distinguished him throughout this national adventure.

July 29, Monday

Letters are pouring in from all over America. Our friends and acquaintances feel that they contributed to the developments and want to express it and share their joy with us.

AUGUST 1, THURSDAY

Ioannis Zighdis and I became close while he was in America. When he arrived in Greece today, he issued an interesting statement mainly addressed to the Greeks of America.

AUGUST 2, FRIDAY

After the junta's self-destruction and the establishment in Greece of a government of national unity, I consider the mission I assigned myself at the end of October 1968, when I arrived in America, to be at an end.

During these years I made efforts, travelled, wrote, communicated with Greek politicians and intellectuals inside and outside Greece, with Americans and Greek-Americans, leaders and common people, more than ever before in my life, more than I ever will again, regardless of what the future holds in store for me.

By rights, I should be able to say "It's over, I have no reason to act or worry for there is a responsible government in Greece that I am certain will lead the country to democratic procedures."

Unfortunately, the fateful error of the second junta created the deep wound on Cyprus and I will have to use my contacts to save whatever possible.

I now have reason to believe that the Greek-Americans, who remained indifferent to or sided with the junta all these years—except for some well-known bright exceptions—will support the campaign for Cyprus. I believe that this time the Greek-Americans will not remain indifferent, but will assist organized efforts, particularly if the Greek government directly or indirectly asks for their help. In these predictions the Greek-Americans did not prove me wrong. Cyprus awakened and united them. Almost all Greek-Americans played leading parts and motivated Congress, which in the case of Cyprus was more effective concerning specific actions taken against Turkey.

With this in mind and feeling that I am obliged to continue the efforts for Cyprus, I spoke with George Rallis, now a minister in the new government, and told him that I was prepared to quit my company—in which I had by now been promoted to an important and responsible position in international operations—and, if they considered it advisable, remain in the United States as ambassador in Washington to organize and direct the Americans and Greek-Americans I know in these critical hours for Cyprus.

Rallis replied, "They are thinking of sending Panaghiotis Kanellopoulos." Then I stressed, "I am not asking for it, I am merely placing myself at the government's disposal,"[6] and added, "I respect and deeply esteem Panaghiotis

[6]Later, in August, when I returned to Greece, Karamanlis himself, prime minister at the time, asked me to remain in America as the government's independent representative to

Kanellopoulos, and it would be a wish come true if he accepts to come to America."

AUGUST 6, TUESDAY
The Davos letter

Davos's letter of July 13, which reached me on July 23, caused me worry, and I wrote Lambrias accordingly.

After forewarding this letter to Lambrias, the Davos issue is now the responsibility of the government.

I hope they decide in a way that is appropriate at this time when the armed forces absolutely need the example set by a leadership that has proved it respects the institutions, the hierarchy and, above all, the sovereign rights of the Greek people. The government's actions will be a lesson for history, to ensure that the tragedy of 1967, which was mainly based on opportunists and cowardly fellow travelers, will not be repeated in the future.

So that it may not be thought that I am eyeing the return of the retired generals—and, therefore, of my own return—to active service, I indicated in my letter to Lambrias that, "I am not proposing the return to active duty of generals, etc."

All of us, individuals and governments, will be judged by impartial history.

Many years have passed since then. Today, as this book is being written, I am obliged to state unequivocally that the government took on a serious responsibility toward history by using Davos at the highest level of military leadership. I had strongly urged Davos to help restore normal conditions in the armed services. Instead of grabbing the chance at the time, he reacted negatively, confirming his blind devotion to the dictatorship and his abhorrence of a soldier's role serving the nation and not a regime that kept the Greeks in shackles for 7 years.[7]

organize the campaign for Cyprus. I thanked him but said that an independent representative cannot carry out such a mission, which can only be handled by the government's official representative, i.e., the ambassador. I stressed that it would be difficult if not impossible for such a representative to exist, in a diplomatic no man's land, appearing publicly and trying to convince American citizens, possibly in opposition to American policy. I recommended to the prime minister that they do not send anyone in such capacity and instead give the ambassador the wherewithal to accomplish the task. I gave the same answer to the Deputy Prime Minister and Foreign Minister, George Mavros, who posed the same question on the same day.

[7]The book by Olympios Dafermos, Το αντιδικτατορικό φοιτητικό κίνημα 1972–1973 (The antidictatorial student movement 1972–1973) was published in 1992. Dafermos, an electrical engineer at Athens University, had participated in the student movement, been persecuted and forced into military service by the regime. In an appendix to the book, the author included a secret order of Davos's, issued on November 30, 1973, to the divisions and other units of the army corps, which fully confirms his devotion to the dictatorship.

The government knew of the Vidalis-Davos correspondence. Despite that, for reasons known only to itself, it proceeded to promote him to the highest levels in the army. Perhaps some in the government, among whom was the late, never to be forgotten Evangelos Averof, as I know from personal communication with him, who felt that my argument with Davos was personal. They preferred however, to ignore the clear content and tone of the two letters and, in particular, Davos's description of all those who opposed the dictatorship as a "despicable camp," which, naturally, included, among everyone else, the prime minister.

Perhaps the government, in its hesitation given the uncertainty of those times, decided that discharged generals who had opposed the dictatorship should not be assigned to leadership positions.

The government's decision was correct, and I, moreover, had repeatedly said and written, "I am not proposing the return of cashiered generals." The distance, however, between this position and the assignment to the top job of the armed forces of a person who had insisted until the last moment upon his pro-dictatorship fanaticism is huge, particularly when there were remarkable generals in active service who could have filled the leadership positions most competently.

It is indeed my responsibility that I did not publicize the Davos letters as soon as I returned to Greece. Perhaps because I did not expect, after everything that happened during the years of dictatorship, that the democratic government would reward its slanderer. Perhaps also because I did not consider it advisable to create further trouble for the national government given the grave threat emanating from Turkey. Maybe history will judge that I acted correctly. Today, however I believe that this was an unacceptable error.

AUGUST 7, WEDNESDAY

Following the arrival today of the new ambassador, who now represents the government, I finally feel that my mission is over and will limit my activities concerning Cyprus just to what, if anything, is asked of me.

Return to Greece

AUGUST 23, FRIDAY

After approximately six years, I am returning to Greece, alone, without the family.

I never doubted that I would return to a liberated homeland, but the emotions I felt at my return surpassed anything I had ever felt before in my life.

Friends and relatives greeted me at the airport.

I addressed the following few words to the gathering:

I am deeply moved and happy to be back among you.

The joy tentatively ruling our souls now at the beginning of the end of a pointless but tragic national trial turns to grief when one considers that the sacrifice of our young at the Polytechnic was not enough, that the holocaust of Cyprus was needed before violence admitted that it had reached a dead-end. But at this moment, it is our duty to look to the future, the future of Greece and the future of martyred Cyprus.

Gazing over the many rough obstacles in the road to this future, I ask you to please allow me to express some simple hopes.

I hope, first of all, that we may learn from the misfortunes of the past. I hope that when blame is assigned—whenever that might be—it be done in a spirit of historical responsibility and justice and not with vengeance.

I hope that we have been convinced that in the future we must rely mostly on our own strengths.

I hope we embrace the need for national unity, not as a monolithic concurrence of political beliefs, that would be suicide, but unity in a national cause, the cause of making and keeping, at long last, the Greeks responsible for the future and fate of our homeland.

I hope we have been convinced that sincere devotion to democracy is not the privilege of some but the right of all Greeks, the product of sacrifices made and struggles fought by the King, politicians, men and women of the arts and letters, soldiers, all of our compatriots and, above all, by the young.

I hope the armed forces have been convinced—and will convince others—that they serve the nation and exist solely to defend our national independence and integrity.

I hope that from here on out we can surround our armed forces, which must rapidly become the model of a national defense organization, with affection.

I hope that no one still yearns to divert the armed forces from their clearly defensive sacred mission. If they do, they must be removed without delay.

I hope all Greeks will assist the government of national salvation in its so difficult task. Our select compatriots of which it is composed have shown and are showing courage and wisdom, facing both the cowardly external challenge and strengthening our defensive capabilities while steering a course towards restoring our free institutions.

Decay, division, hatred, pain, the humiliation of the Greeks, the weakening of Greece, and the disaster of Cyprus were founded in April 1967.

July 24, 1974 lays the foundations of national unity, based on our people, the power of Greece, and the freedom of Cyprus. The road ahead will be long and hard. Our faith in Greece and in the strength of free and united Greeks will prevail. Let us be hopeful.

Thank you.

This, my first return to Greece, marked the end of the mission I had set myself.

This effort was a voluntary offering to the nation in critical times, which, unfortunately, concluded with the tragedy of Cyprus.

I am overjoyed that today I received the greatest recognition I could ever expect for this offering. The recognition from our son and my wife.

At our home in Athens, I found the following letter which they had taken care would arrive before I did:

August 23, 1974

My father,

More than six years have gone by. Years of anxiety, years of struggle with despair. You saw the doors of the cynics closed, those of windbags open, and occasionally some action. With your soul you struggled to turn the tiny spark into flame.

Perseverant although alone, alone but tough, six years of struggle. Struggle with the cynics, struggle with the indifferent, struggle with challenges, struggle with temptation, and always with your own self in uncompromising self-criticism.

Now you are in our poor and abandoned little Greece. Laurels and glory are distant. It does not have riches and finery to give (not that you would want them), but you have your reward already. Our Greece gave you the struggle, the struggle it offers everyone, you grabbed it and it absorbed you. Your occupation and, at the same time, reward, is "the struggle."

Welcome to Greece rising.

Efthymios

Always near you,
Matina

I thank the Lord for this recognition.

CHAPTER 8

1975 (Cyprus)

1975—Efforts Continue, but Now for Cyprus

On August 7, 1974 I wrote: "Following the arrival today of the new Ambassador, who now represents the government, I finally feel that my mission is over and will limit my activities concerning Cyprus to just what, if anything, is asked of me."

I am still in the United States where I have assumed additional duties at the company as Director for International Development.

This position allows me to travel to the Middle East (particularly Iran, Saudi Arabia, and Egypt) and the opportunity to visit Greece and observe first hand the developments there as well as here in the U.S.A.

In the meantime, a dramatic transformation has occurred in the stance of the Greek-Americans because of the Cyprus tragedy, as I noted a year ago.

The Greek-American Institute, headed by Eugene Rossides, a lawyer and former Deputy Secretary of the Treasury (1969-1973), achieved the impossible by getting Congress to accept his proposals to enact an arms embargo against Turkey on December 17, 1974. Rossides, a partner of the law firm Rogers and Wells, was in an excellent position to conduct legal research and gather arguments for Congress to adopt in passing the embargo bill. Rossides's central argument was that the Turks violated the legal conditions attached to the provision of American military aid for defensive purposes when they used American weapons in their offensive against Cyprus. It is clear that Congress's positive stance was based on the legal foundations of the effort, not a national vindication on behalf of Cyprus, or Greece.

The Administration and Kissinger in particular fought to bypass and repeal this Congressional success with all their might. They eventually succeeded on August 1, 1978.

During the confrontation between Congress and Kissinger from the beginning of the year, I wrote to members of Congress urging them to maintain the embargo until Turkey gave in. I feel it necessary to present some of the responses I received from senators and congressmen for the record.

On February 26, 1975, at 10:15 AM Congressman John Brademas called me to say:

a. Rosenthal, Sarbanes and Brademas met with Kissinger two days ago;
b. Brademas's explanation of Kissinger's stance was:
    - He has not applied pressure on Turkey. All his effort is concentrated on increasing pressure on Congress.
    - He is dealing with Congress as a hostile entity in this matter and not as a branch of the American government.
    - They will meet again.
    - Congressman Brademas is not prepared to support resumption of aid without some guarantee that progress will be made.
c. Kissinger's ego has been bruised because he is not in a position to influence Congress and he is not prepared to alter his stance and apply pressure on the Turks as Congress desires.
d. To support his stance, Kissinger is spreading rumors that the Greek government would not be against a resumption of aid to Turkey, without being able to say so publicly. Brademas feels that there is no grounds for circulating such inaccuracies.

We agreed to meet as soon as I return from Greece.

On March 1, 1975, Senator Henry M. Jackson, who helped our efforts to restore normal conditions to Greece a great deal, wrote to me:

> *Thank you for your letter referring to the crucial issues of Greece and Cyprus and for your support of my candidacy for president.*
>
> *I am grateful for your encouragement.*
>
> *I have spoken against the administration's Cyprus policy and joined in Congressional initiatives to limit aid to Turkey.*

On March 4, Senator Robert Taft Jr. wrote me:

> *Thank you for your letter concerning military aid to Turkey.*
>
> *On September 19, 1974, I voted in favor of the Eagleton amendment to the Import-Export Bank bill and stated that the Senate considers that the president ought to declare that Turkey is not entitled to any foreign aid in view of its military action in Cyprus. This amendment passed.*
>
> *As was decided concerning the foreign aid proposal for 1975, military aid to Turkey was stopped on February 5, 1975.*
>
> *You can be certain that I will keep your positions under consideration should bills be resubmitted to the Senate for a resumption of military aid to Turkey.*

On April 30, 1975, Senator John Glenn wrote me:

Thank you for your letter in which you express your opposition to the sale of military equipment to Turkey.

As you know, military aid to Turkey was stopped on midnight February 4, 1975 because President Ford was not able to assure Congress that there had been substantial progress in the negotiations between Greece and Turkey over Cyprus. With bill S846 the Senate Committee on International Relations proposed lifting the ban on military aid to Turkey.

I wrote the following letter to Kostas Karras on June 18:

Dear Kostas,

It has been a long time since we have been in touch with each other.

The Turks are furious with Congress. They are threatening reprisals. At this moment I do not know what will happen but I cannot see the House turning around, despite Kissinger's pressure.

I hope our compatriots have understood that without the aid embargo—an act of historic importance, which was an achievement of our own Brademas, Sarbanes, Rosenthal, and Rossides—no one would be dealing with Cyprus. Not Ford or Kissinger, not NATO or the Turks.

I am not sure they understand many things back home. They are, as a whole, ruled by a political fanaticism, an oversimplified populism, and an effort to diminish values and people.

Let it be.

I received mail not just from those who support our position, that is, the continuation of the embargo. I received letters by some who voted against. For example, on July 25, 1975, Congressman Thomas Luldow Ashley, of Toledo, Ohio, the city we called home for so many years, sent me the following letter:

As you know, the House of Representatives yesterday voted down bill S846 (Senate) for a partial lifting of the arms embargo against Turkey by 223 votes to 206.

From your recent letter I can imagine how enthusiastic you must be with this result. I am also aware that my vote must have been a great disappointment for you. It was very difficult for me to take a position opposed by so many close friends and supporters from the Toledo community. I hope my observations in the House record yesterday will help you understand the reasons behind this very difficult vote of mine. In the final analysis, I had to remain loyal to the national interest as I saw it.

On August 12, I answered Congressman Ashley as follows:

Dear Congressman Ashley,

Thank you for your letter of July 25, 1975. You correctly predicted my deep disappointment with your vote. A man like yourself, dedicated to the ideals of the law and of freedom, obviously raises many questions when he reverses himself on matters of principle.

Certainly I cannot discuss your last statement, that you had to remain loyal to the national interest as you saw it.

Honestly, however, I wonder how supporting the aggression, the illegal use of American arms, the blackmail tactics, and, finally, the uncompromising behavior of the Turks, is in the service of America's national interest.

Unacceptable violence, wherever it may be used, is opposed to the ideals and interests of the free world.

In the long-term, upholding the law, human dignity, and freedom give power to the United States and the Western world. Otherwise, what is the difference between us and the Soviet bloc in their actions in Hungary and Czechoslovakia? We are not justified, I believe, in rewarding aggression, what ever the excuse.

I sincerely believe that you will wish to reconsider your position in the future.

On August 14, 1975, that is, as soon as he received my letter, Congressman Ashley wrote back:

I appreciate your letter of August 12, in which you gave me additional opinions concerning aid to Turkey and I am very sorry that we will not be able to agree on this issue.

You should be certain that I respect your opinion and I hope you respect mine. I hope in the future there will be issues on which we can agree.

In addition to congressmen, the positions adopted against the Turkish action by retired military figures who had remained silent or even helped the Junta when we were fighting against it are also worth noting.

I will mention two examples: General James A. Van Fleet and Admiral E. R. Zumwalt, Jr., former Chief of Naval Operations, who had agitated on the issue of home-porting facilities. The statements by these two top officers are masterpieces of bold criticism against the main proponent of the pro-Turkish policy, Secretary of State Henry Kissinger.

In July of 1975 General Van Fleet sent a personal letter to all members of the House of Representatives and editors of major newspapers.

In this letter he says, inter alia:

As former Commander of the United Nations forces in Korea (1951—1953) and head of the American Advisory Aid Group to Greece (1948—1950), I am writing to express my strong opposition to bill S846, as amended and submitted by the House Committee on International Relations on July 11, 1975, approving the resumption of providing American arms to Turkey.

As someone who has dedicated his career to the armed forces of the U.S.A., I believe that our country and our allies in NATO must be opposed to any act of aggression, whether it is committed by friends or enemies.

I am obliged to condemn the continuing actions of the Turkish invasion against Cyprus and its people. I am obliged to condemn the illegal use of American war materiel in the aggression against a small, defenseless nation and its citizens. Actions such as these constitute a violation of Turkey's bilateral agreements with the United States, NATO, and the charter of the United Nations. Beyond these, Greece, our ally in two world wars and the only surviving democracy in Eastern Europe, is the strategic key to the Eastern Mediterranean and more important than Turkey for the military interests of the United States and NATO. Unfortunately, Secretary of State Kissinger's policy has caused heavy and permanent damage to relations between America and Greece.

It is inconceivable for the government of the United States to succumb to Turkey's threats that it will close our bases there. That would be surrender to blackmail and unworthy of our country.

Consequently, I call for withdrawal of the Turkish occupying forces from Cyprus and the immediate return of the 200,000 refugees to their homes, based on the unanimously passed United Nations Resolution 3212.

General James A. Van Fleet

U.S. Army, retired.

Another example of a military man's objection is the statement made by the retired admiral, E. R. Zumwalt, former Chief of Naval Operations, on the first anniversary of the Turkish invasion of Cyprus.

First, the Admiral referred to General Van Fleet's letter and then continued:

History teaches and I accept the wisdom of the warning given by a great allied leader of WWI, France's Clemenceau, that, "War is too important to be left to the soldiers."

I propose a modern axiom to complement Clemenceau's aphorism. "Peace is too complicated a matter to be left to just one diplomat."

Dr. Kissinger has mobilized his propagandists to convince Congress that America's installations in Turkey are technically more important than America's relations with Greece. This argument is deeply hypocritical because, when the Junta had imposed a military dictatorship over Greece,

> the argument was that the bases in Greece were of vital importance to NATO and the Sixth Fleet. Now, with a democratic government at last restored in Greece, Dr. Kissinger leans towards Turkey. I believe that the interests of America and of NATO require our friendship with both Greece and Turkey. To contribute to the confrontation between these two countries, however, is a dangerously inflammable and divisive foreign policy. If we are, nonetheless, forced to choose between our bases in Turkey and the continued support of American bases in Greece by a democratic government, then, in my judgment, Congress must vote in favor of Greece and against the Kissinger amendment to lift the arms embargo on Turkey.
>
> In my opinion, our existing and possible future bases in Greece are more important for us than our facilities in Turkey.
>
> The present disagreement has been distorted into a political test of power between the administration and what has been described as the "national policy of the Greek lobby." This is an non-American argument at the time when our nation—a nation of immigrants—is entering its two-hundredth year.
>
> Banning future American arms shipments to Turkey is not a "national," and certainly not a Greek issue. It is fundamental American policy based on which, in other times, I have seen the navy used as the means of implementation. The Sixth Fleet was twice ordered to steam in the sea between Turkey and Cyprus as a clear warning from an American president against a Turkish invasion. You should recall that there was no invasion because American policy was absolutely clear. It saddens me to see that there was no policy when Cyprus was invaded last year.
>
> Today only Congress can clarify American policy. That is the challenge of the debate this week over the Kissinger amendment. Seven months ago this policy was examined and the decision was clear. By 199 votes, the House overwhelmingly approved an amendment that imposed the ban on arms shipments to Turkey.
>
> In my opinion, this verdict needs to be confirmed this week with the rejection of the Kissinger amendment, number S846.

I have left for last the excellent—and long—statement by Senator Henry M. Jackson, which he sent me in late May, as it was entered in the Congressional record on May 19, 1975.

The statement expresses the intense concern of enlightened members of Congress about the future not only of Cyprus and Greek-Turkish relations but also about the long-term credibility and prestige of the Atlantic Alliance.

Senator Jackson's statement:

Mr. President, when the Turkish armed forces began their violent occupation of Cypriot soil about a year ago, I steadfastly supported Congressional initiatives aimed at upholding the integrity of American law and restoring the freedom and independence of Cyprus. I believe that the basic foreign aid legislation—which states that American military aid is provided for self-defense and collective security—expresses wise policy. The events of the last ten months provide no basis for exempting Turkey.

The Turkish military *fait accompli* in Cyprus occurred in part thanks to American military aid to Turkey.

Congress supported the aid program to Turkey because it considered that country a substantive member of the collective Western security structure.

That was the only reason Congress approved this program, because the purpose of our aid programs is to reinforce a nation's capacity to defend against an external invasion and not to participate in one.

I am sorry that the president and the Secretary of State chose to make what is now called the "Turkish aid problem" a serious test of relations between the administration and Congress.

They are so intent on "helping" Turkey and they are so slow to realize that Congress meant what it said when it voted to ban aid to Turkey, that they are today asking us to pass a special exemption so they can resume aid. The arguments they have used to justify this special exemption are many and varied—the need for presidential "consent," Turkey's strategic importance, "stability" in the Eastern Mediterranean. The administration, however, ignores the fact that the democratic government in Athens must now bear the weight of what happened in the past, while the North Atlantic Alliance as a whole is weakening. I am concerned because the diplomatic passivity of the United States against the Turkish invasion of Cyprus may now weaken the democratic institutions that with such difficulty and so much hope arose in Greece.

It has never been Congress's intention to intervene in the regular implementation of American foreign policy.

What we insisted upon is that the American position be based on American law—a position that expresses the deep belief of the American people that we must not participate in military adventures that pit one ally against another.

Beyond that, I do not foresee that there is a prospect for greater stability in the Eastern Mediterranean or a restoration of the spirit of cooperation between Greece and Turkey, given that approval of the Turkish military adventure remains the cornerstone of the Ford-Kissinger position.

> The fact is that the Administration has very little to show for its policy. What motive does Turkey have for restraint, when the United States is acting to increase Turkish military capabilities?
>
> Honestly, Mr. President, I believe that there have been very many discussions about the need to satisfy the "national honor" of the invaders of Cyprus and no concern whatsoever from the administration for the victims of the invasion, the uprooted people of Cyprus.
>
> The administration's diplomacy remains oriented towards the Turkish perspective on Cyprus and has failed to present solutions even for the pressing humanitarian problems on the island. Can peace be restored if the refugees cannot return to their homes? Can political stability be established when the once booming Cypriot economy lies in ruins?
>
> The administration's insistence on a policy that gives Turkey the opportunity to further secure its military position on the island will only lead to prolonging the agony of Cyprus.
>
> Therefore, I urge the Senate to stand decisively on this issue on the realistic position already adopted by Congress, a position based on principle. Particularly when it is about the freedom and independence of a small country, I see no reason to be impressed by rhetorical exaggeration and scare tactics. There is still time for the administration to act without delay in favor of an independent Cyprus and a renewed North Atlantic Alliance.

While this was taking place in the United States it was only natural that there would be concern in Athens. On July 14, 1975, I received this telegram from former minister Stelios Allamanis:

> In view of the vote in Congress to resume aid to Turkey, call to action in cooperation with familiar opponents of the junta all the true American friends of Greece STOP A resumption of aid will embolden the barbarian conquerors of Cyprus perhaps to occupy the entire island and completely exterminate Hellenism STOP Further actions against Aegean islands offend the dignity of Greek people and exhaust the patience and self-restraint of our government, rendering Greco-Turkish war and broader Middle East and Balkan conflict inevitable, shattering NATO and humiliating the UN and endangering world peace STOP Hope our struggle is successful against all odds STOP

I responded immediately with the following telegram:

> Thank you for telegram STOP Brought to mind old intense memories STOP Assume all of you know that everything possible has been and is being done STOP Greek-Americans and American friends helping maximum STOP Unbelievable efforts however to overturn Congressional deci-

> sion STOP Despite this they are encountering stiff resistance so far STOP Struggle will not end whatever decision adopted next week STOP Will be in Athens early August STOP

Kissinger has been bitterly criticized for his behavior during the Cyprus crisis and for his insistent and heavy-handed efforts in his many confrontations with Congress over the arms embargo against Turkey.[1]

At the end of his unsuccessful efforts to convince Congress, the artful Kissinger proceeded with a move that led to lifting the embargo. In negotiations with the Turks to renew the base agreements, he publicly offered Turkey military aid worth a billion dollars over a four-year period.

Congress reacted immediately and decisively against this action for a variety of reasons but mainly because the embargo was still in effect and Congress ordinarily does not approve military aid for more than a year or, at most, two.

Kissinger then publicly offered military aid to Greece worth 700 million dollars over a four-year period.

Karamanlis's government then arrived at a difficult but correct decision. It judged that the fate of the embargo was sealed, after so many votes and pressure from the administration. It considered Kissinger's offer attractive and accepted it. This is how the 7 to 10 ratio was created, which is still in effect today, and thus, with tragic irony, was the embargo definitively ended, though only after Greece had won the 7 to 10 ratio.

Throughout all this activity inside and out of Congress, I felt that I had to add my voice publicly at the time when Kissinger's efforts to overturn the embargo were being judged. I wrote my thoughts in a short article that the *National Herald* in New York published on July 20, 1975.

As these lines are being written, 23 years after the Turkish intervention in Cyprus, it is apparent that the continuing American policy of appeasement toward Turkey, despite its crimes on Cyprus and its expansionist provocations, is the essential cause of the continuing division of the island and Turkish intransigence.

These efforts in 1975 were the last I made to help limit Turkey's military capability. They also were my last actions on our national issue. At the end of 1975, my family and I, except for our son who remained to continue his university studies, returned permanently to Greece. From then on, of course, I remained far from public life.

[1]The description of Kissinger's behavior on lifting the embargo is from an article by James G. Pyrros that appeared in the book *Greece under Socialism* by Nikolaos A. Stavrou, professor of political science/international relations at Howard University, p. 236

Epilogue

The history of activities in the U.S.A. to restore democracy in Greece is unknown in its details.

For this reason, the form of this book was designed to help meet the need for historical investigation of this critical period in the life of the nation. The comfort of a general narrative with far fewer details was sacrificed to link events in the precise chronology of their occurrence. This precise chronological link provides the true dimensions of each specific event and assists historical compilation.

The interposition of detailed movements and communications with a host of prominent and unknown individuals and the presentation of very limited information about the author's family and professional life was judged necessary and useful for the historian. We felt that the full picture should be given of the environment in which the activities of a Greek officer who assigned himself an unorthodox and exceptionally difficult mission in the vastness of America were carried out.

We hope that the reader will vindicate this choice of a chronological narrative and the insertion of historically useful detail.

We also felt it necessary, however, to cap the detailed description with this epilogue, a short review of the conclusions arising out of the previous narrative.

I will divide activity against the dictatorship into three sections:

a. The Greeks;
b. The Greek-Americans;
c. The Americans.

I will conclude with a brief discussion of the dictatorship and today's intractable problems.

A. Greeks Against the Dictatorship

Affected by the success of the coup and, especially, by the political unrest before the coup, at first the vast majority of Greeks accepted the *fait accompli* and even welcomed it with relief, albeit with the hope that the diversion would be short. As time passed the regime revealed its true colors, confirming its intention to maintain the dictatorship for a long period, while the hopes of the Greek people that the putschists would lead the country to normal conditions began to fade.

Disappointment began to set in, along with lethargy arising from:

a. the imposition of a police state upon every aspect of national life;
b. the absence of a clear way out;
c. the by now obvious tolerance of the regime by the West and the East and active support for it mainly from the United States but also from France.

The country's political elite, aware of its responsibility for the political instability before the coup, began to contribute, to the extent possible, to instigating some activity against the dictatorship. Unfortunately, up to the end of the regime in 1974, the politicians never managed to unite their forces, something that might have had some effect domestically, especially upon the army, and abroad, mainly upon the Americans.

Former minister Yeorgios Mylonas, in his book *Escape from Amorgos,*[1] *wrote in March 1973:*

> The dictator Papadopoulos often repeated that he had united the country. Undoubtedly, he has. The Colonels have become the common enemy against which the Greek people are united, regardless of their views on the social setup of post-junta Greece. This *de facto* creation of the conditions for a political alliance among all political camps is a fact of utmost importance. If properly cultivated, it could lead to the speedier liberation of the country and facilitate to a great extent the orderly functioning of democratic institutions after the overthrow of the dictatorship. And to think that all this is because of the junta. As the saying goes, no dark cloud without a silver lining.

Instead of capitalizing on this psychological climate, apart from the absence of unity and coordination, most politicians considered that the dictatorship would lead the country sooner or later to a political dead end and so, instead of putting stress on steps that would hasten the regime's demise, worked on partisan positioning for the post-junta period. The result was that the dictatorship was prolonged, culminating in the Cyprus tragedy.

The behavior of a large number of military officers disproved the myth that the entire armed forces were behind the coup. They showed admirable maturity and a spirit of sacrifice, typified by the following actions:

[1] Yeorgios Mylonas, Απόδραση από την Αμοργό, p. 57.

a. their reaction on December 13, 1967;
b. the navy's move in the spring of 1973;
c. internal dissent in various forms, particularly participation in the *Free Greeks* organization—the history of which must someday be written—and the exiling, imprisoning, and discharging of large numbers of excellent and brave men who had proven themselves on the battlefield

In contrast to the category of officers who acted against the dictatorship, many, essentially fellow travellers of the regime, tolerated it, moving up the chain of command into posts vacated by their colleagues. They helped prolong the Junta and share responsibility for the Cyprus tragedy.

The dictatorship deteriorated through the actions of prominent and unknown Greeks inside and outside the country. Greece's young people contributed decisively through uprisings, first at the Law School and then at the Polytechnic.

Among the many prominent Greeks who, despite tremendous difficulties, contributed substantially to the constant harassment and decay of the dictatorship domestically, were distinguished politicians, such as Panaghiotis Kanellopoulos, Yeorgios Mavros, Yeorgios Rallis, Ioannis Zighdis, Panaghiotis Papalighouras, and Dimitris Papaspyrou. Apart from all their other isolated activities, they condemned the raw violations of democratic principles (such as the right to a secret ballot) marring the Junta's referendum, greatly assisting efforts abroad.

The role of the King also was decisive. The main elements of his activity were:

a. The action of December 13, 1967;
b. His refusal to return despite the junta's insistence;
c. The sum of his activities against the dictatorship during his years of exile and the conditions he constantly set for the country's return to normality;
d. His decision to put the question of the monarchy to the verdict of the Greek people after the dictatorship's fall.

I will repeat a central observation.

After the coup's success, all politicians and intellectual leaders were automatically placed into the Junta's enemy camp. Military officers, in contrast, as members of the armed forces, had the choice of participating in power or opposing the regime. Many officers of all ranks did oppose the dictatorship. A gratifyingly large percentage of them were young, with their entire careers ahead of them. These men sacrificed their comfort and their expectations to save the honor of the Greek officer corps. They constitute a bright beacon of integrity, respect for democratic procedures, devotion to duty and to their oath. The submission of the totality of Greek society and its classes to the pervasive violence did not affect many Greek officers who, at a very early stage, chose the path of sacrifice and resistance against the regime.

B. Greek-Americans against the Dictatorship

Given that in Greece itself the behavior of the people, politicians, and soldiers was as described above, one cannot be too harshly critical of the Americans of Greek descent for their lack of interest in the problem.

Secure behind the extremely useful catchphrase, craftily cultivated by the Junta, that the Greek-Americans should not interfere in the internal affairs of the mother country, particularly when the regime justified the coup by saying that it had "saved Greece from communism," the Greek-American community in general behaved in a way that helped the dictatorship in many ways. Mainly, though, it allowed the U.S. administration to claim that the Greek-Americans considered the situation in Greece to be just fine.

There were exceptions to this attitude among many prominent intellectuals and a number of outstanding members of the community. Among the details in the main text of this book are references to a number of prominent people who played a serious role in the effort to degrade the dictatorship. All of them as part of an informal group, acting independently, tried, as I did, to influence American authorities in favor of restoring normal democratic rule in Greece.

Another substantial exception to the overall stance of the Greek-Americans was the venerable Archbishop of North and South America, Iakovos, who, with careful maneuvering constantly tried to affect the position of the American administration on restoring democratic order in Greece.

Of the Greek-American organizations, the largest, AHEPA, took a stance in favor of the junta, with the bright exception of its Supreme President in 1973, Dr. Michael Spirtos.

The *National Herald* of New York was the only Greek-American newspaper to be consistently against the regime.

In general, the Greek-American community was unable, at this point in the nation's history, to realize that the dictatorship was a problem for Greeks generally and not just a domestic political problem in the motherland. Fortunately, this silence or tolerance of the dictatorship gave way in 1975 to a profound change of heart because of the Cyprus tragedy. The Greek-American community undoubtedly has two major extenuating factors in its favor. First, that we Greeks usually ignore the existence of this distant section of our nation and seek it out only in times of crisis, in times of national peril or economic need. Second, we have not taken care to create the belief among all Greeks, in the country itself and abroad, that we all are part of a larger whole, with its own particular nature that must have its own priorities and goals on the world stage.

Obviously, the idea that Greek culture is interwoven with freedom has not been assimilated, and that every deviation from freedom automatically diminishes us as a people.

This stance of the Greeks of America ought to be studied in depth in order to draw the conclusions as to what Greece must do so that the parts of the nation which live abroad can be brought to realize that they, too, are part of the Greek world and have the same obligations and rights in the pursuit of national standing internationally.

C. Americans against the Dictatorship

I will divide this section into three subsections: Congress, the Press and the Administration.

1. Congress

This great institution, the main foundation of American democracy, was a consistent and active opponent of the dictatorship.

As an institution it adopted specific measures and individual members of Congress acted in ways that put pressure on the administration and, indirectly, on the regime to encourage the restoration of democracy.

Some of its greatest moments were:

a. The holding of hearings on specific issues at which members or representatives of the administration were obliged to say, under oath, that they were applying pressure on the regime for restoring normal conditions and that there would be progress at regular intervals, statements that were disproved by events,
b. The legislative effort to stop military aid, capped by the embargo against Turkey following its invasion of Cyprus;
c. The dispatch of fact-finding teams to Greece whose reports were awkward for the Administration and the dictatorship;
d. The provision through Congressional acts of specific opportunities for the American press to express bitter criticism against the Administration.

In general, Congress, as a fundamental democratic institution, reacted systematically against the administration's myopic policy. Congress consistently maintained that the strategic interests of the alliance were best served long-term by restoring democracy in Greece. It proved that it believed that it was in America's interests to fight dictatorships wherever they appeared and to support democracy worldwide.

The different approaches taken by Congress and the Administration strengthened the regime, which, although irritated by the legislature's stance, was supported by the policy of appeasement practiced by the Pentagon and theAdministration.

2. *The American Press*

The press in America, an institution in the service of public opinion in this vast democracy, expresses the beliefs of the people; investigates the reaction of politicians on issues large and small; and responsibly presents the truth as seen by its experienced practitioners.

In general, the American press maintained a clear position against the Administration's policy in Greece.

It is not an exaggeration to say that never before or since have so many top stories been written about Greece. The *New York Times* ran a story or an editorial on the dictatorship in Greece at least once a week.

Apart from the editorials and reports from Greece, the American press expressed its opposition to the Administration's policy and the continuation of the dictatorship with a plethora of caustic cartoons, which captured public feelings about the Colonel's regime.

The American press discomfited the dictators indirectly by supporting the forces arrayed against them and directly by influencing the administration, which was under pressure from the nearly unanimous opposition of the press to its policies supporting the Greek regime.

3. *The Administration*

It has not been proved that the American administration connived in some way with the conspirators concerning the decision to carry out and actually carrying out the April, 1967 coup. It has, however, been proved that the Johnson Administration initially and the Nixon Administration subsequently went beyond mere tolerance of the regime to active support of the dictatorship.

American policy was motivated by the need to serve U.S. interests in the region. Support for the regime, which was seen as meeting its alliance obligations, was grounded on this basis. From time to time, the Administration would whisper that it desired a return to democracy.

Despite pressure from Congress, the press, and allied countries, this policy of successive American administrations, which constituted a shortsighted submission to strategic interests, remained essentially unchanged throughout the years of Greece's enslavement by the junta, its fellow-travelers, and supporters, topped by the dictators' greatest ally, the Pentagon.

Voices were raised in warning against the Administration early on. These voices were many, constant, and from various directions. I will not refer to the voices of prominent Greeks who began railing against American policy from the beginning. I will note just some examples of American opinions raised during the dictatorship.

On July 30, 1969, 50 Congressmen sent a letter to Secretary of State William P. Rogers, in which they said, inter alia:

> Reliable reports show that in junta-ruled Greece, the economy is falling, basic social freedoms are violated, and people continue to be arrested and imprisoned without charges. Further, anti-Americanism is rising, according to reports, because our old friends believe that the United States is the main supporter of a military dictatorship with no popular backing . . .

On October 6, 1969, a *New York Times* editorial wrote:

> The Nixon administration cannot ignore warnings that, in the end, the continuation of the Colonels in power will not protect but will endanger American strategic interests in the Mediterranean while simultaneously crushing the hopes of the Greek people for freedom, honor, and peace.

In February of 1971, the Senate Foreign Relations Committee sent two staff members, James G. Lowenstein and Richard M. Moose, to Greece to study the situation. The unclassified version of their detailed and thorough report was issued on February 26, 1971. The report closes with the following:

> The policy of friendly persuasion clearly has clearly failed. The regime has accepted the friendship, and the military assistance, but has ignored the persuasion. Indeed, the regime seems to have been able to exert more leverage on us with regard to military assistance than we have been willing to exert on the regime with regard to political reform. We see no evidence that this will not continue to be the case.

On October 28, 1967, on the occasion of the Greek national holiday "OCHI" marking the beginning of WWII, Senator McGovern said this:

> After five and a half years, the Colonels have failed to break the spirit of the people. The Greek dictatorship rests on the abolition of elections, a censored press, the imprisonment and torture of dissenters—and on the support of the government of the United States.

On June 26, 1973, Senator Jackson, in a speech to the Senate, said, inter alia:

> Mr. President, some deep-thinking people following the goings-on in NATO—distinguished officers, professionals, military men with just one concern, the security of the West and the Mediterranean region—have expressed their continuing concern over developments in Greece.

These and other similar warnings were not enough to move successive administrations from the original position of providing support for the dictatorship all those years. And when the Watergate scandal broke, everything came to a standstill, with Nixon unable to take any positive initiative and all-powerful Kissinger, who, as an adherent of *realpolitik*, that is, supporting the strong man of the day, ignored all long-term consequences and supported the dictatorship to the end.

Kissinger, somewhat apologizing, confirmed his positions in a recent and deeply significant book. The following excerpt is characteristic:

> In the case of the Greek dictatorship, Kissinger clearly reversed the priorities and instead of supporting "organizations that promote democratic values," supported the dictatorship for reasons of American "national security."

The present book illustrates that, in sharp contrast with the successive American administrations that supported the dictatorship for their own reasons for seven years, distinguished Americans, members of Congress, intellectuals, the press, and ordinary citizens consistently and insistently supported efforts to restore democracy in Greece. The author firmly believes that the time has come, after three decades, for the Greek state to seek out these prominent American citizens who acted against the Greek dictatorship and reward them morally, honoring them for their selfless contribution to restoring political freedoms in Greece. This book can help in the effort to find them.

Finally, the reader will wonder to what extent the Greek side influenced the American stance toward the dictatorship. In the introduction, I presented the basic conditions determining the entire effort, one of which was a positive strategy, that is, an effort to persuade the Americans rather than oppose or ignore them. At the time, the three schools of thought held by politicians of varying persuasions about the Americans were to persuade them, oppose them, or ignore them, and each politician, and each school of thought, had its own arguments.

As to which of these three schools of thought was most effective in influencing the Americans, the answer will be given by history.

D. The Dictatorship and Today's Intractable Problems

As these lines are being written we are faced with a completely new situation in comparison with the years of the dictatorship in Greece. We are faced with an unprecedented democratic awakening. It is estimated that there are now twice as many democracies worldwide as there were 30 years ago.

Democracy won the huge ideological battle of the cold war. Democracy proved in fact to be the "West's absolute weapon that prevailed."[2]

Unfortunately, the soldiers who took power in April 1967 had no awareness of the value of democracy for the political, economic, and social development of the Greek nation and did everything they could to keep it at bay.

Also unfortunately, the coup leaders were not the only ones responsible for the loss of so much time in resurrecting the country. Every Greek shares this responsibility because through misguided actions or damaging failure to take action we provided the golden opportunity to a small group of fanatics to carry out the plans they had spent years preparing. They thereby managed to take power and repress the people for seven years, delaying the country's political, economic, and social development and progress.

Certain foreigners must also share the blame because, in the service of their own interests, they ignored the value to themselves of spreading democracy around the world. They also ignored the agony of the Greeks who wanted to strengthen the domestic front by restoring democratic institutions

The weakness of the divided Greek resistance and the lack of an alternative solution prolonged the dictatorship by encouraging the junta and allowing foreigners to continue supporting it blissfully. The result was the tragedy of Cyprus, which has been festering for the last 25 years.

We Greeks expected a great deal from foreigners and laid the blame for prolonging our national tragedy solely at their feet. Both are proof of how we evaded our own responsibility for:

- The conditions that allowed the dictators to come to power.
- The tolerance and apathy of the many, who expected solutions from others while not pursuing a collective national effort to end the anachronistic regime.

But that belongs to the past. It is our wish that we will learn from this national adventure and create conditions that will allow us to view the future with optimism.[3]

[2]Orestis Vidalis, Το Σύγχρονο Γεωπολιτικό Περιβάλλον και η Εθνική μας Πολιτική (The Contemporary Geopolitical Environment and our National Policy), October 1998, p. 91.

[3]Part of this article was published in the newspaper *Kathimerini* on October 26, 1984, entitled "More popular participation in major decisions."

This wish has become agonizing and is a universal call to face up to the problems that have been mounting in recent years.

The problems and difficulties for our economy and international standing arise from: the disintegration of institutions, the lack of confidence in anyone and in the politicians, the absence of optimism for the future, heartlessness toward the weak, the environment our young people grow up in that fails to emphasize our national heritage and does not urge them toward propriety and decency, and above all, the exorbitant political partisanship that has outflanked and ignored the national interest. In the end, all these converge to undermine all those virtues that kept us upright in far worse periods of wars and national disasters.

This dismal picture is the result of many causes. It is mainly, however, a result of the dictatorship's interference in the country's political life, which, apart from all the other tribulations, did not allow modernization to develop or, mainly, people but also ideas, to be replenished.

Fortunately, in recent years there have been more and more calls for renewal of political thought and practices from serious observers who feel responsible for the country's future. It is urgently necessary to implement renewal and modernization of our political behavior so as to decisively strengthen our domestic front, which is essentially the sole foothold for attaining national goals.

We must be optimistic for the future of this country. Yet it is useful and perhaps even necessary to note the dramatic truths handed down by one of Europe's preeminent thinkers.

The distinguished British historian, Arnold Toynbee, refused to accept that the course of any civilization is predetermined. From his rich experience as a student of history, Toynbee arrived at the aphorism:

> Civilizations are not murdered, they commit suicide. Civilizations are not threatened from the outside but are led to disintegration and decay due to their inability to deal with internal trials. It is not the externals that pose unsurpassable obstacles but the internals. If we do not solve the internal disagreements that threaten our existence, we cannot impose order outside our space.[4]

We will conclude with a proposal and an optimistic prospect for renewing political thought and practice.

We will end this gaze into the future with the reminder that we Greeks have

[4]Toynbee, A. J., *A Study of History.* Abridged ed. by D.G. Somerwell, New York and London, Oxford University Press, 1947, p. 275.

the duty and obligation to secure the maintenance and progress of Greek civilization in the future.

In order to fulfill this duty and, in view of the challenges we are facing as we look toward the 21st century, we must believe that our highest national goals are:

a. Constantly improving the functions of democracy;
b. Decisively strengthening our domestic front by dynamically developing an internationally competitive economy;
c. Achieving the best possible compromise between the two main issues, modernizing our institutions, and constantly improving our standing in the world community;
d. Facing the future with a long-term national vision and long-term planning,without the unfortunate custom to date of solving only daily problems with a short-term partisan point of view.

Postscript

My father's epilogue, written in 1997, synthesized the lessons learned from his anti-dictatorship struggle and his observations on the interaction of institutional forces in the United States that had shaped foreign policy towards Greece.

His analysis is relevant to this day as agonizing choices still persist between the propagation of democratic ideals versus so-called security considerations involving pragmatic accommodation of unpalatable regimes. This perennial dilemma between seemingly abstract principle and short term practicality will continue to challenge policy makers. The policy answer will be shaped by the strategic priorities, the intellect and the personal moral calculus of the final executive decision maker. However, in a vibrant democratic society, such as that of the United States, the executive has to consider the views of public opinion, the press and most importantly the Congress. This interplay provides the opportunity for activists to make their case and to present their side of the argument. This is what Orestis E. Vidalis did in his day and even though his views on policy did not prevail, he drew satisfaction from the fact that debate was not swept under the carpet, as both the influential press and the Congress kept the executive branch of government under pressure and questioned misguided policies towards Greece. In creating and sustaining this pressure on the executive my father certainly played a key, albeit not very visible, role — as he consistently rejected grandstanding and self-promotion. As James Pyrros, Congressman Nedzi's Administrative Assistant, said to my father (page 319) "Your modus operandi is to have your hands everywhere and your fingerprints nowhere."[1]

Today, it would have been gratifying for my father to have seen how accurate, prescient and effective his analysis and argumentation had really been. Firstly, the pressure he sought to generate via the press and the Congress was really felt by the executive and secondly, and more importantly, his arguments were really heard and to a great extent integrated in the analysis of the State Department professionals.

With the benefit of hindsight, given the publication of State Department documents, as well as internal policy discussions with then Secretary of State Kissinger (disclosed and made publicly available after my father died in

[1]Vidalis, Orestis E. *Confronting the Greek Dictatorship in the United States. Years of Exile: A Personal Diary (1968-1975)*. New York: Pella Publishing Company, Inc. 2009. (p. 319)

2001), one can see clearly that Orestis Vidalis' arguments and warnings were reflected in the discourses of the State Department team of Assistant Secretary of State for Near Eastern and South Asian Affairs Joseph Sisco and ambassador H. J. Tasca, who represented the U.S. in Athens for most of the duration of the dictatorship. It is worth citing a couple of characteristic passages from an action memorandum prepared for the review of Secretary of State Kissinger in February of 1974:

"The moderate political leadership in Greece perceives a close identity of interests among Greece, the U.S. and NATO. . . . Its attitude toward the U.S. will, however, be significantly affected by the degree to which it sees us as supporters of military dictatorship. . . . there is probably an inevitable inverse relationship between the ease with which we secure Greek co-operation on security matters now and the ease with which we will be able to secure it from the . . . successor regime. . . ."[2] and

"The hands-off approach (non-involved approach toward Greek internal affairs) probably best meets urgent short-term needs, but it does not provide well for long-term concerns."[3]

The fact that the views of the foreign-service professionals were ignored or short shifted by Dr. Kissinger, does not lessen their validity or relevance to this day. My father, as is clear in his epilogue, understood the role that Dr. Kissinger played and the relatively low importance he assigned to Greece and other small countries in his grand geopolitical chess game.

It is evident, given the documents available today, that the State Department professionals fully understood the long term issues, threats and tradeoffs affecting the region. Sadly, their political boss chose to ignore their counsel. Dr. Kissinger opted, instead, to focus on so-called security issues, which in fact were matters of military convenience that ultimately undercut the legitimacy of U.S. policies in Greece, Cyprus and even Turkey. As a consequence, the scholar-diplomat suffered the embarrassment of the embargo on U.S. military aid to Turkey, which was imposed by a mobilized Congress after the Turkish invasion of Cyprus. It was all part of the price of sidestepping Congressional leaders systematically in the long years of his stewardship over U.S. foreign policy.

[2]"10. Action Memoradum From the Director of the Policy Planning Staff (Lord) to Secretary of State Kissinger." *Foreign Relations of the United States, 1973-1976*. U.S. Department of State Office of the Historian. Washington. 15 Feb, 1974. 10 Aug., 2009. <http://history.state.gov/historicaldocuments/frus1969-76v30/d10>

[3]"12. Minutes of Secretary of State Kissinger's Regional Staff Meeting." *Foreign Relations of the United States, 1973-1976*. U.S. Department of State Office of the Historian. Washington. 20 Mar., 1974. 10 Aug., 2009. <http://history.state.gov/historicaldocuments/frus1969-76v30/d12>

Following the Turkish invasion of Cyprus, Kissinger was in fact obliged to "buy" congressional acquiescence with excessive aid (to the tune of almost $2 billion of American tax payer money) for both Greece and Turkey, a steep increase from previous years. This expensive exercise in military balance perpetuated the conflict situation between Turkey and Greece rather than actively shifting it to a principle based relationship as allies, neighbors and potential European Union partners. One could argue that this was the price the West had to pay since the U.S. had sacrificed its moral legitimacy in the region to the altar of pragmatism. This sacrifice of the "soft" power options has not served the relationship of the U.S. with Greece, Cyprus and possibly Turkey for the past few decades. Today, in the middle of 2009, even the unimaginable is happening, as both Greece and Turkey are using their relationship with Russia to leverage their "long standing" NATO ally, the U.S.

The preface and the postscript to my father's book stand on the proposition that there should be no mindless trade-off of fundamental democratic values for short term military convenience. A complete and thoughtful framework has been offered by Joseph Nye, a distinguished scholar diplomat, who has introduced the conceptual framework on "soft" and "hard" power options and their judicious combination into "smart" power.

It is important according to Nye to play the right game in the right chessboard, being fully mindful that gains on one board can create losses on another. While it is true enough that the U.S. dominates in the unipolar military board, it certainly does not dominate in the economic one and even less so in the transnational relations board. In the era of globalization, no single government can deal with issues that defy borders, such as climate change, epidemics and illegal immigration.[4]

In a thoughtful speech in Athens, June of 2008, Nye explained that following the collapse of the Soviet Union the U.S. went through a period of "triumphalism," with nobody left to balance American power. This led opinion makers, such as columnist Charles Krauthammer, to argue for "assertive unilateralism" as the best guide to American foreign policy. According to "unilateralist" thinking, the United States should first decide what it thinks is right and then let others exercise the option of joining its "coalitions of the willing." In Nye's view unilateralism ". . . has been a disastrous approach to foreign policy" making. Accordingly he proceeded to forecast significant changes in America's foreign policy regardless of the outcome of the November 2008 election.[5] (p. 10) It had become obvious to all that the dominance

[4]Dr. Nye, Joseph. "Leadership and American Foreign Policy" *Athens Forum 2008*. Athens, Greece: The Kokkalis Foundation. 19 June, 2008: p. 11

[5]Dr. Nye, Joseph. "Leadership and American Foreign Policy" *Athens Forum 2008*. Athens, Greece: The Kokkalis Foundation. 19 June, 2008: p. 10

of "hard" policy under President George W. Bush had resulted in failures paid for with vast expenditures of American blood and treasure.

Utilizing Nye's framework on the conduct of U.S. foreign policy during the period of the Greek dictatorship, one can draw an important lesson. America's over-reliance on hard policy options in the military chessboard eroded its credibility and legitimacy in the other two boards. This rendered U.S. leadership more remote, more difficult and, ultimately, ineffective in the Greek-Turkish-Cyprus setting.

One hopes that the current administration, which speaks with understanding and conviction of the multi level combinations of soft and hard power in our multipolar world, will find the way to translate concept into action and assert benign influence and leadership that our world so badly needs.

Efthymios O. Vidalis

With the outstanding friend of Greece Ambassador Henry Labouisse

The humanist, admirer of the Hellenic spririt, and great friend, Dr. Petros Koumantouras

With James Webel at the Naval Officers Club

The sincere friend of Greece General Lauris Norstad

King Constantine at the Third Army Corps. To his right the Commander of the Army Lieutenant General K. Kollias, to his left the Commander of the Third Army Corps Lieutenant General G. Perides and the Corps Chief of Staff Brigadier General Orestis Vidalis

With the Greek Chief of Staff General Athanasios Frontistis

With Walter Silva during a visit at the Third Army Corps in 1967

The great Hellene Panagiotis Kanellopoulos with Admiral Brown

The Supreme President of AHEPA, Dr. Michael Spirtos, presents to King Constantine a commemorative medal of AHEPA

From left to right: Demetris Papaspyrou, Georgios Mavros, Panagiotis Kanellopoulos, Ioannis Zighdis, Panagiotis Papaligouras and Georgios Rallis

Return to Greece

August 23, 1978

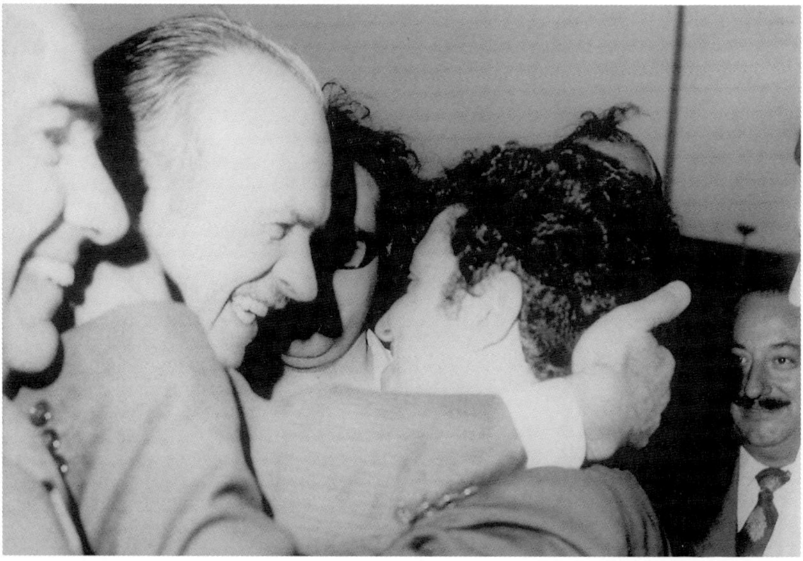

Rejoicing with friends and relatives at the airport after the collapse of the dictatorship.

Kostas Zisiou presenting the secret symbolic seal of an organization of exiled officers who had resisted the dictatorship.

Index of Names

Reader's Aide

The following partial list of names provides some information and clarification for people whose position and affiliation were not clear in the text and may not be known to the non Greek-affairs specialist.

Agris, Peter. Publisher of the Hellenic Chronicle
Alamanis, Stelios. Parliamentary deputy with ERE and minister
Anastoplo, George. U.S. political science professor
Angelis, Odysseas. General, First Chief of Staff under the Dictatorship, Greek Armed Forces, 1967–1968
Antoniou, Dimitrios. Retired civil servant, Vidalis family relative
Arbouzis, Dionysios. General, dictatorship opponent
Arnaoutis, Michael. Major, Aide de Camp to King Constantine of Greece
Aslanides, Costas. Greek Military Officer, Junta member, Deputy Minister of Sports
Athanasiadis, George. Greek publisher of Vradini newspaper
Averof-Tositsas, Evangelos. Prominent politician of ERE and minister of several governments
Bonanos, Gregorios. General, Commander-in-chief of the Hellenic Armed Forces during the dictatorship
Branco, Raoul. Brazilian economist at the UN
Brockles, Andrew. Greek-American businessman in Dallas, Texas
Broumas, Nikos. General officer during the dictatorship
Demetracopoulos, Elias. Writer, journalist, prominent opponent of the Dictatorship residing in Washington D.C.
Deros, Yannis. Greek-American businessman in Chicago
Erselman, Andreas. Brigadier General, Co-leader of the December 13th counter coup.
Fatseas. U.S. government employee
Garoufalias, Petros. Greek Minister of Defense, 1964-65
Granitsas, Spyridon. Prominent Greek journalist residing in New York City
Gratsios. Executive in Onassis shipping company
Horn, Ioannis. Publisher "Political Issues" and *Athens News*
Ieronimos. Archbishop of Greece during the Dictatorship
Javis. Greek-American businessman
Kalatzakos, Aristides. Parliamentary deputy with ERE and minister
Kanellopoulos, Panagiotis. Greek intellectual,politician, Prime-Minister of Greece at the time of the April 1967 coup d'état

Karavia, Maria. Greek journalist
Karousos, George. Greek military officer
Karras, Kostas. Intellectual, ship-owner and anti-dictatorship activist
Kokkas, Panos. Greek Publisher
Koniotakis. Greek Air Force officer
Koumandouras, Petros. Physician, philanthropist, close friend of the Vidalis family
Kousoulas, Dimitrios. US political science professor
Krasas, Spyros. Greek businessman residing in Florida
Kulukundis, Elias. Greek ship owner
Kyriazidis, Nikos. World Bank executive
Lambrakis, Christos. Major Greek publisher
Lykourezos, Alexandros. Prominent Greek lawyer
Makarezos, Nicholas. Military officer, coup leader, Minister of Economic Coordination
Maliotis. Prominent Greek-American
Mangakis, George. Prominent Greek lawyer who defended opponents of the dictatorship
Manolas. Pentagon civil servant
Margaritis, Konstantinos. Greek General of the Air Force
Markezinis, Spiros. Greek Politician, dictatorship Prime-Minister
Maury, Jack. CIA officer
Mavros, George. Greek political leader of Center Union
Mylonas, George. Parliamentary deputy with Center Union and minister
Nianias, Dimitrios. Professor and Parliamentary deputy with ERE and minister
Oikonomidis, Andreas. Professor
Opropoulos, Demetrios. Military officer who was handicapped during his exile.
Papademas, Costas. Counselor, Cypriot Embassy in Washington
Papagos, Leonidas. Chief of Staff of the King
Papakonstantinou, Konstantinos. Parliamentary deputy with ERE and speaker of the parliament
Papakonstantinou, Michalis. Parliamentary deputy with the Center Union
Papaligouras, Panayiotis. Prominent Parliamentary deputy with ERE and frequent minister
Papaloukas, Demetrios. Greek General
Papaspyrou, Dimitrios. Member of Greek parliament, Center Union.
Patilis, Demetrios. Greek officer member of the Junta
Pesmazoglu, Ioannis. Professor and statesman
Pipinelis, Panayiotis. Greek diplomat and foreign minister of the Junta
Plytas, Georgios. Prominent Greek politician and mayor of Athens.
Pollis, Adamantia. Greek-American professor of Sociology
Potamianos, Charalambos. Greek ship owner
Roufogalis, Michael. Lieutenant Colonel, Deputy Chief, Greek Central Intelligence Agency during the dictatorship

SAUNDERS, AL. National Security staff at the White House
SAUNDERS, HAROLD. Undersecretary of the State Department
SILVA, WALTER. US diplomat
SOROKOS, IOANNIS. Greek military officer, served as ambassador to London and Washington D.C. during the dictatorship
SOTIRHOS, MICHAEL. Greek-American businessman and contributor to the Republican party
STEPHANOPOULOS, STEPHANOS. Greek Prime-Minister, September 1965 – December 1966
STRATOS, CHRISTOPHER. Parliamentary deputy with ERE and minister
THEOTOKIS, SPYRIDON. Parliamentary deputy with ERE and minister
TSATSOS, CONSTANTINE. Parliamentary Deputy with ERE and minister, professor
TSILIOPOULOS. Military attaché of the Greek embassy serving in Washington D.C. during the dictatorship
VENIZELOS, SOPHOCLES. Greek Parliamentary Deputy and deputy leader of the Center Union Party until February 1964
VOURNAS, GEORGE. Greek-American Lawyer, dictatorship opponent
VOVOLINIS, COSTAS. Member of the dictatorship government
YEORGALAS, GEORGIOS. Deputy Minister of the Dictatorship
ZISIOU, KOSTAS. Greek military officer, active in the anti-dictatorship movement
ZOITAKIS, GEORGIOS. General, Regent of Greece from December 1967
ZOLOTAS, XENOPHON. Governor of the Bank of Greece